Michael Schulman, Ph.D.
Eva Mekler

# Bringing Up a Moral Child

## Teaching Your Child to Be Kind, Just, and Responsible

DOUBLEDAY
New York  London  Toronto  Sydney  Auckland

A MAIN STREET BOOK
PUBLISHED BY DOUBLEDAY
a division of Bantam Doubleday Dell Publishing Group, Inc.
1540 Broadway, New York, New York 10036

MAIN STREET BOOKS, DOUBLEDAY, and the portrayal of a building with a tree are
trademarks of Doubleday, a division of Bantam Doubleday Dell Publishing Group, Inc.

Previously published under the title *Bringing Up a Moral Child: A New Approach for
Teaching Your Child to Be Kind, Just, and Responsible.*

Lyrics from "I Am a Rock," copyright © 1965 by Paul Simon. Used by permission of
the publisher.

"Incident" from *On These I Stand: An Anthology of the Best Poems of Countee Cullen,*
copyright 1925 by Harper & Brothers Publishers, Inc.; renewed 1953 by Ida M. Cullen.
Reprinted by permission of GRM Associates, Inc., Agents for the Estate of Ida M.
Cullen.

Excerpt from "East Coker" in *Four Quartets,* copyright 1943 by T. S. Eliot; renewed
1971 by Esme Valerie Eliot. Reprinted by permission of Harcourt Brace & Company.

Library of Congress Cataloging in Publication Data
Schulman, Michael, 1941–
    Bringing up a moral child: teaching your child to be kind, just,
and responsible / by Michael Schulman and Eva Mekler.
      p.  cm.
    Rev. ed. of: Bringing up a moral child. 1985.
    Includes bibliographical references and index.
    1. Moral development.   2. Moral education.   3. Child rearing.
I. Mekler, Eva.  II. Schulman, Michael, 1941–    Bringing up a moral
child.  III. Title.
BF723.M54S38   1994
649'.7—dc20   93-23916
CIP

ISBN 0-385-46989-6
Copyright © 1985, 1994 by Michael Schulman and Eva Mekler
All Rights Reserved
Printed in the United States of America
February 1994
First Main Street Books Edition

10  9  8  7  6  5  4  3  2  1

# Contents

# Preface

## HOW TO USE THIS BOOK

This book is divided into three parts. The first part tells you how children actually develop a conscience and also shows you how to teach them moral values. Unlike theorists who try to explain all of moral behavior by a single mechanism, such as *reinforcement* or the *Oedipus Complex* or a person's *stage of moral reasoning,* we believe that moral behavior is based on three basic psychological processes, which we call the three foundation stones of moral development.

Part Two looks at the major forces that work against leading a moral life, such as jealousy, anger, and greed. We offer a variety of techniques for helping children handle their destructive passions in constructive ways, including a program in "love training" designed to help you bring up a child who is inclined to care about people.

In the third part of the book, we cover a number of common moral issues and dilemmas that children typically face at different ages. They range from how to resolve conflicts with friends in constructive ways to adolescent concerns over sex and drugs. Notice we present the problems *by age* and not by "stage." Unlike stage theorists, we do not tell you that your child *should* be doing this or that at a certain stage of development. Instead, we point out what the world will be confronting your child with at specific ages and what your child's concerns will be that might make it easier or harder for him or her to acquire moral standards. In the last chapter we discuss how to help children maintain moral standards in the "real" world, a world that often seems to reward the selfish and unscrupulous.

It is important to read Part One, the "foundation stones" chapters, carefully before going on to the specific problem areas covered in the rest of the book. Once you understand the way in which children learn morality, you'll be better able to teach it in all the various situations you'll see through with your child.

This updated edition of *Bringing Up a Moral Child* contains new sections on such common parental concerns as tattling, racism, and the fear that a moral child will be too easily hurt and taken advantage of in today's harsh and competitive world. The reference notes have also been updated to reflect the latest developmental research.

# Part One

# The Family-Based Program

# 1

# You Can Teach Your Child
# to Be Kind and Just

Concerns about the moral training of children have taken on a new sense of urgency. The traditional sources of moral guidance—religion, the schools, community and family customs—are not as influential as they once were. Yet young people today are confronted by serious moral issues, often at a younger age than ever before. Concerns about drugs and sex are particularly troubling to children and their parents, and crime among our youth is virtually a national epidemic. In today's world, moral training has largely become the responsibility of the parents alone. But many parents are uncertain how to go about it and often ask whether morality can really be taught at all.

At a parent conference, one mother voiced her concern this way:

> It's so hard to know what's right and wrong anymore. Everything is open to question. My own parents were very strict and autocratic with me. I followed orders, or else. But I don't want to be like them. I want my children to understand the reasons behind the rules I give them. But frankly, I'm not always sure myself what my reasons are. So half the time I simply avoid saying anything at all about what I feel is right and wrong. I've never really taken a stand on lying or cheating on tests or marijuana or even household chores. And believe me, all these issues have come up. I just don't know what I have a right to demand.

Another parent described her confusion over what to teach her teenage daughters about sex:

My mother taught me to "save" myself, otherwise a nice young man from a good family would never marry me and I'd turn into a destitute old maid. My daughters would laugh at me if I said the same thing to them. My mother's ideas about sexuality are just not true in their experience. Virginity is not a salable commodity anymore; and, besides, both my daughters are bright and won't need any nice young men to support them. But I don't think they should take sex lightly, either. If there's a rule about what's proper sexual conduct for a fifteen- and a seventeen-year-old girl, I certainly haven't come across it.

A father described his conflict over how to bring up his children to be caring yet tough enough to survive in the "real" world:

I'm a businessman and quite successful. But I have had to do things in business that are exactly the opposite of the way I teach my kids to treat people. In fact, I wouldn't be happy if they knew some of the grimy details of what I've had to do to survive in my industry. Yes, I want my children to be kind and considerate, but I worry that they'll be eaten alive when they have to make it on their own.

Another parent bemoaned her inability to rely on religion for moral training:

I was taught to be good because it was a sin not to be, and God would punish me if I wasn't. I still believe in God, but not in a God that rewards and punishes our acts; and I can't teach my children something that doesn't make sense to me. I wish I could. It would make life easier, but I can't be that hypocritical. And they wouldn't accept it anyway. The other day my sixteen-year-old daughter came home from church after hearing one of those standard sermons against premarital sex and said, "With a world full of war, famine, and disease, God couldn't possibly be wasting His time keeping track of people's sex lives." My oldest boy doesn't believe in God at all, and he hasn't turned out any less moral than the others—unless you believe that not believing in God is immoral, which I don't. Don't forget, the same folks who brought us Saint Francis also brought us the Inquisition.

Parents and their children have traditionally been embedded in a network of family, community, and religious institutions, all of which contributed to the moral upbringing of the children. It was once common for parents, children, grandparents, and even great-grandparents to live close by, sometimes sharing one roof. But the nuclear family is now, for the most part, independent and isolated, removed from geographical, cultural, and religious roots. More and more the family is forced to take up the task of the moral training of children on its own.

Yet most parents are uncertain about what to do and experience serious self-doubt ("Am I too old-fashioned?") and guilt ("Am I hurting my child psychologically?").

The child-rearing experts—pediatricians, psychologists, psychiatrists—have often only added to parents' confusion. For years experts warned them not to stifle or "traumatize" their children, that discipline would somehow produce an inhibited or neurotic child. "Permissiveness" was the catchword of the day. Today the "disciplinarians" are raising their voices again. They call for the reassertion of traditional values and the resurrection of the obedient and innocent child. Where the permissives were concerned about keeping children free of neuroses, the disciplinarians are interested in bringing up children who do their chores and keep out of trouble.

In this book you will not find a call for either permissiveness or discipline, because neither approach touches on parents' real concerns. The issue is not how restrictive and controlling parents should be. It is, rather, *how to bring up a moral child.* By *moral* we mean, simply, a child who strives to be kind, fair, and responsible. This is what parents are really after. They've learned the hard way that permissiveness doesn't work—character and conscience don't simply spring into being, and kind and considerate children are no more likely to be neurotic than anyone else. They've also learned that strict discipline is not the path to morality, that you can't rely on children to be good merely because they are afraid to be bad.

Today's parents, like those of the past, are interested in bringing up children who *want* to treat others well, who are genuinely concerned about other people's feelings, and who *choose* to do good even when they can get away with doing bad. They want a practical and effective family-based strategy for bringing up a moral child in today's world. That is what you will find in this book. It is written for parents who are interested in an overall program for bringing up a moral, caring child, as well as for parents whose children already have any of a number of character problems, such as lying, stealing, cheating, cruelty, etc.

The procedures do not depend on religious training; nor are they based on any moral training program in the schools. The focus is on the family and on the parent as teacher. We cover moral behavior, such as helping and sharing; moral feelings, such as empathy and love; and moral understanding, in the form of personal standards of conduct. You will also find what we believe is a comprehensive theory of moral development.

This is a practical book, but the practices we recommend grow out of a particular theoretical framework. It's important that you understand this framework since you will certainly encounter child-rearing situations that we haven't discussed. Armed with clear and concrete principles, you will be able to adapt our program to meet these challenges.

Lastly, you will find that our program and theory rest on a solid foundation of psychological research in moral development. Since the early decades of this century, researchers have been gathering evidence on the causes of moral thought and action. Their collective efforts make a scientific understanding of moral development possible and permit us to approach moral training as applied science. As you will see, this body of research provides support and direction for our program.

## A NEW THEORY OF MORAL DEVELOPMENT: THE THREE FOUNDATION STONES

A moral child is one who strives to be kind and just. Notice that the words *kind* and *just* both refer to how our behavior affects other people. Morality, of course, is concerned with how we treat our fellow humans. We call children kind when they strive to help others. We call them just or fair when they treat people without bias or favoritism, when they try to see that everyone, including themselves, is judged according to the same rules, shares burdens equitably, and receives what he or she deserves. When children are kind and just, we will also find that they behave responsibly toward others and try to keep their promises to them. To use an everyday example, a kind and just youngster will do his household chores not because of expectations of reward or punishment, but because he acknowledges and accepts his fair share of household responsibilities and recognizes that others suffer when he is neglectful.

People and societies certainly disagree over what actions they consider kind and fair. For instance, a capitalist and a socialist will have very different conceptions of what a fair wage is (to the pure capitalist it's the market value of one's labor; to the pure socialist it's based on need). And while there is general agreement that morality implies *not doing harm,* there is far less consensus on what our moral obligations to others are. Different societies, for example, define an adult's responsibilities to his or her aging parents in different ways. Even when people agree on what they mean by kindness and fairness, they may disagree over how best to accomplish these ends. Even common charity can be viewed as doing more harm than good, as reflected in the adage, "If you give a man a fish, he can eat for a day; if you teach a man to fish, he can eat for a lifetime." In other words, misguided charity may make people dependent. But such disagreements are questions of policy, not morality; they are disagreements over the best way to be kind. You can oppose a person's policy, but if you judge her intentions to be honorable—that she is truly interested in doing good—you will still consider her kind and moral.

**Morality defined.** Moral behavior has two components: Its intention must be good, in the sense that its goal is the well-being of one or more people; and it must be fair or just, in the sense that it considers the rights of others without prejudice or favoritism. Helping my friend gain an unwarranted advantage over others may be kind to him but it is not fair, and thus not an instance of moral behavior. Treating everybody equally cruelly may be fair, but it is not kind and, therefore, it is not moral. Conversely, we consider an act *immoral* if it seeks to harm others or gain an unfair advantage over them. A person's acts may be moral, immoral, or amoral—the last referring to behavior not performed specifically to benefit or harm others.

Intention is crucial when judging the moral standing of an act. When we say that something a child did was well intentioned, we mean that she did it without being threatened or coerced and that the primary reward for her was that it enhanced the well-being of another person. In everyday language one might say that the child did it voluntarily, because it was the right thing to do. We can never be totally sure what the real payoffs are to someone. We can only try to make good guesses by observing what a person does and how her behavior is affected by different outcomes. If we see that a person who treats another kindly doesn't seem to be gaining anything directly for herself or operating under any threat, we will assume that she is concerned with the other person's welfare. But if, when the opportunity presents itself, he runs off with the other person's life savings, we will probably infer that he was just pretending to be kind in order to gain that person's trust. Putting it in more formal psychological terms, we judge an act to be well intentioned when it appears to be reinforced by the enhanced well-being of the person to whom the act was directed.

*Moral motivation.* Do people really ever act solely for the benefit of others? Can we really be that selfless? A better way to ask this question is: Can people gain pleasure simply by giving someone else pleasure or by alleviating another person's pain? They most certainly can. Most of us have known this pleasure in our lives, whether through giving to a child, a spouse, a friend, or even a stranger. Giving is a great joy. And, as psychologist Robert Weiss has shown, easing someone's pain is, in and of itself, an effective positive reinforcer. He found that people work harder and faster on a task when their only payoff is reducing the discomfort of someone they've never met before.[1]

Admittedly, children can be brought up in ways that make them too insecure or angry or greedy or cynical to care about anyone's needs but their own. But, without doubt, any normal child has the capacity to find pleasure in the pleasure of others. *Experiencing gain at someone else's gain is the essence of moral motivation.* A person who helps someone because she cannot bear to witness human suffering or because she feels it is her duty and her self-esteem depends on it, is certainly gaining something herself from her act of kindness. But these are exactly the kinds of gains that make us call her behavior moral.

There have been, to be sure, philosophers (Hobbes) and psychologists (Freud) who have seen human beings as intrinsically self-centered and uncaring, having nary a kind impulse except through the civilizing forces of family and society. But research evidence argues against this dark vision. To cite just one study, a team of psychologists observed twenty-six children, from three to five years old, during thirty hours of free play in a preschool setting. The record shows that during that time the children engaged in approximately 1,200 "altruistic" acts including sharing, cooperating, helping, and comforting.[2] The so-called "civilizing" forces, in fact, often work against morality: three-year-olds have no racial prejudice.

Caring appears to be as natural to human beings as aggression, and from an evolutionary point of view, this makes good sense. Human beings have not evolved as solitary creatures. For our early ancestors the survival of an individual depended very much on the survival of his or her group. An intact group was better able to hunt and gather food, build shelter, and defend itself from enemies and predators than individuals on their own. When an individual cared for and protected the members of his group, it made the group more likely to stay together and survive, and, in turn, increased that person's own chances of staying alive. Inclinations to be kind and just, which promote the welfare of our fellow group members and keep our group intact, have, through natural selection, become an intrinsic part of being human because they have had survival value.

Moral behavior is indeed so crucial to human survival that processes to bring it about have evolved in all three major behavioral systems: the action system, the reaction system, and the self-control system (psychologists call these the operant, respondent, and cognitive systems). This brings us to the heart of our theory of moral development. Moral motivation is acquired through three psychological processes, which we call the three foundation stones of moral development. They are: 1) internalizing parental standards of right and wrong action; 2) developing empathic reactions to other people's feelings; and 3) constructing personal standards of kindness and justice. Each process is based on one of the three major behavioral systems and each has its own positive and negative emotional states. The negative states, shame, guilt, and self-loathing, can be very powerful sources of self-control.

### Internalizing Parental Standards of Right and Wrong

When we say that the child internalizes parental standards, we don't mean that he merely obeys his parents' rules to avoid punishment. We mean he has come to define certain actions as *right* or *wrong*, based on his parents' rules, and has learned to apply to himself the same words he has heard from his parents on how to behave properly. In other words, what a child internalizes are the *shoulds* and *shouldn'ts* he's heard his parents utter, such as "Share your toys," "Don't hit," and "Consider other people's feelings." At early stages of internalization the child will actually think those words when faced with temptations, and he'll often picture his mother's or father's pleased or disappointed face in anticipation of their reaction to how well he lived up to their standards.

Whether internalization takes place depends on how clearly and consistently parents state their rules and also on what they say and do when their child follows or fails to follow the rules (such as praising and scolding him in timely and appropriate ways, and teaching him "nicer" ways to satisfy his needs). It also depends on whether they have treated the child in ways that foster his feelings of love for them. Children internalize the rules of loving parents much more readily than those of cold or abusive parents.[3] It is the child's need to receive love from and give love to his parents that motivates him to adopt their standards of good and bad behavior. When he disappoints them by breaking one of their rules, he feels ashamed, unworthy of their love and afraid of losing it. This is far more painful to most children than fears of a spanking or losing a week's allowance. A child who is only afraid of punishment will hesitate to break a rule only if he thinks he'll get caught. The child with internalized standards of right and wrong may not care about the feelings of the playmate whose toy he is grabbing, but he does care about Mommy's and Daddy's feelings about whether he is "good" and he may give up the toy to feel worthy of their love.

## Developing Empathic Reactions

Our second foundation stone of morality is the child's miraculous ability to react with empathy to someone else's feelings. Empathy refers to a person's feeling bad over someone else's unhappiness and good over another's joy. Empathy is surprisingly common in children and appears to be an inborn capacity to recognize and "feel" other people's emotions. But like any inborn capacity, it varies from child to child. It contributes to morality because when a child feels someone else's joy and pain, *he* winds up feeling good when he makes them feel good and bad when he hurts them. This bad feeling is called guilt. Because of empathy a child can understand—without anyone telling him—that harming others is bad and comforting them is good.

## Acquiring Personal Standards

The third foundation stone of morality is the development of personal standards. Ultimately a child's sense of right and wrong must rest on her own standards of how people should treat their fellow human beings and what kind of person she wants to be. Once a child has acquired personal standards, right and wrong are no longer based on the approval of others. The child's actions are then under the guidance of her own ideals, and she will even begin to evaluate her parents' rules and those of other authorities according to these new standards. When she violates one of her own rules, she feels *ashamed of herself,* and it doesn't matter if no one finds out. Since ideals involve long-term goals, a child's willingness to rely on her own standards depends greatly on the confidence she has in her ability to reason about the long-term effects of her actions. Without that confidence she will tend to look to authorities and "experts" to tell her what is right and wrong.

## MORALITY CAN BE TAUGHT

Morality is something that parents can teach, both by setting up conditions that foster empathy and by teaching standards of kindness and justice in various direct ways. In other words, children are susceptible to moral instruction in all three moral domains. But, unfortunately, our species did not evolve only the capacities for caring and justice. Man the hunter and man the hater are just as much a product of our evolutionary past.

Every day, newspaper headlines remind us of how cruel we can be to each other: "Youth Gang Sets Fire to Subway Clerk," "Death Squads Slaughter Villagers," "Teenager Murders Old Woman," "Toxic Wastes Dumped Near Community Water Supply," "Man Kills His Child," "Child Kills His Father," and on and on. World military spending is over a trillion dollars a year.

Watch young children in a playground. They alternate so quickly and easily between friendly and aggressive behavior. One moment they are laughing together and running about gleefully, the next moment they are pushing and screaming at each other. Some well-timed and sensible instructions from parents can make an enormous difference in whether the friendly or the fighting side of the child is encouraged.

To a child, the presence of another child is a signal. He or she can be a signal for fun, or danger, or "Let's see what she has that I can take," or "I'll show him who is in charge here." When we call a child moral, we mean that the presence of others has become a signal to attend to and be concerned about those other individuals' needs and feelings. The earlier parents start teaching this to their children, the better. Moral training gets harder as children get older, but there is no reason to believe it is ever too late.

### Do Children Have an Inborn Moral Sense?

Sometimes in family counseling sessions, when we are talking about *teaching* morality, a parent will ask, "But isn't a moral sense something a child is either born with or not?" This is a question that philosophers have debated for centuries. It cannot be answered with a simple yes or no. Children *don't have to learn* to feel empathy when they see others suffering. They are born, in varying degrees, with that ability. But a child *can be taught* to attend to people's feelings more closely so that empathy occurs more often and more easily. Also, because children won't feel empathy for someone they are angry at or whom they've learned to define as alien or "not us," if you teach your child to deal with his anger constructively and encourage a broad definition of "us," you will be setting the conditions for him to experience a great deal more empathy.

Again, children prefer some things without learning—some smells, some sounds, some tastes—over others. Ranking stimuli is natural to them. Morality involves the ranking of different ways of treating people: treating people kindly and justly is considered better than using or harming them. Whether a child applies her natural tendency to rank experiences to the area of social behavior and whether moral actions get the highest rank (as opposed to, say, actions that lead to increased power or wealth), depends on learning.

Lastly, without being taught, children recognize the relationship between cause and effect. If a smile is regularly followed by a kiss, whenever they see a smile, they'll expect to be kissed. Personal standards are statements about cause and effect. They say a) do this, b) under these conditions, and c) these consequences will follow. Personal moral standards usually involve taking into consideration long-term consequences, such as benefits to the community at large. But children have to *learn* to care about long-term consequences; whether a child develops personal moral standards depends on whether this learning has taken place.

In sum, there is no innate moral sense, but a child comes equipped with a number of unlearned capacities. Through the proper experiences, these capacities will serve as a base upon which a moral sense or conscience can develop. Our moral training program is designed to help parents provide their children with these experiences.

## Are Nice Kids Wimps?

In workshops and counseling sessions parents often say that they don't want their child to become so nice that he or she turns into an easy mark for others, too easy to take advantage of. They point out that they don't want their child to harm others or get into trouble but, they add, the world is a competitive and dangerous place and they don't want their child's concern for others to put him or her at a disadvantage. Well, *are nice kids wimps?* Are compassionate and caring youngsters at a disadvantage in the "real" world?

The evidence says no. Many studies attest to the fact that kind children are among the most popular and successful. Children who treat others well out of compassion or principle—because they are sensitive to other people's feelings or have a sturdy sense of right and wrong—are generally nobody's pushover. They are not easily coerced and not an easy mark. And this is true whether they are five or fifteen. Moreover, their peers recognize and appreciate them for their moral qualities.

Think about it. We don't honor moral heroes (Gandhi, Martin Luther King, and others, both eminent and ordinary) because they were easy to push around. Moral individuals are the strongest among us. We honor them for their courage and perceptiveness, not their weakness or naïveté. And it is the same with children.

Researchers have found that youngsters who were most often chosen by their classmates as "best friends" were among the most altruistic and sensitive to what others were feeling. Other studies report that children want their friends to be truthful, cooperative, helpful, encouraging, trustworthy, and fun; and they don't want them to be touchy, sarcastic, two-faced, or aggressive. These findings have been confirmed for children from preschoolers to adolescents, boys and girls, blacks and whites, in well over a dozen studies.[4]

What's more, moral children are among the least likely to be taken advantage of. One reason for this is that their sensitivity to others tends to make them good at reading people's motives. In addition, if they do get fooled they aren't as likely to feel demeaned by the experience as are children whom we call "pleasers." Pleasers are nice to others, not out of compassion or principle, but as a way to make friends. They lack confidence in their appeal so they give others their toys or money, or their time, or their sexual favors as a way to get peers to like them. In other words, they are not really *giving,* they are *trading.* When the peer doesn't reciprocate, the pleaser is left with nothing and usually feels humiliated.

In contrast, children who give of themselves out of true caring or a personal sense of the right way to treat people—while they may feel bad if deceived—will more readily understand that it was the dishonest person who was demeaned, not them. They can still take pride in their generosity. Any child can be victimized, and many children will experience rejection. But moral children have a strong sense of who they are and what they stand for, and this actually makes it easier for them to weather life's storms and uncertainties.

## A CRITICAL LOOK AT THE MAJOR THEORIES OF MORAL DEVELOPMENT

When psychological discussions of moral development take place, the names Sigmund Freud, Jean Piaget, and Lawrence Kohlberg inevitably come up. Since the advice that parents get from psychotherapists and educators, as well as from "parenting" books and magazine articles, is often based on these theories, it's important for parents to know something about them—including their flaws.

### Sigmund Freud

According to Freud, a child has no natural inclinations toward kindness or justice, and empathy has no place at all in his theory. Concern for others, he says, can come about only after the child's more fundamental selfish and aggressive impulses have been suppressed and transformed through the "resolution of the Oedipus Complex" at about the age of six or seven.[5]

Unfortunately, Freud never tells us how to treat children so that the Oedipus Complex is resolved constructively. And many studies show that children behave kindly toward others long before the age when the Oedipus Complex is supposed to be resolved. In fact, from the very beginning of their social lives with playmates—even at the age of two—children are much more affectionate than aggressive.[6] Kindness that is motivated by empathy—that is, pure and simple concern for others—is as much a part of a child's nature as selfishness.

Despite its shaky foundation, Freudian theory was a major force behind the permissive child-rearing practices of recent decades. A fundamental tenet of the theory is that when children's hostile impulses are brought under excessive control, neurosis breaks out. Although the theory never spelled out exactly which parental practices constituted excessive control, and though there was hardly any evidence to support it, a generation of parents began to worry that if they disciplined their children they would risk turning them into neurotics.

## Jean Piaget

Piaget's theory of morality actually covers only one aspect of moral development. As he says himself in his major work on morality, "Readers will find in this book no direct analysis of child morality as it is practiced in home and school life or in children's societies. It is the moral judgment that we propose to investigate, not moral behavior or sentiments."[7]

So Piaget was not looking at what leads children to treat others kindly or cruelly. He was only interested in what children think about right and wrong. For example, when he writes about lying, he doesn't deal with what influences children to lie or tell the truth; only with how children of different ages define and evaluate lying.

Another difficulty with Piaget's theory is that even within its limited scope, other psychologists don't, for the most part, confirm his findings. For instance, he said that when young children judge the "naughtiness" of an act they are more affected by how much damage was done than by the intentions of the person doing the damage. Other psychologists generally find the opposite: even for very young children, a person's intention is the most important element in evaluating an act. Moreover, it doesn't take a psychologist to know that Piaget was way off the mark when he said that young children, from about the age of two to six, regard their parents' rules as "sacred and untouchable, emanating from adults and lasting forever." Would that it were so. Contrary to Piaget's claim, young children question rules, judge some as unfair, and demand that rules they don't like be changed.[8]

A central premise of Piaget's theory is that children go through well-defined stages of moral development and that we shouldn't expect much in the way of moral behavior at early stages. Most research, though, does not support the idea that children go through clearly defined stages of moral development.[9] In this book we cite study after study showing that young children reason and act in much more moral ways than Piaget recognized and that they are not egocentric as he claimed. Moreover, because Piaget was looking for universal stages of moral development, he hardly focused at all on why some children are more moral than others; nor did he suggest what might be done to spur children whose moral sense was developing slowly. He was, in fact, against doing anything to accelerate passage through the moral stages which, he believed, occurred naturally out of the child's everyday interactions with peers. Thus, formal moral training for children was explicitly not encouraged.

### Lawrence Kohlberg

Lawrence Kohlberg's theory is an extension of Piaget's work on the child's understanding of justice and he, too, only focuses on judgments, not behavior.[10] As odd as it sounds, given it's prominence, his theory is not at all based on the observation of how children treat one another in real life settings. Among the questions you *won't* find addressed in Kohlberg's work are how children come to care about behaving kindly, why a youngster feels sad or guilty when she realizes she's hurt a friend, what makes a child stand up for a smaller child who is being picked on, why a three-year-old will comfort a hurt playmate without anyone telling her to, and what parents can do to promote kindness and fairness in their children. Kohlberg's basic procedure is to describe hypothetical moral dilemmas to children (should a poor man steal a drug to save his dying wife?) and ask them what would be the right thing to do, and why. He claimed that as children get older they go through a series of stages in their reasoning about what the best action is in these various dilemmas. But what these stages represent is not at all clear since in thirty-five years of research it's never been established that as children proceed through Kohlberg's stages they actually *treat* people more justly or kindly. Indeed, studies show that three-, four-, and five-year-olds can be very kind and are often fair. And they often give solidly moral reasons for their actions. Nancy Eisenberg-Berg and Cynthia Neal found that when they asked four- and five-year-olds to explain why they had been kind to someone, many referred to the "needs" of the person they had helped or to friendship, or simply to the fact that they wanted to help or share. Contrary to Kohlberg's theory, virtually none of these preschoolers said they helped because of fear of punishment or desire to gain a reward, answers that would have corresponded to Kohlberg's Stages 1 and 2, the stages in which he places preschoolers.[11]

Among other evidence showing that scores on Kohlberg's test don't reflect moral behavior is a study that compared the moral stage scores of delinquent ("sociopathic") preadolescents in a correctional facility to normal children of the same age. The difference was slight. Both groups were at the same Kohlberg stage, with the normals only a shade higher up the stage than the sociopaths.[12]

Kohlberg acknowledged that having a high moral development score does not mean that you will be a nice person. As one of his colleagues, Thomas Likona, put it in a book based on Kohlberg's theory, "we can reach high levels of moral reasoning and still behave like scoundrels."[13] If one can be immoral and still have a high Kohlberg moral development score, then Kohlberg's test cannot be measuring anything very central to moral development.

When it comes to child-rearing, stage theorists, like Kohlberg and Piaget, tell parents and teachers not to expect much from young children because they haven't reached "mature" stages; they also say that special training won't move a child through the stages more quickly since you can't (or shouldn't) fight nature. But many studies find that young children behave just as morally as older children.[14] And since a child's stage score doesn't correlate to any significant degree with moral behavior, knowing your child's stage won't tell you anything about how he is likely to treat people. As children get older they score higher on Kohlberg's stage test, not because they become more inclined to treat people kindly and fairly, but because they can better analyze the long-term consequences of the pro and con choices in the ethical dilemmas on the test. The cruellest lawyer is, without question, going to get a higher stage score than the kindest eight-year-old.

## Reinforcement Theory

The main premise of the reinforcement approach is that if you want a child to treat others well, give her something she wants whenever she does. In the language of behavioral psychology, you can increase the frequency of the behaviors we call *kind* and *just* by positively reinforcing them when they occur.[15] We have some doubts about the effectiveness of this approach.

Reinforcement programs have been applied in family settings, in group homes for delinquents, in classrooms with disruptive children, and in various other institutions—but with limited success. The programs typically report short-term gains, but few long-term improvements.[16] When the reinforcement program ends, the negative behavior generally returns.

We suggest that the reason reinforcement programs have such limited success is because simply reinforcing (or punishing) a child will never lead him to classify some actions as "right" and others as "wrong." It only teaches him what pays off and what doesn't. When the payoffs change—for example, when a child leaves a group home and returns to his neighborhood, there's no reason for him to abide by the former rules. If he's only been exchanging his "good" behavior for objects or privileges and not out of love for the rule-giver or because he's come to care about other people's happiness or unhappiness, then if someone offers him a higher reward to be cruel, that's what he'll be. Effective moral education doesn't merely use the same old reinforcers (money, privileges) to try to control bad behavior, but instead strives to change *what the child finds reinforcing.* The goal is a child who is reinforced by (and who will try to bring about) good feelings in others. Then the child's good behavior will be *self*-initiated. He will then have a conscience *for all seasons,* not available for sale to the highest bidder.

# 2

# Internalization: The First Foundation Stone —How You Can Help Your Child Internalize Your Moral Values

Imagine you are a teenager. You have been invited to a large party. You know some of the guests. Others are strangers. You leave the party room and go to the foyer closet to get a pack of gum from your jacket. You notice an open handbag on the floor and see that it contains a wallet with a sizable number of bills. For a moment you feel an impulse to take some of the money. But an inner voice says no. An internal debate begins. "No one would know it was me." Again the inner voice says no. The second voice persists: "But I really could use some extra money this week. And anyway, someone stupid enough to leave her money around like that deserves to get ripped off. It'll be a good lesson for her. And if I don't do it, someone else will."

But the first voice gets firmer: "It's wrong to steal. If I want to teach her a lesson, I could find out whose handbag it is and suggest that she put it in a safer spot." You wonder how much money is there. "Seems like a lot. She won't miss a small part of it." The inner voice asks, "How do you know? Maybe it's all she has. Or maybe she took it out of the bank for something important. It doesn't matter whether she'll miss it or not. It's her money, not mine. Am I going to let myself turn into the kind of person I complain about and detest when friends tell me they've been robbed? Am I going to make her feel the way Susan felt last month when her bag was stolen in a restaurant?"

The internal debate ends with a clear and forceful "No!" And you walk out of the room to find the owner of the bag, feeling bad that you were tempted, but good that you did the right thing.

Everyone has, at one time or another, experienced such immoral impulses—times when we desperately want our own desires fulfilled even if it means causing pain to others. We may want more money or sex or status, or we may be seeking revenge or simply wish to be left alone. At those times we are tempted to hurt those who have what we want or who stand in our way by deceiving or attacking them, or taking what they own; or we may hurt them out of negligence because we are so wrapped up in our own interests that we forget our responsibilities to them. Fortunately, though, most of us, most of the time, don't pursue our desires with so singleminded a focus that we wreak havoc on those around us.

What stops us from acting on these temptations? What leads us to consider the needs and points of view of others before blindly pursuing our own ends? The answer is surprising. Most of the time we simply talk ourselves out of our selfish pursuits. An inner voice argues against our destructive impulses. It sounds deceptively simple, but the development of self-control over destructive impulses—of what in everyday speech is called *conscience*—depends largely on what a child learns to say to himself during moments of temptation. Research has established that both children and adults can and do regulate their physical and intellectual behavior through self-instruction[1] (reminding oneself of *"i before e except after c"* is a simple example). The same holds for moral behavior.

For decades psychologists have been asking, How does a child "internalize" rules of conduct and values? Our way of asking this question is, How does he or she acquire a moral inner voice? We also want to know what can be done to see that this voice speaks to him or her forcefully and dependably.

We will use the term *internalization* as a label for this process of learning moral self-instruction. But we do not agree with psychologists who believe that a child internalizes his parents' standards out of fear of punishment or conditioned anxiety.[2] These may keep a child (or adult) well-behaved, but not because he has come to accept and want to live up to his parents' standards of right and wrong —which is precisely what internalization refers to. When a mother says of a child, "He won't do it because he knows he'll get hit," she means something very different from when she says, "He won't do it because he knows it's wrong." Moreover, if the only reason a child keeps his nasty impulses in check is because he has an anxiety attack when he doesn't, we are a lot more likely to think of him as neurotic than moral. A number of studies on the early development of internalization have shown that one- and two-year-olds are more likely to internalize parental directives and follow rules without constant reminders or threats when parents treat them with warmth and sensitivity, explain their rules clearly, and don't rely on physical punishment.[3] As we shall see, internalization has a lot more to do with love than with fear.

## WHAT IS INTERNALIZATION?

Parents are always telling a child, in one form or another, "Do this because it's good" and "Don't do that because it's bad." When a child begins to give these same instructions to herself, we say that internalization has taken place. The words of the parent are now those of the inner voice of the child. Internalization, as we define it, refers to the learning of standards of behavior, not just rules. For instance, if a child *hasn't* internalized a standard against hitting, she may still refrain from hitting if she's learned that her mother will spank her if she hits. But once she's internalized the standard, she won't hit because she tells herself that hitting is *bad*. Then she won't hit even if she can keep her mother from knowing; or if she does hit she'll know she did something she shouldn't have, and will often confess even without being asked. When we hear an exasperated parent complain to a child, "Every time I turn my back on you, you get into trouble," we know that internalization has not taken place.

Internalization provides the first stage of self-control over selfish and aggressive impulses and is accomplished when the inner voice speaks to the child *before* he takes an action. If the voice speaks only after a misbehavior has occurred, the child's inner experience will be closer to "Oops, I did it again and now I'm in trouble," than to "Mommy said it's bad to do that" or "Mommy will be pleased if I do this" (or "disappointed if I don't"). The inner voice tells him what he should and what he shouldn't do.

Young children often go through a stage when the inner voice is actually audible; you can hear them prompting or scolding themselves out loud. For example, after reprimanding a three- or four-year-old for taking things that aren't hers, a parent might actually hear the child say to herself, "Don't take. Bad," as she pulls her hand back from reaching for a playmate's toy. In time, self-instruction becomes private, although at times even adults scold or cajole themselves out loud.

During a child's first years, internalization is based primarily on his love for his parents, on his desire to please them, and his terrible distress when they are unhappy with him. Four-year-old Tommy may be quite content to play with his toys alone and ignore his sister's pleas to share in his fun. He may not feel empathy for her unhappiness or understand any general principles of sharing and responsibility. But he knows that mommy wants him to share, that she is disappointed in him when he doesn't, and that when he shares on his own initiative she tells him he's a good boy. So he shares. Sharing is good because mommy said so.

When a child has internalized standards—when he "knows right from wrong"—he doesn't behave well simply to reap external rewards or avoid punishment (neither of which would be considered moral reasons). Something is added with internalization: the child begins to judge his own behavior (for instance, whether or not he shares with others) as "good" or "bad," and he feels proud or ashamed of himself, depending on whether or not he lives up to his parents' rule to share. He will even apply their rules to others,[4] and tell a playmate that a rule is right "because my mommy said so." It is then fair to say that he has begun to acquire moral standards or *values*. Sharing has become a "good" thing to do.

Psychologists would say that sharing has acquired reinforcing value (it is a "learned" reinforcer). The child has come to value sharing because it leads to his parents' approval, and because not sharing evokes their disapproval. When parents generally treat their child lovingly, their disapproval contrasts sharply with what he is used to and is often sufficient punishment by itself. Warm parents who give their children clear rules and affectionate approval for following them, as well as firm correctives for transgressions, tend to raise children with strong consciences.[5]

There is another reason why a child will internalize her parents' rules. Being good is a way for her to express her love for them. Children feel love very intensely and go through phases of incredibly strong attachments to parents. One aspect of a child's love for her parents is empathizing with their feelings, which leads her to want to make them feel good. One way to do this is by following their rules; it is her gift to them, a way of saying, "You are good, so your rules must be good."

Internalization is only the first step toward what we would call an adult conscience. Ultimately, the child must empathize with and care about the feelings of his siblings, playmates, and anyone else he interacts with, and not treat them well only as a byproduct of his love for his parents. Some children show strong empathic feelings for others during their earliest social contacts, when they are two or three, while others need to be taught to be sensitive to people. As we will see in the next chapter, children can learn to be more empathic.

There is another way that children need to go beyond internalization: Their parents' rules must become *their* rules, which can only happen if they understand and appreciate the reasons for the rules. When that occurs, we say the rule has become a *personal standard* of the child. A rule like "Everyone deserves an equal chance," will then be followed because it leads to good consequences, and not because parents or any other authority say it should be followed. At that point, the strongest preventive to rule-breaking is no longer the child's concern about disappointing his or her parents and losing their love, but loss of self-love.

## WHAT PARENTS CAN DO TO PROMOTE INTERNALIZATION

Children must learn three things for internalization to take place. These are: (1) what words to say to themselves; (2) in what situations these words should be said; and (3) what the outcomes are of succeeding or failing to control their actions. These must be learned. How do you teach them?

### Give Clear Rules and Reasons

If you want your child to learn what to say to himself, you must make your instructions very clear. The statement, "Share your toys," leaves open to interpretation the meaning of the word *share*. Does it mean to let someone else play with your toy for as long as you do? Or does it mean to play with the toy together? Clearer instructions are "Take turns playing" or "Whoever goes first can play for five minutes, whoever goes second plays for seven minutes," or "Flip a coin to pick who goes first today; the other one will go first tomorrow."

By giving your child specific instructions and concrete examples, he will learn quickly what you want him to do and how to do it. "Remember, Billy—be nice to your cousin Jennifer when she comes over tonight" is not a clear statement of how Billy should behave toward his visitor. "Don't forget to ask her what she wants to see when you're selecting a television show," or "Remember, she's not supposed to eat ice cream, so don't make fun of her when she has fruit for dessert" are statements that define for Billy what you mean by "nice," and also clarify for him what he must or must not do to fulfill your instructions.

As a parent you have a choice. You can refuse to explain the reasons behind your commands and, in effect, teach your children that being good simply means being obedient, or you can teach them that being good means striving for certain openly stated values (such as "Everyone should have an equal chance to have fun"), and that the purpose of the rules (such as, "Take turns at the game") are to bring those values about.

There are some very practical reasons for choosing to explain your rules to your child. First, when a child learns values—not just what to do, but why it is proper to do it—her "good" behavior is more likely to extend to new situations, including those in which you are not present and have no direct input (for instance, when she is out with friends or away at camp).

For example, in the illustration above about sharing toys, Tommy's mother can teach him, simply, that sharing is good and mommy wants him to share. Or she can teach him that if he doesn't share his toys, he will hurt his sister's feelings, and that mommy wants him to care about the feelings of others for some very *good reasons,* which include that everyone feels hurt at times (him too) and needs someone to help them feel better, and that the world becomes a happier place to live in if we all watch out for and try to help each other. His lesson, then, is not simply to please mommy by sharing for some unclear or arbitrary reason, but to please mommy by learning to pay attention to the needs of others. This goal can then guide the child's behavior in a great many different situations.

When parents make clear statements of reasons, a child learns that they care about his intentions as well as his actions. Simply handing over a toy because mommy said so is not enough. Wanting others to have fun and adopting a caring point of view are the important lessons to be learned.

Even preschoolers can begin to understand the lessons that everyone is equal, feels similar frustrations and joys, and deserves the same chance at the good things available in life. You can communicate this with such statements as "We share toys with others because we want everyone to have a good time playing," or "Having a good time is the reason for playing, and everyone should have the same chance to have a good time."

Grade-school children can learn that everyone has different tastes and that being nice means respecting differences and finding compromise solutions when differences cause conflict (say, over what TV program to watch). An older child can be taught how important sharing is to the quality of life in, and sometimes the very survival of, a community—whether that community consists of a group of friends, a family, a nation, or the whole human race.

Another important reason for teaching a child the reasons behind rules is to fortify her against those who would influence her to act in selfish and uncaring ways. When a child is young, if parents simply issue commands to her about what to do and what not to do and provide approval when she is obedient and disapproval when she isn't, she will usually accept the rules and follow orders. But during her preteen and early adolescent years people outside the family start to have a strong effect on her. The influence of peers, teachers, coaches, television characters, etc., begins to supplant the influence of parents. If she has not learned values, but only a particular set of actions to please her parents, she will readily discard those actions if they conflict with the one's encouraged by the newly influential people in her life.

What's worse, if the one principle she has internalized is that a good person is one who is obedient to authority, she will be easy prey for new and possibly unscrupulous authority figures who wish to use her for their own ends. Encouraging mindless obedience will not prepare a child for the difficult moral decisions she will have to make in her life.

The more fully you explain the reasons behind your rules, the more quickly your child will develop personal standards to help her resist the ill-intended influence of others. When she understands why a rule exists and what good is expected to come from following it (other than mommy's approval), she can then see for herself whether these expectations are confirmed and the rule is worthwhile. If living up to a rule is supposed to make life better, and it doesn't, then the rule needs to be re-evaluated, regardless of who it came from. Teaching reasons thus sets the framework for the transfer of power over the child's behavior from the parents to the child.

A child's earliest use of language reflects an understanding of causality and of other people's feelings, so you can start giving your child reasons for your rules even before he or she is two. One recent study recorded twenty-eight-month-olds saying such things as, "I'm hurting your feelings 'cause I was mean to you," "I nice? I get to ride horse again?" "I give a hug. Baby be happy," "Me can do it. Me good girl," and "Katie not happy face. Katie sad." Almost all the children in the study used the words "good" and "bad"; most used "have to" and many used "supposed to." Thus, by the time a child is two and a half years old, he or she has all the essential ingredients for understanding rules and reasons. Moreover, during these early years children begin to give reasons to explain and justify their behavior in disputes with parents and siblings.[6] By allowing your child to state his case you show him respect and can commence a dialogue about what are acceptable and unacceptable reasons for one's treatment of others.

There are effective reasons and ineffective ones. Effective reasons stress the impact of the child's actions on others—whether they are harmful, helpful, or fair. We recall one mother who was having trouble with her twelve-year-old daughter in a number of areas, including getting her to phone in when she was returning home late from school or from visits and outings with friends. When we asked if she had explained to her daughter why she wanted her to telephone, she said yes: "I told her that I'm her mother and I have a right to know where she is." But merely claiming a right is hardly an adequate reason. She might have told her daughter that she worries about her when she is late, which is both unpleasant and interferes with her own activities at home. She might also have said that since she takes her daughter's schedule and needs into account when she makes her own daily plans, and since her time is valuable, she wants to be consulted before any changes in the schedule are made.

Research shows that children want to be given reasons for rules. But parents should not expect much success with simplistic explanations that only assert that some behavior is "good" or "the right thing to do," without explaining how that behavior actually affects the well-being of others.[7] Few children accept every rule passively. Even a two-year-old will squawk about a rule he thinks is unfair to him (for instance, if it bars him from doing something he sees his older brother or sister doing).

To be sure, sometimes, when upset, it's easy to forget to give a child reasons. One day, when our daughter was three, we discovered that she had colored with crayons on a wall in our recently repainted bedroom. We gave her a clear and firm instruction (while probably pointing an angry finger at her): "Don't color on the walls. You can only color on paper." The next day she did it again. This time the reprimand was harsher: "We told you yesterday, you are not allowed to color on the walls . . ." A few days later, she did it again. As the anger was rising up we realized we had never told her why we didn't want her to color on the walls. So we gave her our reasons—we told her how we tried to make the room beautiful, reminding her of Mommy's hard work in making the curtains and about how we all pitched in to prepare the room for the painting. I'm not sure she fully understood or agreed with the aesthetic aspects of the explanation, but she clearly appreciated the respectful way we addressed her—and she never colored on the walls again.

### Teach a Caring Point of View

You obviously don't want to have to break down the injunction to "Be nice" into a string of specific instructions every time your child interacts with someone. Before long, you want him to be guided by his own sensitivity to people's feelings and desires. But before that can happen, he must first *notice* people's feelings, understand what gives rise to them, and take upon himself responsibility for making those he interacts with feel good. In other words, you must teach him a caring point of view.

One format for teaching this is to ask your child to come up with his own plan for how to be nice to someone, say, his visiting cousin. That way he'll have to think about what she does and doesn't like and pay closer attention to her emotional changes, including subtle ones, when they spend time together. By discussing his plans you can correct any misconceptions he has about her, and also compliment his accurate observations and good ideas. A child is much more likely to carry out a plan when he's participated in conceiving it. Ultimately you want him to internalize the general rule, "Be nice to others," and to understand that to do so he must attend to their feelings—even when he might not want to.

Let's look at a problem that came up in the Larsen family that illustrates the value of teaching a caring point of view. The Larsens' twelve-year-old son, Jack, and nine-year-old daughter, Annie, usually got along well. But recently Jack had friends over for a weekend. The boys excluded Annie from their activities, barring her from Jack's room. Annie, feeling rejected and having no one to play with, became angry and teary, which only made things worse. The boys then made fun of her, and Jack complained that she was ruining his weekend.

Mr. and Mrs. Larsen told Jack and his friends to "be nicer" to Annie, but the problem continued. They considered ending the sleep-over, but were reluctant to take away an activity that the boys enjoyed so much. They scolded Jack, but realized that from his point of view there was a real conflict of interest. They explained Jack's point of view to Annie and told her to play on her own, but she continued to feel hurt and angry.

What Mr. and Mrs. Larsen had not yet taught Jack was precisely what he could do in this situation, including what his responsibilities to his sister were and how he might balance them with his own desires of the moment. Obviously, "Be nicer to your sister" was not sufficient. Jack, in a sense, was two people. When alone with his sister he was a caring brother. When he was with his friends, he saw Annie as an intruder and an obstacle to his fun. He had to be taught precisely what to attend to and what to say to himself to resolve this conflict.

Mrs. Larsen began Jack's "observation training" by asking him if he could tell when Annie was unhappy. He said, "Yes, her face looks like this," and proceeded to mimic her unhappy expression. His mother then told him he had to be mindful of Annie's feelings. He could not simply ignore her unhappiness because it interfered with his fun. She asked him if he liked to see Annie smile. He said he usually did, but protested that it would ruin his fun to include her in all his activities. "She's only nine—and she's a girl."

Mrs. Larsen explained to Jack that each member of the family had a responsibility to all the others—"That's what it means to be a family." Jack was told that even though he was able to enjoy himself in the evening without the company of his sister, he still had to fulfill a responsibility toward her. He was the older brother and she depended on him, so his responsibility—and his challenge—was to change her sad face into a smiling one without spoiling his own evening.

He acknowledged that there were some activities Annie could join in. He agreed to invite her to join in for one hour of the evening's activity, and said he would speak to her about which games would be the most fun for her. Annie was delighted at the invitation. She said it was all right if the boys wanted to play without her, as long as she had some fun too (and, we believe, felt secure about her brother's love).

Jack learned that he was expected to attend to the feelings of others even when he might not want to; that when his actions produced unhappiness in someone else, he should take it as a cue that a problem needed solving. He also learned that reasonable compromises are possible and necessary for everyone's needs to be considered. Mr. and Mrs. Larsen learned that they had to take responsibility for *teaching* caring rather than merely demanding or expecting it.

Teaching a child to observe others in a sympathetic way can be a regular part of his or her moral lessons—not only when some conflict occurs. What does a child see when she looks at people? Does she view them as similar to herself—to be treated as she wants to be treated? Or does she see them as objects to serve her desires? Does she translate what she sees into an understanding of their needs and hopes and fears? And if so, does she use that information for their benefit or to take advantage of them?

The lion stalking the gazelle isn't interested in the needs of its prey. It doesn't care about the gazelle's terror or its panic to protect its young. If the lion is aware of these aspects of the gazelle at all, it is only to use them as a way to better predict the gazelle's movements. To the lion the gazelle is simply a meal. When a mugger sees an old woman with a handbag walking down a lonely street, his reaction to her is similar to the lion's response to the gazelle: the old woman is immediately seen as prey. If she shows fear, it is a good sign. It makes her more defenseless. As an ex-mugger stated in a recent *New York Times* article on street crime, "They were simply people to be taken. I didn't feel any bond with them."

People victimize each other in many ways—most of them, fortunately, with less serious consequences than assault. But it is all too common for individuals to see others as objects to be exploited. A businessman who knowingly sells defective, useless, and even dangerous products sees his customers as prey; he feels no bond with them.

You can teach your child to perceive another person sympathetically, as a life to be enhanced, and not merely as an object to be used or manipulated. There is evidence that the more similar we believe people are to us, the more sympathetic and kind we are to them.[8] So start by making sure your youngster understands that other people have feelings and desires just as he does, and that these deserve consideration equal to his own.

A child also has to be aware that what others desire in a specific situation and what makes them feel good may be different from what she desires and what makes her feel good. If you give her the instruction, "When you want to help others feel good, it's important to understand *their* likes and dislikes," you will be drawing her attention to such differences between people and encouraging her to use this information for altruistic ends. This same message can be stated in more concrete terms to help her overcome specific problems with people. For instance, if her relationship with her brother is making her unhappy, you might say, "If you want to show your brother that you love him, pay attention to what *he* wants, because it's different from what you want."

You can start teaching your child to be sensitive to other people's feelings during his second and third year. Even two-year-olds understand that other people have feelings, and by four a child can be quite good at recognizing situations that make people happy, sad, angry, and afraid. By that age a child is certainly capable of recognizing that his own behavior can make people feel good or bad. The more you focus your child on people's feelings, the more likely his own natural empathy will be aroused and the more helpful he'll want to be. This desire to be helpful will, in turn, stimulate his interest in learning even more about people since, by the age of five, children understand that to be "a good helper" you have to know what a person needs."[9]

**THE SHERLOCK HOLMES GAME.** A concrete procedure for teaching your youngster how to observe others carefully and become sensitive to their feelings is the Sherlock Holmes Game. It's useful for children in the five- to nine-year-old range. Start by making it clear to your youngster that the purpose of the game is to teach her something important, something to carry into her daily life. Then introduce the game in the following way:

> We are going to play the Sherlock Holmes Game. Sherlock Holmes was a famous detective who was able to solve crimes that no one else could solve. His secret was that he looked at people very carefully. Because he took the time to look, he saw things that no one else saw, and he could tell whether or not the person had committed the crime. We are going to learn to use Sherlock Holmes's method of looking at people. But the people we are going to observe haven't committed a crime. We want to look at people we know and figure out how to be as nice as possible to them. In order to be nice to them we first have to figure out what they like and what they dislike.

After this introduction, ask your youngster to choose a person he knows well and likes, and who is available for direct observation. Then restate the goal of the game: "Let's see if we can figure out what makes [the person chosen] happy or unhappy. To do that we need to know what he likes and dislikes." (For parents who are not comfortable with this kind of formal procedure, the same ends can be accomplished in informal everyday conversations. For instance, you might say "Let's do something nice for Uncle Harry today. Let's figure out what he likes and dislikes and then we'll know what to do.")

Make up a chart with the following categories:

**The Case of** (*name of person*):

| Likes | When? | Why? | How Do You Know? |
|---|---|---|---|
| Dislikes | When? | Why? | How Do You Know? |

Then ask your youngster to think of activities or things this person likes or dislikes, when and why he or she likes or dislikes them, and what "evidence" he has observed to support his conclusions.

You can help him get started by giving examples of what you yourself have observed about this person, starting with the statement, "I'll give one example, then you'll give one." Once your youngster has learned how to play, you can fill in an item in one column, and ask him to fill in the other columns. For example, you might insert "Loud television" in the *Dislikes* column, and have him fill in when that particular person objects to loud television and why.

At times your child may have only a vague feeling about someone. He might say, "I'm not sure why, but I think that Uncle Harry doesn't like Aunt Jean (his sister-in-law). Help him clarify his suspicions by asking him what specifically he has seen or heard that makes him feel this way. Suggest what clues to look for in the future that might confirm or disconfirm his feeling.

The following is an example of a chart with some items filled in:

**The Case of Uncle Harry:**

| Likes | When? | Why? | How Do You Know? |
|---|---|---|---|
| Talking to Grandpa | After dinner | Likes old stories | Asks questions about the past. Listens quietly. |

| Likes | When? | Why? | How Do You Know? |
|---|---|---|---|
| Gardening | Weekends | Likes to figure out best way to make things grow. Likes fresh vegetables. | Spends lots of time in garden. Says, "Wait till you taste these tomatoes." |
| Pizza | Supper | Tastes good | Eats a lot of it. Smiles when it arrives. |

| Dislikes | When? | Why? | How Do You Know? |
|---|---|---|---|
| Being late | For movies | Won't know story | Refuses to go if late |
| Loud TV | After work | Tired | Grouchy |
| Aunt Jean | Anytime | She's critical and bossy | He walks out of room when she walks in. Frowns when she talks. |

The final part of the Sherlock Holmes Game involves helping your youngster take the step from observation to action. In the above Case of Uncle Harry, seven-year-old Martin was asked, "What can you do to make Uncle Harry feel good?" His parents told him that for each item on the chart he should think of something he could do to help his uncle obtain what he likes and avoid what he dislikes. Martin came up with the following: "When Uncle Harry is listening to grandpa's stories, I'll play quietly in another room or listen along with him"; "I'll ask him if he needs help gardening"; "I'll be ready on time.when we go to the movies"; "I'll turn the TV down when he comes home from work."

Martin came up with some ideas about how he could help Uncle Harry feel better about Aunt Jean. But his parents felt that aside from the fact that it was unlikely that he could do anything to improve their relationship, both his aunt and uncle would consider Martin's efforts an intrusion into their affairs. Martin's parents told him that although he must take responsibility for the way he treats others, he would be invading their privacy if he tried to change the way they treat each other unless they asked him to.

Martin was now confronted with his first moral conflict: It's good to try to help others, but sometimes helping becomes an invasion of privacy. Martin would also have found himself in the midst of a moral conflict if his parents wanted him to be helpful to his uncle in ways that he felt were unfair to him (if, for example, it used up all his free time). We'll return to a detailed discussion of moral conflicts in a later chapter.

## Be Consistent

Your child can't learn rules of behavior if the rules keep changing. What you consider right and wrong should not be dependent on your moods or whims. If it is wrong to tease a classmate today, it should be just as wrong tomorrow. It shouldn't be wrong today merely because you are in an irritable mood. It shouldn't be passed over tomorrow merely because you are preoccupied. The rules should be consistent, as should the consequences of living up to them or breaking them.

Internalization requires consistency; otherwise, instead of focusing on standards of behavior, your child will monitor your moods to see if today is a day she can get away with something or if it's a day she's likely to be punished by you for no apparent reason. Inconsistency teaches a child that standards are not very important to her parents, at least not as important as the moment-to-moment stimuli triggering their moods. She also learns that her parents are self-centered and unreliable. When parents are inconsistent about moral rules, children tend to lose respect for them, and often come to resent them as well.

For the sake of consistency, it is important when stating rules about behavior to specify the situations in which they apply. Is it always wrong to hit someone? What about self-defense? Often parents scold a youngster one day for hitting someone, and scold him again the next day for not defending himself against a bully. If parents do not specify when it is and is not permissable to hit someone, the result will be a hurt and confused child.

In an important early study on the family factors associated with aggressiveness in children, "inconsistent discipline" by parents was strongly linked to high aggressiveness in grade-school boys. The consistency between parents was also an important factor. Parents who were in conflict about how to raise and handle their child were far more likely to have a seriously aggressive child than those who agreed on child-rearing practices.[10]

Parents would do well to present a united front to their child when it comes to discipline and teaching moral values. Otherwise, the child is torn between which parent to please. He also quickly realizes that by seeming to take one parent's side he hurts the other and exacerbates the conflict between them. This is a very painful and confusing position for a child. A common "solution" to this no-win circumstance is for the child to cynically undermine all rules by playing one parent off against the other. When parents absolutely cannot agree on a rule, the best thing to do is to openly agree to disagree; that is, to present their differences to the child, explain their reasons, and let him discover and decide what *he* would like to do. This will only work if neither parent punishes the child, even obliquely, for going the way of the other parent. A child *can* learn that people can see things differently and still handle their disagreements reasonably and respectfully.

## Be Forceful and Persistent

Mrs. Green was an activist. She fought for the downtrodden in many ways and on many fronts. She was actively involved in politics, participated in a number of social conscience organizations, and tried to conduct her daily life in accordance with her moral principles. She was a forceful speaker at both public meetings and social gatherings. Yet with her own children she was surprisingly timid and irresolute.

Her son, Josh, was an energetic and attractive ten-year-old who knew quite clearly what he liked and didn't like. And one of the things he liked to do was taunt his neighbor and classmate, Sammy. Sammy was overweight and Josh liked to call him "Tubby" and "Fatso," knowing full well that this hurt Sammy's feelings. Sometimes the two boys played well together, but on more than one occasion when Sammy came over to play, Josh would order him out of the house because he was "too fat." Sometimes other playmates would join Josh in the taunting.

Mrs. Green was a very compassionate woman and it pained her to hear her son tease Sammy. Ordinarily, if she felt that some person or group was being mistreated, she would staunchly fight in their defense. But her efforts on Sammy's behalf were not very forceful.

She asked Josh if he would like it if someone made fun of him. He said he wouldn't but that he wasn't fat. He added that if someone did make fun of him, he would have to learn to take it. His mother's only reply was "It's not nice to make fun of people," and that she'd prefer that he didn't. She told us that she believed that her son had to make up his own mind about how to treat people. She remembered resenting her own mother for constantly nagging her about

everything under the sun and didn't want to inflict the same unpleasant experiences on Josh (and, perhaps, risk his coming to resent her). She also said that parents had no right to impose their
values on their children. To do so, she felt, was a form of tyranny.

This same Mrs. Green who was determined not to nag her own
son about something she truly believed in—not hurting others—was
ready at a moment's notice to nag any government official, corporate or union executive, or newspaper editor when she felt they were
hurting others by their actions. In these situations she was firm and
persistent, and would never say that these people in positions of
power should be left to make up their own minds.

There was a serious and tragic consequence of the way Mrs. Green
was handling Josh: she was bringing up a child she didn't like. She
enjoyed his enthusiasm and intelligence, but more and more she
was growing to dislike his character, his "heart," as she called it.
And more and more she began to mistrust his intentions toward
others.

Where was Josh supposed to learn values if not from his parents?
Imposing values seems so unpleasant, so authoritarian; yet Mrs.
Green was ready and willing to preach and teach her beliefs anywhere—except in her own home. She may have been nagged too
much by her own mother, and there are certainly many areas of
child behavior that parents might best leave to the child's own taste
and judgment; but how your child treats other people (including
yourself) is too crucial to be handled with a laissez-faire attitude.
When a child is young, his thoughtless or downright nasty behavior
usually has only limited consequences for others. As he gets older,
his potential to do harm increases markedly.

When a child is inclined not to behave morally, parents must let
him know clearly and forcefully just how important it is to them that
he treat others well, and that their good feelings toward him depend
on it. They should insist that, regardless of his inclinations, his actions must either benefit others or, at the very least, not harm them;
otherwise, *they* have a responsibility to those he might harm (as well
as to him) to curtail his freedom. The research evidence is quite
consistent on this matter. Permissive parents who don't insist that
their children live up to moral rules tend to have children who are
aggressive, self-centered, and irresponsible.[11]

What might Mrs. Green have done? For one thing, she might have
taken a lesson from herself. Although she said she was against nagging and power tactics, she employed them quite readily when Josh

refused to do his homework or said he didn't feel like going to school. At these times the rules were made quite clear. Josh *had* to. If he refused, she did not hesitate to communicate her disapproval. She explained the importance of doing well in school, and expressed anger at his misbehavior. She told us that she was willing to be forceful about school because Josh was too young and inexperienced to understand the importance of education and make his own decisions in this area. We find it astonishing that she considered him experienced enough to make his own decisions about how he should treat others.

Mrs. Green won the battle over schoolwork without ever hitting Josh. She didn't have to. Because he wanted her approval and was upset by her disapproval and because she was clear and consistent in this area, an insistent tone of voice was all she needed to get Josh to capitulate. Having to hit or spank a child in order to make him behave is usually a sign that important opportunities for training have been mishandled. It is likely that Josh would not have continued to mistreat Sammy if his mother had insisted that he stop and let him know how sad it made her feel for Sammy and how much it bothered her, that she couldn't feel pride in Josh when he treated others badly, and how good it made her feel whenever she was proud of him. As we'll see shortly, she could also have taught him a strategy for self-control and given him some specific lessons on how to be a friend.

If you don't let your child know what pleases and bothers you about the way she treats others, and don't insist that she treat others well, then she will never know what kind of conduct you value, or that your values have real importance in your life. If you value people who are kind—and if you want your child to develop the same values—then she cannot be spared the moral judgments of her actions. Your praise of her acts of kindness should be enthusiastic, just as your condemnation of her unkindness must be resolute and persistent.

Dispassionately telling a child that it is wrong to hurt someone isn't likely to be effective. You can, of course, gain some control over her behavior by taking material things away from her or punishing her when she misbehaves (you won't take her to the circus), or offering her an incentive for behaving better in the future (you will take her to the circus). But what moral lessons are you teaching by setting up a relationship between the way she treats other people and whether or not she goes to the circus next week?

If you reward and punish your child in an impersonal manner without letting her know how much her behavior pleases or upsets you, she will never learn that mistreating others is a different kind of offense and much more serious than, say, not making her bed or arriving late for dinner. If you refuse to take her to the circus as a way to teach her to be more responsive to the feelings of others, then it's crucial for her to understand that the reason you are not taking her is because you can't enjoy being with her and don't feel she deserves to have a good time when she has been intentionally mean to someone.

Dispassionately delivered reasons, rewards, and punishments simply will not teach your youngster the importance of being kind to others. Effective moral training has to depend on your relationship with her; that is, on your openly expressing your honest feelings toward her—whether they be of love and joy or shame and sorrow— whenever she is kind or unkind to others.

As a general rule, communicating feelings that will make children feel guilty or ashamed should be reserved exclusively for moral training, for teaching them about the natural consequences of treating others kindly or cruelly—never over matters of social convention or taste such as hair-length or masturbation. In other words, shame can be used both constructively and destructively.

**The role of shame.** A child's experience of shame consists of his inner voice telling him he did something wrong, plus uncomfortable bodily sensations, plus images of the upset looks on his parents' faces and their disapproving words to him when they learn about his misdeed. A child who feels ashamed after hitting a playmate in anger may not care about the pain he caused the playmate. His concern is with those who made the rules against hitting—his parents. He feels ashamed because he has done what he has been told is bad to do by someone he loves and admires and whose love and admiration he wants.

But shame is not the simple fear of rejection. It's not only the child's anticipation of exposure and disapproval that upsets him. He also recognizes that he has violated a trust and has made himself undeserving of love. He wants to maintain his parents' good opinion of him, but also wants to feel he deserves it; he wants to *be* a "good boy." That is why children who are feeling shame often confess. Psychologists Robert Sears, Eleanor Maccoby, and Harry Levin, in their classic treatise on the development of conscience, provide a touching example of this need to make things right through confession.

INTERVIEWER: We'd like to get some idea of how Sid acts when he's naughty. When he deliberately does something he knows you don't want him to do when your back is turned, how does he act?

MOTHER: Very seldom does that. But a few times he has done something that he shouldn't do, that I don't know anything about, if I'm in the other room, he just can't hold it in very long. And finally he comes in to me and he says, "Mother,"—and I'll say, "What?"—"I did something I shouldn't have done." Instead of leaving it and getting away with it, he usually comes and tells me what he's done. He usually comes, I mean, and it's not very long after he's done it. He can hardly hold it in to himself, you see.[12]

Contemporary child-rearing practices are generally opposed to parents using shame to influence a child's behavior. Our position is that for any of us, child or adult, shame is a natural and unavoidable reaction when we violate values that we share with people who are important to us—people we love and admire, and whose love and admiration we want. When you share values with others, it is as if you and they were part of the same team with the same ideals and goals. When you violate the values, you feel as though you've betrayed your teammates, and shame is the natural reaction.

Therefore, whether or not you intend to use shame as a disciplinary technique (by saying to your child, "You ought to be ashamed"), whenever you teach your child values you are automatically setting up conditions for him to feel ashamed if he violates those values.

Some parents feel they can and should prevent their child from ever feeling shame by giving unconditional love; that is, by assuring her that whatever she does, no matter how selfish or cruel, they will never love her less. But in fact, unconditional love is a myth. There certainly are parents who never stop loving their child, in the sense of feeling protective and caring about her happiness. But other aspects of loving a child—respecting her or cheering on her goals or enjoying her company—these all depend on how she behaves.

The loss of love is a natural and proper reaction to immoral behavior. If parents don't teach this to their child in the home, he will be ill prepared for the world outside. Nowhere else will he find unconditional love. In the world outside the family, ostracism and loss of love are the natural consequences of cruelty, stealing, cheating, etc. It is important that a child's experience within the family not be so different from the outside world that he gets a distorted picture of the common rules of social exchange.

We have all seen parents who are afraid to be genuine with their children, who put up with treatment from them that they would never tolerate from anyone else. These parents usually have good intentions; they want to be understanding. But they believe that they will traumatize their children or make them insecure if they discipline them. Unfortunately, their permissiveness and failure to define what are acceptable and unacceptable ways to treat people (including one's parents), does a disservice to both themselves and their children. The consequences to the children are particularly severe since few people outside the family will be as tolerant of mistreatment as the parents.

Most of those who take issue with shame in child-rearing are really concerned that children not be made to feel ashamed of certain specific kinds of behaviors, feelings, or thoughts—those that are deemed natural and harmless. For example, masturbation, among other sexual practices, was once widely considered sinful and good grounds for shaming a child. In recent decades, our society has increasingly removed sexual practices from the moral sphere. Less and less do we base our judgments of a person's character on his or her sexual behavior, or on any behavior that causes no harm to others.

Without question, moral judgments should never be made about behavior that does no one any harm. This is an important theme that will recur many times in this book. But we disagree with those who argue that children should never have to feel shame or fear loss of love from parents regardless of what they do. We believe these are essential for teaching self-control to children who hurt others intentionally. Indeed, in the Sears, Maccoby, and Levin study mentioned before, and in more recent research as well,[13] the children with the strongest consciences were the ones whose parents were the warmest and most accepting, and who used "love withdrawal"— they expressed their disapproval and disappointment emphatically and emotionally—when their children behaved immorally.

Be assured that while we are recommending that children be held responsible for the harm they do, we definitely *are not* recommending bringing up a child in a harsh environment—quite the contrary. Since internalization depends on children's love for their parents, values are best taught in a loving atmosphere—one in which "good" behavior is taught systematically and affectionately, and not just expected from the child and punished when it fails to appear; an atmosphere in which parents communicate the importance of moral values firmly and only criticize specific behaviors, never the child in general; and one in which parents provide ample opportunity for children to correct misbehavior and feel good about themselves.

Since most children care very much about how their parents feel about them—usually more than they care about circuses, allowances, and other material incentives—you have a pretty powerful tool with which to influence your child (at least until adolescence, when it is rivaled by the power of peer approval). Because it is so powerful, you must be careful about how and when you use it. If you tell your child that it hurts you when she doesn't eat everything on her plate or when she wears her hair differently than you like, you are misusing the word *hurt*. These actions certainly don't hurt you in the same way as when you witness her being intentionally cruel. Your need to stop her cruelty certainly can't be equated with your need for her to finish her supper or look neat.

If you want to change a child's behavior in areas that really don't hurt anyone, that are not moral issues but are matters of taste or convention, the more neutral disciplinary techniques are appropriate—take away television time or the circus or her allowance. But don't take advantage of her feelings for you by playing on her sympathies or by withholding your affection for her over any and every kind of misbehavior. This won't help her learn the difference between real moral issues and matters of changing taste and convention. You want to be adamant when it comes to cruelty; but flexibility is worth considering when it comes to household rules like making the bed—especially if you want your youngster to feel that she is a full-fledged member of the household with some decision-making rights.

Turning everything into a moral issue and playing on your child's feelings as a way to control her will, if you succeed, overly restrict her freedom of action. Children have to learn to say no to their parents, but it's hard to say no to a parent if you believe it will hurt him or her deeply. If, when she gets older, she discovers the difference between true moral issues and all the other times she denied her own desires to prevent causing you "pain," she is likely to resent you and turn against you. She will probably then use up most of her and your money complaining to her psychotherapist about it.

## Set Up Well-Defined, Dependable, and Instructive Consequences

One of the best-established principles in psychology is that behavior is affected by its consequences. When behavior is rewarded it tends to occur more often in the future. When it is punished, it occurs less frequently.

There are many aspects of a consequence that contribute to its effect on behavior. These include the size of the reward or the severity of the punishment and how quickly and dependably the reward or punishment follows a behavior. The most important consequences for a child are his parents' approval and disapproval, both of which are crucial to the internalization process. Material rewards (money, toys, etc.) and physical punishment are not recommended. For instance, if your children's play often erupts into fights, you'll have better results in the long run, if instead of offering them a dollar to play cooperatively for an hour, you sometimes tell them *when they are playing cooperatively* how good it makes you feel to see them enjoying and being kind to each other, and even how it fulfills hopes you've always had for a close, joyful family.

Two general principles that we do recommend for setting up effective consequences are: (1) establishing consequences that are dependable and signaled clearly; and (2) the "undoing principle," which offers a framework for setting up natural consequences that allow children to remedy their misdeeds.

*1. Establishing clearly signaled and dependable consequences.* Clearly signaled and dependable consequences let a child know exactly what is expected of him. The anecdote we use to illustrate this does not come from a situation involving parents and children, but from a quite surprising observation at an amateur boxing match between teenagers.

Athletes generally accept the rules of sports as fair since the rules apply equally to all contestants. But some contestants try to get away with breaking or bending the rules. One of the ways boxers do this is by getting an extra jab in at their opponent after the referee has told them to break a clinch. Ordinarily, referees do more than signal a break verbally; they move right in on boxers in a clinch and physically direct them to move apart, watching carefully for sneaky jabs.

At this particular boxing event there were a series of matches and four different referees during the course of the evening. Three of the referees handled the clinches in the typical hands-on manner. But one ref was different. He never touched the fighters. When he said break, they instantly moved apart.

There was something startling about the immediacy of the young boxers' response to his signal. These were inner-city teenagers, some with histories of antisocial behavior, with what some psychologists would label "lack of impulse control." Yet here they were, in the middle of all this passion and violence, scrupulously adhering to the rules of the game.

There was a good reason for this. At the start of the fight this referee made it very clear to the boxers exactly how he would handle the clinches. He told them precisely what he expected of them and what the consequences would be if they did not follow the rules. He said that he would call out "Break" just once, and that if a boxer failed to step back immediately or attempted to land a blow after the signal, he would be disqualified on the spot. The boxers knew from the referee's reputation that he would most definitely enforce the rules—and they handled the clinches accordingly.

This is an unusually vivid demonstration of just how effective consequences can be when they are signaled clearly and occur dependably. In a family setting, too, children respond well to clear signals and dependable consequences. The general form for parents to follow is, If you do A, B will follow (for instance, "If you and your brother start hitting each other, the two of you will have to be separated for the rest of the evening"). Then, if A occurs, make sure B follows.

Keep in mind, though, that as in sports, consequences work best when children agree that the rules are fair and the rewards and punishments appropriate. Children, as well as adults, try to resist rules that they believe have not been established for the mutual benefit of all but, rather, as a way for others to gain at their expense. You'll see this kind of resistance in a child who complains that his parents don't "understand" him—which usually means he believes they've set up rules and consequences without taking important needs or goals of his into account. We will come back to this problem of setting up fair rules and consequences later, and will borrow and put to good use some effective negotiation and "participation management" strategies from the field of organization psychology.

We'll take our boxing example a step further to clarify how consequences contribute to internalization. If the young boxers adhered to the referee's rules only because they didn't want him to disqualify them, they might be expected to try to get away with rule-breaking whenever a more lenient referee oversees a match. There would be no internalization. But, say one of the boxers knows the referee from the local recreation center and admires him; the fact that the referee takes the rules of fair boxing so seriously may very well lead the youngster to adopt the rules as his own, regardless of who referees his future matches. Internalization would be even more likely if, after the match, the ref said to him something like, "You're a good, clean boxer. I like that."

As we've pointed out, when someone that children admire approves of them for following a rule, they are inclined to perceive that rule as good. Adults are subject to the very same process, which we see when junior corporate and military personnel and fraternity pledges increasingly adopt the economic, social, and political values of their superiors.[14]

**2. The "undoing principle."** Normally parents punish a youngster's misdeeds by imposing some kind of restriction on him, such as taking away his allowance or a favorite toy, or banning TV for some period of time. The child then must passively wait out the duration of his "sentence."

In some situations, however, it is possible and advisable for children to actively remedy their misdeeds. We call this the "undoing principle:" If a child steals, he must return the stolen object or make restitution for the loss; if he lies, he must confess and tell the truth. In most situations—particularly when a child is a "repeat offender" and knows full well what the rules are—it will benefit him to have to face someone he has harmed and try to correct the wrong.

We believe that requiring a youngster to undo a misdeed provides her with very important lessons. First, she can experience a sense of positive accomplishment when she takes constructive actions to undo a transgression. Second, she learns that she is a responsible being and cannot be protected by parents from the repercussions of her misdeeds. Third, "undoing" allows her to start with a clean slate in the eyes of her parents (and, one hopes, the person she has wronged).

It is important for parents to remember that once their youngster has made amends she has earned the right to be considered a trustworthy person again. One transgression does not constitute a life of crime. But if parents harp on the event or continue to show their mistrust after the child has made restitution, she will feel permanently stigmatized and come to believe that any positive efforts on her part are futile.

Mrs. Philips discovered that her nine-year-old daughter, Vickie, had, in a moment of anger, stolen some Magic Markers from her friend, Polly. The year before Vickie had taken some candy from a local store without paying for it, but since that was the first time she had stolen anything, her mother thought it would be sufficient to explain to her why it was wrong to steal. She pointed out that Vickie was stealing from a person, not a store, that the owner worked hard for his money and that it wasn't fair for someone to come along and just take his things without paying. "Wouldn't you feel bad if someone stole your favorite doll?" her mother asked. "Would you want to make someone feel bad like that?" Often a simple explanation like that will suffice.

But now Vickie had taken something again, and more serious steps seemed necessary. Mrs. Philips told her daughter she would have to bring the markers back and apologize for having taken them. When Vickie said that she didn't want to do that, her mother replied that stealing was both wrong and against the law, but that she could make an effort to make amends for the theft. Otherwise, more serious steps would have to be taken, including informing the police. With markers in hand and head hung low, Vickie went off to her friend to make her apology.

A few minutes later Mrs. Philips received an angry telephone call from Polly's father. He was shocked—but not at the theft. He was shocked that a mother could "traumatize" her daughter in this way. "Do you know what kind of damage this could do to her?" he asked.

In this situation, without question, Mrs. Philips gets our vote. Some parents feel that forcing their children to "face the music" by directly confronting the person they have wronged will somehow result in a permanent psychological scar. This fear is an outgrowth of various psychological theories that attribute adult emotional problems directly to unhappy childhood experiences. Unquestionably, the events of childhood affect later development, but there is little evidence to support these childhood-traumatization theories.

On the contrary, our experience has been that children respond well to parental discipline and even punishment, so long as there is some reasonable relationship between the child's misdeed and the parents' reaction. Making Vickie return the pens was, of course, a kind of punishment, but it was a punishment designed to *teach* her that there are natural consequences when you are caught harming someone (the other person will like and trust you less), and that there are better, more constructive ways of getting what you want than stealing. Vickie also learned—and this cannot be overemphasized—that her mother attached great importance to her behaving honestly.

There was a contrast effect at work here that had a crucial bearing on the effectiveness and "healthiness" of the training. Mrs. Philips was a very loving mother. She enjoyed her daughter and communicated her pleasure in words and through lots of physical affection. So Vickie understood that if her mother became stern or harsh, it was because a serious infraction had occurred. She trusted that her mother was on her side, was not arbitrary in her reactions, and had open and just motives. Sternness coming from a parent whose everyday manner is stern, harsh, or self-centered could not have had this same effect.

Mrs. Philips was also wise enough to know that her daughter's training would not be completed by simply insisting that she return the stolen items. The embarrassment of having to confess might make Vickie think twice about stealing in the future, but it would not teach her what to do in similar circumstances when filled with anger (which she said had been her motive for the theft). There was also obviously a friendship at stake, so Vickie needed to learn how to apologize constructively—in a way that would be honest but would also maintain the friendship between the girls.

Mrs. Philips started by asking Vickie exactly what she wanted from Polly that prompted her to steal the markers and what she now wanted. The youngster admitted that although she was still angry at her friend, she did want to remain friends. She said she hadn't really wanted Polly's markers, but only wanted to hurt her because Polly ignored her when other girls were around—"and this wasn't the first time." She said that her feelings were hurt, but that she didn't know how to get Polly to change. This understanding formed the basis of the apology. Her mother explained that for friendships to last, they have to be based on honesty, on a willingness to take the risk of letting your friend know when she hurts you, and on a sincere interest in understanding your friend's point of view.

When Vickie went to Polly's house she admitted to her that she had taken the markers in anger. She then explained why she was angry, and that she took the markers because she was too embarrassed to say that she had felt hurt. She added that she knew she was wrong to take them, promised never to do anything like that again, and hoped they could still be friends and try to figure out how to overcome their problems. By apologizing in this way Vickie took responsibility for her actions, was given the opportunity to make amends, and made a first step toward learning how to resolve conflicts with peers in a constructive manner.

### Provide Good Models

Children learn from observing. If they see you treat people kindly and justly it will confirm for them that you truly value kindness and justice. Many studies show that children become more generous and helpful and adhere to rules more steadfastly after they've seen another child or adult behave that way. Unfortunately, they are also prone to follow bad models. Moreover, if you preach goodness to your child but he sees that you don't practice it, the research evidence suggests that he will be more influenced by what you do than by what you say.[15] As he gets older, he's also likely to resent you for being a hypocrite.

Often by simply observing how you behave toward people, your child will understand the moral rule behind your actions. But sometimes it's helpful to put into words what you are doing and why—for example, to explain to her why you are returning a grocery item that was mistakenly placed in your bag, or returning money to a clerk at the supermarket who gave you too much change. If you think about it you'll be surprised at the moral implications of many of your everyday actions that your child witnesses. If she understands the rules guiding your actions, she'll be able to apply them to her own behavior, even though the situations she encounters may be different from yours.

Something else worth putting into words is the good feeling you get from living up to moral standards. Psychologists Elizabeth Midlarsky and James Bryan have shown that children are especially prone to imitate someone's generosity when that person has expressed how good it made her feel to help others.[16]

It is also important to point out other good models to your child —both adults and children. Be careful, though, that you don't communicate this in the form "He's good. You're bad. Be more like him." That will only make your child feel bad and he's likely to resent the person you want him to learn from. He'll more readily accept your bringing good examples to his attention if you praise only the specific actions of the other person and explain why you want him to learn them. Also explain to him that we all learn from other people, that it's a way to get smarter faster because everybody doesn't have to make the same mistakes.

An interesting and effective application of observation learning was described in a recent report of a study of young children (twelve to thirty-six months of age) in a day-care center. When a child behaved aggressively (hitting another child), destructively (breaking a toy), or disruptively (having a tantrum), the caregiver first explained to him what he did wrong and how he should have behaved. For example, if he took a toy away from another child, he was told "No, don't take toys from other children. Ask me for the toy you want." Then the caregiver took him to the side of the room, comforted him if he seemed upset, and told him to sit there for a short while and observe how other children asked for a toy when they wanted one.

Within about a minute the caregiver asked him if he was ready to resume play and if he knew how to ask for toys. If he indicated yes, he was returned to the play area and as soon as he engaged in the correct behavior, he was given enthusiastic praise ("Good! You asked for the toy you wanted"). If the child failed to indicate he was ready to behave correctly, the caregiver left him alone for another thirty seconds and then asked him again if he was ready. This observation learning procedure proved far more effective than simply correcting the child and then redirecting his attention, which was the usual way disruptive behavior was handled.[17] Parents can easily adapt this approach to their own child's play activities with other children.

Keep in mind that characters from stories, both real and fiction, are good sources of moral models for children. One parent helped her daughter think through moral dilemmas by asking her what she thought her favorite character in a storybook series would do in a similar circumstance. Another parent helped his child understand moral courage by relating the story of Jackie Robinson, the first African-American to play professional baseball, and Pee Wee Reese, a white teammate who quickly befriended Jackie, paving the way for other players to accept him on the team. One parent used the Scrooge story (in Charles Dickens' "A Christmas Carol") to help her son recognize his selfishness. The boy, who loved and was moved by the story, had to admit that he was more like the miserly and miserable Scrooge of the first part of the story than the generous, loving Scrooge that he becomes.

### Teach Children What to Say to Themselves and When to Say It

Parental approval and disapproval can motivate a child to change his behavior, but in and of themselves won't teach him something new, since in order for parents to approve or disapprove the behavior must already have occurred. Consequences can only bring about new behavior slowly, through what psychologists call *shaping,* which is similar to the old "you're getting warmer" game. Direct instruction that describes and demonstrates the desired behavior is a much more efficient way to teach. Giving your child detailed behavioral rules and instructions for attending to people's feelings are two examples of direct training. You can also teach him in a direct way what to say to himself in order to make sure he actually does attend to people as he has been taught and follows the rules he's learned. In other words, you can instruct his "good inner voice" directly in order to make sure it says the right thing at the right time.

Let's return to Mrs. Green, Josh, and Sammy to illustrate what could be done to teach Josh self-statements to make him more sensitive to Sammy's feelings.

The first step in teaching self-statements is to define exactly what Josh should say to himself in order to change his behavior. If he is presently saying anything at all to himself when he has the urge to make fun of Sammy, it is that it's all right to do so. His behavior will change if he tells himself something different, something like, "If I call Sammy fat, he will feel bad, and it's wrong to make people feel bad." His mother can actually have him rehearse this—first out loud, and then to himself. She could begin by saying:

> Sammy is your friend and I know you like him. But sometimes you are mean to him. It's as if part of you is telling yourself "Be nice to Sammy," and another part is saying, "I don't care about him" or even "I like hurting him." Everybody feels divided like that at times—adults too, me too. And there are times when the mean voice sounds a lot louder in our head than the good voice. That's when we need to remind ourselves with all our strength to do the right thing and not let ourselves hurt someone on purpose. When you feel an urge coming on to be mean to Sammy, that's when that good voice has to speak right up and say, "If I call Sammy fat, he will feel bad, and it's wrong to make people feel bad." In

other words, it's important for us to expect to hear from these mean voices inside us because they are going to be there. When we're ready for them they won't get the best of us.

Okay, now imagine a time when you might be tempted to make fun of Sammy. (After he acknowledges that he has thought of a time.) Okay, now say out loud what the good voice is supposed to say. (After that.) Good. Now imagine that same situation again, and tell yourself the same thing, but only in your head this time.

Some children will enjoy the attention you give them during this kind of training. Some will resist it, particularly an older child who is trying to assert his independence. If you make the effort—even if your child balks at going through the step-by-step rehearsal—you'll more than likely have made your point. You will have demonstrated how important the issue is to you and given him a procedure for gaining self-control. It's not necessary to insist on the rehearsal if he really seems unhappy about it.

Josh is not always unkind to Sammy—only some of the time. It's helpful to know *when* in order to better prepare him to use his new self-statements when they are most needed. Does he taunt Sammy primarily when he gets frustrated about some goal of his own? Does he make himself feel better by showing his superiority and power over his friend? Or does he mistreat Sammy primarily when he is afraid he might have to share some activity, toy, or person with him? Perhaps he's afraid that the other kids will look down on him for being Sammy's friend.

If his parents recognize a pattern in the occasions when he is mean to Sammy, they can remind him of what to say to himself at just those necessary moments and also shape his self-statements to fit the instigating circumstances precisely. For example, Mrs. Green could say to Josh: "You're upset now because you struck out in the Little League game this morning. Now is the time when you need to be careful not to do or say anything to hurt Sammy's feelings. If you start to make fun of Sammy or feel yourself about to, I want you to *tell yourself* not to do it and remind yourself that it is wrong to try to make yourself feel better by making someone else feel bad—and that making Sammy feel bad won't improve your batting average."

A reminder: When you try to discern precisely when your child behaves badly toward someone, it is important to remember that you will never be making more than a guess. It should be a guess based on careful observation, but don't be too pushy about your explanation. If your child disagrees with your hypothesis, tell her what you've observed that has led you to your conclusions; but it isn't usually necessary to convince her that you are right in order to teach her when and how to make proper self-controlling statements.

As we have seen, a child can gain control over and inhibit unkind urges by learning *what* to say to herself and *when* to say it. She can also learn to internalize statements that promote helpful actions. The other side of "Don't hurt others" is "Do something to make them feel good."

With this in mind, Mrs. Green could instruct Josh that one of his responsibilities in being Sammy's friend is to help him feel good about himself. A conversation between this parent and her son might run something like this:

MRS. GREEN: You've been a bad friend to Sammy. You can start to undo that by being a good friend to him. (Recall the "undoing principle.") One way to be a good friend is to help your friend feel good about himself. Think of a time when Sammy doesn't like himself.

JOSH: When we're playing baseball. He's not a good hitter and sits out most of the time.

MRS. GREEN: Would he like himself more if he was a good hitter?

JOSH: Sure.

MRS. GREEN: When he strikes out, what happens?

JOSH: The kids on the team get annoyed with him and make fun of him.

MRS. GREEN: Now how can you be a better friend to Sammy?

JOSH: I can try to help him hit better and tell the other kids not to say anything when he strikes out.

MRS. GREEN: Good. Do you really think you can do that?

JOSH: Sure.

MRS. GREEN: When he doesn't get a hit in a crucial game, you're going to get annoyed with him and then it's going to be hard to remember to be a good friend and continue to be encouraging. So let's practice what to say to yourself then. Imagine you're playing an important game and it's Sammy's turn at bat and he strikes out. Try to feel how annoyed you'll be. Then say to yourself, "Sammy's trying his hardest and he probably feels terrible now. I'll tell him it's okay and that we'll just practice some more." First say it out loud; then imagine the scene again and say it to yourself.

If Josh is going to teach Sammy to hit, it would be important for his mother to emphasize to him the power of praise. Children fall so easily into criticizing each other and calling each other names like "stupid" and "dummy." But in teaching skills like baseball, praise works much better than criticism. In baseball there is already a natural and obvious negative consequence for "misbehavior"—missing the ball. Adding criticism is unnecessary. A child can learn to teach effectively and even have fun doing it—if he or she is taught an effective way to teach. Basically, this consists of (a) breaking down the task to be learned into small steps that can be mastered with a little practice ("Hold your bat back so you can be ready for the ball." "Swing straight." "Follow through on your swing."); (b) giving instructions on what to focus on in order to master each step ("Remember to feel the pull on these muscles as you hold the bat the correct way." "Watch the ball."); and (c) praising even the slightest improvement.

For Josh, playing with Sammy could take on a new focus. Instead of becoming frustrated by playing with someone unskilled, he could experience the challenge of testing both his knowledge of the game and his skill as a teacher. He could also experience the good feelings that come from making his mother proud of him because he has learned to be a responsible friend.

Of course, the ultimate goal is for Josh to be good—not because he's pleased his mother, but because he sees his friend's pleasure. But reaching that goal depends on his development of empathy for Sammy—a process that can be slow for some children.

Before leaving the topic of internalization we'd like to share one of our favorite examples of the process. It is said of Jawaharlal Nehru, the first prime minister of India, that whenever he was confronted with a difficult political decision, he would remember and try to be guided by these words of Gandhi:

> Whenever you are in doubt or when the self becomes too much with you, try the following expedient: Recall the face of the poorest and most helpless man you have ever seen and ask yourself if the step you contemplate is going to be of any use to him. Will he be able to gain anything by it? Will it restore to him control over his own life and destiny? In other words, will it lead to . . . self-rule for the hungry and spiritually starved millions of our countrymen? Then you will find your doubts and your self melting away.

# 3

# Empathy: The Second Foundation Stone—How You Can Foster Empathy in Your Child

It was Bernard's seventh birthday and his second-grade teacher, Mrs. Lester, was slicing through the homemade chocolate layer cake she had brought to school to celebrate the occasion. The children lined up, plastic forks in hand, waiting to be served. Soon it was Amy's turn, and as Mrs. Lester handed her a piece of cake, Amy asked if she could give her piece to Ronnie, a shy boy who was sitting by himself in the corner. To Mrs. Lester's "Don't you like chocolate cake?" Amy whispered, "I do, but Ronnie doesn't think anybody in the class likes him. That's why he didn't come up for cake. Maybe he'll feel better if I bring him some and sit with him for a while."

It was 3:30 and Mrs. Robbins looked out the window and saw her daughter, Mandy, and three of her friends arguing as they walked home from school. When Mandy came in she was crying and immediately burst out with, "They're firing Mr. Skelton."

Mandy was in the fourth grade at a private school and Mr. Skelton was her math teacher. "He's a good teacher," she exclaimed. "And he tries hard. But the kids don't listen to him and they make fun of him. It's not his fault if they don't learn anything."

Mrs. Robbins had met Mr. Skelton at Parent's Day. He seemed bright and caring, but appeared a bit awkward and, she had to admit, did seem somewhat comical in an absentminded-professor sort of way. She remembered hearing one of the other parents blame her son's poor math grades on Mr. Skelton's inability to maintain discipline in the classroom, but she hadn't heard anything about him being let go.

Mandy asked her mother to call the school to see if she could do anything. "I just told Harriet and Barbara and Tommy that I'd never talk to them again if they made fun of him anymore. They think I'm crazy, but I feel so bad for him when they do that. He shouldn't have to lose his job because some dumb kids don't know how to behave themselves. The only teachers they listen to are the mean ones. But, Mommy, he's a very good teacher, and he's a very nice man—and it's just not fair."

When Mrs. Richmond came back from the supermarket at 11:00 A.M. she was surprised to find her son, Joey, at home. He had recently started a summer job as a mechanic's assistant at a local automobile repair shop. Joey, who was seventeen, loved working on cars and already knew quite a lot about them. He was excited to have an opportunity to learn about many different kinds of cars and to work with the latest professional equipment. Today was the beginning of his second week on the job.

"I got fired," Joey said a bit sheepishly. His surprised mother asked what happened. "They told this guy that they fixed his car. I knew they didn't—so I told him so. All they did was adjust the carburetor to make it sound better, but the whole engine's going to die in a couple of hundred miles. Instead of telling him, they charged him for things they never did and told him it was okay. I felt funny. I didn't know what to do. When he mentioned he was taking his family on vacation tomorrow, driving up to Canada, I pictured them all being stuck on the road somewhere with their hood up and their vacation ruined. So I told him—and they fired me. After that, I would have quit anyway."

Evelyn shocked herself. She couldn't believe she had actually stolen a pocketbook. A moment ago she was sitting in the public library working on a report for her seventh-grade history class. She looked up and saw an unattended pocketbook across the table next to a pile of books. She looked around. There were three or four people at other tables, all busy at work. "She must be in the stacks," Evelyn thought, and a strange excitement ran through her body. "I'll take it," she said to herself. She quickly gathered her belongings, glanced back and forth around the room, lifted the bag, and walked briskly out the door.

Now she was running down the street with her heart pounding to the thrill of danger. She ran into the park and found a bench on a deserted pathway. Now she would open the bag and see what treasure her bravery would yield. First, the wallet: seventeen dollars—not bad. There was a pretty leather key case, and her favorite perfume, and makeup she liked, and a pen, and some clips and ribbons, and a photo album with pictures of friends and family and a dog, and. . . . Suddenly Evelyn began to feel a sinking sensation in her chest. She started to cry. "How awful that girl must feel now. How could I be so mean?"

The everyday items in the pocketbook, and the photos had brought into vivid focus for Evelyn that she had stolen the pocketbook from a person, a girl just like herself. She realized how hurt and angry she would feel if someone had done that to her. She sat on the bench a long time, imagining her victim's reaction to the discovery that her bag was missing; she pictured the girl's sad walk home and her explanation to her parents. Through her tears, Evelyn noted her victim's name and address on the identification card in the wallet. She went to the house, rang the doorbell, put the pocketbook down and ran away. From across the street she watched the girl's look of surprise as she picked up her bag. She saw her face fill with happiness and relief when she found all the contents intact. As she watched Evelyn wished she could say something to her about what she had learned, and wondered if they could become friends; but she felt too ashamed to really consider confessing.

From what we see on our television sets and read in our newspapers, and from so many of our own daily experiences, it is easy to become pessimistic about human nature. We witness man's inhumanity to man everywhere we look. But the four incidents just described tell a different side of the story. People do care about others. They do help others, sometimes at considerable cost to themselves. Caring and helping don't usually make headlines, but they do happen all around us all the time.

The protagonists in each of the four stories had something important in common. Each experienced the feelings of another person. They weren't simply cool and rational observers of others; but in some remarkable way they actually felt the experience of the other person—from the inside, as if it were happening to them. We call this marvelous ability to feel for others and put ourselves in their place *empathy*.

Empathy is the second of the three foundation stones of our moral-training program. Its significance for moral behavior is that it allows us to feel pleasure at other people's joy and pain at their suffering.

Because of empathy, our own actions toward others have a powerful emotional effect on ourselves. If you experience another person's suffering and if he is suffering because of something you did, then, in effect, you have hurt *yourself* by hurting him. When you feel empathy for others, your actions toward them boomerang back on you. You feel good if you are good to them and bad if you hurt them. Therefore, when we experience empathy it becomes in our own interest to treat others well. The particular kind of distress we experience when we hurt someone we "feel for" is referred to as *guilt* or as having a guilty conscience. Conversely, when we bring joy to someone we empathize with, their good feelings fill us with joy.

## THE EXPERIENCE OF EMPATHY

One of the wonderful aspects of empathy is our helplessness in the face of it. We don't *decide* to feel for someone; it just happens to us—virtually reflexively when the conditions are right. And when we feel for someone, we don't want to hurt that person—our inclinations are all helpful. In fact, it's painful *not* to help. Anyone who has been unable to ease the pain of someone he or she *felt for*—a parent with a hurt or sick child, for instance—knows how intense the psychological discomfort of empathy can be.

The experience of empathy is based on imagining how someone else feels and putting ourselves in his or her place. This was demonstrated in a study some years ago by Ezra Stotland at the University of Washington.[1] Stotland's subjects observed a person reacting to heat applied to his hand. The "victim" was actually Stotland's assistant, trained to act as if he were feeling pain. When subjects were told to focus only on the movements that the assistant made, they reported little empathy for his suffering. But when Stotland instructed them to imagine either how the assistant felt as the heat was applied or that they themselves were undergoing the heat treatment, subjects did experience empathic discomfort.

Stotland's findings, along with those of many other researchers, demonstrate that simply prompting a child to imagine how another person feels or to put herself in that person's place are highly effective ways to arouse empathy in her.

One way to clarify what the experience of empathy is like is to contrast it with sympathy. When you feel sympathy you care *about* the other person; when you experience empathy you *are* the other person. For example, a friend of ours is sympathetic to the misery of both Catholics and Protestants in Ireland and can understand both their positions. He abhors the killing on either side. But he is of Irish Catholic descent and he cannot help his personal identification when members of that faction are harmed. He *becomes* them and feels their pain more acutely. We know others who have a similar division between their empathic and sympathetic reactions when they hear broadcasts of Israeli and Palestinian war deaths. They regret the killing on both sides, but losses on one side will evoke a stronger, more personal identification and mourning.

Empathy is most easily aroused for the suffering of people with whom we identify, with those who we recognize as people like ourselves. Military combat trainers know this and do their best to prevent their soldiers from feeling empathy for the "enemy." Combat trainers will, for example, try to dehumanize the enemy by attributing all sorts of atrocities to them. Political leaders often do the same when they want the general citizenry to accept their designation of who their enemies are; a standard ploy has been to associate "our side" with God and "their side" with the devil.

Whom we identify with is not just limited to national or ethnic affiliations. During the Vietnam War, many Americans empathized with the Vietnamese in the sense that they experienced the suffering of a foreign people as their own. They *were* the Vietnamese. In fact, in a study of California college students in 1971, more laudable traits were attributed to the Vietnamese people than to Americans.[2] Antiwar movements in the past have generally been idealistic (war is bad on principle) or self-protective (it's not our problem), and they were not very widespread or effective. The vigor and persistence of the Vietnam War era antiwar movement may have been due to the personal sense of tragedy that many Americans felt when they read about the slaughter of these distant people with whom they shared a common humanity.

### Empathy Motivates Kindness

Empathy leads to altruism. When we feel for people, we want to act on their behalf. We want to protect them from harm, ease their suffering, make them happy. This relationship between empathy and altruism has been confirmed many times by research psychologists. They have evoked and measured empathy in various ways and usually found that high empathy leads to more helping, increased sharing, and a greater willingness to sacrifice in order to promote someone else's well-being.

What is exciting about these studies is that they demonstrate how easy it is to get people to be concerned about others. Without doubt, we can be a very nasty species; but these various findings offer evidence that our inclinations to do good are just barely below the surface, ready to come forward.

For example, psychologists Miho Toi and C. Daniel Batson[3] found that they could generate empathic feelings just by altering the focus people had while listening to an interview. They then went on to demonstrate that empathy does, indeed, lead to altruism. Toi and Batson's subjects, students at the University of Kansas, did not know they were participating in a study on empathy. As far as they knew, they were recruited to evaluate pilot tape recordings of a new campus radio interview program. Their task, they were told, was to adopt "a specific listening perspective . . . because how people listen can influence their reactions to broadcast materials."

Students heard an interview with a schoolmate who said she had broken both her legs in an accident and was having a hard time keeping up with classwork. The "listening perspective" was the way Toi and Batson tried to arouse empathy. They assigned one group to an "empathy" condition and asked them to focus on the feelings of the person being interviewed. The other subjects were asked to gather only objective information about the interviewee.

After hearing the program, the listeners were given the opportunity to volunteer to help the interviewee with her schoolwork. Toi and Batson's main findings were that the "empathy" subjects reacted with much more compassion for her and considerably more of them volunteered to help than those in the "objective" group. The researchers concluded that empathy for someone in trouble produces a strong urge to help.

In another study, B. Leiman secretly filmed kindergartners and first-graders as they watched a short videotape in which a child becomes upset upon discovering that his prized marble collection has been stolen.[4] The tape ended with a close-up shot of the child's sad face. Some viewers showed sadness on their own faces as they saw the child on the tape learn that his marbles were gone. Others did not react noticeably. Leiman used the degree of sadness on a viewing child's face as a measure of the amount of empathy he felt.

After the tape, the children were given a choice: they could play with an Etch-a-Sketch toy or they could turn a crank on a machine that issued marbles, *all* of which would go to the boy they had seen on the film. The results were clear: Children who were visibly moved during the tape cranked out many more marbles than those who were not. As in the Batson experiment, this study found that when you feel for someone in pain, you also feel impelled to do something to help him.

The Toi and Batson, Leiman, and many other studies on the connection between empathy and altruism demonstrate that fostering a child's empathic reactions to the experiences of others is an effective way to get her to treat people more kindly. When children don't act on their empathic feelings, it is usually because they don't know how to or aren't sure they are allowed to.[5]

## The Origins of Empathy

The capacity for empathy is obviously something we are born with. And just as obviously, it doesn't develop in everyone to the same degree. Parents with more than one child often report that one seemed, from his or her earliest years, to be more sensitive to others, more concerned about people's feelings. Parents also find that some children seem, without special training, to be more aware of their impact on those around them; they seem to know that they have the power to hurt others as well as make them feel good.

Often parents have no idea how their child got that way, or why another child turned out "less feeling." It's not uncommon for a parent to say that a child was just "born with a good (or bad) heart." Empathy, like most human traits, is evidently not distributed equally among the human race. Some children, like seven-year-old Amy, who shared her cake with a classmate, do indeed seem to have come into the world with a larger dose of whatever it is that makes us respond empathically to our fellow humans.

Child psychologists have observed empathy in children at very early ages—well before they are two. Martin Hoffman, one of the leading researchers on empathy, tells the story of a thirteen-month-old child who, upon seeing an adult look sad, responded with a distressed look of his own, and then "offered the adult his beloved doll."[6]

Some psychologists speculate that empathy begins virtually at birth, tracing its roots to the "empathic distress cry" emitted by infants even on their very first day of life when they hear another infant crying. Interestingly, in studies of the empathic distress cry, newborns weren't as prone to cry when they heard a computer-generated copy of crying, or even a recording of themselves crying; they weren't just responding to loud noise. They were able to tell the real thing—a member of their species in trouble—from a simulation.

As early as their second day of life infants appear able to differentiate sad, happy, and surprised expressions on an adult's face. By three months, they not only discern mood changes in others, but their own emotional states are affected by them. By the time children are two years old they are able to make the connection between what people feel and the causes of their feelings, which enables them to take actions to purposely make people feel better or worse. Psychologists Inge Bretherton and Marjorie Beeghly recorded some conversations of two-year-olds that confirmed how adept they are at connecting emotions to their causes. Two of their examples are "Maybe Gregg would laugh when he saw Beth do that" and "You sad, mommy. What daddy do?"[7]

Another observation of Martin Hoffman's illustrates this understanding of causality in a child who was only fifteen months old: "Michael was struggling with his friend, Paul, over a toy. Paul started to cry. Michael appeared concerned and let go of the toy so that Paul would have it, but Paul kept crying. Michael paused, then gave his teddy bear to Paul, but the crying continued. Michael paused again, then ran to the next room, returned with Paul's security blanket, and offered it to Paul, who then stopped crying." Hoffman's interpretation was that "Michael . . . could somehow reason by analogy that Paul would be comforted by something that he loved."[8]

It's clear that between twelve and thirty months of age, children spontaneously begin to display behavior that definitely deserves to be called empathic. They seem to be moved by the happiness or sadness of others, often trying to give comfort when they see someone in distress. They also become increasingly aware of the various kinds of feelings that people have and what causes them and they even begin to engage in "reparative behavior," trying to make amends when they realize that they are the cause of someone else's pain.[9]

By four, children have a good enough understanding of emotions to accurately play-act other people's circumstances and emotional states. They'll play at being mommy driving the car and even play getting angry at a bad driver who cuts them off. This ability to take on another's perspective is crucial for moral development as demonstrated in a recent study with preschoolers. The researchers, Robert Stewart and Robert Marvin, gave these young children a test to measure how well they understood another's point of view and also recorded which children came to the aid of a younger sibling in distress. The children who did try to give comfort (about half did) were usually the ones who scored high on the perspective-taking test.[10]

As a child's language skills develop she becomes able to feel empathy for others without having to witness their experience directly. She can feel for people just by being told about them. She will then witness their experience in her imagination. No doubt this unique human attribute has contributed enormously to our species' survival, and, as a by-product of its survival value, it is probably why we enjoy stories and plays. As we shall see, a child's ability to empathize with the fictional and historical characters she reads about opens up many opportunities for moral training.

## WHAT PARENTS CAN DO TO FOSTER EMPATHY

Since empathy involves putting ourselves in someone else's place, it follows that for any of us—child or adult—the more information we have about a person's experience, the more likely we are able to feel empathy for him, feeling bad when he feels bad and good when he feels good. There are three levels of knowledge we can have about people's feelings. The first is simply observing what they are feeling (anger, joy, etc.). Beyond that, we can understand the immediate causes of that feeling (they got tired, they won the lottery, etc.). At the third level we have an understanding of how a particular experience fits into a person's life as a whole, with its ongoing struggles and strivings.

Sometimes just witnessing someone's emotional state is sufficient to arouse a child's empathic feelings. If he sees someone crying, even if it's a stranger, he may start to cry himself and make an effort to comfort the person. A number of studies demonstrate that this basic empathic reaction to simply observing distress in others is quite common in children. In fact, even just telling children about the plight of others, say "poor children," is usually sufficient to get them to donate some of their own belongings.

When a child is spontaneously compassionate in this way, there is obviously no need for parents to do anything extra to bring on empathic feelings, except, when necessary, to expand his or her awareness of what people might be experiencing. One study reports that a particularly effective way to do this, and induce altruism, is to ask children leading questions that direct them to make their own discoveries about people's needs and feelings, and how they might be helped.[11]

Parents can support their child's compassionate inclinations by letting him know that they are pleased with his sensitivity to others, and by assisting and guiding his efforts to give aid. Sometimes parents worry about their child being too empathic, too easily upset by others' misfortunes. The best way to handle this is not to "harden" him by turning him into a cynic or embarrassing him for his tender feelings, but rather to help him put his feelings into action and teach him that even small acts of kindness can make a great difference in people's lives.

There will be times, though, when even a generally compassionate child won't spontaneously focus on another person's feelings, at least not from that person's perspective. For instance, when a child's interests conflict with someone else's, her own perspective may be the only one she recognizes, and without any hesitation she may ignore or knock the other person out of the way. She may know quite well that she has hurt the person, but may not care, or may even be glad. At those times she needs some firm instructions to attend to the other person's feelings and consider her actions from that person's point of view. Martin Hoffman and a number of other researchers have shown that parents who consistently react to their children's misbehavior by focusing them on the feelings of the person they have harmed tend to have children who evince a better understanding of other people's perspectives and who are more empathic and altruistic.[12]

In one recent study psychologists Carolyn Zahn-Waxler, Marian Radke-Yarrow, and Robert A. King observed that children (one-and-a-half- to two-and-a-half-year olds) who were the most caring and helpful had mothers who reacted to their harmful acts with emotionally toned explanations that forcefully pointed out the ill effects of what they had done and stressed how wrong it is to harm someone. They quote some effective reprimands including, "You made

Doug cry. It's not nice to bite''; "Don't you see you hurt Amy—don't ever pull hair''; and "When you hurt me, I don't want to be near you." These mothers generally combined internalization and empathy training techniques, giving their children firm instructions to focus on other people's feelings.

One reminder: As we pointed out in the last chapter, stern reprimands work best when they contrast with the way parents usually treat their child. In the study by Zahn-Waxler and her colleagues, the mothers who were the best moral trainers were themselves the most "empathic caregivers," showing great concern for their children's "hurts and needs." These researchers also caution that "physical restraint and physical punishment" were not associated with high altruism in children and that simply giving a child "prohibitions without explanations" worked *against* the development of altruism.[13]

A child is better able to put himself in someone's place and thus is more likely to feel empathy for that person when he knows not only *what* the person feels, but *why* he feels as he does. If a mother tells her son in a harsh voice, "Turn down the stereo," he can be pretty sure what she is feeling. Her tone of voice will communicate her irritation and perhaps even convey a warning that he'll be punished if he doesn't do what she asked. Scolding and threatening may get her what she wants for the moment, but they won't get her son to care about her peace of mind.

If she wants empathic understanding from him, she'll have to provide him with the information he needs to understand her, and not expect him to read her mind and then get angry when he doesn't. She might, for instance, tell him, "when the stereo is that loud, it makes me physically uncomfortable and I can't concentrate on my work" or "I need to relax for a while after work and I can't when the music is that loud." These messages would let her son know the specific needs behind her reactions to his loud music and give him the opportunity to accommodate her out of compassion rather than fear.

It's a mistake to assume that your child will automatically regard you as a person with feelings like his. When his desires and your desires conflict, empathy from either of you will be hard to come by. If you only give him commands ("Turn down the stereo"), the pressure on his behavior is all from the outside—from you as the authority. If, instead, you tell him the full story about what you are feeling, sharing with him what your needs and experiences are and letting him know how his actions make your life easier or harder, you will be setting up the conditions for him to get inside your experience and feel empathy for your needs. Once empathy is aroused, the pressure on him to behave well will come from himself. Empathy will then serve as an impetus for *self*-control.

Unless a child understands why someone feels the way he or she does, his ability to ease that person's pain or make him or her feel better will be very limited. In addition, because people don't always show their feelings or describe them very clearly, frequently the only way to ascertain someone's emotional state is by surmising it on the basis of information about what he has gone through. For instance, eleven-year-old Lilly thought that her friend, Judy, was snubbing her when she passed her in the school hallway without a word and then failed to return a phone call. But Lilly understood these incidents differently a few days later when she found out that Judy's parents had just separated. Then she no longer took Judy's neglect personally.

Certainly by the time children are eight years old they can appreciate this kind of extenuating circumstance and make accurate guesses about a person's feelings on the basis of information about what he's recently experienced. They are even capable of forgiving someone who mistreats them if they learn that the person was ill or having personal problems.[14]

You can use virtually any discussion about people to educate your child about feelings and their causes, and their connections to how people act. For instance, if he asks why his recently widowed aunt is selling her country home and moving back to the city, you can explain that she feels lonely living by herself without any family nearby, and that her old house makes her sad because so many things in it remind her of happier days in the past. Then you can be open to further questions.

Too often, and without good reason, parents keep children in the dark about why adults feel the way they do. A typical conversation might go something like this:

MOTHER: Aunt Esther is feeling sad, so play quietly tonight.
CHILD: What made her sad?
MOTHER: Never mind. Just do as I ask.

When parents keep the causes of emotions secret from their child, they are not helping her develop either compassion or a more mature understanding of human feelings. They are only giving orders. Her aunt's sadness may then become merely a burden and an inconvenience as far as she is concerned. The most effective information for arousing empathy is information about what a person is striving for and the struggles he is having in reaching his goals. It is a device well known to writers. The more they tell us about a character's pursuits and setbacks, the more likely we are to empathize with that character, even if he or she is a villain. Only by knowing a person's hopes and struggles can we truly understand his or her joys and disappointments.

For instance, for decades now, every Christmas, television viewers have turned on Frank Capra's *It's a Wonderful Life* and been moved by George Bailey's conflict over his sense of duty and his longing to free himself of obligations so he can pursue his dreams. Would any of us want to hurt George Bailey? But it's not only noble characters we feel empathy for—not when great writers have their way with us. For over forty years, theatergoers have empathized with the plight of Blanche DuBois, who took a streetcar named Desire to a world in which she didn't belong. We can empathize with her need to recapture a lost youth even though she lies and schemes and tries to manipulate those around her. Perhaps only Shakespeare could make us feel for a character as cruel as Richard III, but by letting us in on Richard's moment-to-moment "objectives and obstacles" (to borrow theater vocabulary), he certainly does.

These writers' techniques are so powerful that children can be induced to empathize with anything from a cartoon mouse (good old Mickey) to an inanimate object, as in the classic story of *The Little Engine That Could*. Children apparently have a biologically based readiness to respond empathically to virtually anything, once they view it in terms of its strivings and struggles.

It's not that children don't know the difference between living beings and inanimate objects. They certainly do and ordinarily treat them very differently. It may be illogical to feel sorry for something that you know doesn't really have feelings, but children do just that. Once they come to view an inanimate object as being involved in some kind of struggle, empathy overpowers logic.

Adults, too—and with surprising frequency—will feel for the "plight" of an inanimate object: navy men will try to rescue a battle-scarred warship from an "undignified" scrapping. A friend of ours feels guilty whenever he returns to the rural home of his childhood because when he was ten, he broke branches off an old tree that "had made it through a lot of hard winters and earned the right to live out its natural life without anybody disfiguring it."

Like a good writer, parents can guide their children into the inner experiences of others. Like the reader of a good story, the child's reaction to seeing the world from other people's perspectives will be to understand and empathize with their hopes, joys, and sorrows.

## Role-Playing, Guided Imagining, and Role Exchanging

One of the most effective ways to help your child experience the world from someone else's perspective is through *role-playing,* which refers to the process of imagining that you are someone else, seeing the world through his or her eyes and behaving as he or she would behave. When a mother says to her daughter, "Imagine how your brother feels when you take his toys away," she is, in effect, asking her to role-play.

When role-playing is used in a structured way, with *guided imagining,* it is a particularly effective tool for getting a child to understand and care about a person's strivings and struggles. In guided imagining you focus your child on evocative details of the other person's experience.

For example, suppose your child makes fun of the way one of his schoolmates looks—perhaps a neatly dressed but not conventionally attractive boy in his class. Start by sitting him down in a quiet place. If he refuses, be forceful and persistent so that he understands how important it is to you and how much you disapprove of his insensitivity. Then ask him to close his eyes and imagine himself in the place of his schoolmate getting ready for school in the morning. As this boy, he selects his nicest clothes, combs his hair carefully—in general, tries to look his best and hopes he'll have a pleasant day at school and that his classmates will like him. And all goes well until he meets up with—guess who?—who deliberately tries to make him feel bad. Then ask your child to describe what he (as the boy) thinks and feels after he is insulted.

This kind of detailed imagery is far more effective than simply reminding your child that "It's not nice to make fun of people." The more details you create for your child, the stronger the impact should be.

In the example above, role-playing is used for remedial purposes, to prevent a child from repeating an insensitive act. Role-playing may also be used for a more general kind of sensitivity training by simply selecting a person the child knows—even someone he has only read about—and having him imagine various circumstances and struggles in that person's life. This is particularly useful in helping a child understand and overcome fears and prejudices against people who come from different backgrounds.

The power of role-playing to increase sensitivity and improve behavior was demonstrated a few years ago in a carefully executed study by Michael Chandler of the University of Rochester.[15] He found that delinquent children who learned general role-playing skills committed fewer crimes than a group of similar children that did not have the training. The children—all between eleven and thirteen years of age—were serious offenders: "All had multiple contacts with the police [and] had committed one or more crimes which would have constituted felonies if committed by an adult."

First Chandler confirmed that the delinquent children had poorer "perspective-taking skills" than a comparison group of nondelinquent children; the delinquents had a great deal of difficulty describing incidents from any perspective but their own, while the matched nondelinquents had little difficulty switching perspectives.

The role-playing training consisted of having the youngsters "develop, portray, and record brief skits involving persons of their own ages [in] real-life situations," and then videotape them. Chandler's assistants gave the children feedback on the accuracy and quality of their depictions.

To show that any improvement in behavior was due to learning role-playing skills and not just from the activities and social contacts, Chandler set up a comparison group of delinquent children who made animated and documentary films that weren't focused on people, and did not engage in any role-enactments.

At the end of ten weeks the children with the role-playing experiences scored substantially higher on a perspective-taking test. Those without role-playing training improved only slightly. Of greater importance is the finding that during the eighteen-month period following the training, *the group with the role-playing experiences had half the number of arrests than they had during the eighteen months before training.* There was barely any change in the other group.

Chandler suggests that a child's antisocial behavior may stem from his inability to see the world from anyone's point of view but his own. His study demonstrates that this deficiency is correctable.

Other studies have also demonstrated the value of formal role-playing training.[16] In one, Ronald Iannotti of Marietta College in Ohio worked with six- and nine-year-old children from middle-class backgrounds. Like Chandler, Iannotti used skits as a format for training, assigning each child a different role in a story—one, for instance, about some boys who found a wallet and had to decide what to do with it. Various scenarios were developed for each story, either by the children themselves or by the adult leader. Sometimes the children physically enacted the role; sometimes they just described what they would do as their character in the story.

To make sure that the boys understood the motives and feelings of the characters they portrayed, the leader asked them such questions as "Why did you do what you did? Why do you feel that way? What will you do next?" To focus the boys on the feelings of *others*, the leader asked, "How will they feel? What is he/she thinking about you? How would you feel if you were . . . ? What would you do if you were . . . ?"

To test the effects of the training, Iannotti set up an "altruism" test at the end of the training session. Each child was given some candy to keep and was also told about a poor boy whose birthday was coming up. The children could eat all their candy themselves or donate as much as they liked to the poor boy.

Iannotti found that the six-year-old children with role-playing training were more generous than an untrained comparison group. Almost none of the untrained children donated candies, whereas, on the average, the trained children gave away more than half of their sweets. The nine-year-olds were already pretty adept at seeing things from other people's perspectives and were quite generous even without the role-playing training. But, in general, those who were the best role-players were also the most generous—just as other research has found that children who are adept at taking on other people's perspectives tend to be more cooperative and less selfish than children who are weak in this skill.[17]

Keep in mind that the children in the Chandler study were *not* specifically trained to reduce their criminal behavior, and those in the Iannotti study were *not* taught to be generous. Improvement in these children was a result of learning to see the world from someone else's point of view.

For parents the primary lesson of these role-playing studies is to make this kind of training a part of your child's formal moral instruction. Choose someone for her to role-play and ask her to imagine herself living through some of the circumstances of that person's life. Prompt her understanding of the person she portrays with the same kind of questions asked by Iannotti—Why did you do that? How do you feel? How do others feel?—all to be answered from the perspective of the person she is portraying. Start the training when your child is between four and six years of age. The results will be a more understanding and compassionate youngster.

Another technique for sensitizing a child to someone else's perspective is *role-exchanging.* In role-exchanging two people sit facing each other and discuss some area of mutual concern. But each responds as if he were the person facing him—in effect, stating and arguing for the other person's point of view. This is an effective way to help two people resolve a conflict since it forces each to see the issue dividing him from the other's perspective. When you argue for another person's position, it becomes clear whether or not you really know what his or her concerns are in the conflict between you. Each party can then correct each other's misconceptions.

For instance, a brother and sister were having a conflict because she refused to lend him money. He said he was angry at her stinginess and hurt by her mistrust. Their parents set up a role-exchange session for them. At one moment in the discussion, the boy, while portraying his sister, found himself saying, "I didn't lend you the money because I know when you borrow from your friends you never pay them back." Once he had unwittingly taken on her perspective he understood that she had legitimate reasons to refuse him, and he was forced to relinquish the position that she was selfish and uncaring.

On another occasion an ongoing conflict between two sisters over television programs ended when the older girl, enacting the role of her little sister, heard herself saying, "I know I'm only eight, but there are programs that I like and don't like—*the same as you.*" The older child had never really understood before that her sister truly cared about her choices. She had just considered her a pest.

You can use role-exchanging not only to overcome conflicts between siblings, but also to resolve conflicts between yourself and your child.

## Fostering Empathy in Everyday Situations

You can turn everyday events that arise in the normal life of your child into occasions for empathy training. For example, we have already described how even the way a parent tells her child to turn down the stereo can point his attention toward her needs and feelings and give him information about his impact on her. In this section we'll discuss some common family situations and concerns. (The handling of more extreme and destructive behavior is saved for later sections of the book.) Some of these examples will, on the surface, seem to be discipline problems, but what we usually think of as discipline problems do often turn out to be based on a lack of sensitivity to others.

**MELISSA.** At a family party on a recent Friday evening, Arthur spent a good deal of time with his six-year-old daughter, Melissa. They danced together, played tickle games, fed each other pieces of cake, and so on. Late in the evening, Melissa ran over to Arthur saying, "Swing me, swing me." So Arthur held Melissa's shoulders, his wife lifted her feet, and up into the air went the delighted little girl.

After a few tosses, Arthur said, "Enough." Melissa cried out, "No, Daddy. More." He put her down, bent down to her and said, in a lovely fusion of warmth and firmness, "That's all for now. You took a nap this afternoon. I couldn't do that because I had to work all day. I'm tired now and I want you to understand why we can't play anymore." Melissa smiled and said, "Okay, Daddy." She hugged him and ran off to some friends in the next room.

The way Arthur handled Melissa's exuberance may seem obvious, hardly worth mentioning. Yet we are constantly surprised at how poorly parents handle such everyday situations. Arthur didn't get irritated with Melissa or scold her. He didn't *expect* her to know that he was tired. What he did do was tell her very clearly what he was experiencing and why he no longer wanted to play. By pointing out that she took a nap in the afternoon, he reminded her of what it feels like to be tired. Most importantly, he let her know that he expected her to care enough about his feelings to end the game without a fuss. His tone of voice and the direct contact he made with her conveyed that even though he wasn't going to fulfill a momentary need of hers right now, he still loved her.

Keep in mind that at this moment Arthur was asking his daughter to care more about his feelings than her own. We guess that she hugged him to let him know she understood, and to confirm that everything was fine between them.

**HAROLD.** Let's contrast Arthur's handling of Melissa with another incident at the same party. Seven-year-old Harold tugged at his mother's skirt. "I want to go home," he whined. His mother, who at that moment was enjoying a chat with her husband and another couple, told Harold to wait. "We'll be ready soon," she said.

A few minutes later Harold tugged and whined again. His mother leaned over to her husband and relayed Harold's message. "In a little while," the husband replied impatiently. After Harold's third interruption, she said to her husband, "We'd better go. He's getting cranky." The father, barely suppressing his irritation, gave in: "All right. We'll go," he grumbled. The evening was salvaged, at least for a while, when the woman they were talking to took the liberty of asking Harold if he wanted to play with some toys upstairs. Harold assented and was led to the toybox and an hour's distraction.

In all this there was no lesson for Harold. He was behaving self-ishly—but so were his parents. No one was taking responsibility for anyone else's feelings. Harold's parents did not appear to be con-cerned with why he was having a bad time at a party where other children were enjoying themselves. Did Harold need to learn how to make friends? Was he feeling tired or sick? Was he confused about what he was permitted to do in someone else's home? Was he feel-ing insecure around so many strangers? Instead of trying to find out what Harold needed, he was treated as an intruder—to be held at bay as long as possible.

What Harold's parents should have done was let him know that they cared about what he was feeling, and, at the same time, that they wanted *him* to care about what *they* were feeling. Even if at that moment they were unable to figure out how to help Harold enjoy the party more, they still could have dealt with him more respect-fully, and taught him to become more responsive to their needs. At the least, they could have taken him aside and engaged in a dia-logue like this one (always best in private):

PARENTS: We know you want to go home and we feel bad that you aren't having a good time. But we don't get to see these friends very often and we really want to talk with them.

HAROLD: But I want to go home.

PARENTS: We know. But lots of times Mommy and Daddy do things to make you happy. And sometimes you have to do things to make us happy. That's only fair.

HAROLD: Will we go home soon?

PARENTS: We're not sure. We'll leave as soon as we're finished. But if you disturb us every few minutes we can't enjoy our talk. Remember when Eloise [Harold's sister] kept bothering you while you were coloring? Well, that's how we feel when you tug at us while we're talking. So find someone to play with now. We'll let you know as soon as we're ready to go.

Reminding Harold of the incident with his sister would be particularly helpful. A child can't empathize with someone unless he understands what that person is experiencing, and often a good way to give him this information is to draw an analogy to something he has gone through himself.

Remember, though, that if all Harold's parents were to do whenever his and their needs conflicted was to ask him to put off what he wants for the sake of what they want, Harold will inevitably come to the conclusion that his parents don't *really* care about his feelings; it's highly unlikely that he will then care very much about theirs. When parents take a child to a party, one of their responsibilities is to see that he learns how to have a good time there.

**DAVID.** Thirteen-year-old David came home from the playground complaining, "I don't want Andrea following me around." Andrea was a nine-year-old neighbor and friend of David's sister. "What happened?" his mother asked. "She kept coming over to me in the playground. She says dumb things. The other kids started making fun of me!" "What did they say to you?" "Oh, they're idiots. Things like, 'David's robbing the cradle,' and 'David's got a real short girlfriend.'"

David was angry. His mother continued the questioning: "Why do you think Andrea kept coming over to you?" "How am I supposed to know?" His mother persisted: "Come on, think about why." "I guess she likes me," he muttered. His mother agreed. "I guess she does, too. In fact, I think she has a crush on you." "Maybe, but she's such a pain," David exclaimed. "Just because she came over to talk to you?" "But then my friends make fun of me," he moaned.

David's mother felt she had to teach her son some important lessons about sensitivity to others and selecting friends. "Well, maybe they're not such good friends," she suggested. "You called them idiots yourself. Tell me, did they make fun of Andrea?" "No, I told them to shut up." His mother was pleased. "Why did you tell them that?" "Because I didn't want her to be hurt." "Good," she said. "It's important to remember that when someone likes you, it means you can hurt her very easily. But it seems that you already knew that, and I'm glad."

David was clearly torn between his concern for Andrea's feelings and his desire for approval from his friends. His mother wanted to support his empathic inclinations, and encourage him to choose kindhearted friends. She asked, "Do you really dislike Andrea?" David had to admit that he didn't. "She's okay. She's really a pretty good kid."

"Well," his mother said, "then what you have to do is figure out what to say to your friends so that they'll understand that one person letting another person know that she likes him isn't something to make fun of. It may take some courage to say that to your friends. But I think most people want to be nice; they just need some encouragement. And if they are real friends, they'll care about your feelings. If they don't care, well, that's a good thing to know, isn't it?"

David thought about it for a moment, and agreed: "If they want to act like idiots, I don't want to be their friend." His mother felt that her lesson had gotten through.

**JAY.** As we mentioned earlier, hitting a child for misbehavior is usually not the best way to teach kindness. But not long ago we observed an incident that was an interesting exception. In the following anecdote we also introduce a new and useful technique: *empathy self-control training.*

Tony was very physical with his two sons, Joey, ten, and Jay, eight. He hugged them a lot and liked to play rough-and-tumble games with them, like tag and mock wrestling. The roughhousing was always controlled and the boys enjoyed playing. But sometimes Jay, who was quite robust, got carried away with his own enthusiasm and hurt his older brother or even his father. He would hit them in a vulnerable spot or bend a finger back too far or squeeze them too tightly.

On a few occasions, Tony told Jay that he was playing too roughly. "Games are for fun. If you hurt someone you spoil the game." Jay always said he was sorry. The reason for Jay's excesses became clear when on one occasion he blurted out that he hated to lose. His father had done his best to see that everyone won about an equal number of times, but Jay, perhaps compensating for the fact that he was the smallest player, continued to be an overzealous competitor.

His father's lecture on playing within the rules of the game ("You don't really win if you break the rules") had a short-lived effect.

Tony's next tactic was to end the game abruptly whenever Jay lost control. He told Jay, "I don't want to play with you when you try to hurt me or your brother." This worked. Soon Jay began to play with more regard for his family members. But his father noticed that when Jay played with his friends, his old desire to win at any cost emerged, and more than once a friend went home crying.

Tony decided that a different kind of lesson was needed. The next time he saw his son hurting a playmate, he went over to him. "This is what it feels like when you do that," he said, and let Jay have a dose of the same pain that he had just inflicted on his playmate. Jay yelped, "Ow, that hurts." As his eyes filled with tears, he added, "Okay, I get it."

Tony had never hit either of his children, and he was worried about whether he had done the right thing. He asked our advice. We felt that he was giving Jay an important lesson about the impact of his behavior on others, and assured him that what he had done would probably have a beneficial effect. We recommended that later, in a calm moment, he discuss with Jay the lesson he wanted to teach him.

Later that day he explained a very crucial point to Jay: he hadn't hurt him to punish him. He had done it because he believed that Jay did not understand what it felt like to be hurt by someone. He added that he had enough faith in Jay to believe that once he did understand how bad it felt, he would be very careful not to hurt anyone intentionally again. Jay said he didn't want to hurt anyone and that he would try very hard to play more carefully.

This lesson did lead to an improvement, but once in a while Jay's need to come out on top still overpowered his growing sensitivity to others. Jay claimed that sometimes, in the middle of a game, it was hard to remember to be good. So we helped his father work out a program of empathy self-control training to teach Jay that whenever he sensed that he was about to hurt someone he should immediately imagine what it would feel like to be the recipient of whatever pain he was about to inflict. Empathy self-control is similar to the self-instructional techniques we described in the internalization chapter, but here, instead of the child presenting himself with a rule, he presents himself with an image. The training is carried out in two steps. In Step 1, the parent provides the signal that self-control should begin. In Step 2, the child provides his own signal.

Tony began the first step of the procedure by telling Jay he was going to help him learn to remember to be good, even when he was in the middle of a game that he wanted very much to win. "Let's make a pact," he began. "If I see that you are about to hurt someone, whether it's me, your brother, or one of your friends, I'll say the word *think*. When you hear that word, I want you, right at that very moment, to imagine what it feels like to be hurt in the same way that you are about to hurt someone else." Jay agreed.

The father continued, "Okay. Let's try it once. We'll pretend we're wrestling. I'm on top and you want to get away. You begin to get wild and are just about to poke me in the eye (which Jay had done once). I say, "Think," and right then you imagine what it would feel like if you got poked in the eye." Jay grimaced and said, "That would really hurt." He hugged his father and in a sad voice exclaimed, "I don't want to poke you in the eye, Daddy."

Only twice during the next few weeks did Jay have to be reminded to "Think." Both times he restrained himself from hurting his playmate. After the last occasion, he seemed ready for the final phase of the self-control training.

His father told him he was proud of the way he was playing with his friends now, and that he was ready to learn to say "think" to himself whenever he felt he was about to hurt someone. They rehearsed this a couple of times, going through the motions of a game in which Jay gets carried away, is about to hurt someone, and then reminds himself with the word "think" to imagine what it feels like to be on the receiving end of whatever punch, squeeze, or pinch he was about to inflict. His father tells us that the procedure worked.

The opportunities for empathy training in everyday situations are endless and can take many forms. You can draw your child's attention to good examples of empathic people, including, we hope, yourself. When you share your own empathic feelings for others with your child, he will learn the importance you attach to caring about people's feelings—and there's evidence that this makes for more empathic children. Since peer pressure often encourages children to be tough, sharing your own empathic feelings with your child can help him overcome any embarrassment he may have about his own tender feelings. In general, children tend to become more empathic when they are around empathic people, particularly when they themselves have been the recipients of empathy-based kindness.[18]

Examples of caring people can come from many places. They can be people your child knows personally or has read about or seen on television. You might point out how loved and admired these individuals are because they are caring.

On the evening we are writing this, the nightly news—usually a voice of doom and gloom—had three separate stories of people reaching out to help others. One was about a mother's milk bank set up by nursing mothers who volunteered to share their milk with orphaned infants who could not tolerate formula. Another story was about veterinarians who were working feverishly to save some wild pelicans whose beaks had been maliciously broken. A third item concerned a group of high-school students who formed an organization to help friends who drove when they drank. One of the organizers said he felt guilty when he didn't do anything to stop a friend from driving while drunk.

Aside from pointing out caring people to your child, ask him to think about whether the people he knows are "good" people, in the sense of whether they feel for others and treat them kindly. Also, encourage him to consider an individual's capacity for empathy when he is choosing his friends.

Below is a checklist of principles to use for empathy training in everyday situations.

1. Draw your child's attention to people's feelings. Ask him to imagine how he would feel in their place.
2. Let him know what the impact of his actions are on the feelings of others, including yourself.
3. Explain why people feel the way they do.
4. Make clear (or encourage him to discover) what actions he can take that would be more considerate.
5. Let him know that you expect him to be considerate, that it is important to you.
6. Let him know that you understand and care about *his* feelings and try to offer him a way to get at least some of what he wants —if not now, then in the future.
7. Don't expect him to read minds. Take the time to explain.
8. Help him understand other people's feelings by reminding him of similar experiences in his own life.
9. Help him resist the influence of people who discourage or ridicule his empathic feelings.

10. Give him approval when he is considerate. Show disappointment when he isn't.
11. Use self-control empathy training to teach him to imagine himself in someone else's place whenever he is inclined to hurt that person.
12. Share your own empathic feelings with him.
13. Point out examples of people who are empathic and those who are not, and communicate your own admiration for kind-hearted people.
14. Stress the good feelings that come from caring about other people.
15. Encourage him to consider a person's capacity for empathy when selecting friends.

If you foster empathy in your child, he will treat others kindly for the best of reasons—not just to please you or some authority or gain some end or meet some principle, but simply because it feels good.

## EMPATHY AND GUILT

When a child harms someone for whom she feels empathy, she experiences guilt. Since guilt is painful, she hurts herself when she hurts that person. So, if your child feels empathy for you and you follow our advice and let her know when she hurts you, you are, in effect, purposely making her feel guilty. Should you ever do that? Isn't guilt bad?

Our answer to the first question is an unqualified *yes*. Guilt is a powerful inhibitor of selfish and cruel behavior because it's the natural outcome of hurting someone you feel empathy for. The only way to eliminate guilt is to eliminate empathy.

Isn't guilt bad? Yes *and* no. There is good guilt and bad guilt. Guilt is good when it inhibits behavior that is intentionally unfair or destructive to others. It is bad when it blocks a child's legitimate self-expression and self-assertion, and when it *unfairly* forces her to forego her own desires for the benefit of someone else. What is fair and unfair to ask of a child? What are her obligations to others? What are your obligations to her? There is no way for a parent to avoid making these difficult judgments.

Let's take a situation in which fairness is easy to decide. Suppose your child beats you at chess and you feel terrible at losing. In a sense his victory has hurt you. Should you let him know and make him feel guilty? Virtually all parents would say no, that it would be unfair to the child. We take for granted that anyone playing a game doesn't want to lose and we ordinarily consider it unfair if one player claims that his unhappiness over losing deserves special consideration.

How about if your child wants to go on a camping trip with her friends and you know you will worry about her all weekend? Should you make her feel guilty to keep her from going? What's fair in this situation is harder to sort out. Should your child be expected to take responsibility for your worrying about her? We think she should— but only to the extent of demonstrating that she can meet the normal challenges of a camping trip and that both she and her companions can be trusted to handle risks prudently. If she meets these responsibilities, then we think it *would* be unfair to prevent her from going by making her feel guilty.

But why is it unfair? Because in every relationship there are obligations to be met—some stated, some understood. One way we judge if a person is treating others fairly is by whether or not he is meeting his obligations to them. In a chess game, as in most competitive games, players are obliged to rely on their skills to win. Trying to win by making your opponent feel guilty for beating you violates this obligation. With regard to the camping example, we believe that parents have a general obligation to help their children pursue their own interests and develop their potentials as fully as possible. If worried parents permit their own discomfort to interfere with their child's reasonable pursuits, then they are failing to meet their obligation to foster their child's development.

As children get older, they spend more time away from home, become increasingly influenced by outsiders, and start to form opinions that may be contrary to those of their parents. It is easy for parents to feel hurt by what they view as the "loss" of their child. Parents may even feel betrayed ("We've given him so much"), or just worried when the child is out of sight. At those times many parents are tempted to control their children by making them feel guilty for their independent inclinations. This is the suffocating guilt that psychotherapists build lucrative practices upon. This type of guilt makes a child less of a person—less competent, less curious, less creative, less daring—than he might be. It also leads to resentment—if not immediately, then later—when the child comes to blame his parents for his inadequacies.

If you believe, as we do, that one of the primary obligations of parents is to encourage their child's independent interests and help her develop the skills she needs to pursue those interests confidently, then you will want to do your best to resist the temptation to use guilt to control your child's independent strivings. Ask yourself what kind of person you want her to become. If she wants to go camping, think about whether you prefer a child who is curious about nature and comfortable in it, who enjoys the kind of intimacy and camaraderie that often develops between campmates—or whether you want a child who caters to and adopts your fears. If you are worried that she might get hurt on a camping trip, think of ways to help her acquire safe camping skills rather than simply imposing restrictions.

The question of fairness will come up over and over again. Perhaps, as a moral training lesson, you want your child to devote part of his free time or income from his part-time job to helping others. Is that fair? If so, how much time or money? And which others? The primary guiding principle for answering these questions and discovering what *you* think is fair is to ask yourself what kind of person you want your child to become, what traits and abilities you want him to develop. In getting him to meet his obligations, we reiterate, save guilt tactics only for situations in which they are appropriate: when your child hurts you or someone else intentionally, or when he ignores his legitimate and defined responsibilities to you and others because of selfish pursuits.

*Can a child be too empathic?* Many parents ask this question out of worry that their child's feelings for others might reach a level or take a form that will be self-destructive. Empathy can become excessive or misguided. One sign of this is when a child feels guilty for things that are not her fault. Sometimes this happens when one sibling is clearly more talented or intelligent or popular than another. The more successful one, say, the younger of two sisters, may then assume that every success she has only makes her older sister feel bad. She might then see to it that she achieves far less than her potential (although she might never actually make a conscious decision to do so).

If you see that your child is diminishing her own abilities in order not to hurt her sibling's or anyone else's feelings, you should explain to her that her talents or abilities are not faults to feel bad about, that she is not doing anything wrong by fulfilling her own potential, and that one can't raise others up and make them different than they are by making less of oneself. There is no problem feeling sorry for someone who is disappointed in her own achievements, and there may be ways to bolster that person's morale by helping her do better or helping her appreciate herself in new ways. But placing limits on one's own accomplishments is self-destructive and doesn't really help anyone else at all. (Parents should be aware that a child might also undermine her potential out of fear that she might lose her sister's love if she surpasses her. If it's fear of rejection that seems to be operating rather than empathy, point out to your child that someone doesn't really love you when, out of envy, she wants you to achieve less than you can. Diminishing oneself doesn't work either as a way to give love or to earn it.)

Another indication that empathy is excessive is when a child feels so sorry for others that he lets them take advantage of him. Being moral means being fair, but that includes being fair to oneself too. For example, a teenager was always being "hit on" by a schoolmate for money. When the boy's parents learned that he was "lending" money to the friend on a regular basis, they asked why. The boy explained that he felt sorry for his friend because he was from a poorer family and was always broke.

The boy's parents said that they were glad he was sensitive to other people's needs and that it was his decision whether to give his money away, but they wondered if the friend was taking advantage of him. As the discussion ensued, it was revealed that the friend had not made any effort to earn money through an after-school or week-end job, and it wasn't because he was putting in a lot of time on his school work. "How does he spend his time?" the parents asked. "He generally just hangs out with the kids at the luncheonette," the boy replied. The boy ultimately concluded that the friend was asking others to take responsibility for improving his situation while taking no responsibility for doing so himself.

Children should be made aware that there are individuals who try to take advantage of other people's compassionate feelings. For example, unscrupulous salesmen use various ploys to exploit people's empathic feelings to sell them things they don't want or can't afford, and there are people who will try to play upon a person's sympathies to gain friendship, sex, or virtually anything that they want and know the person would not ordinarily give them.

Children can learn this without becoming overly suspicious and self-protective if they are clear about their own responsibilities and rights. They can be taught to ask themselves, "Do I really have any responsibility to give this person what he needs?'' and ''Is he living up to his responsibilities to himself or to me?'' For example, he might ask himself, ''Should I feel sorry for Brian and give up my position as second-baseman to him because he never gets to play there, when I worked hard to earn that position and he didn't?''

## TEACHING EMPATHY THROUGH EXERCISES

Here are a number of techniques you can use in a regular and systematic way to promote empathy. They will sensitize your child to people's feelings and teach her that she can and should make others feel good. If you set time aside for these exercises, she will understand that they are important to you. With a child between three and six years of age, you may want to call the exercises ''games,'' but make it clear to her that she is learning ways of treating people that she should apply in her everyday life.

**WHO NEEDS MY HELP?** This exercise teaches your child to recognize when others need her help and what kind of help they need. Start the exercise by setting up the chart below. The chart is a convenient way to focus a discussion, but if you don't like charts, you can talk the steps through instead. Begin by writing in the name of someone (the ''target-person'') with whom your child interacts.

**Who Needs My Help?**_____

| When does he/she need help? | Why does he/she need help? | What help does he/she need? | How can I help? | When I helped. |
| --- | --- | --- | --- | --- |

There are three purposes to this exercise. The first is to stimulate empathy in your child by prompting him to think about the needs of those around him. The second aim is to foster accurate judgments so that empathic feelings really reflect the other person's experience. Third, this exercise encourages your child to take the big step from knowing and caring about someone else's needs to actually doing something to help that person.

When you ask your child *When does he/she need help?* he will have to think of specific times and places in the target-person's life. This will tell you about your child's perceptions of the other person and give you the opportunity to correct any misconceptions he may have.

For example, twelve-year-old Sean was angry with his fourteen-year-old sister when she refused to play their usual game of Monopoly on Tuesday night. Her laconic "I don't feel like it," led him to believe she was bored with him, and he was upset. He didn't know that she was anxious about her upcoming entrance exam to a performing arts high school, and he hadn't noticed that she had been preoccupied for days.

Sean's father worked through the *Who Needs My Help?* exercise with him, and he was able to correct his son's misinterpretation of the event. He also helped Sean switch his concern from his own disappointment to how he could be a good brother and help his sister during this tense time in her life. Through his father's guidance, Sean offered to do some of his sister's household chores for a week so that she could have extra time to practice for her audition.

The next question on the chart, *Why does he/she need help?*, asks the child to think about the causes behind the target-person's needs. Some causes will be obvious, such as "Grandma needs help on the stairs because she's old and gets tired quickly." Other causes will be more subtle or beyond the child's knowledge. As we've discussed, whenever possible, parents should explain the circumstances behind people's feelings to their children, but sometimes the person involved may want this information kept private, and sometimes parents will decide their child is not yet ready to understand certain unpleasant facts of life without being unduly upset by them.

There may be legitimate reasons for keeping a child in the dark about why someone feels the way he or she does; but keep in mind that the less information he has, the more unreasonable and unpredictable people's mood changes will seem to him. Often parents ask themselves, What is the gentlest way to tell a child about some of the harsher realities of life? A better way to phrase this question is, What do we want our child to learn from this incident?

We were reminded of this ourselves a short while ago when some friends asked our advice about how to tell their seven-year-old son that his godfather had committed suicide. They assumed the boy would overhear conversations about the suicide and they wanted to tell him the unpleasant news themselves, in as gentle a way as possible.

Unfortunately, no gentle way came to mind. But when we asked ourselves what the boy could learn from this incident, a framework for telling him became clear. The man's suicide was a shock to everyone. He had never spoken of any serious problems, even to his closest friends, and generally seemed cheerful. Only in his suicide note did he reveal how troubled his life had been. There is a lesson in this for child and adult alike. One of the things most of us learn is what to do when we are unhappy. We turn to old friends or seek new ones, we go back to activities that gave us pleasure, or seek out new projects. We remind ourselves of past accomplishments and resolve to seek a better future. It seems that this man who took his own life hadn't learned any of these ways to help himself when he was sad. In particular, he hadn't learned to seek comfort from his friends.

We suggested to the parents that when they tell their son about his godfather's suicide they turn it into a lesson about what to do when feeling sad, and how sharing feelings with family and good friends is a way to get comfort when it is needed. Feeling sad and needing comfort are experiences that a seven-year-old can certainly understand.

The third question on the chart, *What help does he/she need?*, is designed to get your child to take the target-person's perspective so that the help she gives is the help the target-person needs. Even five-year-olds have been shown to understand that to be a good helper you must be aware of the needs of the person you want to help.[19]

In the fourth column, *How can I help?*, your child indicates what help he is capable of giving. You can point out things he is able to do that he hasn't thought of. Or you may have to clarify that certain problems are beyond his ability to remedy. For example, if a friend is upset because he didn't make the school soccer team, there may not be too much your child can do to cheer him up besides offering a sympathetic ear and a few consoling words.

The last column is used to note the dates when you child makes an effort to help. Praise such efforts. If it becomes apparent to you or your child that the target-person's needs are not what they seemed or have changed as a result of the actions taken, this should, of course, be discussed and, if necessary, a new course of action planned.

**WHAT DID I DO?** This exercise serves some of the same purposes as the *Who Needs My Help?* exercise. It, too, focuses the child on the needs and feelings of others, improves his understanding of their experiences, and encourages him to take positive actions on their behalf. In addition, this exercise makes the child directly aware of the impact of his own actions on the good and bad feelings of those around him.

Give your child the following chart, one for each day of the week:

Date _____

| What did I do today that made _____ feel good? | Why? | What did I do today that made _____ feel bad? | Why? |
|---|---|---|---|
| | | | |

Fill in the blanks with either a specific person's name or with the word *Anybody*. If your child is having an ongoing conflict with someone in particular, it is useful to insert that person's name in the blank. Using this technique will teach him that he has the power to break the cycle of negative exchanges ("You hurt me, then I hurt you, then you hurt me, then . . .") by taking a positive action toward the other person.

If both parties to a conflict, such as a brother and sister or a parent and child, fill in each other's names on their charts, and then discuss their answers to the *What did I do?* questions, they will quickly see that the root of their conflict is an insensitivity to each other's feelings. When both sides give each other feedback on what actually did make them feel good or bad, both will learn how they have to treat each other in order to end their conflict.

Fill in the blanks with *Anybody* when you want to encourage your child to think about the impact of his actions on any and all of the people he deals with during the course of a day. This will reveal whether he is treating some people better than others—perhaps being nicer to friends than family members or vice versa. Also, a child who complains that everyone is against him will have to acknowledge his own contribution to his misery if he is faced with a series of blank columns that reveal that he hardly ever does anything to make anyone feel good.

Parents will have to do the recording for young children before they are able to write. Older children should keep their charts with them and record their interactions with the target-person as soon as possible after they occur.

The charts can be discussed every day or every few days or once a week. We recommend a daily discussion when you first start using them. With younger children—between three and seven years old—discussions should continue on a daily basis. Whenever possible, the target-person should be present to give your child feedback. In order to make it easier for both your child and the target-person to recall the details of their interactions, the time and place of each event should be recorded.

At this point your child has only been required to *record* her actions towards others. If you then feel that the way she treats people needs improving, the next step is to hold her directly responsible for making others feel good. You can do this by establishing a minimum number of positive actions per day to be recorded on the "feel good" side of the chart, and the maximum number of negative actions you will tolerate on the "feel bad" side.

Make sure your expectations are realistic. Ask for only gradual changes. If she commits an average of five hurtful acts per day, you'll get better results if you set the requirement first at two rather than zero. Increase the standard each week. What happens if your child meets the standard? Or fails to meet it? Should there be consequences set for success or failure?

Of course there will be consequences. There are, in fact, several kinds of consequences that will affect a child's behavior in this exercise. For instance, you will presumably be pleased if she meets the standards you set and disappointed if she doesn't. Communicate your reactions to her so she knows that your concern about how she treats others is serious.

If she fails to meet the mark, set up a new goal for the next time period. Together, work out a framework that will make it easier for her to succeed next time. She might need a shorter interval between discussions, perhaps only half a day. Or she might need you to signal her when good opportunities to be nice to others arise, or when she needs to curtail an impulse to be mean. Children as well as adults tend to react by habit in familiar situations. Often we fail to recognize an opportunity to do something differently. By signaling a child that a different behavior is possible, you help her break dysfunctional habits. If you then let her know why you gave her a signal at a particular moment, you help her see familiar situations in a new light and make it possible for her to start signaling herself.

When you and your child look for solutions to her behavior problems together, you are letting her know that you share responsibility with her for her actions and that you take seriously your obligation to teach her "good" behavior. We believe that half the battle in moral training is won by parents simply conveying to a child their sense of responsibility for and commitment to bringing up a moral child.

What about consequences in the form of incentives? Should you set up "contracts" as part of this exercise so that she gets something she wants if she meets your standards and loses something if she doesn't? If your approval and disapproval are not sufficiently important to her (and in some parent-child relationships they will not be), then more concrete consequences will have to be used.

When parental approval and disapproval aren't important to a child it is usually for one of the following reasons: her past caring behavior may not have received sufficient credit and approval; she might be angry because she feels that you have been unfair to her in some way; she may not have learned positive ways of getting what she wants; or she may have learned that "bad" behavior pays off (for some children the only way they get time and attention from a parent is by doing something wrong).

To carry our discussion of reward and punishment forward from the previous chapter, let us remind you that when your goal is to instill moral feelings, the incentives must be social. Simply giving a child money or toys to induce her to treat someone well will not make her care about other people's feelings except as a means to an end.

Therefore, it's crucial that any concrete rewards you give must be tied to social consequences. You can do this by making it clear to your youngster that the concrete things you give to, or do for, her, such as volunteering to drive her and her friends to the movies or reading a story to her or participating in a game she enjoys, are all done out of the affection you feel for her—and that your feelings toward her are affected by how she treats people. She needs to understand that you can't enjoy doing things for her or spending time with her when you know that she is insensitive to people's feelings and doesn't care if she hurts them.

These social consequences are so important to communicate because what you ultimately want her to care about is the effect of her actions on people's feelings. Therefore, let her know right from the start that the incentive contracts are only temporary and are merely a tool to make it easier for her to change her behavior. Explain that they must be phased out because, as a member of society, she is obligated to care about the feelings of others without extra payoffs.

Once your child actually does something that makes others feel good, one hopes that the way they express their good feelings and the way they treat her will make her want to treat people well more often. These are the consequences that you hope will ultimately motivate your child's behavior, but she can only experience them if you first get her to actually carry out kind actions.

**WHAT WILL I DO?** In a variation of the *What Did I Do?* exercise, change the question your child must answer to *What* will *I do to make* ——————— *feel good (or bad)?* By changing *did* to *will*, you force your child to define and acknowledge his intentions toward others and plan his actions in advance.

What should you do if he says that he is going to make someone feel bad? Well, first try to understand his reason. For example, he might want to get even with someone for something that person did to him. You can usually defuse his desire for revenge by helping him understand the other person's actions from his or her perspective, for example, by asking him to think about what needs or fears may have prompted the other person's behavior.

Understanding people won't change them and it still may be necessary for your child to protect himself from them. But in most cases he will no longer feel impelled to invest his time and energy in getting even, and he may be able to come up with a constructive plan for improving the relationship—which takes us to the second step for helping your youngster overcome his inclinations to hurt others: Teach him a *constructive* way to resolve his conflicts with others.

Start by explaining two important principles to him. The first is that it isn't the other person as a whole that he finds objectionable, but just some of the things that person does. Second, he needs to understand that you can't get people to treat you differently unless you are willing to treat them differently.

With these principles in mind, ask him to define which actions of the other person need changing. Once this is done, the two of you can work up a program to influence that person through constructive means. One constructive approach is to try to negotiate with the other person using a cooperative strategy (or, as some professional negotiators call it, a "win-win" strategy). The goal of a cooperative negotiating strategy is not to beat the other person or to get him to yield as much as possible while holding to one's own position as rigidly as possible. It is to find a solution that benefits and satisfies both sides.

When negotiation won't work, another kind of constructive approach involves using positive reinforcement to change the other person's behavior. An excellent example of the effectiveness of this approach is described in a study by Susan Rovet Polirstok and R. Douglas Greer of Columbia University.[20]

They taught a highly destructive eighth-grade girl to positively reinforce her teachers to get them to treat her more to her liking. Before the training program, almost all exchanges between the girl and her teachers were unpleasant and hardly a day went by that she was not sent to the dean's office for using abusive language toward them.

The researchers convinced her that there were legitimate ways to make the school environment more pleasant for herself. They asked her how she wanted her teachers to treat her and got her to think about what her teachers needed from *her*—something she had never considered before. She agreed to try to improve her relationship with each teacher by taking the responsibility to make him or her feel appreciated. The researchers and the student worked out a set of simple reinforcers for the teachers, including looking at them when they spoke, nodding to show understanding of what they said, smiling at them and saying, "Thank you" or "Fine" or "Right" after they finished speaking. Her teachers were not told that they were the targets of a reinforcement program.

The results were extraordinary. Within just a few weeks, her relationships with all four teachers had taken a significant turn. She was treating them better and they were treating her better. Pleasant exchanges were now far more frequent than unpleasant ones. Her teachers began to comment on her newfound "maturity" and "remarkable socialization." The cycle of mutual disapproval was broken because the student learned that interaction between people, even between children and adults, is based on exchange, and that *she* could take the initiative to transform hostile exchanges into positive ones.

Parents, too, can teach their children to try to overcome conflicts through mutually beneficial exchanges. A child *can* learn that when things don't go his way he has other options besides passive self-pity or overt hostility—that he really can take control over his destiny in constructive ways.

Sometimes increasing your child's understanding of people he dislikes or teaching him that he can use positive means to change the way they behave will not diminish his inclination to hurt them— they'll still remain the "enemy." When this happens you will need to give him some straightforward behavioral rules about how to treat people he just doesn't like. Two such rules are (a) "If you don't like a person and can't figure out any way to get along with him or be his friend, then keep away from him as much as possible," and (b) "If people try to hurt you, protect yourself from them, but don't become like them by plotting to hurt them back."

We've just considered some preventive measures to take if your child indicates on the chart that she intends to make someone feel bad. Are there things you should do when she notes that she intends to make someone feel good?

There are, in fact, some ways you can help her turn her good intentions into actions. One is to make sure her understanding of what the other person likes is accurate. Remind her to select her actions on the basis of what she has actually witnessed about that person rather than simply guessing or projecting on the basis of what she herself enjoys. As George Bernard Shaw said, "Do *not* do unto others as you would that they should do unto you. Their tastes may not be the same."

Lots of things can happen between the time your child states his intention to make someone feel good and the moment when he is supposed to carry that intention into action. He can become angry at the other person, or feel shy and vulnerable to ridicule, or he may simply forget. The second way you can support his good intentions is by helping him anticipate and prepare for these obstacles.

First have him plan out *exactly what he will do* to make the other person feel good, including when and where he will do it. If you feel that he is likely to get sidetracked before carrying out his plan—for example, because he'll probably get angry at the person he plans to make feel good—then you should teach him what to say to himself when he gets angry so that he can keep his commitment.

For example, he may decide to do something nice for his brother but may also get angry at his brother virtually every day. Prepare him for this. First, explain that when he lets himself get angry at his brother, without thinking, he is letting his brother control him. He can, however, choose how *he* wants to treat his brother and take the responsibility for improving their relationship. If he is willing to make this choice, have him imagine a situation in which his brother angers him; then have him rehearse a self-instruction like, "I know I'm angry at him now, but I'm going to do what I said I would. I'll . . ." (have him state his intention). A number of studies confirm that when children set constructive goals for themselves in this way and rehearse what they'll say to themselves when angered, they are indeed able to control their reactions.[21]

One question that worries parents whose children frequently mistreat people and seem to have little or no feeling for others is whether there are true psychopaths or sociopaths who are totally incapable of empathy. We doubt it. We've noted that there may be biological differences in people's capacity for empathy, but whether some children come into the world without this capacity at all is impossible to prove. As William Shirer has pointed out, even Hitler and his cohorts felt compassion for members of their families.[22]

Some children appear to need a larger dose of empathy training than others, but it would be self-defeating to begin work with a difficult child assuming that he can't possibly learn to feel for others.

There's evidence that even serious criminals can be reached, in the sense that they can learn to feel empathy for people that they ordinarily see only as prey. A recent television news item featured a confrontation between inmates of a Westchester prison and crime victims. In emotional tones, the victims told the prisoners how severely their lives had been damaged by the crimes that had been committed against them (not by this set of prisoners).

By and large the prisoners defended themselves, justifying their crimes with their own stories of poverty, family abuse, drug addiction, and racial bigotry.

At the end of the meeting, something interesting happened. The moderator asked the crime victims if they felt the meeting had been of value. They said no. The prisoners appeared upset by this response. One prisoner said she was hurt, "really hurt" to hear that. But why should she care? Why was she *hurt* by the negative reactions of the victims? We believe it was because now the "victims" were human beings to her, people with struggles and pain not very different from her own, not anonymous members of a privileged class. She seemed to want them to know that she saw them differently now, and that she felt a bond with them as fellow sufferers. At the time of the show there was no data on the long-term effects of these kinds of confrontations on the recidivism rate of the prisoners. But on that particular occasion, in that very unlikely place, some unexpected sparks of empathy were kindled.

# 4

# Personal Moral Standards: The Third Foundation Stone —A Guide to Helping Your Child Develop Personal Moral Standards

The internalization of parental standards and the development of empathy provide two sturdy pillars upon which to build a moral training program. But they are not enough. This chapter will teach you how to help your child develop personal moral standards that he believes he *ought* to live up to—regardless of the approval or disapproval of others, and even when he doesn't feel empathy toward those he interacts with.

Imagine the following conversation between an adult and a child:

ADULT: What if a boy in school was eating crackers and another boy asked him for some and the boy with crackers said, "No." Do you think that it's okay for him to say no?

CHILD: They're his crackers. He doesn't have to share if he doesn't want to.

ADULT: If a teacher saw this, do you think she'd say anything?

CHILD: She might say it was good to share, but I don't think she'd force him to. Not if they were his crackers.

ADULT: Do you think it's okay to take all your clothes off in school if it's very hot?

CHILD: No, I don't think so.

ADULT: What if the school says it's okay?

CHILD: Well, then it would be okay if someone wanted to, but I think everyone would laugh at him.

ADULT: If the school said it was all right and a teacher saw a boy take all his clothes off on a hot day, would the teacher say anything to the boy?

CHILD: Not if the school said it was okay.

ADULT: What if a boy wanted to go on a swing in the school playground and all the swings were occupied—is it all right to push another kid off?

CHILD: No.

ADULT: What if the school said it was okay?

CHILD: No, he should wait his turn.

ADULT: Even if the school said it was okay to take a swing by pushing someone off?

CHILD: It doesn't matter. He should wait.

ADULT: If a teacher saw him push someone off, would she say anything?

CHILD: Yes, she'd say he was bad and tell him he couldn't have the swing.

ADULT: Even if the school rules permitted it?

CHILD: Well, she might let him take it then. But some teachers wouldn't care what the school said. They'd know it was wrong and try to stop him anyway.

Psychologists Donna Weston and Elliot Turiel[1] asked children between the ages of four and eleven these kinds of questions in order to study what children think about different kinds of rules. The dialogue above does not reproduce their format exactly, but we believe it captures the essence of their procedure. Their findings are eye-opening. Almost all children, even four-year-olds, said that pushing another child off a swing was wrong. By the age of nine, a majority of children said it was wrong even if the school approved of pushing. By eleven years of age, ninety percent of the children said it was wrong to push, regardless of school policy. Lastly, almost all children in every age group believed that a school should not make a rule permitting children to hit each other.

These are very important findings. They tell us that by four years of age almost all children believe in a rule against using force as a way to get what you want; and by the time they are nine, most children uphold the rule against using force even when an adult says that force is allowable.

This study demonstrates that for a majority of nine-year-olds and virtually all eleven-year-olds, the rule against using force to get one's way had become a personal standard—a rule to be upheld regardless of who else agrees with it. Similarly, a majority of children at every age level (even the four- and five-year-olds) had acquired a personal standard about private property; they believed that the child with the crackers had a right to refuse to share. Although most children were critical of his selfishness, they defended his right to dispose of his property as he saw fit; and they believed that a school should not set a policy that would take away this right.

Most children even distinguished moral standards, like those about not using force and private property rights, from conventional standards, such as rules about clothing and undressing. The legitimate authorities (teachers and school officials) did have a right to establish rules about conventions, but moral standards transcended authority. Moreover, children are much more accepting of their parents' enforcement of moral rules (such as a rule against stealing) than conventional rules (such as rules about chores).

Children, even very young ones, clearly do learn and come to believe in moral rules. Our own observations are consistent with these findings. For instance, the first two moral rules that most children in our culture acquire and accept (even though they don't always live up to them) are "Don't use force to get your way" and "You can do what you want with your things, but you need permission to use someone else's." These are usually learned before a child is five.

Once moral rules become personal standards, they exert a powerful influence on behavior. A single precept, such as "Do unto others as you would have them do unto you," will affect a child's behavior in a great range of circumstances—*if* he believes in its value and has learned to remind himself of it when he is about to harm someone. Living up to one's own standards gives one a sense of personal integrity.

## WHY PERSONAL MORAL STANDARDS ARE NEEDED AND HOW THEY WORK

When right and wrong are defined by others, whether they be parents, teachers, or political, religious, or business authorities, morality is based on obedience, loyalty, and dependency—on earning approval as a good child, a good party man, and a dutiful member of the flock. If a child has never learned to evaluate the morality of an action for herself according to principles that she understands and believes in, she remains forever vulnerable to the control of any new authority that enters her life, regardless of how ill-intentioned that authority may be. Nor can parents count on the arousal of empathy every time their child is faced with a decision about how to treat others—for example, when she interacts with a competitor.

Ultimately, we want our children to treat other people well because *they* want to, because they have developed their own standards of moral behavior that tell them it is the right thing to do. If you want to feel confident that your child will treat other people kindly, fairly, and responsibly, you will have to help him develop personal standards of kindness, fairness, and responsibility.

Personal standards affect our actions in the same way that internalized parental standards do: Both are statements that we make to ourselves when we are faced with moral decisions—decisions on whether or not to take actions that will help or harm someone. But personal standards differ from internalized parental standards (or those derived from any authority) in that the motivating force behind them is not approval from others. We may have first learned our standards from parents or teachers or friends or books, but now we remind ourselves of them because they define a way of living with other people that we believe in ourselves. They are rules of conduct that are sustained by our *imaginations*—because we can imagine what it would be like to live in a better world in which kindness and justice prevail. Thus, when we have personal moral standards, the consequences that keep us striving to treat people kindly and justly are our own judgments of whether our actions are bringing that better world into being.

History teaches us that moral standards can become the most powerful force in a person's life. Every country, every religion, every ideology has its roster of righteous men and women who lived their lives or gave up their lives for the sake of ideals.

In western culture, the Ten Commandments contain perhaps the best-known moral standards. The Bill of Rights of the American Constitution—in particular the First Amendment rights to freedom of religion, speech, and assembly—is another well-known attempt to specify how men (organized as a government) should treat their fellow men. *Do unto others as you would have them do unto you* is the most universally accepted moral standard. It exists in various forms in every major world religion and ethical system.

Moral standards are only one of many kinds of rules or precepts that we live by. In fact, much of human behavior is governed by rules (some of which are codified as laws), and much of a child's education is devoted to teaching him his culture's collective body of rules. Most of the time these rules work to his and to society's advantage. Indeed, it is only through the transfer of rules to children that each generation need not rediscover and reinvent everything, from the wheel to the Bill of Rights.

We'll use the game of tennis to illustrate how rule-governed behavior works, focusing on the standards that players follow in order to play better, including "Bend your knees when you hit the ball," "Keep your eye on the ball," "Step into the ball," and "Get your racket back early." Those of us who have had even one tennis lesson can testify that these precepts for successful play work. But they only work when they become signals to us *as we play*.

How do we learn to use them? First, the instructor tells us what they are ("Bend your knees"). Then we practice in order to actually experience how they affect our playing. Initially, the instructor gives us our signals. He calls them out to us as we are about to hit the ball. After a while we begin to signal ourselves—often just a moment too late. With more practice we begin to signal ourselves before it's too late to hit the ball properly. And, finally, the same external cues that the instructor responds to, such as the position and speed of the ball and the movements of our opponent, become all the signals we need, and verbal reminders are rarely necessary.

At the start of tennis lessons we adopt the standards because the teacher tells us to—he is the authority. But if they work, they become our personal standards. In a final phase, the serious tennis player will often begin to formulate his own principles, developing procedures for himself that are based on his own physique and temperament, or ones that anyone can use because they are based on general insights into how to play better.

Moral standards operate pretty much the same way. We usually first learn them from other people, starting with our parents. As children we often need reminders to do what is right. After a while we learn to remind ourselves of the rules. And, with experience, we generally do learn to treat others pretty well, usually without having to consciously state the standards to ourselves—although sometimes, when we want something badly or are angry or frightened, we do need to revert to verbal self-reminders.

After a while, as we gain experience in human relationships, we see for ourselves whether our standards work or not, whether they seem to bring about a more decent way of life. If we believe they do, then the moral standards we have been taught by others become our own personal standards. Finally, as we learn more about human capabilities and what makes people happy and sad, we may be able to formulate new principles about the best way to live with others.

There is another important similarity between how tennis and moral standards work. When we start learning tennis we are taught not to expect immediate results; we are taught to be patient. Every so often, though, we do connect with the ball properly and feel the increased power and control of a well-executed stroke. From a solid shot once in a while, we can imagine what it will be like to play well all the time, and this keeps us going. Otherwise our frustration might overwhelm our efforts.

We must learn patience in the moral sphere also. Even when we live up to our moral standards, the whole world doesn't instantly become what we want it to. But once in a while we connect and suddenly we see how a simple act of kindness can improve the quality of life. Parents need to point out enough examples of the good effects of moral actions to keep a child from becoming overwhelmed by cynicism, and to keep the image of a more decent world alive for him.

## WHAT PARENTS CAN DO TO FOSTER PERSONAL MORAL STANDARDS

Children and adults live up to a standard—any kind of standard—because they believe it will lead to a desirable outcome. A tennis player reminds herself to bend her knees as she strokes *only* when she believes it will make her hit the ball better. Similarly, a child will come to remind herself of the Golden Rule—to treat others as she would like to be treated—only when she believes that when she does so, a desirable result will follow, at least in the long run. A rule is valued only when it leads to an outcome that is valued.

So, the central task of parents in fostering personal moral standards is to convince their child that if she lives up to those standards, desirable outcomes will follow. Once she believes this, the standards will be her own. She will want to live up to them.

How do you get your child to believe that good things follow from living up to moral standards? *Through reasoning.* Your task as a parent is to convince your child that A (following moral standards) leads to B (good outcomes). Whenever we try to convince anyone of anything in the form *A leads to B,* we do so by using two elements of reasoning: logical arguments and visible evidence.

## The Power of Reasoning

Let's illustrate how you can reason with your child so that he will accept the Golden Rule as a personal standard, will want to live up to it, and will remind himself of it when he is confronted with decisions about how to treat other people. For this to happen, you'll need to convince him that living up to the Golden Rule is in his own interest.

First, let's see what is implied in the Golden Rule. Ask yourself how you want others to treat you. Well, among the things we assume you want is for people to keep their promises to you and not try to frighten or hurt you or take your belongings. You presumably also want them to consider your needs and desires (for friendship, safety, sustenance, comfort, etc.) when you interact with them. Now, why should you or your child treat others in this way? Why should you keep your promises to them and refrain from frightening or hurting them or taking what is theirs, and why should you consider their needs and desires?

There are many reasons to give a child for living up to a moral standard like the Golden Rule or any other moral standard, but ultimately all reasons need to be subsumed under one grand reason: *When you live up to moral standards you are leading the best life a human being can lead.*

Let us explain. We have described four kinds of consequences that follow from treating people well or badly: (a) the practical consequences of getting treated well or badly by them in return; (b) feeling that those we admire are proud or ashamed of us because of their approval or disapproval; (c) experiencing empathic good or bad (guilty) feelings; and (d) knowing that our actions have helped or hindered the creation of a better world. Each of these is a good reason for treating others well, and should be taught to your child. But none of them will make him feel ashamed *of himself* or lose respect *for himself* when he mistreats others.

But this is precisely what people say they experience when they violate a personal standard of moral behavior. They explain their striving to live up to moral standards with expressions like, "I couldn't like myself or live with myself otherwise," or "Because I would hate myself if I didn't." It is only the fifth consequence we mentioned—knowing that our actions are consistent with our definition of the best kind of person to be—that makes us feel ashamed or proud of ourselves for the way we have treated others. For example, a person can feel guilty for hurting someone without feeling ashamed of himself if he believes his actions were for a good reason. He will only feel guilty *and* ashamed of himself when he knows he has hurt someone and has also failed to live up to his vision of how the best kind of person would have behaved.

Once a child believes that there is a best way to be, he will want to be it; and he will feel bad about himself when he isn't. This occurs because children, by and large, like, and are reinforced by, feeling competent in whatever they do. Some psychologists have called this the competency motive or the drive for mastery.[2] They have observed that children, from a very young age and without special training, want to be good at what they do and readily develop standards of achievement for their behavior.

Thus your child, like every child, has a natural tendency to rank his or her behavior on a scale of competency or excellence. Whether your child applies this scale to his or her moral behavior will depend largely on how strongly you stress the importance of "moral achievement" (in comparison to athletic achievement, academic achievement, financial achievement); that is, on your teaching him or her that the best kind of person to be is a moral person.

By the time children are old enough to be taught moral standards like the Golden Rule (between three and four years of age), they are capable of caring about standards of excellence for virtually any type of behavior. Research shows that the evaluative categories, "good" and "bad," are already very important for three-year-olds, and they readily apply these categories to their own actions. Other studies show that children rise to the standards that adults set for them. When adults set high standards and live up to them themselves, and when they accustom children to working long and hard for distant goals, the children set similarly high standards for their own behavior and work more persistently in the face of obstacles.[3]

As a species we seem not only to have a need to be competent ourselves, but we are also prone to be moved by others' strivings for excellence. Recall how strongly children react to the story of the little engine that could, and remember the evocative beginning of the film *Chariots of Fire* with the runners on the beach. All we are shown in the film are men striving, young men filled with purpose, and we are moved. Indeed, one can make a good case for there being survival value in having ideals of excellence. When a person strives *not* just for an immediate material outcome (say, hunting for food), but to attain a level of excellence (becoming a great hunter), he will master skills that are likely to serve him well if survival becomes an issue (when food becomes scarce).

You can lay a foundation for the growth of personal standards in your child by supporting her competency motive through statements such as "Do your best" and "Be your best" and by praising her for persistence and effort when she strives to master new tasks. Point out and praise other people's strivings for excellence and provide a good example yourself. Obviously, to promote the development of personal *moral* standards, the most important area to encourage your child to do her best in is the moral area.

A note of caution: Some care needs to be taken when you encourage your child to do her best. If your real message is "Do better than everyone else," or if you push her to do better than she is capable of, or if you turn every activity into an achievement situation and disparage pure play and fantasy, you may wind up inadvertently discouraging striving by making it too painful and frustrating. Similarly, if you show impatience because of the time it takes for your youngster to master something or the number of steps he or she must take along the way, you will undermine the child's natural joy in exploring, discovering, and mastering his or her world.

Parents, of course, need to do more than simply assert that living up to moral standards is the best way to live. They need to support this statement with sensible reasons. There are three good reasons you can give: **1)** because it is practical; **2)** because it feels good to do good; and **3)** because it builds a better world. The reason "Because it makes mommy and daddy proud of you," as we've seen in Chapter 2 on internalization, is useful for young children, but in order for personal standards to develop it must eventually be supplanted by the other three reasons.

***Living up to moral standards is practical.*** You can justify the Golden Rule to your child by explaining that if he treats others the way he doesn't want to be treated—that is, badly—they will be inclined to treat him badly. And explain that if he treats them the way he wants to be treated—well—they will be inclined to treat him well.

By and large, explanations in terms of practical consequences will be supported by your child's own day-to-day experiences with others. He will witness on his own that hitting doesn't usually settle a

disagreement, it usually escalates it; and that sharing is often reciprocated. He will learn that what social scientists call the "norm of
reciprocity" generally holds. Studies with children and adults show
that people do try to help those who have helped them.[4] It's useful
to point out his own natural inclinations to return kindness and to
retaliate for mistreatment, and explain that others have similar reactions to the way he treats them.

You can give your child practical reasons during her very earliest
social exchanges as long as you present them within a framework
she can understand. A practical reason in support of a rule against
hitting might be expressed to a five-year-old in this way: "If you hit
him, he's going to get his older brother to hit you, and then you'll
have to get your friends to beat up his brother; and then his brother
will get his friends to fight your friends; and soon all we'll have is
lots of fighting and everybody will hate each other and be afraid of
being beaten up all the time. Then you'd have to spend all your
time scared and planning how to get even, and there'd be no time
for play or anything enjoyable."

If you notice that in a particular relationship, say with a friend,
your child only thinks of himself, remind him to tell himself, "I will
treat him the way I want to be treated"—which means considering
the friend's needs and desires, not literally what your child would
want if he were in the other person's shoes. Then explain why in the
long run it is more practical for him to take the person's needs into
consideration.

A practical reason to give a child for helping his brother might be,
"If you help your brother carry his project to school, he'll be more
inclined to loan you his bicycle." A practical reason for respecting
his brother's belongings could be, "If you take David's baseball
glove without asking permission, he will feel he has the right to take
something of yours, and then you'll both be miserable and just go
on fighting with each other."

Children are generally responsive to these kinds of practical explanations, and they don't need a lot of convincing because they
usually find that in the long run life is, in fact, more harmonious
when moral rules are followed. For instance, two in-school programs
virtually eliminated the highly disruptive behavior of grade-school
children by "punishing" them with the assignment of writing essays
that covered 1) what they did wrong; 2) what happens that they
don't like when they behave that way; 3) what they should do in
similar circumstances in the future (say when they feel impelled to

call out during a lesson); and **4)** what good things follow when they behave appropriately. A similar group of disruptive students that was "punished" by having to write essays of the same length on neutral topics hardly improved at all, indicating that the improvement of the first group was due to what the students learned through their own essays about the practical consequences of their behavior.[5]

Interestingly, before the assignment of the essays, the disruptive children were not very adept at describing the practical consequences of appropriate and inappropriate classroom behavior; in contrast, children who were generally well behaved gave accurate descriptions of "both immediate and delayed consequences."

By the time your child is nine or ten he can understand that he, like every human being, survives only through membership in a community—that each of us depends on others for aid, comfort, and the practical necessities of life. But a morality that is based solely on practical considerations and exchanges is not likely to be very reliable since it is based only on self-concern. In fact, it's barely a morality at all since right and wrong are of no consequence, only what is expedient for one's own gain. Benefiting others is then not a reinforcer; it's merely a means to an end.

More than practical reasons are needed because, in truth, there are many occasions when one can violate moral rules and gain some advantage with little likelihood of incurring any practical cost to oneself. Kindness certainly is not always reciprocated and cruelty isn't always avenged. History and personal experience teach us that lots of bad guys have done pretty well for themselves when only practical consequences are taken into account. When exchange is the *only* reason for the standard "Do unto others," your child may wind up modifying it to read "Do unto others . . . unless you are smart enough or strong enough to get away with doing otherwise."

***It feels good to do good.*** If your child is inclined to feel empathy for people—either because of the way you brought her up or because she just seemed to come that way—a good reason to give her for doing good unto others is because she will feel good when she does good and bad when she does bad. And you can say just that to her: "You would (or wouldn't) want to be treated that way and you know that *you* are going to feel good (or bad) if you treat her that way." Various studies do indeed show that people feel good after doing good, and that they also like themselves more.

You can bolster your empathy argument for following the Golden

Rule by reminding her of past incidents when her actions toward others made her feel good or bad: "Remember how sad you felt when you knocked Johnny down and hurt him?" or "Remember how good you felt when you saw how happy Nancy was the time you let her join your game?" Empathy-based reasons will be very effective for a child who already tends to see things from other people's perspectives, but who often does so only *after* she acts, when it is too late.

For a child who doesn't tend to feel empathy very often, empathy reasons are less likely to work. But virtually all children, unless they have had an exceedingly harsh upbringing, have at sometime in their lives known the good feeling that comes from making someone else feel good. Never forget: Children are capable of great love. They love to give love.

Katherine Banham Bridges, in her classic paper on the development of delight in infants, describes the beginnings—in surprisingly young children—of what we believe deserves to be called the joy of giving.

> An eleven-month-old baby takes great delight in laughter, not only his own but that of another. He will laugh in order to make another child laugh, then jump and vocalize and laugh again in response. At twelve months of age he will repeat any little action that causes laughter. He is becoming increasingly affectionate. He puts his arms around the familiar adult's neck and strokes and pats her face.[6]

In another section she describes "the parental affection and almost self-sacrificing care shown by four-year-olds for their much younger playmates."

Children are clearly able to experience delight at someone else's joy. Sometimes, when they have become too self-centered, they need to be reminded that doing good feels good, too, and that living up to the Golden Rule will bring them pleasure.

You can start using empathy reasons even before your child is two. They are particularly useful for teaching the private property rule, which is usually one of the first that parents want their children to learn. Before children are about three years old they are used to fairly free access to objects in the home, except for dangerous or easily breakable items. But as a child starts to maneuver more and more independently in his or her environment and encounters objects that belong to others, ownership often becomes an issue, particularly between siblings.

Suppose you take your child to a public playground and he spies an intriguing-looking toy and proceeds to play with it or simply take it. First state the private property rule to him: "You can't just take that. It's not yours." Then give an empathy reason: "If you take it, it will make Jane (the owner) feel bad. Think how you'd feel if someone just walked over and took away your (mention his favorite toy)." Then take him with you to return the toy to its rightful owner. It's always best if he actually replaces the toy himself. Don't forget, though, that he does not yet know the rule, so be firm but not harsh in the way you instruct him. You are giving information, not reprimanding. These are hard lessons for a child to learn, so teach them sympathetically.

It's also worth remembering that one reason children resist rules is because, too often, their parents only tell them what they *aren't* allowed to do, and don't take the time to teach them the proper ways to obtain what they want. For instance, a child is more likely to adhere to the private property rule when he is also taught that he can ask for a person's permission to use his or her belongings. You can do this by explaining, "That's Jane's, but she might give you permission to play with it. Come, let's ask her if you can use it." Once your child knows how to ask permission, you can send him on his own with the reminder, "You must get permission first."

***Living up to moral standards helps to build a better world.*** As we said before, children are moved by striving. So teach them about *moral* striving. Make them feel that they are a part of the great human struggle to build a better world, a more ideal world in which there is more love, justice, and creativity, and less fear, pain, and suffering. Teach them about the great moral leaders of the past so they feel a sense of continuity with man's struggle to build a better world throughout history. Why live up to moral standards? Because we build a better world that way.

Having an ideal or purpose is a reinforcer for human beings and feels good as well. The opposite—cynicism, aimlessness, and hopelessness—are sorry conditions. Once we have a vision of a better world toward which we can strive, we will work to keep that vision alive. You can inspire your children to take on moral ideals by giving them a vision of the virtues of a more humane world and convincing them that they can help bring that world into being.

Only human beings are inspirable. What it takes is an awareness of a better condition to strive toward and a belief that we can reach it. One might say that we are the inspirable species.

Once a child has a moral ideal, his self-esteem will depend on whether or not his actions foster that ideal. He will remind himself of the Golden Rule and adhere to it because it helps bring about the world he is striving toward. He will try to resist temptations to violate the Golden Rule because now he wants to be reinforced by "good" outcomes and not by "bad" ones (such as illegitimate gain at other people's expense). A teenager might, for instance, enjoy proving that he is the toughest kid in the neighborhood, but if he has a moral ideal, he won't like himself for caring about being tough and for provoking other children into fights just to confirm his toughness. In the psychologist's terminology, the moral ideal has become a stronger reinforcer than proving his toughness.

Among the most dramatic and well-documented instances of the power of ideals on children is found in the work of the Russian educator, Anton Makarenko. Makarenko developed schools for delinquent children and teenagers in post World War I Russia. These young people were either orphaned by the war or abandoned by their parents during the period of economic and social upheaval following the communist takeover. Many were criminals. Few had any semblance of normal social behavior. Makarenko believed wholeheartedly in the ideals of communism and geared all his pedogogical strategies toward the Leninist goals: the creation of the new Soviet man and a totally cooperative society. Why do your job? Why share the burden? Why learn? Why be fair? There was one answer: Because we are building a better world.

And according to American researchers of this period of Soviet education, the technique succeeded. Makarenko started with an assortment of thieves and rogues, and transformed them into committed and productive members of Russian society. James Bowen described his philosophy: "Makarenko felt that the child's (criminal) past was no part of its future and he adhered strictly to that principle throughout. . . . His view was always directed toward the future . . . the vision of a better world that they could achieve by their own unremitting group effort was held before them."[7]

Most of us brought up in western democracies are not likely to share Makarenko's image of the ideal man as someone who totally subordinates his own vision and interests to those of the group, nor his image of the ideal society as a unified and disciplined collective. His practical achievements, though, should confirm for us that most children are indeed ready and willing to live by moral standards once they believe that their efforts can bring about a better future.

As a child's language abilities develop, as she becomes better able to connect present acts with distant outcomes, and as she accumulates more and different kinds of experiences with people, she will become more and more responsive to "idealistic" reasons for living up to moral standards. During adolescence she will be increasingly affected by reasons that point out her relationship to society at large and her and every individual's responsibility toward building a better society based on standards of kindness, justice, and personal liberty.

In the following discussion a mother uses what are essentially idealistic reasons to convince her son, who had a habit of "borrowing" people's belongings without asking, that it's important to respect other people's property. It began when she noticed him playing with a tennis racket that wasn't his:

MOTHER: Where did you get the racket?

SON: It's Ronny's.

MOTHER: Did Ronny say it was all right to use it?

SON: He wasn't around. It was in front of his garage.

MOTHER: You must have really wanted to play with it badly to just take it.

SON: Well, yeah. I wanted to practice against the wall, and my racket is broken.

MOTHER: I know how much you love tennis, but to just take it without permission? I understand that you wanted to practice, but do you think that's as important as respecting someone's property?

SON: But he's not using it now. I won't break it.

MOTHER: That's not the point. It belongs to him. Who has the right to decide who uses it?

SON: I guess he has the right. But you're always telling me to share. Shouldn't Ronny share?

MOTHER: I think he should. But sharing is voluntary. Neither you nor Ronny should be forced to share because someone just takes your things. Maybe Ronny *is* sharing. Maybe he left it there because he promised another friend that he could use it. Put yourself in his place. Would you like it if he just took your things when he wanted them without asking you?

SON: I wouldn't care.

MOTHER: Come on. Think about some of the things you really like. What about your bike?

SON: Well . . .

MOTHER: In any case, the point isn't how *you* feel about *your* things; Ronny may not be like you. He may be very protective of his belongings, and since they're *his* you have to respect that.

SON: I guess so.

MOTHER: It's a good rule for a lot of reasons. Without it you'd never be able to plan ahead to use something of your own—somebody might come along and borrow it without permission. Or you might take care of your things in some special way that somebody else wouldn't know about.

SON: Well, I guess that it doesn't make any sense to call something yours unless you decide who can use it and when they can use it. I'll return it and call him later. I'll ask him then.

When you use reasoning to support a standard, your goal is to convince your child that, in the long run, living up to the standard produces more desirable outcomes than violating it. You also want him to develop a general habit of thinking about the long-term consequences of his actions and to have good reasons to fall back on in case others try to influence him to abandon his moral standards.

Never underestimate a child's ability to understand reasons, nor his interest in being given reasonable explanations. Children start understanding and using reasons as soon as they start to talk.[8] A number of psychologists have demonstrated that children are able to understand both empathy and practical reasons for sharing and helping by the time they reach four years of age, and that these reasons do, indeed, guide their "prosocial" (or positive) behavior. In one such study on preschoolers, Nancy Eisenberg-Berg and Cynthia Neal report that when children explain why they helped, comforted, or shared with others, among the most common reasons they give are the needs of others, mutual benefits, and friendship.

In another study—this time with kindergartners—most children who shared candy with a classmate said they did so for empathic reasons ("I gave so he'll be happy," "So he won't be sad," "If I don't give, he won't have"). Those who shared for empathic reasons *gave more* candies than the few children who said they gave only for practical reasons: because they hoped their classmate would reciprocate ("I gave to him so he'll play with me").[9]

Other research shows that children place great importance on the reasons behind rules. This was clearly demonstrated by political psychologist June L. Tapp in a worldwide study of children's ideas about rules. She discovered that by the time most children reach five years of age they believe that rules and laws can be changed if they are more harmful than good; and that by the time they are eight, most believe that it is right to break a rule that leads to harming people or injustice. As one fourth-grader put it, a rule is good if it is "not something that takes away your freedom." On the basis of her findings that children care a great deal about the reasons for rules, Tapp urges parents to "explain to children *why* a rule is instituted (she coins the lovely phrase "persuasion to virtue").[10]

## Reasons Work Best in Democratic Families

Psychologist Glen Elder surveyed thousands of adolescents from Ohio and North Carolina and found that when parents explained their rules and decisions, their children were much more likely to follow those rules voluntarily than when they were imposed without explanation.

But Elder also found that giving reasons worked best in democratic families where the child had considerable input about rules and decisions (but not the final say), as compared to autocratic families where the child had no say, and permissive families where the child did pretty much whatever he wanted.

In democratic families the child followed the rules because he believed his parents' reasons made sense. When a child felt his parents' explanations weren't sound, he wasn't expected to simply accept them; they were open to discussion. Moreover, children who were raised democratically and given reasons for rules turned out to be the most self-confident and independent adolescents. They also had the most admiration for their parents and wanted to be like them; and they believed that the rules their parents taught them to live by were good rules. In other words, their parents' moral standards became their own personal standards.

Both adults and children are more likely to adhere to standards and consider them fair when they have participated in creating them.[11] In business this is called "participation management"—and companies that use it usually report an increase in both employee morale and productivity. One important lesson your child will learn from participating in rule-making is that in order to set up rules that everyone accepts, it is necessary to compromise and be sensitive to the needs of others. Also, once a child has helped formulate the rules that he must live by, it becomes difficult for him to play the role of the disgruntled victim, reacting either helplessly or rebelliously to rules imposed on him by others.

One reason democratic approaches work is that seemingly opposing viewpoints are often reconcilable if they are expressed openly and made clear. Once parents and children understand the reasons behind each other's positions, they can correct each other's misinformation and look for mutually satisfactory solutions. Putting into words what each person wants and feels is an important first step toward resolving family conflicts. Even if differences remain, an honest sharing between parent and child will have taken place, each will understand the other better, and the feeling that children often have that their parents are arbitrary and unreasonable will have been allayed.

### Common Moral Standards and Reasons

Following are some examples of common moral standards and the reasons that parents can give to support them. All the reasons below are practical—they argue that breaking the rule makes life difficult or dangerous or less pleasant in the long run.

In addition to these practical reasons, parents should always state empathic reasons ("How would you feel if . . . ?" "Remember how you felt when . . . ?" or "Wouldn't you want someone to help you if . . . ?") and also give their children "better world" reasons that explain moral standards as standards of excellence which foster the best human qualities.

Not everyone will subscribe to all the standards and reasons we list. Our purpose is not to tell parents *what* to teach their children, but rather to offer examples of standards that are commonly accepted in our culture. They do make sense to us, but what is important is that you teach your child standards and reasons that make sense to you—ones that *you* believe in.

| STANDARD | REASON |
|---|---|
| Influence others and settle differences through compromise or persuasion. Don't use physical force or | If you force others into doing something that you want but they don't, they will resent you, avoid you, and try to |

coercion to get your way. Might does *not* make right.

undermine your power over them. They are also likely to retaliate.

If you force others into accepting a bad idea, you, as well as they, will be stuck with its consequences. You will also lose their respect.

If others are afraid to disagree with you, you lose out on their knowledge and creativity. They will resent you for suppressing them and look for ways to escape your influence.

If you agree to do something, do it and do it well. Keep your promises.

People count on your doing what you promised and they may be harmed if you don't.

They will no longer trust your word and will prefer sharing activities with people that they can count on.

Treat others fairly. (Judgments of fairness are based on whether people get what they deserve. But there are different criteria for evaluating what is deserved, such as, we all share equally, one's share depends on one's contribution, one's share depends on one's need, and one's share depends on one's rank or status. So try to establish criteria of fairness in advance and settle disagreements over what is deserved through compromise.)

When people believe they have been treated unfairly, they feel abused and angry and often seek revenge. Unfairness in a group or organization lowers morale and members' commitment to group goals.

Be helpful when someone is in need. Don't hit someone when he or she is down.

We are all down sometime or other. That's when we need others most. It is unlikely others will be there for you unless you are there for them.

Don't take advantage of someone's weakness. Encourage people's strengths.

Taking advantage of a person's weakness usually requires either deception (as when you flatter someone who is insecure) or exploitation (as when you fleece someone who has come to you for aid). Both lead to anger and a desire for retribution when the victim learns the truth.

Be sensitive to people's feelings. Don't make fun of others.

If you set a precedent of making fun of others, you may someday be on the receiving end of someone else's jibes.

We usually make fun of others for the most superficial reasons (an odd nose or walk or speech pattern) and thus deprive ourselves and our group of potentially valuable friends.

Tell the truth. (One exception that most people would subscribe to is, if you are being threatened or oppressed by a person or group or a government, you may have to lie to protect yourself or your loved ones. Also, there are lies that people call "white lies," which are told to others to protect them, and not for the purpose of taking advantage of them in any way. Many people

Once someone catches you in a lie, it is very hard to win back his or her trust; and, typically, he or she will spread the word to others that you are untrustworthy. You lie to cover up something you have done or intend to do. You won't have to lie if you do only what you are proud of doing, and don't let others force you to hide what you feel proud of.

do not consider this type of lie to be immoral, as long as the information withheld is not something the person needs to know in order to make his or her own decision about something.)

| | |
|---|---|
| Consider the goals and desires of others, and try to help them reach their goals. Share and be helpful. | If others find that they benefit from interacting with you, they will want to interact with you again; and often they will reciprocate your kindness. |
| Be honest and trustworthy. Don't take someone else's property without permission. | If you take people's property, they will ostracize you in order to protect themselves; also, they may feel justified in taking your things and both of you will be unhappy. |

When teaching rules and giving reasons, keep the following in mind:

• Remember that practical reasons in and of themselves will not inspire your child toward concern for others. They only focus him on the long-term consequences to himself of living up to moral standards. But when practical reasons are joined with "better-world" and empathy reasons, your child will come to value moral standards because they make the world a better place for everybody, including himself. Then he'll feel good about himself when he lives up to them, regardless of who approves or disapproves.

• Emphasize the *prescriptive* side of standards focusing on what to do rather than the *proscriptive* side which focuses on what not to do. Researchers have found that children are better able to translate moral principles into concrete positive actions when they are taught the positive side of moral rules. "Tell the truth" is better than "Don't lie."[12]

• Don't expect that by simply stating reasons to your child she will automatically follow the rules of her own volition. You must make good behavior a requirement. Moral rules must be *rules,* not suggestions. The motives that make a child behave destructively or irresponsibly are usually strong and urgent. Even a young child will generally understand your explanation for why she should be kind, fair and responsible, but when she wants something badly, the benefits of moral action will often appear remote and uncertain in comparison to the immediate gratification she can get by grabbing something she wants or punching someone who annoys her. In family discussions, the agenda should not be whether to treat people well, but only how to best accomplish it.

• When giving reasons for standards, prepare your child for the counterarguments he will hear from other people. You may teach him to be considerate, but be assured that someone else will tell him that it's a dog-eat-dog world and that the only sensible rule to live by is, "Do unto others *before* they do unto you." While you teach him, "It's not winning that counts, but how you play the game," he'll learn from others that "Winning isn't everything—it's the only thing." Indeed, such self-centered standards have come into fashion lately.

If you want to inoculate your child against arguments that are contrary to the standards you hope he'll live by, you should forewarn him about such counterarguments, and explain why you disagree with them.[13] Doing this will have the added good effect of forcing you to clarify your values for yourself.

• Don't assume that your child thinks of rules as bad. Children generally don't, particularly when the rules are justified by good reasons.[14] Since a child is a relative stranger in the world, everything is new and exciting for her. And also scary. Good rules help her navigate through hidden obstacles and pitfalls. They tell her how things will turn out if she behaves in certain ways. Also—and this is of great importance—rules can make her feel that she is surrounded by people who know what they are doing and who can guide her. They help her feel secure.

• When you give a child reasons for rules, he learns that the value of a rule lies in the good that follows from living up to it and not from who said it. Make it clear that your reasons are based on your experience in life and not on your having any godlike or absolute knowledge of right and wrong. Teach your child that you are simply a more experienced traveler through life than he is, and that your obligation as a parent is to share with him what you have learned. Then he'll be less likely to resent you when he finds, as he inevitably will, that you don't have all the right answers. He is also less likely to accept anyone else's claim to complete authority or knowledge.

### "I Like Myself When I'm One of the Good Guys"

Once a child agrees that living up to a moral standard will produce a better future, she will hold people, including herself, in esteem only if they live up to that standard. Thus, her self-esteem will now begin to depend on whether or not she lives up to her standards, and she will begin to think of other people as "good" or "bad" according to their adherence to those standards—and she will want to place herself among the ranks of those who are good.

The child will want to be able to apply the same kinds of good words to herself about her own actions as she applies to those of other good people. In contrast, when she has done or is on the verge of doing things that only bad people do, she will be forced to condemn herself with the same opprobrium that she has used to condemn them.

The way these good and bad labels work is described well by a salesman who said,

> There is a salesman in our company who's a real rat. He doesn't care what he says to people as long as he makes the sale and comes out with a few extra dollars. Sometimes when I've had a bad week selling, I find myself starting to sound like him—really preying on any weakness I can spot in order to get customers to sign and commit to lots of extras. But then I tell myself, if I continue that way, I'll have to think of myself as a rat, just like him—we'd be identical, two rotten peas in the same pod. Well, that's usually enough to stop me. A couple of times I kept pushing for the sale, and when I got it I felt terrible. It's important for me to think of myself as a decent person.

A good motto to teach a child is "Don't be what you hate." Also give your child lots of examples of good people, people who try to live up to moral standards. As any Sunday School teacher knows, your child will be moved by stories of people striving to do good. And once he adopts a moral standard as his own, he will want to feel that he belongs with the "best" people—best in the sense that they strive to treat others well. Research by Milton Rokeach and his colleagues has confirmed that you can motivate people to strive to live up to their ideals by giving them information on how they have fallen short of those ideals in the past or that they aren't living up to the standards of those they admire.[15]

The only moral heroes most children learn about nowadays are cartoon and television characters like Batman and various "bionic" creatures. Few parents make the effort to provide their children with instances of real-life heroes beyond those the child might learn about in religious training. Make this effort. It will enrich the both of you.

But first you will have to define for yourself which people you think stand for moral values. Be careful to teach your child that you are calling a person good because he or she lived up to moral standards, and not vice versa: Slavery doesn't become good because Thomas Jefferson owned slaves.

If you claim you're too busy to think about such things, you will be missing out on an opportunity to provide your child with important lessons. It will be much easier for her to act in terms of her moral standards if she knows that others have done so. Their acts can inspire her and teach her what has worked in the past. They can help her feel that she is part of an ongoing human struggle to create a more benevolent and just world.

## Attributing Good Intentions:
## An Effective Way to Criticize

Children, like adults, have interests that compete with doing what they know is right. They want material things or power or revenge, and sometimes moral standards are overlooked or overwhelmed. But you can use your child's desire to like himself and maintain his status as a good person as a way to motivate him to live up to his standards.

Not too long ago we observed an elementary school teacher do this by saying the perfect thing to a six-year-old boy. The boy's classmate, Brigit, had come up to the teacher, face full of smiles, to show her some drawings she had just completed. The little boy, Albert, was standing near the teacher's desk and when he saw the drawings he promptly remarked, "They stink."

Brigit's smile vanished. The teacher took Albert aside, bent down to him and said, "You may not know it, but that hurt Brigit's feelings because she really worked hard on those pictures. Now, I'm sure if you knew that you were going to hurt her feelings, you wouldn't have said that about them. I don't think you'd ever want to be that kind of boy, would you?"

Albert swallowed, and with his face down, he muttered, "No." His teacher then took his hand and said, "Come, let's take a good look at her pictures together, and we'll each tell her which one we like best.''

The teacher did not simply scold and disapprove, although her approval was certainly at stake for Albert. What she did was remind him of a standard he already understood, but that had not yet become a guiding principle for his actions. Even though she didn't state the standard formally, her reminder that *It's bad to hurt people intentionally* came through very clearly.

Albert was induced to apply this standard to his actions because of two things his teacher did:

1. She attributed underlying good intentions to him (''I'm sure if you knew that you were going to hurt her, you wouldn't have said that''). By doing this, she was granting him membership in the good persons' ''club''—a membership she assumed he desired. If he continued to ignore the standard, he'd lose his ''membership''—not just because his teacher disapproved of him, but because the categories ''person who intentionally hurts others'' and ''good person'' are mutually exclusive. Research on children's understanding of logic shows that even five-year-olds can understand the idea of mutually exclusive categories.[16]
2. She asked him to define the kind of boy *he didn't want to be* (one who intentionally hurts others). By doing this, she was forcing him to choose whether or not he wanted to keep his status as a good person. If he did, he'd have to use the standard as a guide for his behavior toward Brigit, as well as his future behavior toward others.

The importance of attributing good intentions as a way to induce children to live up to standards is supported by a number of studies. In one, boys and girls seven to ten years of age, played a miniature bowling game to win marbles, which could then be cashed in for toys. An adult attendant told each child that he or she could donate some of the marbles won to poor children so that they too could have prizes. The game was set up so that all children received the same number of marbles and most children did donate.

Afterward, the adult said to some of the children, ''You shared quite a bit. I guess you shared because you're the kind of person who likes to help other people.'' This was the attribution of good intentions message. Other children were told, ''You shared quite a bit. I guess you shared because you thought I *expected* you to.'' Later, when the children bowled again, those who had received the ''good intentions" message donated more marbles than those who had received the "expectancy" message. Even two weeks later when the children played again, many more of those who had received the good intentions message donated part of their winnings.

The researchers concluded that "children could be induced to behave more altruistically if they were able to attribute their good behavior to the fact that they were the kind of people who cared for others." Another study of good attributions found that pupils who were told by their teacher that they were the kind of children who tried to be neat and clean littered less than children in a comparison class who were just told that they ought not to litter. Other studies have found similar "good intentions" effects on reducing cheating, increasing cooperativeness, and extending children's ability to be patient.[17]

The children in these various studies obviously already knew and agreed with the standards—they believed that it was good to share and be neat, honest, cooperative, and patient. But children often want all the prizes they can get, and they typically prefer to rush off to meet friends at the end of class rather than take the time to throw their trash in the wastepaper basket. However, once a child has been awarded a "good" label, he risks losing it if he fails to live up to it. He will no longer be able to think of himself as "good."

We need to stress that in these studies the primary thing at risk for a child was her judgment of herself—her self-concept. For instance, children in the "neat" class were never criticized for littering. Nor were they praised for any specific neat acts. They were only given statements like, "Our class is clean and would not do that" (leave litter around like the previous class). But soon the children in the "neat" class not only were criticizing and picking up after each other, they also "castigated the teacher for her desk being the only messy one in the room." They were proud of their good label ("the neat class") and they weren't going to let their teacher, who had been the initial labeler, undermine their pride.

There is a principle for parents in these attribution studies: *Praise the child and not just the act.* (Contrast this to an earlier stated principle: Criticize the act, not the child.) When she's kind, tell her you're glad she's a kind person. Give your child "good" character labels so that a "bad" act can cost her the label she wants to apply to herself. But never lead a child to believe she has lost a "good" label irrevocably. It's important for children to learn that morality is a daily process, not a state that one attains or loses forever. If a child comes to believe she can never deserve to think of herself as a good person, she may take a "what's the use" attitude and conclude that since she has nothing to lose she might as well give her selfish impulses free rein.

Should a child ever be given a "bad" label? Our recommendation is *no*. Obviously, if a child understands the meaning of a "good people" category, he will also understand its opposite, the "bad people" category. The best way to handle the "bad" category is to present it as the place one can wind up if one doesn't do good things. For example, when the teacher said to Albert, "I don't think you'd ever want to be that kind of boy [who hurts people], would you?" she was implying that if he continued to hurt others, he would have to be considered the kind of person who hurts people.

The following are some other attribution statements you can make when your child engages in bad behavior. Each implies the possibility of consignment to the bad-guys club:

"I'd hate to think of you as the kind of person who doesn't care if he hurts people."

"That's just the way_____treats people. You don't like her because of that, so I know you don't want to be like her."

"Think about a person you like and a person you don't like. I'm sure that's not the kind of thing someone you like would have done."

There is evidence that the attribution effect is strongest for children who are at least eight years old.[18] At this age, they are beginning to define the kind of person they are, in terms of both their interests (I like arithmetic) and character (I am a kind person).

The following are some other useful ways to handle criticism if your child has violated a moral standard:

• Acknowledge that you understand that what he was after was important to him (for example, practicing tennis). Never belittle his interests.

• Compare the outcome she was after (satisfying some immediate desire) with the more serious and longer term outcomes that follow from failing to live up to the standard. Your argument should stress cause and effect; If you do A, B follows—and some B's are better than others.

• Don't expect your child to know a rule he hasn't been taught.

Don't blame. Teach firmly but lovingly. It is not the child that is bad, it is only some particular actions of his.

- Use questions in the form of "What would happen if . . . ?" so that she recognizes the value of the standard on her own. You want her to agree with you, not merely follow orders.

- Use examples from your child's own experience to support your argument, or cite other analogous, real-life events—using language he can understand ("The king of France thought that because he had a strong army he could treat people any way he wanted and could take whatever he wanted from them. But when enough people felt he was being unfair they joined together and . . .").

- Construct hypothetical situations to support your explanations ("If you hit her, her older sister will hit you . . ." or "What if a man came into daddy's store and took things without paying for them?").

- Use empathic arguments and evidence based on feelings your child has had in the past or can easily imagine. ("Remember how you felt when . . . ?" or "How would you feel if . . . ?").

- Use stories and fables to illustrate a point. For instance, a rule against making fun of others could be supported by reminders such as "Remember how the ugly duckling was mistreated just because he looked different?" Stories that describe circumstances that are similar to the child's allow her to see beyond her own immediate needs and evaluate a situation less subjectively. It then becomes easier for her to understand how another person feels.

- Don't be neutral. Let him know that the standard is important to you.

- Be open to her counterarguments, and never, never be afraid to acknowledge you were wrong about something.

- If, after a discussion, you don't accept his reasons and he doesn't accept yours, don't hesitate to insist that he live up to the moral standard you are trying to teach him—whether he likes it or not. But make sure he at least understands your reasons for upholding the standard. He may reconsider later.

- Practice what you preach. Otherwise your child is likely to follow your practices and will think of you as a hypocrite.[19]

## STANDARDS TO TEACH AND STANDARDS NOT TO TEACH YOUR CHILD

There are many different standards that deserve to be called moral because they define an "ideal" way of living with one's fellow man. But they are not all equal. "We must purify the race," can be considered a moral standard, as well as "Kill the infidels." But these are standards that we assume (and hope) all readers would reject. We reject them on moral grounds because we judge some moral standards to be better than others, depending on the outcomes they seek to produce—that is, we value some outcomes more than others.

Moral standards can be a great source of good. But history has also taught us that people do very cruel things to each other in the name of moral standards. How can we make sure our children don't fall prey to standards that encourage harming others?

There are some standards that have emerged out of human conflict and misery to meet this very need to protect society from moral zealots, as well as from ill-intentioned people who camouflage their selfish or cruel purposes with moral rhetoric. One of these standards is, *All men and women, regardless of race, religion, and nationality, have equal rights.* If you teach your child this and tell her about the horrors that people have suffered when this standard has not been honored, she will be less likely to follow leaders who want to harm people simply because they are different. She will understand that when the Golden Rule says, "Do unto others . . ." there can be no restrictions as to who those others are—it cannot mean *only* other Americans or Caucasians or Aryans or Christians or Jews.

Similarly, if you teach your child that everyone has a right to believe or not to believe in whatever he or she wishes, he will be less likely to try to harm or restrict those who don't believe in his religion or political or economic system. And if you teach him that everyone has a right to say and write what he or she believes, he won't want to join those who see conformity and loyalty as the highest virtues; nor will he view dissent as dangerous.

These moral standards are, of course, codified in the Bill of Rights of the American Constitution. The First Amendment, for example, reads:

Congress shall make no law respecting an establishment of religion, or prohibiting the free exercise thereof; or abridging the freedom of speech or of the press; or the rights of the people peaceably to assemble, and to petition the government for a redress of grievances.

Among the goals of the American Constitution, as set out in its Preamble, are "to establish justice," "to promote the general welfare," and "to secure the blessings of liberty." Whenever people strive for these goals they tend to rediscover the same kinds of moral standards. As early as 50 B.C. the Roman statesman, Marcus Tullius Cicero, wrote "Only in states in which the power of the people is supreme has liberty any home." Seventeen hundred years later, in 1690, John Locke, the English political philosopher, wrote, "The liberty of man in society is to be under no other legislative power but that established by consent of the commonwealth." Almost a century later, in 1776, under the guiding hand of Thomas Jefferson, the American Declaration of Independence asserted that "Governments are instituted among Men, deriving their just powers from the consent of the governed." One hundred and seventy-two years after that, in 1948, the United Nations, by a unanimous vote, established the Universal Declaration of Human Rights. Article 21 states, "The will of the people shall be the basis of the authority of government."

We see that across thousands of years, in the ongoing human struggle to find standards to live by, the same principle keeps reappearing: All individuals have an equal right to participate in making the laws that they will live by. There are many other such principles. For instance, you will find the freedoms of religion, speech, and assembly that were set forth in the First Amendment of the American Bill of Rights, restated almost two centuries later in the United Nations Universal Declaration of Human Rights. People and governments do not always do what they believe is right; but there is surprising agreement across centuries and cultures about the best way for human beings to treat each other.[20]

If you teach your child these basic moral standards, she will be less likely to abuse others or ignore their plight during those times in her life when she is filled with anger or prejudice, or when she wants something desperately or simply wants to be left alone. When you teach her these principles, teach them well so they aren't learned merely as a set of empty slogans. Psychologists Gail Zellman and David Sears found that a majority of the California school children they questioned (ages nine to fourteen), agreed with the statement: "I believe in free speech for all no matter what their views might be." But when it came down to concrete instances, whether a communist, a Vietcong, or a Nazi should be allowed to make a speech in the community or hold a meeting, very few children said yes. Other researchers report similar findings: When we don't like what a group stands for, many of us are quite willing to restrict the freedom of its members. Indeed, one study found that a majority of Americans were against allowing people to publish books against our government or make speeches against God.[21]

Zellman and Sears argue that children can, in fact, be taught to live up to high standards of freedom and equality and to extend basic liberties to unpopular groups. But they conclude that for the most part, "political socialization fails to teach the true meaning of American democracy . . . to convey the unique and desirable feature of the American system, namely its tolerance for diversity and individual liberties."

These issues may sometimes seem far removed from the day-to-day concerns of your family; but, ultimately, all our lives and families are profoundly affected by the climate of freedom and justice in our society. So we urge you, teach your child these standards of freedom and equality well.

There are some standards that are commonly taught to children in the name of promoting morality, but which we believe actually make it difficult or impossible for a child to live up to more basic moral standards. Two common ones are teaching a child to be ashamed of his thoughts and feelings, and teaching him that obedience to authority is a virtue in itself.

**"A bad thought is like a bad deed": The misuse of shame.** We recommend that you do not teach your child that a bad thought is like a bad deed. In fact, we strongly recommend that you teach her that there are no such things as *bad thoughts*. Teach her never to make moral judgments about her own thoughts because they have no consequences for others—only her actions do.

It's important for parents to understand that when a child feels someone is treating him unfairly, so-called "bad thoughts" (angry, revengeful thoughts) are perfectly natural and to be expected. Children, like adults, cannot help what they feel, but children can become frightened of being punished or shamed for having the wrong kinds of feelings. When this happens children will often resort to denying that they have thoughts or feelings that have been labeled "bad." Having to lie to parents about important and troubling thoughts leads to feelings of alienation and mistrust for both child and parent. And even if a child manages to keep his "bad thoughts" secret, he may wind up living out his entire life hating himself for being a "sinner in his heart."

A more serious consequence of labeling thoughts and feelings as bad is that the child may begin to deny them *to himself;* that is, he can feel angry and revengeful and not know it. Sigmund Freud, of course, pointed this out long ago. He wrote that a child will repress self-knowledge when he has an excessively harsh super-ego (Freud's term for conscience) that condemns his feelings and thoughts.[22]

But how can a child not know what he is feeling? How does this kind of self-deception come about? It happens because the child has learned to avoid applying accurate labels to his feelings. For instance, ordinarily we learn to say we are angry when we have certain thoughts, images, and bodily sensations, which include an awareness of who we are angry at and what the person did that provoked us, as well as thoughts about gaining satisfaction by doing him or her harm.

But a child who has learned that it is bad to be angry may come to avoid applying the label "angry" to his feelings. He will still have all the experiences to which the word "angry" ordinarily refers, but he will shun the label because he doesn't want to hate himself for being a bad person. On occasions when the experiences (the thoughts or body sensations) that would ordinarily be called "feeling angry" are too strong for him to ignore or when they are forced on his attention by others, he will still try to avoid self-hatred by mislabeling them with a more acceptable label. Even after actually harming someone he might say, "I didn't mean to hurt her feelings. I only wanted her to understand my point"—and he will believe it. As far as he is concerned, he was not angry.

Psychologists would then say that his motivation to do harm was "unconscious," meaning that they believe that his behavior was directed toward, or reinforced by, certain ends (say, making his sister cry), while he insists that he was after something more benign (making a point).

Children need to know how to take constructive action when in the throes of destructive impulses—and this process must start with their full recognition and acceptance of those impulses and the feelings and thoughts that accompany them. They must be able to acknowledge without judgment that they wished harm to someone or imagined hurting him or her. Only then can they begin to analyze the frustrating circumstances behind their feelings and try to attain their goals in constructive ways. Only then does self-control become possible. (Note that our understanding of unconscious motivation is not based on the Freudian view that we all possess—and are possessed by—a secret mind that controls us. Freud worked at a time when it was generally believed that what we do is determined by conscious choices. When he found that people don't always choose to do the things they do, he looked for another explanation. But he couldn't break free from the idea that behavior is determined by choices, and merely invented an invisible, "unconscious" chooser who inhabits and controls us without our knowledge.)

Let's say your child has rageful tantrums whenever she is thwarted or disciplined. You certainly don't want to give in to them, but you also don't want to make her ashamed of her feelings. At a calmer time, let her know that it's all right for her to feel angry, but not all right to act on those feelings to harm anyone. Also, tell her that she can do more than simply rein in her impulses; she can learn to take constructive actions to overcome frustrations. You can teach her how by rehearsing self-instructional procedures with her: First have her imagine an occasion when she can't get something she wants and then, when she begins to feel the anger building up, have her practice reminding herself to be constructive.

Then have her practice the following steps: **1)** calming herself by relaxing her arms and shoulders while slowly exhaling as much breath as possible; **2)** trying to understand the other person's point of view; **3)** trying to think of a reasonable compromise ("I give you something you want and you give me something I want"); and **4)** looking for other strategies for getting what she wants (such as earning her own money to buy something you don't want to pay for, or proving she can handle a later bedtime responsibly by agreeing to get herself up and ready for school on time for a whole week without making everyone miserable or falling asleep in classes).

*"Always obey authorities": A standard that leads to trouble.* We honor the great moral leaders of history not because they slavishly obeyed authorities, but because they upheld high principles—often in defiance of authorities or laws that they considered unjust. If morality were simply based on doing what authorities and laws command, black Americans would still be riding in the back of buses. Indeed,

America would still be an English colony. Too often laws are made by those with wealth and power to serve their own interests.

We honor the "man for all seasons" whose principles cannot be purchased or frightened or commanded away. We dishonor the man who justifies his actions with the words, "I was just following orders." In the past fifty years these have become words of ignominy. We have all witnessed the horrors that can happen when people are brought up to believe that their highest moral responsibility is following orders. You need to teach your child to be able to say no.

The danger of teaching a child to blindly obey authorities is, of course, that authorities may ask him to do the most awful things. In 1891, Kaiser Wilhelm II of Germany addressed a group of army recruits:

> . . . You have sworn fidelity to me, you are the children of my guard, you are my soldiers, you have surrendered yourself to me, body and soul. Only one enemy can exist for you—my enemy . . . it may happen that I shall order you to shoot your own relatives, your brothers, or even your parents—which God forbid—and then you are bound in duty implicitly to obey my orders.[23]

Here is a case of blind obedience that is much closer to home. In 1969, Mike Wallace of CBS News interviewed an American soldier who participated in the roundup and slaughter of hundreds of unarmed civilians at My Lai in Vietnam. When asked why he did it, he answered: "Why did I do it? Because I felt like I was ordered to do it." When asked how he brought himself to shoot babies, he replied, "I don't know. It's just one of these things . . . the mothers was hugging their children and . . . Well, we kept right on firing."[24]

We are all shocked when we read about events like these. We ask ourselves how people could do these kinds of things. In the early 1960s psychologist Stanley Milgram, reacting to the horrors of the Nazi death camps, set out to study why people hurt other people simply because they are ordered to by someone in a position of authority.

Through an advertisement in a local newspaper, Milgram recruited ordinary individuals from various walks of life to participate in a psychology experiment for a modest fee. In the laboratory each subject met the experimenter and a person who was introduced as another subject, but who was actually the experimenter's paid assistant. The subjects were told that the study was on the effects of punishment on learning, and that one subject would serve as the learner and the other would be the teacher. Teachers were told to give increasingly severe electric shocks each time a learner made a mistake. It was arranged so that the real subject invariably became the teacher with the task of giving the shocks.

After a certain number of mistakes and shocks, the learner, who was strapped to the shock device, yelled to stop the experiment or screamed as if in pain. When a teacher said he or she wanted to stop giving shocks or when he or she asked what to do, the experimenter said, "The experiment requires that you continue." That's all. He did not threaten in any way or offer them any incentives to go on.

Yet go on they did. As Milgram put it, "the results of the experiment are both surprising and dismaying. Despite the fact that many subjects experience stress, despite the fact that many protest to the experimenter, a substantial proportion continue to the last shock of the generator. Many subjects will obey the experimenter no matter how vehement the pleading of the person being shocked [or] how painful the shocks seem to be."[25]

Why did these very ordinary people carry out such orders? Milgram suggests a number of reasons, including a sense of obligation to the experimenter, politeness, the awkwardness of withdrawal, and the tendency to become absorbed in the narrow technical aspects of the task. But he felt that the most significant cause was that the subject relinquished personal responsibility: "He sees himself not as a person acting in a morally accountable way, but as the agent of an external authority . . . his moral concern now shifts to a consideration of how well he is living up to the expectations that the authority has of him."

Over half of the forty subjects delivered the full range of shocks, proceeding through and past the set of levers marked "Danger: Severe Shock," to the last three marked "XXX." Most of the subjects gave over twenty shocks—well into the "Intense Shock" range on the board. Only a few resisted and quit the experiment before reaching this point.

Milgram confirmed in various ways that his subjects were not deviants or sadists, they were ordinary people who could be expected to believe in the moral principle, "one should not inflict suffering on a helpless person who is neither harmful nor threatening to oneself." Presumably because they did believe in this principle, most subjects showed extreme signs of discomfort as they administered the more powerful shocks: they sweated, trembled, stuttered, bit their lips, laughed uncontrollably, groaned, and dug their fingernails into their own flesh. Most complained and asked permission to stop.

Milgram concluded that "Even when the destructive effects of their work become patently clear, and they are asked to carry out actions incompatible with fundamental standards of morality, relatively few people have the resources needed to resist authority."

Man's inhumanity to man is very old news. The surprising and dismaying aspect of Milgram's study is how little pressure was needed to induce ordinary people to violate common standards of how people should be treated. Milgram's concern was with people's "resources" to resist authority. This is our concern too: What can parents do so that their child will be able to resist those who would lead him to be cruel?

## FOSTERING MORAL INDEPENDENCE: TEACHING YOUR CHILD WHEN TO SAY NO TO AUTHORITIES

Let's see what we can learn from a subject in Milgram's study who resisted the experimenter. Mr. Rensaleer, a thirty-two-year-old industrial engineer, quit the experiment shortly after the learner started to complain of pain. When Mr. Rensaleer refused to push the next lever, the experimenter gave his regular reply:

EXPERIMENTER: It is absolutely essential that you continue.
MR. RENSALEER: Well, I won't—not with the man screaming to get out.
EXPERIMENTER: You have no other choice.
MR. RENSALEER: I *do* have a choice (*incredulous and indignant*). Why don't I have a choice? I came here on my own free will. I thought I could help in a research project. But if I have to hurt somebody to do that, or if I was in his place, too, I wouldn't stay here. I can't continue. I'm very sorry. I think I've gone too far already, probably.

Later, when the experimenter interviewed Mr. Rensaleer and asked him who was responsible for shocking the learner against his will, he said, "I would put it on myself entirely." He explained:

I should have stopped the first time he complained. I did want to at that time. I turned around and looked at you. I guess it's a matter of . . . authority, if you want to call it that; my being impressed by the thing, and going on although I didn't want to. Say, if you're serving in the army, and you have to do something you don't like to do, but your superior tells you to do it. That sort of thing, you know what I mean?

One of the things I think is very cowardly is to try to shove the responsibility onto someone else. See, if I now turned around and said, "It's your fault . . . it's not mine," I would call that cowardly.

Clearly, Mr. Rensaleer holds himself accountable for the way he treats people. Contrast this with a man who obeyed the experimenter all the way to the highest shock levels. This man blamed the learner and the experimenter. His justification was that the learner "agreed to it, therefore [he] must accept responsibility." But, he added, "the biggest share of the responsibility" goes to the experimenter. About his own responsibility? "I merely went on. Because I was following orders . . . I was told to go on. And I did not get a cue to stop."

Milgram's study leads us to our first principle for fostering moral independence.

**PRINCIPLE #1.** *Teach your child that he and only he is responsible for the consequences of his actions.* This principle is dramatically illustrated by the reminiscence of another man who refused to obey authority. He was a German citizen who risked his life to rescue Jews from the Nazis. He described the moral training he received as a child to psychologist Perry London.

> I came from a poor family . . . My mother said to me when we were small, and even when we were bigger, she said to me . . . "regardless of what you do with your life, be honest. When it comes the day you have to make a decision, make the right one. It could be a hard one. But even the hard ones should be the right ones." My mother . . . always in life she gave me so much philosophy. She didn't go to high school . . . but so smart a woman, wisdom, you know.[26]

London interviewed twenty-seven Christians who risked their lives to save Jews. Almost all described a strong attachment to a parent who taught them about their responsibility to others. Later research with many other rescuers confirmed that for most, their extraordinary moral commitment stemmed from the moral education they received from their parents.

There is a strong connection between accepting responsibility for our actions and how we treat others. For example, college men who indicated on a questionnaire that they believed they were personally responsible for the effects of their actions were also the ones who most fully lived up to their moral codes and who were rated by their dormmates as the most considerate and helpful.[27]

Sometimes it's risky to make a decision on your own. And sometimes it's just very easy to go along with authorities or friends or the latest trend. Often parents will have to convince their children that it is ultimately in their own interest to think for themselves. Here's an example of a mother who did just that:

SALLY: All the kids at school are excited about the election for school president tomorrow afternoon.

MOTHER: Really? Who's running?

SALLY: Adrienne against Mary. I'm voting for Adrienne.

MOTHER: Why did you choose her?

SALLY: Well, all my friends said that they were voting for her.

MOTHER: Is she the best person for the job?

SALLY: Well . . . I guess I'm not sure.

MOTHER: What qualities do you think a class president should have? What does she have to do?

SALLY: She supervises the student fund committee—so she should be a good planner and a good moderator.

MOTHER: What else?

SALLY: And she represents our school at the district conference—so she should be up on school issues and a good debater.

MOTHER: Anything else?

SALLY: A lot of the younger kids look up to the class president so she should be someone who will be nice to them and make them feel like they're part of the school.

MOTHER: Is it important to you that the president be someone who can do the best job?

SALLY: Sure.

MOTHER: Do you think it would be better if the principal appointed the president?

SALLY: Oh, no. The kids get to see sides of each other that the principal doesn't see. And sometimes the class president has to even argue with the principal. No, it's important that the kids elect her.

MOTHER: Well, do you think your friends considered the requirements of the job carefully when they chose Adrienne?

SALLY: Maybe not. They probably chose her because she's lively and funny.

MOTHER: Does she also have the other qualities needed for the job?

SALLY: I'm not sure.

MOTHER: Then do you think you're ready to decide who to vote for?

SALLY: I'd better give this some more thought. And I have some questions I want to ask both Mary and Adrienne tomorrow morning. I think it's best if I make up my own mind on who I'll vote for.

MOTHER: One more question. Were you voting like your friends because you thought they might not like you if you disagreed with them?

SALLY: I didn't think about that at the time. But maybe. But I don't want them to like me just for going along—not when I think their decision is wrong. Then they're not really liking *me*, are they?

Notice that Sally's mother did not tell her what to do. If she had simply said, "Think for yourself," all Sally would have learned was that her mother wanted her to behave in a certain way. "Think for yourself" would remain her mother's rule, not hers. And as psychologist Jack Brehm has demonstrated in his research on "psychological reactance," many of us can be quite contrary (even ornery) when other people—including our parents—tell us what to do without adequate reasons.[28]

Her mother's strategy was to let Sally discover the reasons why she should think for herself by prompting her into asking herself questions about what was important to her (having a competent president), how to best bring about what she wanted (electing someone with the best skills), and what might be the outcomes of the two alternatives open to her (thoughtlessly adopting her friends' choice of candidate versus evaluating the candidates on her own). Sally filled in the rest.

PRINCIPLE #2. *Build your child's confidence in his or her ability to make good decisions.* A child who doesn't have confidence in his own judgment is easily manipulated by others. He will look to authorities for certification. As Milgram described it, Mr. Rensaleer became "incredulous and indignant" when the experimenter told him he had no choice but to go on. It's as if he were saying to the experimenter: "Who are you to tell me what I should or shouldn't do?"

The German citizen in London's study also had confidence in his own judgment. In another part of his interview he indicated that, although he wasn't raised religiously, he took the *protest* part of his Protestantism seriously. As he put it, "Protest is Protestant. I protest." His religion taught him that his own heart is the final authority on what is right and wrong, and that once he decides that something is wrong, he is obligated to protest.

One way to help a child gain the confidence to act on his own initiative is through warmth, or *nurturance,* as researcher Ervin Staub calls it. In one of Staub's studies on this topic, an adult played a game with each of a number of kindergarten children in a room alone for about ten minutes. In the "nurturance" condition, the adult chatted in a warm, friendly way, smiled frequently and complimented the child often. Children in the "neutral" condition were handled in as businesslike a manner as possible without smiles or friendly conversation from the adult.

When the children were later left alone in the room, they each heard a crash from an adjoining room which was quickly followed by sounds of a child crying. Staub confirmed his expectations that the children who had been treated warmly would take the initiative to help the (supposedly) hurt child next door. Indeed, while very few of the children who had been treated neutrally went next door to give aid, more than 25 percent of those who had been treated warmly did go to help.[29] Given that these were five-year-olds in a strange circumstance, that's a pretty sizeable percentage.

Staub theorized that warmth works because children who are treated in a friendly manner aren't afraid that they will be punished for taking an independent action. Treating children warmly gives them the confidence to rely on their own judgment.

In our own family-therapy practice we commonly find that children of cold or harsh parents are afraid to take virtually any kind of spontaneous action, including helpful ones, because they are afraid that their parents will find some fault in what they have done and criticize or punish them.

In one such case, Mr. Gorden, a widower, was determined to bring up his children "strictly." Unfortunately, in practice, strictly meant that he jumped down their throats every time they did anything that deviated even slightly from his narrow standards. He always focused on what they did wrong, never on what they did right or better. He gave them no room to learn from their mistakes. All three of his children were afraid of him. In family-therapy sessions, they all looked at their father constantly to see if he was approving or disapproving of what they were saying.

With great trepidation his sixteen-year-old daughter complained that he was impossible to please. She said that he lectured her and her brothers on being helpful to others, but on one occasion, when she helped an elderly woman get off a bus and the bus driver—presumably not knowing she intended to get back on—drove off with her schoolbag, all her father did was scold her for being careless. He did not acknowledge her kindness at all.

The children agreed that everything they did seemed to break some rule, and they all expressed fear about doing anything without first getting permission. (Of course, Mr. Gorden then criticized them for lacking initiative.)

The lesson here is, if you want your children to have confidence in their own judgments, make them feel good about themselves by praising their attempts at independent thought and action; acknowledge even small steps toward independence. Don't make them feel stupid. Give them the freedom to make mistakes. In fact, teach them to expect to make mistakes, and not to be thrown by them. Teach them that one learns from mistakes. Don't simply condemn them for failing. Remember, *the more faith your child has in his own competence, the more willing he will be to rely on his personal standards when faced with moral issues.*

Here are a couple of examples of what to do and what *not* to do if you want your child to develop confidence in his judgment. We recently saw a mother in a playground hit her son after he had bruised and scraped his leg. As she hit him she said, "I told you not to go on the big swings." She was probably reacting out of honest concern for her child, but the pain in his leg had already given him a clear message about the danger of the big swings. She was hitting him for willfulness and disobedience. If you have a willful child—meaning one who likes to think for himself—don't try to beat him into submission. Of course, you want to feel you can rely on him to obey your rules, but you'll accomplish this better if you make sure he understands why the rules exist.

This mother had given her child an order about the swings, but we assume she had neglected to demonstrate how difficult it would be for him to mount one. Most children are not stupid or self-destructive, and if you take the time to teach them about what they are and aren't capable of doing, they'll usually get the point.

This mother would have been more helpful if she had first given her son the comfort he wanted and then started his lessons on how to master the big swings (such as teaching him to sit in the middle of them and to hold the ropes firmly). Even if he was many months away from being able to use them alone, his sense of failure could have been turned into one of partial mastery. When a parent can't take pleasure in her child's desire to master his environment and get a kick out of each step along the way, then she and her child have a serious problem. Showing your child that you enjoy seeing him learn is one of your major obligations as a parent.

Mr. London decided to teach his "lazy" fourteen-year-old son carpentry. He gave him some wood and some tools and told him to build a simple bookcase. Periodically he checked on the boy's progress. "Don't hold the hammer there, hold it up there," was his first comment. "Look, you're not thinking," was his second.

Mr. London was neither patient nor warm. He was only critical. He never prepared his son for any step along the way, nor did he explain in advance how to "think" about building a bookcase. He wasn't teaching—he was testing. And since the boy had never built anything before, it was inevitable that he would fail every test. The "lesson" ended quickly with frustration and mutual bad feelings toward each other.

Along with nurturance or warmth, you can bolster your child's confidence in her decision-making ability by giving her direct experience and training in how to make decisions. Children who are brought up to do only what they are told, without questioning and without the freedom to make any decisions on their own, cannot be expected to have much faith in their own ability to make reasonable choices.

There are two types of decisions that we all have to make: those that primarily affect ourselves (personal decisions), and those that have important consequences for others (moral decisions). With regard to personal decisions, most adults would never let anyone tell them what to eat or what to wear or when to go to bed. Yet many children have to fight for the right to make any of these kinds of decisions for themselves. In some families, the first time they get the chance to do so is when they go off to college or move out on their own.

Parents do need to teach their children about healthful eating, and may want to encourage them to taste a variety of foods for the children's own ultimate pleasure. They may want to make their child aware of conventions and fashions in clothing, and of the effect that one's clothing has on others. They will usually also want to help their child set up productive cycles of waking and sleeping so that he or she has sufficient energy for work and play. But too many parents fail to think through the goals behind their rules, or pay enough attention to the unique personality and temperament of each individual child. They simply issue orders. If a child doesn't like an order, but is not permitted any say in the matter, then his or her only options are either to defy it or blindly obey it.

When should a child be given the right to make these kinds of personal decisions on her own? As soon as you feel she can evaluate the important factors that go into making a choice so that she doesn't jeopardize her health or future. At that point the choice should be hers. It is true that children often opt for immediate satisfaction without thinking about the long-term consequences. They may want to eat only pizza and ice cream, or to pursue some interest at the expense of their school work. Parents obviously have to keep their children in touch with the long-term consequences of their actions; and since children can be very impulsive, parents will at times have to make firm demands ("You may not leave until all your homework is finished") or impose restrictions ("No, you may not go downtown alone").

If parents make very clear to both themselves and their child the real purposes behind their rules and restrictions, they will usually find that some rules are unnecessary and that their child will be far more willing to accept restrictions than they would have sus-pected.[30] Also, when you state the purposes behind your restric-tions, it becomes apparent what skills your child needs to master before he can have the freedom he wants. For example, before you let your child decide for himself whether he can go shopping down-town on his own, you will want to feel sure he can handle public transportation and bustling crowds, that he knows travel routes and how to read bus or subway maps, that he deals with money well, that he can interact prudently with strangers and that he is aware of potential dangers and can react to them sensibly. When you break the requirements down in this way, you may realize that your child is, in fact, physically and mentally ready to master the necessary skills. At the least, you can give him a reasonable explanation of why you don't feel he is ready for the freedom he desires.

When children are treated as if you really believe that they are intelligent beings, they will often show surprisingly good sense. It's easy to behave irresponsibly when someone else makes all the deci-sions for you.

Keep in mind that our ultimate concern is with a child's ability to be guided by personal *moral* standards and not with rules about his or her daily habits and tastes. But we feel it is important to discuss decision-making in day-to-day matters because a child's trust in her moral judgment does not spring up from nowhere. The more competent a child feels about her ability to make sensible judgments in any area of her life, the more trust she will have in herself and her personal standards when making moral decisions.

Let's look at a common daily dilemma—bedtime. What time should a child go to sleep? Many families have endless squabbles about this, with endless negotiations for a half-hour more—as if there really were some universally correct sleep time. Obviously there isn't. It depends on the child's sleep needs, and children, as well as adults, have different needs. It also depends on the demands the child must face the next day. If a child who goes to bed late is grouchy and fuzzy the next day, that's a good reason for an earlier bedtime.

But what if he's fine? Why shouldn't he then be given the freedom to decide for himself? If you simply say to him, such and such time is the "proper" bedtime for nine-year-olds, he'll either feel you are being unreasonable because you can't explain to him *why* it's proper or he'll acquiesce and assume that authorities have the right to define arbitrarily what is proper and improper. Neither is what you want your child to believe.

Many parents admit that an important reason for an early and regular bedtime for a child is to give themselves some free time and privacy. When their children are awake, parents are often on constant call: "Mommy, do this"; "Daddy, he hit me"; "How much is six times four?" If you need free time and privacy, tell your children. There's no reason to hide this from them, or give them confusing messages about bedtime because of it. It won't make them feel unloved or resent you. On the contrary, it should make them more understanding and appreciative of the efforts you make to meet their moment-to-moment needs throughout the day.

So many family problems arise because parents have a hidden agenda and try to cover up their real motives with confused messages that must appear arbitrary and unreasonable to their children. Psychologists have found over and over again that children become more responsible, kind, and self-reliant if they are brought up in democratic homes where they are given sensible reasons for clearly defined rules, held accountable for living up to the rules, and encouraged to participate in family discussions and decisions, including discussions of moral issues.[31]

Open discussions about the real reasons behind your decisions make compromise and creative solutions possible so that both of you can get at least some of what you really want. If you want your child to go to bed early because you need free time and privacy, you can work out a compromise with him: He can stay up later if he stays in his room and engages only in quiet activities, and if he scrupulously respects your "alone" time. That way you teach him that with freedom comes responsibility.

With regard to setting a regular bedtime for your child or wake-up time on weekends, remember what while some children seem to need and like regularity, others fight it their entire lives. There's no evidence that living by a schedule makes children more productive or creative or content. Try to recognize and respect the individual needs of your child. Living by the clock is often practical, but don't try to sell it as a moral virtue.

**PRINCIPLE #3.** *Teach your child how to evaluate reasons on his or her own.* A three-year-old girl was riding in a car with her grandfather. It was evening and she could see the full moon through the trees as they drove along the road toward her home. She noticed that the moon appeared to be moving in the same direction as the car. The child had never seen this before, so she asked her grandfather why the moon was moving tonight. Her grandfather, not up on the latest research on motion parallax, said that the moon follows all good little girls to make sure that they get home safely. The child pondered this explanation for a few moments, and then turned to her grandfather and asked, "But what about the good little girls who live in the other direction?"

Clearly the grandfather's explanation wasn't good enough for this bright girl. She thought of an exception that undermined his theory, and then she knew that his reasoning was faulty. When children have confidence in their own ability to reason, they become more questioning and more resistant to passive acceptance of explanations and orders. They also become more tolerant of diverse views.[32]

Without this confidence it's easy to simply go along with the authorities or experts because they *must* know more than you do. As one acquaintance once put it, "I go along with whatever the president says. He has all that information and all those expert advisors. Who am I to contradict him?" This attitude takes for granted that the authorities and their experts always have admirable goals and infallible judgment. Young children tend to assume this.[33] But even a casual reading of history reveals how important it is to teach our children to be less credulous and more probing.

Children need to feel that they know how to evaluate whether an action that someone tries to persuade them to take is or isn't the right thing to do. You can teach your child that a good strategy for evaluating the merits of persuasive arguments involves two steps: First he must define his own goals and then he must evaluate whether the action that someone wants him to take will bring those goals about.

There are no objective criteria for evaluating values. Which ones your child chooses will depend largely on which values you have stressed in his upbringing and the kind of example you set for him. This was confirmed in a study by Martin Hoffman who found that parents who stress such "altruistic" values as "showing consideration of other people's feelings" and "going out of one's way to help other people," were the ones most likely to have children who "care about how other kids feel and try not to hurt their feelings," and who "stick up for some kid that the other kids are making fun of or calling names."[34]

Once your child defines what he values, he is then in a position to decide whether or not a particular action—like shooting the kaiser's enemies when told to, or helping a classmate cheat on an exam, or voting for a particular candidate—will bring about the outcome he desires. In order to decide whether a particular action will lead to a particular outcome, it's important to make sure the outcome is defined very concretely. Everyone wants a more just world, but Hitler's idea of justice may not be the same as your child's. A few years before the Civil War, Senator John C. Calhoun defended slavery with the argument, "There never has yet existed a wealthy and civilized society in which one portion of the community did not, in point of fact, live on the labor of the other."[35]

But when one portion of the society is wealthy while the rest live in abject poverty, is it in fact a "wealthy" society? And can a society with slavery be called "civilized"? Is a society with great buildings, elegant clothes, and lavish balls more civilized than a society that aspires toward universal justice?

A good example of how the word *freedom* can be twisted to mean whatever the speaker wants it to mean comes from the Soviet diplomat Andrei Vishinsky, who said:

Freedom of speech, of the press, of assembly, of meetings, or street parades, and of demonstrations are the property of all the citizens of the USSR, fully guaranteed by the state upon the single condition that they be utilized in accord with the interests of the toilers and to the end of strengthening the socialist social order.[36]

Free speech evolved to mean exactly the opposite of the freedom to say only what someone else decides is in the interest of a "social order." But *freedom* is a word that people like to hear, so politicians use it and hope nobody notices the distortions.

Even if your child is convinced that the goal someone wants her to pursue is a good one, she'll still need to evaluate whether the actions she is asked to take will in fact lead to that goal. Have similar actions been successful in the past? Are there better ways of reaching the goal, ways that are less costly, dangerous, or harmful to people along the way? Research shows that even six-year-olds have the reasoning skills necessary to make these kinds of evaluations.[37]

In practice, it's often difficult to judge the merits of a persuasive argument on our own. For instance, candidates ask us to vote for them on the basis of their economic and military policy—areas most of us are not expert in. Therefore, an especially useful tactic for evaluating persuasive arguments is to seek out counterarguments. These might come from friends, teachers, newspapers, books, etc. In general, if we expose our children to only one side of important issues—for instance, in politics, only the liberal side or only the conservative side—we are not helping them learn how to evaluate issues (and most political issues are moral issues at their core). They will only be able to blindly affirm party doctrine. Recall our acquaintance who argued that the president is the best informed. There may be some truth to that. But there are other people who are also very well informed and we can look to them for counterarguments. It is one of the advantages of living in a system with free speech and more than one political party. Indeed, many governments go to great lengths to keep citizens from forming their own opinions by controlling the information they have access to. Secret operations, censorship, and restrictions on where citizens may travel and which foreigners may enter, are used to make sure that viewpoints contrary to official pronouncements are never heard. Such practices are intrinsic to totalitarianism, but even in democracies, our own included, they are not uncommon.

You can give your child practice in evaluating persuasive arguments by applying the strategy we outlined above (defining values, defining terms, judging the likelihood that the recommended action will work, and seeking counterarguments) to newspaper editorials and any kind of advertisement. Work through the process together. Being able to evaluate arguments is particularly important for children approaching their teen years. From then on, more and more, they will be the target of arguments trying to persuade them to support some policy or buy some product.

# Part Two

# Bad Kids, Good Kids, and Better Kids:

### Overcoming the Forces That Compete with Morality

# 5

# Bringing Up a Loving Child: A Guide to Overcoming Jealousy, Fear, and Hate

One way to bring up a moral child is to bring up a loving child. When we say, "I love," we ordinarily mean two things: One is that we value those we love, in the sense that we get pleasure from being around them, look forward to seeing them, and visualize and think about them when they are not around. We value people for lots of reasons, including how they look, what they say, and what they do.

The second aspect of loving is empathizing with the feelings of those we love. We feel good when they do and bad when they don't, which motivates us to want to be kind to them, help them achieve their goals, and protect them from harm.

Before we say "I love," we usually need to experience both value and empathy. If we only value someone, say, for aspects of his or her looks or personality, but don't find ourselves empathizing with that person's feelings, we use words like *infatuation* and *admiration* rather than *love* to describe our experience. Similarly, we would not say we love someone whom we don't particularly enjoy or want to spend time with, even though we find ourselves empathizing with his or her feelings.

Types of love, of course, differ. The love for a wise old aunt feels different from the love for a brand new bride or groom—because what we value in the two people is different.

As poets and songwriters are always telling us, loving is a glorious experience. It feels wonderful—and this is how it contributes to morality. Doing things for the person we love comes without effort.

When we feel empathy for people, we feel compelled to treat them well, to help and protect them. But empathy in and of itself can sometimes be a burden, compelling us toward actions that we would really prefer not to take. Loving, though, is more than just empathy; it feels good right from the start and doing things for the person we love is a pleasure.

This chapter is devoted to helping your child become a more loving person. It will help you teach him to value people.

## LOVE CAN BE TAUGHT

Donna hated her baby sisters. That's how her mother described it. Donna was an energetic and robust two-and-a-half-year-old. Her sisters were six-week-old twins.[1] Donna attacked them whenever she got the chance. She threw books and ashtrays into their cribs and tried to knock the cribs over; once she was caught just as she was about to stab one of them with a pencil. That's when her mother, Mrs. Linden, decided to seek psychological help.

When Mrs. Linden and Donna arrived at our office, the mother was wearing a wristband. She explained that she had beaten Donna so severely for attacking the twins that she had sprained her own wrist. Donna showed no obvious signs of abuse. She seemed to be cheery and enjoying this outing with her mother. While Mrs. Linden gave background information, Donna alternated between exploring the objects in the office and sitting on her mother's lap, hugging her tightly. Twice she said, "I love you, Mommy." Mrs. Linden reprimanded her for touching things in the office, for singing, and for marching about. She only told her what not to do, not what she could do.

Donna readily went with an assistant to play with some toys in the next room and Mrs. Linden proceeded to describe the situation at home. She had tried to prepare Donna for the birth of the twins, but was unable to give her much time and attention during the last month of pregnancy. She had a difficult time with the births and spent two weeks in the hospital while Donna stayed with her grandmother in another city.

Donna hadn't liked the twins from the moment they arrived home. Mrs. Linden began to sob and explained that caring for the twins took all her energy. She had very little time left over for Donna. Her husband ran a store and was hardly ever home to help her. She said that Donna's usual strategy was to attack one of the twins while the other was being bathed or fed. Mrs. Linden felt that if something wasn't done Donna would kill one of her little sisters.

Obviously Donna was jealous of the two intruders who were monopolizing her mother's time. Attacking the twins might just get rid of them, and if not, at least it was getting her some attention from her mother. It was better to be hit than to be ignored. Clearly we needed an immediate solution in order to protect the twins, but Donna's needs had to be considered as well. She was only two-and-a-half years old and needed to feel secure about her mother's love. This was not just Donna's problem—it was a family problem.

When faced with either an individual or family problem, the two most important questions a psychotherapist must answer are, *What behavior do we want to eliminate?* and *What behavior should replace it?* The first question is usually the easier of the two. In this case there was no doubt that we wanted to end Donna's attacks on the twins. The second question usually takes a bit more thought. We certainly did not believe that hatred between siblings is inevitable or that the best one can do is suppress it or deflect it in some way. Our goal became clear: We wanted to replace aggression with kindness. We decided that the best way to do this was to replace Donna's hatred of her sisters with love for them.

Beating Donna had not stopped her attacks. More severe beatings might (if the mother's wrist would hold out), but only at the cost of turning Donna into a terrified and even more hate-filled child. So we devised a plan to get rid of Donna's aggressive behavior. Mrs. Linden was told to place some masking tape on the floor about four feet from the cribs on all sides. She was to tell Donna not to cross the tape without permission and not to throw anything across it. If she did, she would be put in her room by herself for five minutes.

We told Mrs. Linden it would not take long for Donna to test the new rule and cross the tape, but the four-foot span between tape and cribs should provide enough time to retrieve Donna before she could do harm. She could increase the distance if necessary. Mrs. Linden was skeptical: If beatings didn't work, how would putting Donna in her room work? We explained that beatings gave Donna something she wanted: contact with her mother. Putting her in her room would eliminate this contact. Psychologists call this procedure "time-out from reinforcement," meaning that instead of punishing a child for misbehavior, you set up a defined period of time when the child cannot get something she ordinarily wants and has access to.

We suspected that the time-out would not succeed for long unless it was coupled with a program for getting Donna to love her sisters. So we asked Mrs. Linden to buy a lifelike doll. She replied that Donna had lots of dolls and seemed to take pleasure lately in smashing them apart. We suggested that this was probably a sign of her resentment toward the twins and it was also an indication that no one was teaching Donna to behave kindly and gently. This doll was not to be given to her. It was only to be used for teaching. At this point Mrs. Linden protested that she didn't have the time. We reassured her that she would not have to spend any more time teaching Donna than she was already spending chasing, hitting, and yelling at her. Only now her time would be used more constructively. We also stressed that Donna would never behave differently unless she were treated differently, and that we, the psychologists, could not make her behave. It would have to come from her parents. She agreed to try.

We told Mrs. Linden to tell Donna, in as affectionate a tone of voice as she could muster, that they were going to play a game that would teach her how to be kind and gentle, and that they were going to use the new dolly for this. First, she was to show Donna how to pet the doll gently by stroking it gently herself. If Donna was too rough, she was to guide her arm, handling her tenderly, providing lots of encouragement, and giving praise, hugs, and kisses when Donna's behavior became more gentle. We wanted Mrs. Linden to provide her daughter with a model for gentleness by the way she instructed her. We told her not to scold Donna if she became too rough, but just tell her that they couldn't continue playing if she hurt the dolly and that they would have to try again later. Three ten-minute training sessions per day were scheduled.

As soon as Donna mastered petting the doll gently, they could begin the powdering lesson, followed by the kissing lesson, the cleaning lesson, tucking in, washing hands, turning over, etc.

As Donna mastered each lesson, the next step was to have her engage in her newly learned activity at the same time as her mother was attending to the twins. While Mrs. Linden cleaned and powdered one twin, Donna was to stand right at her side (where she could be watched if any doubt remained about her intentions toward the infants) and clean and powder her doll. The final step was to have Donna demonstrate her new skills on the twins. She was to become her mother's helper. She was ready for this big step four days after the initial meeting and met the challenge with eagerness and ease.

Mrs. Linden also followed through on our instructions to teach Donna to be sensitive to the changing needs of the twins. She did this by saying things like, "This cry means she's hungry, that cry means she's gassy," "We have to hold her head up because she isn't strong enough yet to hold it herself," and "When she's quiet like that it means she's happy."

The direct lesson in all this was to teach Donna how to behave gently toward her new sisters. But of equal importance was to get her to experience the twins as a source of pleasure. Soon they were no longer the nasty creatures that took her mother away from her; they were now links to shared activity with her mother. Donna had to be sent to her room for crossing the tape only twice, and by the second day of training all aggression against the twins had ceased.

After a few weeks Mrs. Linden called to say that she was sure that Donna loved the twins now, and referred to them as "her" twins. She added that she herself was actually enjoying Donna's companionship while tending to the twins and felt much more spontaneous affection for her. We asked her what she meant by the word *love*. She explained that she believed that Donna was not treating the twins gently in a mechanical way or only to gain approval, but that she now got pleasure from being with her baby sisters and cared about their welfare. She became upset when the twins cried, and was concerned about their comfort. Mrs. Linden felt that Donna could now be trusted with the infants because her intentions toward them had changed.

Donna changed to a remarkable degree in a very short time. Our experience has shown that this is not unusual. Small changes on the part of parents in the way they handle discipline and affection can produce great changes in children. This shouldn't be surprising since loving simply feels so much better to a child (and most adults too) than hating. Right now, stop and think of something endearing about someone you love. You probably can feel a smile start to form on your face. Feels good, doesn't it?

Donna's case was originally published under the title "Love Training." We want to underscore the message of that title most emphatically: *You can train a child to love.* You can do it by teaching loving behavior, by reinforcing loving behavior when it occurs, by openly and firmly disapproving of antagonistic behavior, and, most impor-

tant, by setting up situations that stimulate your child's natural inclinations to find pleasure in, and feel compassion for, others.

## HOW PARENTS CAN TEACH LOVING BEHAVIOR

Donna's mother used the doll for this. Many children need to
learn, in a very structured way, how to behave affectionately. (Lots
of adults need to learn this, too.) Even when a child doesn't intend
to do harm he often won't realize how easily people can be hurt,
both physically and emotionally. The first time your child does hurt
someone, it pays to give him the benefit of the doubt. Assume he
didn't know better and take the time to explain to him how to be
nice to someone and how vulnerable we all are.

Children not only need to learn how to express physical affection,
but many need to be taught how to express affection verbally. This is
a particularly important issue in early adolescence. Teenagers often
go through a phase when they are very disrespectful toward their
parents. They will say very little, and what they do say often takes the
form of a grunt, a whine, or an accusation. A typical answer to a
question will be "I dunno" or "Nothin'." Parents can be very hurt
by this unexpected brusqueness. Their once-pleasant child is now
talking to them as if they were his enemies. It is especially painful if
they haven't used a similar tone of voice with him.

Let your child know how you want him to talk to you. Tell him
that he has a right to voice a complaint, but should do so with
affection and respect. Remind him that the way he talks to you
should reflect your whole relationship and not just his momentary
frustration, and that it hurts you when he talks to you as if you were
his enemy. If he does feel you have become his enemy, then both of
you need to talk about it so that you can find ways to communicate
the love you feel for him.

Many children adopt a curt, hostile tone not so much out of any
real hostility toward parents as out of their need to test their adolescent "tough guy" style. This style will usually disappear if it is
nipped in the bud. One set of parents we know were having an awful
time dealing with the way their fourteen-year-old son talked to them.
Almost everything he said had a disdainful tone to it. The boy's
favorite aunt solved the problem by appealing to his vanity and
sense of humor. One evening she told him she was going to mimic
everything he said in order to show him how he looked and
sounded when he put on his tough guy act. It wasn't long before he

was laughing heartily at himself. Then he said, "Do I really sound that dumb?" Everyone nodded in the affirmative and Mr. Tough Guy was heard no more. Appealing to a child's sense of humor is a wonderful device for giving him feedback on his behavior while at the same time defusing a conflict. We will come back to this useful technique later in other contexts.

There are many occasions when you will be able to give your child specific instructions on how to behave affectionately. For example, when she is going to a family party you might remind her, "Your cousin Cynthia is shy. She's not sure that other kids like her. So when you see her, she'll feel good if you find something nice to say to her. If you like her dress or her hair, tell her so. Or find something else you like about her—like how smart she is—and let her know." You might add, "Cynthia usually sits on the side and just watches the other kids play. I think she'll feel really good if you ask her to be your partner in some of the games."

A good teaching technique to use with even a four- or five-year-old child is to set the problem for her and let her come up with her own solutions. You might say, "Your cousin Cynthia is shy and will probably find it hard to join in any games with the other kids. What can you do to make her feel more comfortable and help her have a good time?" Setting the problem for your youngster to solve is particularly useful when you anticipate that she is not going to be comfortable carrying out your suggestions, or when she resents being told what to do. She may come up with something even better.

When you ask your child to figure out how to behave affectionately and thoughtfully toward someone, you will be teaching her more than to simply mimic some words or actions that you've given her. You will be letting her know that when she interacts with others you want her to think about the interactions from their points of view and to consider how she can make them feel valued and cared about.

## Reinforce Loving Behavior

Recall that Mrs. Linden had to learn to praise Donna and give her hugs and kisses when she behaved affectionately. Too often parents ignore children's good behavior and only pay attention to them when they're bad. Most children crave attention and if they only get it when they do something destructive, then you can be sure that they are going to be destructive more often.[2] Your child wants your approval. Give it to him when he expresses affection, and he will express affection more often.

Sometimes parents reinforce the opposite of loving behavior. Sometimes without fully realizing what they are doing they reinforce hostile or disrespectful behavior. This happens mostly with boys since the conventional masculine identity does not include tenderness and vulnerability. Fathers often want their sons to turn into "real" men, which they think means being rough and tough. You may not consciously encourage your son to be a tough guy, but that's what you're doing if he sees that the hockey players you most admire are the ones who start all the fights, or if he picks up that the happiest times in your own youth were when you and your buddies had brawls with other guys.

There's a big difference between teaching your child how to defend or assert himself and instilling in him the need to prove his worth and manliness by beating up someone else. Children who have this need, male or female, go looking for fights. They can only feel good by making someone else feel bad.

If it's important to you that your children be physically tough, consider putting their toughness in the service of a benevolent cause—one that will encourage them to feel and express affection for others. They might, for example, join a community service organization that provides older citizens who live in dangerous neighborhoods with young people to accompany them on walks. Or perhaps there is a community rescue squad or some other local organization working to aid or protect people. In a world in which there is so much real danger and real injustice there are far more productive ways for youngsters to affirm their physical prowess and courage than in senseless combat. Compare the courage and manliness of the toughest hockey player fighting for an evening's entertainment (and an increase in salary) to the courage of Mahatma Gandhi or Martin Luther King, who never raised their fists in violence, but put their lives on the line over and over again in the service of love and justice.

## Disapprove of Antagonistic Behavior

Children need to learn which are the acceptable ways of getting what they want and which ways are unacceptable. When a child tries to get what he wants by hurting or using someone, he is communicating the opposite of love. He is saying to that person, "I don't value or respect you and I don't care about what you want or what you feel. You are simply a means to an end." Make it as clear as you can to your children that hurting and using people are not acceptable ways of interacting with them.

Parents expect a certain amount of fighting between children, but they are often shocked when they learn that their youngster has been manipulating and using another child. Mrs. Burton was pleased, though somewhat surprised, that her fifteen-year-old son, Darryl, had befriended one of the unpopular boys in the neighborhood. But she became suspicious of his motives when she noticed that Darryl always had much more spending money than his allowance and Saturday job added up to. She didn't want to believe that her son was using his new friend for money—that he was, in essence, selling his friendship. To her disappointment, she overheard Darryl in a telephone conversation that confirmed her suspicions. He described the unpopular boy as an easy mark and outlined his strategy for bilking even more money out of him.

In a counseling session, both parents admitted that they had been aware for some time that Darryl was selfish and self-centered, but they felt he didn't do *really* bad things. Darryl was moody but also a real charmer, and it had been easier to ignore his "little misdeeds" than confront him with them. Among the "little misdeeds" they encountered were stealing "just some change" at his job, paying someone to write "just a few" school essays for him, and, as a "practical joke," putting glue in the keyhole of a classmate's locker on the day he was to try out for the school swimming team. They also suspected him of stealing his grandmother's watch.

The Burtons agreed that Darryl needed to learn to be more caring about people's feelings. We worked out a program in which they would finally express disapproval of his misdeeds. First, they sat him down and enumerated the items they knew about. Then they apologized to him for having neglected his moral training and confessed that they had not met their responsibility to him. They stated that they believed he did these things because he didn't really care how other people felt, and that they saw it as a family problem to be solved together. They told him they were resolved to do their best to change his behavior, acknowledged that it would be hard on all of them, and said they hoped he would cooperate.

The Burtons set up a tight program in which Darryl had to account for all his money and all his free time. His homework was checked nightly and assignments were confirmed with his teachers.

The "What did I do today that made someone feel good . . . or bad" charts were given to him daily. At first he was required to fill in at least two items per day on the "feel good" side. Over the course of six weeks the requirement was increased to five per day. They told him they would check on whether he was filling in the form truthfully by contacting some of the people whose names he had filled in each week. They promised to do their best not to embarrass him with friends, but that if he failed to cooperate and meet the requirement, they would feel obliged to let his friends know about the program and why they initiated it. His parents stressed one goal: They were determined to do everything they could to see that Darryl began to be concerned with what he could do for people, rather than how he could use them.

Darryl resisted each step of the way. By the time a youngster is fifteen he has usually learned lots of strategies for getting around his parents. He knows how to make them feel sorry for him, make them feel guilty, frighten them with threats of dropping out of school or of running away, etc. Darryl knew all the tactics and used them.

The only way to succeed in influencing a bright and determined teenager is by communicating clearly and calmly that you will outlast him; that you are not interested in power over him for its own sake and are not out to harm him; that you are, in fact, quite willing to tailor your program to suit his needs so long as he provides clear evidence that he has made progress toward the goals you have set; and that you believe that turning him into a caring person is the most important thing you can do for him and for the society in which you all live. He must see how important this is to you—that you will spend entire nights up with him if necessary, that you will take off from work to meet with teachers, that you will do *whatever* has to be done.

Mr. and Mrs. Burton told their son that they did not want to take away his allowance or job, but that they would do both if he did not provide them with the details of how he spent his money and free time. At first he refused. But he capitulated when they picked up the phone to call his employer. He threatened to run away from home. They said that that would upset them because they loved him, but they would have to meet their responsibility to him anyway. One night Darryl didn't come home. When he returned the next evening, quite exhausted, his parents told him that they were too upset with him to discuss anything about his whereabouts the night before (which seemed to disappoint him), but they did not let him go to sleep until he finished both nights' homework.

The Burtons' persistence paid off. Little by little Darryl got into the habit of thinking about how he could benefit the people he interacted with. He had to think about it to meet the chart requirement. And after four months his parents realized that focusing on other people's needs no longer seemed to rub against Darryl's grain. They gave him days off from keeping his daily record and chart; after six months they phased both out entirely.

We believe that the details of this program—the charts and homework, for example—were important, but we also believe that what made them effective was the Burtons' insistence to Darryl that they were willing to do everything they could to make him a caring person. The emphasis wasn't on discipline. It was on morality. Darryl began to see that his parents were motivated by love for him and concern for the people he dealt with. Ultimately, he changed because of their love and determination, not because he feared the specific consequences set up in the program.

## How to Encourage Loving Feelings in Your Child

What makes us love? We love people and things that give us pleasure. When Mrs. Linden said Donna loved the twins she was, in effect, making a prediction about Donna's future behavior toward the infants. She was saying that Donna's kindness to them no longer depended on outside forces. She could be trusted now because she *enjoyed* taking care of them. Once the twins ceased to be an obstacle between her and her mother—indeed, once they became the key to shared activities with her mother—they became a source of pleasure for her.

We believe that children have a natural inclination to derive pleasure from members of their own species (and from puppies and various other species as well)[3] and to empathize with their feelings —that is, to feel love for them—unless one or another kind of obstacle, such as fear, rivalry, and hatred, gets in the way. Observant parents know that children start out liking people. During the first weeks of life infants begin to smile to the sound of a human voice; and by their fifth week they smile when they see a human face. In fact, the human face is the thing that makes babies smile the most during the first few months of life.[4] Babies just love faces.

Moreover, children commonly display great affection and real concern for others at a very young age. In a study of eighteen-month-olds, child psychologist Harriet Rheingold and her colleagues observed that virtually all the children "on their own initiative—without prompting, directions, or praise . . . share toys with others including mothers, fathers, and unfamiliar adults." It was also common to see these children offering food and other objects to parents, siblings, and other children. We have observed this kind of sharing to be common in eleven- and twelve-month-olds. In a second study, Rheingold found that almost all children between the ages of eighteen and thirty months spontaneously, promptly, and cheerfully offered to help an adult (either parent or stranger) who was engaged in household chores. Other research shows that preschoolers appear happy when engaging in prosocial behavior, such as sharing a toy with a playmate.[5]

Many children begin to express affection by the time they are a year old, and by fifteen months most children clearly show affection for each other. You can see them holding hands, sitting close to one another, hugging, petting, and smiling at each other. Between twelve and twenty-four months children begin to play together and they usually do so very nicely, even with a child they have never met before. Psychologists have also reported that the overwhelming majority of interactions of two- to five-year-olds are affectionate. For example, most exchanges during a free play period in a nursery are friendly and helpful; few are aggressive. The aggressive exchanges may be the ones that get the most notice, but they happen far less often than friendly play.[6]

***Giving love fosters love.*** One of the best ways for parents to reinforce and foster a child's loving inclinations is to make him or her feel loved. Children who feel loved by their parents tend to like other children and be liked by them in return.

The evidence is quite clear on this. Martin Hoffman found that parents who spent time playing, conversing, joking with, and reading to their children had children who were friendly, generous, and affectionate. Other researchers found that children who came from "affectional" families were the ones most likely to be judged by peers, teachers, and youth-group leaders as friendly, honest, responsible, loyal, and morally courageous. Still other studies have confirmed the other side of this same coin: children who feel rejected by their parents are more likely to be aggressive and unaffectionate.[7]

How can you make a child feel loved?

• One way is to show your child that you get pleasure from her presence. If she comes into a room and you smile because when she's there the world seems a better place, she'll know she's loved. If your mood changes for the worse when she is around, or if she can never pull you out of a bad mood, she'll quickly learn that she is unimportant or a burden to you.

• Your child will know he's loved if you are sensitive to his needs when the two of you are together. He will not feel loved if too often you are too busy, too nervous, too depressed, or too tired to give your time and attention to his needs. Sometimes he will want you to help him accomplish something, and sometimes he will simply want to spend time with you, playing or going for a walk or just chatting.

A father once asked us what to do about his ten-year-old son who every weekend kept pestering him to play chess. (The father was divorced and only saw his son on weekends.) The father was a serious chess player and said it wasn't any fun to play with a ten-year-old. He wanted their time together to be entertaining for him, too— which meant that they spent most of their weekends as spectators, sitting side by side at a sports event or a movie. Unfortunately, the father wasn't able to have any fun just seeing his son enjoy himself or helping his son master a new skill.

We suggested that the only way he could gain any pleasure from the time they spent together would be by focusing on what his son needed from him, which included love, companionship, instruction, and encouragement. Since the father was a high achiever, we recommended that he set goals for himself in order to engage his own need for accomplishment. For example, he could plan to teach his son a new chess opening or commit himself to doing something to raise his son's self-esteem. We emphasized that he was to think of these as goals for himself and not as tasks for his child. His son was certainly motivated to learn chess from him, and if the boy was slow in mastering something, the father was to take it as a sign that *he* needed to improve as a teacher. It didn't take long before the weekends were more fun for both of them.

Try to become more aware of what your child needs from you. You might try a variation on one of our empathy charts from Chapter 3 and ask your child to fill in and show you his answers to "What did my parents do today that made *me* feel good . . . or bad?"

• A child will know she is loved if her successes make you feel good and her failures make you feel bad. Then she'll know you care about her goals and are on her side. This doesn't mean you have to approve of and support everything she does. If you give her good reasons why you don't support a goal of hers, she'll know that your disapproval or lack of enthusiasm is not because you don't care. On the contrary, she'll learn that you don't support a particular goal because you *do* care about her—which brings us to our next point.

• Your child will feel you love him if he knows you care about his future and the kind of person he is becoming. Letting a youngster do whatever he wants may seem like an act of love, but it is often simply neglect. At times your child may resist your attempts to make him meet his responsibilities to others (he won't be in the mood for team practice) or to his own future (he won't want to do his homework). But if you explain your reasons and stay pretty consistent, in the long run he will understand that your persistence is a sign of caring. Be careful, though. He'll also recognize if your persistence derives less from caring than from your own insecurities ("What will the neighbors think?"), or from your concerns about status ("I want everyone to see that *my* child is a winner"), or your power needs ("You'll do what *I* say").

Insisting that your child be responsible is important, but don't expect her to behave like a perfectly running machine. For instance, she might feel that she needs a day off from school because she wants a break in routine. If it's not a critical day for exams or special assignments and if her grades are okay, consider her request. Businesses recognize this need and give their employees a certain number of sick leave or personal days. Schools don't, but perhaps they should.

• A child will feel loved if he knows that you need his love. Two brothers, nine and six years old, began to display tantrums and other kinds of misbehavior when their parents separated. Both parents were very concerned about showing their children that they were still loved and that "the family" would continue even though their father would no longer live at home. Because of their concern and guilt and their own problems in adjusting to the separation, both adults became solicitous and permissive with their children, and very unsure of how to handle their misbehavior.

When we asked them what they felt was important to the family, they responded that everyone should feel a sense of mutual caring and responsibility. They had taught their children that in their family everyone cares for everyone else, that it was essential that everyone feel loved and protected, and that each child have as much responsibility as the parents to be sensitive to and care about the needs of the other family members. These parents were forgetting this now. They were so concerned that their children feel loved that they were neglecting to insist that their children *give love* as well. The sense of the family could continue only if the obligations of all family members to each other continued, and if the parents communicated that they needed very much to receive their children's love at this difficult time. By letting their children know how much their love was needed, these parents confirmed to their children how much they *were* loved.

Given the high rate of divorce in our society, it's worth mentioning here that research finds that the impact of divorce on a child's social and emotional well-being depends most heavily on whether or not a loving relationship between the child and his or her parents continues. As one research team expressed it, "The negative effects of divorce were greatly mitigated when positive relationships with both parents were maintained."[8]

• Children feel loved when you share your thoughts and feelings with them. It lets them know you find them worthy to talk to. Let your child know what thrills you, whether it's the smells in the country on a summer morning or a passage from a book you are reading; but don't insist that he have the same reaction. The goal of intimacy is not agreement; it is sharing. Share some of your fears and frustrations also.

• You also let children know you love them by treating their thoughts and feelings with respect. It communicates that you recognize them as people with independent identities and the right to their own opinions and preferences. We recall a mother who belittled her son's taste in music. She liked opera. He liked rock, which she felt was "mindless." Music was important to both of them and it was a sore spot in their relationship. She accused him of listening to rock just to be in with the other kids. In a family-therapy session, it emerged that the son thought all opera singers sounded alike. He couldn't hear the difference between one tenor and another, and he suspected that his mother only liked opera because it was "cultured." He enjoyed all the different "sounds" of rock music. To him it was more innovative. This surprised his mother since to her all rock music sounded alike.

They were given a joint homework assignment: to spend a week educating each other about the music they liked—which they did with some enthusiasm. Their music preferences didn't go through any immediate transformations, but they came away with more respect for each other, and in the future they were less prone to impugn the motives behind each other's preferences.

• It also helps if you tell your child you love her and tell her some of the specific things you love about her. Touches, hugs, and kisses —as long as they aren't forced on a child at times when she doesn't want them—convey your physical pleasure in her.

• Respect your child's temperament. Some children, of course, are easier to love than others. Most parents find that one of their children is just plain nicer than the others—and seems to have been born that way. Researchers have begun to recognize that children have inborn temperaments that make some easier to handle and get along with than others.[9] So it may be that one reason affectionate parents have friendly children is because their children started out with friendly temperaments and their parents found it easy to be affectionate to them. At the same time, our clinical observations have led us to believe that heaping doses of love, wisely dispensed, can turn a difficult child—as in the case of Donna—into a loving child.

When we decide to have children, nature makes us no promises. We don't always get one whose temperament is compatible with ours. Our job is to commit ourselves to doing the very best we can with what we get. We should also remember that from the child's point of view, we may not be a great bargain ourselves. Sometimes we're lucky and come up with a child whose temperament is just what we would have chosen. If not it doesn't mean the child isn't fine. He may be just wrong for us. You may want an outgoing, playful child and have gotten one who is quiet and self-contained— which might be perfect for someone else; or your wild and messy monster may be someone else's idea of what "real boys" are supposed to be like.

As the various procedures in this book show, you can teach a child to care about and respect your needs (for him to be less messy, for example), and you can stimulate and reinforce behavior that makes him more fun for you. But you will both be happier if you recognize and respect his particular and natural tendencies. If yours is an active child, running and jumping and waving his arms about may feel really great to him, but you may not want him to express that need whenever the spirit moves him. If you take the trouble to find a good time and a good place for him to let his exuberance run free, it'll be much easier to teach him where and when to be calm and controlled. And you'll like each other a lot better as well.

***Help your child experience the pleasure of cooperative play with other children.*** Your child will like other children if he finds playing with them fun, and you can help him understand that play is only fun when everybody cooperates—that is, when everyone lives up to the rules of the game and is concerned that each playmate has fun too.

Most youngsters start to play cooperatively during their second year of life. By three, most are ready to observe basic cooperative rules like taking turns. By five they are capable of cooperating in competitive games and can understand and adhere to rules regarding boundaries and scoring. As Jean Piaget noted, competitive games are possible only if all players *agree to cooperate* in obeying the accepted rules of competition.[10]

But sometimes selfish, possessive impulses are stronger than any inclinations to cooperate. That's when parents can help a youngster discover the pleasures of cooperating. For instance, a three- or four-year-old will be less intent on taking and keeping possession of a ball once he discovers how much fun it is to roll or toss it back and forth with another child. On a recent visit to a toddler playcenter we saw a wise caregiver turn the difficult lesson of learning to share into a lesson about the fun of playing together. Her charge had just gotten off a rocking horse but immediately got back on as he saw a little girl approach it. The caregiver said to him, "No. Jenny was about to get on the horse and you had finished with it. So let her have it. You can ride on that horse over there." He whined and pulled at the first horse. The caregiver lifted him onto the second horse, saying, "You have to share. You can ride this one." He did, but with an angry scowl on his face. She saw this and promptly pulled his horse over to Jenny's saying, "Come on, let's see how much fun we can have riding together." She synchronized their rocking, made up a little story about riding through the park together, and quickly had both children playing happily together.

You may have to remind your child of cooperative rules a number of times before they stick. Be patient as well as persistent. She may be struggling with strong impulses that she is not used to controlling. Some children, for example, find waiting their turn particularly frustrating. Sometimes this can be remedied by focusing the child on the alternating aspect of shared activities: "Now it's Tommy's turn to throw and your turn to catch, so stand there and get your hands ready." Sometimes it will help if you focus her on her playmate's goals: "Tommy threw the ball this far before. He's going to try to throw farther this time. Let's see how he does." And sometimes you will simply have to make clear that the other players want to play as much as she does, and that waiting for one's turn is a necessary part of the game that everyone has to endure. (In a later chapter we'll discuss what to do when these methods don't work.)

Virtually any object or activity can form the basis of a cooperative activity. For example, giving a child a piggy bank is a time-honored technique for teaching youngsters about thrift and how to plan for long-term goals, as well as providing them with their first experience of financial independence ("It's your money. You can buy what you want with it."). Children get very excited when they watch their savings grow and anticipate reaching their goal. By establishing a *joint* piggy bank with another child, you can give your youngster the additional experience of setting shared goals. You can establish a joint account for two or more of your children or a child and one or more of his friends (with the permission of each friend's parents, of course). Ask the children to select a goal they all want and can use cooperatively, and give each veto power over the choice so that every child truly wants what has been chosen.

Along with the usual economic lessons that children learn via a piggy bank, a joint piggy bank will give each child practical experience in working out a cooperative enterprise. They will have to define such things as what happens if one child is unable to make payments or decides not to. They will also need to come up with an agreement for how they will share the object once enough money has been saved to buy it. Children usually discuss these issues very seriously, and if you charge them with the requirement to be fair, meaning everyone is treated equally, they will make an effort to see that everyone's opinions and desires are taken into consideration.

This kind of long-term joint project in which children work together and are dependent on each other for something they all desire can establish close bonds between them.

## OVERCOMING A CHILD'S FEAR OF PEOPLE

*Cautious children.* Children differ in their tendency to like and trust people. For reasons that appear to have more to do with each child's inborn temperament than with any pleasant or unpleasant early experiences, some children greet new people with enthusiasm and trust, while others are wary and reserved.[11] Psychologists Alexander Thomas and Stella Chess, who together have done extensive research on children's temperamental differences, refer to the cautious types as "slow to warm up" children. The temperamental differences are nicely illustrated in the lovely movie *Harold and Maude.* Harold, a shy, reclusive adolescent, is taken under the wing of Maude, a warm and high-spirited elderly woman who makes friends with everyone. Upon observing Maude's total ease with a group of strangers, Harold says to her in amazement, "You sure have a way with people." She replies matter-of-factly, "Well, they're my species."

Not all children are equally at home with other members of their species, and parents will have a problem if they try to push their slow-to-warm-up child to be the center of attention and the life of the party. The child will, of course, also have a problem. It's important that you be aware of your own wish for a particular kind of child. Slow-to-warm-up children *will* warm up to people if they are given time and support and some instruction. But if they are only criticized or embarrassed because of their cautious nature, they'll begin to see all social situations as negative events to be avoided.

If your child is wary of social situations, prepare her for them in advance. Let her know what to expect and how to interpret other people's behavior. A child doesn't have to learn to "make friends" when she is at home among family members. Everybody has either always been there or is ordinarily very welcoming to her. But knowing *how to make friends* becomes a real concern when she goes out among strangers in the playground or classroom.

Take the case of Kenneth, a ten-year-old boy who was diagnosed by the school psychologist as a school phobic. Kenneth became frightened in school and did his best to get out of going. The psychologist's report speculated about "separation anxiety"—meaning fear of being away from his parents. But we learned that during the summer months Kenneth happily spent weeks away from his parents when he visited cousins on their farm. His problem was not fear of separation, it was fear of strangers. The family lived in a fairly isolated rural locale and had moved three times in the past five years. The boy had been to three different schools. When he entered a new classroom all alone and saw all the kids chatting and playing together, he felt instantly that no one liked him; then he started to cry and ran out of the room. That immediately got him labeled as a crybaby and an oddball, and made it unlikely that any of his schoolmates would approach him.

What Kenneth needed to learn was *the time it takes to make a friend and what to do to make a friend.* Friendship usually arises from sharing activities with someone, so we suggested that he volunteer for the school movie projection squad. He did, and made his first friend there. He also needed to rehearse simple first-meeting skills, practicing how to introduce himself and ask questions about the other child so that his focus would be on learning more about him or her and not on how he himself was coming across. Being self-conscious means, quite literally, that you are focused on yourself and whether or not people like you. Once our "school phobic" got past agonizing over whether *he* was liked, he could "see" his schoolmates clearly enough to find things he liked in them and he in turn became more likable.

Here are some guidelines to follow if your child is slow to warm up to people or frightened of them:

• Don't simply force him into social situations on the assumption that sooner or later he'll learn how to handle them on his own. He may, but, like Kenneth, he may become terrified and compound his difficulty with peers by appearing to be a misfit.

• On the other hand, don't let him avoid social situations. He does need to enter them, but he also needs to be taught how to cope with them.

• Don't ridicule your child for his fears.

• In the beginning, it may be helpful to accompany him when he enters new situations, letting him know he can come and talk to you if he feels frightened. If he comes to you too often, set up a time requirement: he can come and talk to you only after ten minutes have passed. Lengthen the time period gradually.

We were able to arrange for Kenneth's mother to come to school in the middle of the morning and his father to come in the middle of the afternoon. The guidance counselor arranged a room for them to meet in for a few minutes between periods. This seemed to reassure Kenneth that he wasn't simply being thrown among strangers for the day. After a week-and-a-half he told his parents that they didn't need to come anymore. He said he no longer had time to meet them between periods because he was too busy delivering movie projectors to classrooms.

• Teach your child what to expect in new situations. Teach him that making friends takes time and that other children are often just as shy about starting a conversation as he is. It doesn't mean they don't like him, just as it doesn't mean that he doesn't like them.

• Teach him social skills. These include how to introduce himself to new people; how to ask them about themselves so he can learn about them and show them he is interested in them; how and when to compliment someone; how to invite someone to do something with him; how to join in on games and activities. It's of great benefit to socially withdrawn children to have social skills broken down this way. A good teaching technique is to play-act social situations together, switching roles periodically, so you can model each skill for him (such as, what to say when introduced to a new person), and he can then rehearse it.[12]

Two other techniques that have been effective in helping children overcome "extreme social withdrawal" are (a) modeling the child's fear and (b) using "specific reassurances." When a child is afraid of people (or anything else), simply telling her "There is nothing to be afraid of" rarely calms her. Obviously, to her, there is something to be afraid of. *Modeling* her fears means putting into words what you think she might be feeling, as if you were feeling the same thing. For instance, a mother might say to her socially fearful five-year-old, "Come, let's go join the circle game with those children." If she hesitates, the mother can quickly voice the child's fear: "Wait a second . . . what if they won't want us to join in and tell us to go away?" This is where *specific reassurances* come in. The mother might then say, "They all look so friendly and are nice to everyone who joins in. I'll bet if we join the circle and clap our hands like everyone else, they'll be glad to have us playing with them."

• Explain to your child that not everyone is nice, and not everyone will like him; but that if he is friendly and helpful most children will want to be his friend.[13] Also explain that people seek out others for friendship because they value things about them—because they are smart or funny or attractive or helpful or good at doing certain things. Making friends becomes easier if you develop attributes that others value.

• Have her practice "confidence skills" to help her make it through scary times. Two effective procedures we originally developed for actors to use for overcoming stage fright are the *Confidence Stimulus* and *Confident Hero/Heroine* exercises. We have used these same techniques to help both children and adults overcome a variety of everyday dysfunctional fears.

Start the *Confidence Stimulus* procedure by asking your child to think of a person, place, or object that makes him feel confident and good about himself. It might be a parent or grandparent or a pet, or a baseball glove, or a treehouse, or ballet slippers. Then have him practice using this confidence stimulus. First he imagines himself in social situations that make him anxious. Shortly after he starts to feel anxious, tell him to replace that scary image with the image of his confidence stimulus, imagining it with all his senses (sight, smell, etc.).

The goal is for scary situations to become a signal to him to start thinking of his confidence stimulus. You can help this process along if, when you are with him in a situation that makes him anxious, you remind him to think about his confidence stimulus for a few moments. Once he finds that this calms him he'll use it on his own.

In the *Confident Hero/Heroine* procedure, the child first selects someone whom she thinks of as confident (daddy, mommy, Wonder Woman, a sports figure). Then she imagines that she becomes that person—that he or she moves right inside her for a little while to help her overcome her fears, taking over her muscles, her eyes, her thoughts. Have her practice this by asking her to imagine a scary social situation, and then imagine how she will behave in that situation when her hero or heroine is inside her to help out. The last step is for her to bring her hero or heroine with her right into the troubling situation. Since children generally like to play "pretend" games, you may find them eager to use this technique.

**Wariness of strangers.** Sometimes parents inculcate an excessive fear of strangers by the way they teach their children about the potential dangers of people. Of course, there are dangerous people, and there is every reason to instruct youngsters not to go off with strangers and that some areas of the community may be unsafe to walk in. But remember your goal is to teach him or her to take sensible precautions and to know what to do if dangerous or uncertain situations arise. In a similar vein, crossing the street is dangerous—unless one knows how to read traffic lights and watch out for cars. We assume you want your child to be skilled at crossing streets, not afraid of them. We also assume you want your child to know how to protect himself from dangerous people, but not to be afraid of people in general.

When you inform your child about the dangers that she might encounter, also make clear that she can rely on most people for help if she needs any; that most people will want to be kind to her. If she gets frightened or lost, she can ask a storekeeper to call home or the police station for her. When you tell her where she can and can't go alone or even with friends, and why these restrictions are necessary, also explain that there are really only a few bad people around the community and that they ruin things for everybody. Take your child for a walk around the community. Introduce her to shopkeepers, mailmen, policemen, playground attendants. Point out something interesting and nice about each person she meets—about his or her job or personality or ethnic background, family, or uniform. This will help her feel that she is part of a community: friendly people know her and she knows them.

Children gain confidence in their ability to handle unexpected dangers if you give them well-defined instructions—for instance, if you tell them never to go off with anyone without asking your permission, even if it's with someone they know. Explain that anyone who cares about them would want them to get permission first. You might even make up a code word in case you ever have to send someone for them unexpectedly. Another good safety lesson is to teach a child if anyone tries to force him or her to leave without permission, to say out loud "I don't know you. Leave me alone. I don't know you. Help." That way passersby will be alerted.

Most important, if you focus your child's attention on the many and various likable and interesting qualities of people—from their grand strivings to their funny little habits—and if he sees that you like people, he is bound to become a people-liker too.[14] You needn't hide the flaws of humanity from him, but your stress should be on our merits and our occasional magnificence.

## OVERCOMING RIVALRY AND JEALOUSY

Rivalry is another obstacle to love. A child's first fights arise from rivalry over objects, territory, and parental affection.[15] He may want a toy that someone else is using or want to keep the one he has all to himself. He may want to sit on a particular chair or have exclusive rights to his favorite corner of the sandbox. He might want complete possession of his mother's lap or the sole right to bring his father the mail. All children have at least a touch of the "Me, me" syndrome.

Most young children don't seem to take pleasure in injuring a rival. They just want him or her out of the way so they can get what they are after. Correspondingly, most rivalry conflicts between young children don't carry over into permanent hard feelings. They scream and struggle over a toy one minute and are happily building a sandcastle the next—and this is true of siblings as well as playmates.

Rivalry can, however, produce enduring feelings of dislike and a desire to do harm when the rival seems to always stand in the way of one's goals. Thus, as a child grows older and becomes more aware of her ongoing needs and desires, she will often hold a rival responsible not only for her present frustration, but for the unhappiness she anticipates in the future as well. Thus, an older child might hold a grudge against someone who beat her out for a prize or a position on a team or a boyfriend.

Some amount of rivalry or competition is inevitable. But it is not inevitable to hate or try to harm a rival. There are a number of valuable lessons you can teach your child in order to prevent this.

*Teach your child about fairness.* Fairness means taking turns and sharing limited resources. It means receiving only what you deserve. It is based on everyone being equal and having the same rights to enjoy things, places, and people. At first your child will understand that fairness is good because you say it's good. But it won't take long before he understands that it's good because it's the best way for everyone—including himself, to find pleasure and peace of mind. Fairness can become extremely important to children at a very young age—even by the age of four if you let them know that you expect them to be fair. Moreover, research shows that by age six, youngsters have become quite adultlike in their criteria for judging what is fair and what isn't.[16]

When you see your youngster being unfair after you've taught her what fairness means, hold off on scolding her. First try asking her if she's being fair. This may be sufficient to remind her to apply the rule of fairness to her current activity. It also allows her to feel that *she is making a choice* to be fair. Then you can praise her if she makes the right choice.

***Teach your child to be a good sport.*** Sportsmanship means adhering to the rules of competition and not using illegitimate tactics to gain an advantage. It also means treating your rival with courtesy and respect. Sportsmanship, whether in sports or in other areas of life, puts the focus on *how* a person competes and not whether he or she wins.

Your child will come to care about sportsmanship if you teach him that the real rival in any competition is himself. In reality, all he can do is strive to do his best. Whether or not he beats his rival is merely a by-product of his own striving. Teach him that if he loses to someone else, it makes no sense for him to hate that person for doing his or her best. If winning is important, the only sensible response is to try to do better next time. A rival can set a pace or show what levels of achievement are possible through effort. But parents need to help their child learn to care about self-improvement rather than beating someone else.

"Bad sports" are usually shunned because they try to win through inappropriate means, like cheating, temper tantrums, fighting, and "sour grapes" complaining, what they cannot win through skill. Children are quite capable of understanding that they can feel bad about losing and still like and respect the person who beat them.

***Teach your child to be a good loser.*** This is an important aspect of sportsmanship. It's not only important how you compete, but also how you lose. Being a good loser means you acknowledge the end of the competition, show respect for the winner (a handshake at the end of a match is common), and will do nothing illegitimate to alter the outcome. Explain to your youngster that if she is a bad loser (or an ungracious winner, for that matter) she will lose the respect of her peers (and her parents).

***A reminder for parents: Don't compare your child to other children.*** When you make comparisons, someone gets put down as inferior. Statements like "When he was your age, your brother could swim the entire pool" or "How come Johnny made the team and you didn't?" do not help a child improve his skills. They only make him feel bad about himself and often resentful toward the person to whom you are comparing him.

Parents need to recognize the uniqueness of every child. Not every child will have the same motivation, temperament, strength, coordination, or intelligence. Too often parents try to fit a child into a slot that is absolutely wrong for him. The result is a discouraged and resentful child and disappointed parents.

A friend of ours grew up in an area where hockey was the major sport. But he didn't like the rough physical contact. He resisted his family's attempts to force him to follow in his older brother's footsteps. They threw it up to him that his brother had been the top scorer on the high school team. They also ridiculed him for pursuing "sissy" figure-skating, which he loved. His parents never went to see him skate until he was a college senior and was competing for a national championship. He won the competition and his parents seemed truly proud of him then, but he found it hard to overcome years of feeling resentful that they had never really made an effort to see who *he* was.

When we discourage you from comparing your child to other children, we don't mean that your youngster can't learn from observing others. On the contrary, you want him to observe what people, including his peers, do that makes them succeed, and also what they do that makes them fail or get into trouble. Helping your child recognize that someone has a skill worth analyzing and learning will not make him feel unappreciated, helpless, or resentful as long as a negative comparison isn't implicit in your instruction.

*Another reminder:* The more secure your child feels about your love for her the less threatened she will be by your affection for others—as when a new baby arrives or when you praise her brother or sister.

A difficult time for many youngsters is when a single parent talks fondly of a new mate. If a child feels threatened, she will not be able to empathize with her parent's happiness. To help your child feel secure in such potentially threatening situations, make sure she knows she's appreciated and loved, and that her place in your life is never in jeopardy. Whenever possible, make her feel that she is a participant in any venture that affects the family, including a new mate for you. Remember, whatever affects the family directly affects *her* well-being. Discuss your plans with her so she doesn't feel uncertain and left out, and let her know that you need and want her on your side. By doing so you will be sharing more of yourself with her, communicating what you expect from her, and reaffirming her importance in your life.

*Sibling rivalry.* In the psychology literature, sibling rivalry gets a lot more attention than sibling companionship and love. But sibling love is actually more common. The truth of this was demonstrated recently in a study in which parents left siblings alone in an unfamiliar room with an adult stranger. The average age of the younger child was fourteen months; the average age of the older one was three-and-a-half years. In more than half the pairs, the older children acted "to reassure and comfort their younger siblings in the absence of the mother. . . . Common responses included approaching and hugging the infant, offering verbal reassurance of the mother's eventual return, and carrying the infant back to the center of the room to distract him or her with toys."[17]

Parents unwittingly encourage sibling rivalry when they compare a child to her brothers or sisters. When one child feels that her parents love her less than they do her siblings, everyone in the household suffers. You can avoid this if you make a real effort to see that each of your children feels appreciated for his or her unique qualities. It will help if you spend time with each child alone, the two of you just getting to know each other.

It's also important not to let your own guilt about favoring one child make you overly permissive about the misbehavior or selfishness of another. Neither child will benefit from this. You definitely can and should let each of your children know what you enjoy about him or her and what you don't, so long as you focus on *each one's* actions without comparisons to anyone else. There's nothing wrong with telling one child you will enjoy him more if he makes an effort to be helpful around the house or if he bathes more often. Your children are less likely to start tallying how much you love them if you convey to each that love isn't something you put on a scale and compare. Every love is unique and it's not a limited resource—there's enough to go around for everybody.

Another antidote for sibling rivalry is to stress the specialness of being someone's brother or sister and the responsibility that comes with that special relationship. Many parents would be happy if their children just "got along." You'll do better if you make it a requirement that they not merely get along, but that they actively take care of each other. Make it their responsibility to be on each other's side. When this is the rule, the issue in an argument isn't "Who did what to whom first?" It's "What do each of you have to do to make the other feel loved?"

## PREVENTING PREJUDICE

It is a sad fact of life that children all over the world are taught to hate people who are different from them. Any difference will do. Children are taught to hate people of a different religion, tribe, nationality, skin color, economic class, political system, clan, region —you name it.

Prejudice becomes particularly frightening when it is invested with moral zeal, when we are taught that the people we are supposed to hate deserve to be hated, and indeed that it is righteous to hate them. When we come to believe that hatred is the path to virtue, our moral feelings are recruited in the service of destructive goals. When we are exhorted to fight a "holy war" in the name of our religious or political beliefs, moral action is no longer defined in terms of kindness and fairness. *We* are the true believers and we are moral only if we destroy the "enemy."

This kind of "moral" hatred is commonly fostered by political and religious demagogues who try to maintain their hold on followers and cover up their own ineptitude or greed with horror stories about outside agitators and "evil" aliens who they claim are at the root of all problems. Unfortunately, nationalistic and fundamentalist religious movements in many parts of the globe are again legitimizing hatred of and violence toward outgroups.

Psychologists and sociologists have described various factors behind people's hatred of those who are different from them. One reason is that the hated group serves as a scapegoat: we blame them rather than ourselves when things go wrong. This explanation is supported by studies (and daily news reports) that show that attacks on minority groups increase during hard times. For instance, Carl Hovland and Robert Sears found that the number of lynchings of blacks in the South went up whenever economic conditions declined. For some people, prejudice is the path to self-esteem: no matter how low their personal status or how unsuccessful their lives, they can always feel superior to members of a downtrodden and despised minority. Sexual rivalry has also been a common theme in hate literature: the despised group wants "our women" and they are accused of possessing uncontrollable sexual urges and engaging in all kinds of debauchery.[18]

These various psychological and sociological factors do not in and of themselves produce prejudice in individuals or communities.

They only fan the flames of hatred that have already been ignited through more direct instruction. When parents or peers apply ugly, inflammatory words like "evil," "demonic," and "depraved" to a foreign group, children become conditioned to fear and loathe the individuals belonging to that group.[19] When children hear adults exalt the superiority (and justify the special privileges) of their own group in comparison to the inferiority and ignobility of other groups, a new generation of haters is in the making.

Too often parents communicate to their children that there are three types of people in the world: *us,* whom we treat well; *them,* whom we don't really care about but are willing to coexist and do business with, and the *enemy,* whom we are supposed to shun or destroy. Anything is permissible with the enemy. You can burn them alive, kill their children before their eyes, use them for horrifying medical experiments. Moral rules don't apply to them and, unfortunately, the technology of our "higher" cultures provides us with tools of torture and mass annihilation undreamed of by our hunter-gatherer forebears. As Amnesty International and the U.S. State Department survey on human rights woefully report year after year, torture of "the enemy" is business as usual in most of the world.

When we disagree with people who are part of *our* group, we try to reason with them, or, at worst, we take them to court and, for the most part, abide by the rule of law. When New Jersey and New York argue over taxes or water rights, they don't dispatch armies along the Hudson. They go to arbitration or court. Unfortunately, international laws and courts aren't taken seriously in the same way. When we disagree with people who are *not us,* might makes right.

Sometimes we are shocked by how casually people are willing to inflict pain on those they have defined as the enemy. Some years ago we were with neighbors watching a television news report on border skirmishes between Russian and Chinese troops. One of the group, a bright young chemist, said, "Wouldn't it be great if they knocked each other off with an atomic war?" He was serious. He gave no thought to the hundreds of millions of deaths or the agony of those left alive. They were "the enemy." Their agony was not his concern. Oddly, his friends considered him a "nice guy" and he thought of himself as a good Christian, although he said he thought that Christ's call to love one's enemy wasn't "practical" in our day and age.

One certainly needn't look at anything as dramatic as warfare and international rivalries to find shocking instances of total disregard for the welfare of "foreign" people. At a recent hearing of the Federal Consumer Product Safety Commission on whether U.S. companies should be allowed to sell to other countries products found too hazardous to be sold here, a manufacturer's spokesman pointed out the money that could be made through such sales (he described it as the U.S. placing "a higher priority on competitiveness"). He referred to safety standards as "cultural issues." One commissioner disagreed strongly with this decision, stating that "Things that cause asbestosis here are going to cause it anywhere." He went on to note that among the dangerous products likely to be sold abroad if the agency permitted it are pajamas treated with the fire-retardant Tris, which has been shown to cause cancer, and "probably an awful lot of paint containing lead, spackling compounds with asbestos, [and] a miter saw in which blades went flying off."[20] Presumably the misery of foreign children suffering from cancer or lead poisoning and the agony of their parents is not a concern of certain manufacturers, or at least not as high a priority as "competitiveness."

**Extend the boundaries of who is "us."** When someone is a member of "our" group we are prone to treat him or her well. As a tribal elder in an African village put it, "Even if he is your enemy, as long as he is of your tribe, it is bad to steal from him."[21] Who is *our* tribe? Who is *us*? It's a critical question because the record is consistent from the Old Testament to today's newspapers—as soon as some people are seen as "not us" we feel free to treat them badly. When they are "not us" we can steal from them or make them slaves, and even take their lives without moral compunction. There is probably no more important lesson you can teach your child than that "us" is all of mankind, all races, all religions, all nationalities. Thomas Paine said it well: "My country is the world, and my religion is to do good."

When people are defined as "not us" we tend to interpret their actions in the worst possible light. Sociologist Robert Merton described this inclination to judge an action as good if it is committed by an admired member of our group, and bad if done by someone from a group we dislike:

> The very same behavior undergoes a complete change of evaluation in its transition from the in-group . . . to the out-group. . . . Did [Abe] Lincoln work far into the night? This testifies that he was industrious, resolute, perseverant, and eager to realize his capacities to the full. Do

the out-group Jews or Japanese keep these same hours? This only bears witness to their sweatshop mentality, their ruthless undercutting of American standards, their unfair competitive practices. Is the in-group hero frugal, thrifty, and sparing? Then the out-group victim is stingy, miserly, and penny-pinching.

This kind of irrational thinking obviously has to be overcome if we are ever to live in harmony with others. Research shows that when we recognize a common group identity with others, we are more likely to find cooperative solutions to our conflicts with them.[22]

When we teach our children that their group is mankind it doesn't mean that we want them to like or accept everything that people do. In any group we belong to there are people and policies or practices we may support or oppose. We may still prefer our particular religion or political system. But it does mean that we will teach them never to mistreat people because they are a different color or do not believe in our God. And it means we will not claim superiority to someone because he or she was born across the ocean or on the other side of the tracks. We will still want our children to be able to protect themselves from people who want to harm them, whether they live down the street or across the globe, but hating will never be "holy"; and another's agony will never be a reason to gloat.

***Teach your child about the similarities between different kinds of people in the world.*** Emphasize what she has in common with those who may appear very different from her because they look different or have different habits and lifestyles, or pray to a different God. Psychologists have found that we are inclined to like and help people whom we perceive as similar to us, and we are less likely to harm them.[23]

Social psychologist Milton Rokeach found that a white person's racial prejudice against blacks could be overcome if he believed that the black person's values were similar to his own. This study was done in the early 1960s when racial prejudice was far more socially acceptable than it is today. Still, whether a white person chose to work with or spend free time with blacks or other whites depended more on whom he believed he shared values with than on color. Another more recent study also found that shared values could overcome the color barrier: white college students preferred as roommates blacks who had similar values to theirs over whites who had different values.[24]

Unfortunately, most of the time we don't look at how we are similar to "foreign" people. We focus on our differences. You can change this if you teach your child that while people's customs may be very different, those customs are all expressions of common human needs. All religions, for example, regardless of their particular rites and rituals, try to answer questions about the mystery of existence and they all offer a code for how people should treat each other. We needn't accept a particular religion's answers in order to respect its quest and recognize its similarity to our own. It may not offer a path we would choose for ourselves, but we can certainly share the earth in harmony with those who find sense and comfort in it.

We can look for similarities in any aspect of culture. In his classic book, *The Nature of Prejudice,* Gordon Allport described the "neighborhood festival" technique developed by Rachel Dubois as a successful tool for repairing "the ravages of prejudice in the community":

> It consists of reminiscences on the part of all present concerning experiences in childhood. All who compose the group—Armenians, Mexicans, Jews, Negroes, Yankees—are invited to compare their recollections of autumn days, of fresh bread, of childhood pleasures, hopes, punishments. Almost any topic will bring out the universal (or closely similar) values of all the ethnic groups.[25]

These discussion topics are all about ordinary, everyday experiences that, to some degree, we all have in common, regardless of our background. Your child is likely to have a school or neighborhood acquaintance from a different background. If it is appropriate, have her invite a "foreign" child over for a chat or a meal after school. Stimulate her curiosity about that child's background. He or she might know unusual games or crafts or have interesting stories to tell.

You can help your child develop an understanding of, and an interest in, other peoples by showing him that you, too, are interested in learning more about the different kinds of people in the community. Take him to parts of your neighborhood or to other communities where people come from different backgrounds. Explore their food, their churches, their mannerisms, and their arts and crafts. It will be an enriching project for both of you.

The father of a four-year-old told us that one day his son came home from nursery school and, while recapping the day's events, said, "I don't want to play with Lee." When asked why, he explained that Margaret, a classmate, said, "Lee is Chinese; he's not like us. And his eyes are funny." The parents were flustered, but felt a need to take action. For one thing, they didn't like Margaret and they thought that Lee was the nicest and brightest child in the group.

Their message to their child was very clear. They said, "Lee looks funny to you because there aren't many Chinese people around here, but there are lots of them in other places. In fact, there are more people in the world who have Lee's kind of eyes than people who have our kind, and we would look funny to them if they had never seen us before. Their eyes see as well as ours do, and they are just as nice people as we are. Hasn't Lee been nice to you?" The answer was yes. "That's what's important, not whether people look alike."

That weekend they took a walk through their city's Chinatown. The boy was amazed at "all the Lee's" walking by. He tried on a little Chinese hat in a gift shop and asked if he could wear it to school on Monday to show Lee. The father told us that he and Lee became close friends after that.

When you try to prevent your child from developing prejudice, you will, of course, have to deal with your own prejudice. But that can be accomplished for the sake of your youngster and the world that he and all children will inherit. A man we know is quite open about his hatred of blacks. He grew up in a rough urban area and spent his youth fighting blacks almost daily. His father was shot and killed by two black teenagers while they were robbing his store. But one evening in his home, he stopped a guest from telling an antiblack joke. His children were nearby and he said he didn't want them to grow up hating or making fun of anyone. He knew he had trouble seeing blacks as individuals and he knew why. But he wanted his children to have a different experience.

***Teach your child to appreciate the differences between people.*** People do differ from each other in many respects. We can react to those differences with fear and disdain or with interest and respect. The uniqueness of each culture enriches mankind. Diversity, as any ethologist will tell you, has survival value. The more kinds of abilities and traits that a population can call upon to solve its problems, the more likely it is that a solution will be found.

Expose your child to *human* culture, not just the narrow culture she was born into. In the history of every race, nationality, and religion, there are extraordinary achievements. It will be harder for your child to think of a people as inferior after she has learned some highlights of its history and civilization. Museums, books, and television are all good resources for material on different cultures. It's very important that our children recognize that different groups have different perspectives on the same events. For example, Native Americans do not consider Columbus and other European explorers heroes. Our schools are beginning to incorporate such different cultural perspectives into their curricula. Also, help your child understand and appreciate things that seem strange to her ("They eat seaweed, ugh!"). Many of us have a tendency to dismiss things that are unfamiliar. You might have to do some homework yourself. Remember that when you explore new areas with your child you will also be getting to know more about each other. One of the reasons for the emergence of a "generation gap" between parents and children is that they have nothing to say to each other. They only talk about "business": school grades, chores, bedtime. Exploring the diversity of human creativity together will help bridge that gap.

The goal is not for your child to give up his own cultural identity; nor is it for him to like everything about other cultures. He may not like a culture's music or its political system. The goal is for him to learn that our way is not the only way or necessarily the best way (think of the thousands of American businessmen eagerly reading books on Japanese management practices). He needs to learn that other cultures can be a source of knowledge and pleasure for him and that more often than not, when you make an effort to understand another people, you will find things to like about them.

This was confirmed by research done at New York University in the early 1940s. Students who took a course in racial contributions to American culture, in which they did research on the achievements of different ethnic groups, had less prejudice at the end of the course than at the beginning.

In another study from the same period, white high school students in Illinois were formed into committees and assigned research topics on "Negro life," including access to housing and jobs, treatment by the police, and achievements in art and science. (It's worth remembering that at that time blacks were not recognized for their achievements in athletics since they were not allowed on any professional teams in any sports in America.) The students, many of whom had voiced anti-black feelings before the assignment, became more sympathetic to blacks and their struggles. In fact, they concluded from their investigations that there was an urgent need for better medical care and more adequate housing for blacks in the community.[26]

An eloquent case for extending the boundaries of who is *us*, of which others we are willing to stand up for and protect, was made by Pastor Martin Niemoeller, a German clergyman during the Nazi era:

> In Germany they first came for the Communists, and I didn't speak up because I wasn't a Communist. Then they came for the Jews, and I didn't speak up because I wasn't a Jew. Then they came for the trade unionists, and I didn't speak up because I wasn't a trade unionist. Then they came for the Catholics, and I didn't speak up because I was Protestant. Then they came for me. And by that time no one was left to speak up.[27]

***Foster empathy for people from other backgrounds.*** Help your child understand the lives and struggles of other people from their points of view. Books, films, and television can be of assistance here. More and more the popular media are breaking out of traditional stereotypes and showing minority and foreign peoples as full-fledged human beings engaged in the same struggles as everybody else.

The value of stories for reducing prejudice was confirmed by psychologists who found they were able to reduce anti-black feelings in prejudiced white second- and fifth-graders by reading them stories in which a black child was the hero.[28] From their evidence they concluded that "young children's racial attitudes are fairly malleable."

Seek out materials that will let your child feel the feelings of those who are different from him. The following poem by Countee Cullen is a poignant example:

### INCIDENT

> Once riding in old Baltimore,
>   Heart-filled, head-filled with glee,
> I saw a Baltimorean
>   Keep looking straight at me.
>
> Now I was eight and very small,
>   And he was no whit bigger,
> And so I smiled, but he poked out
>   His tongue, and called me, "Nigger."

> I saw the whole of Baltimore
> From May until December;
> Of all the things that happened there
> That's all that I remember.[29]

**Teach your child that all people are dependent on each other.** Benjamin Franklin's famous warning to the Continental Congress in 1776, "We must, indeed, all hang together, or most assuredly we shall all hang separately," is worth remembering today. Franklin was convinced that the survival of any one of the thirteen colonies depended on all of them putting aside their differences, recognizing their mutual dependency, and working toward common goals.

In more recent times, social psychologists Muzafer and Carolyn Sherif confirmed that when groups appreciate their dependence on each other and strive toward common goals, conflicts between them do indeed tend to dissolve.[30] The Sherifs divided children in a summer camp into two competing groups. As expected, before long a good deal of intergroup hostility emerged in the form of name-calling, fighting, and raids on each other's cabins. Simply bringing the groups together for meals and other social occasions in the hope that increased contact would lead to increased friendliness didn't improve relations. The children now flung flood at each other along with their insults.

What did work was creating a common or "superordinate goal." The Sherifs manufactured some "common predicaments" (a break in the water pipe, a stalled food delivery truck) that affected both groups and could only be remedied if the entire camp pitched in and worked together harmoniously.

By having to work together for common goals the groups gradually began to alter the strictly competitive perspective from which they viewed each other. Friendships emerged between members of the different groups and intergroup cooperation began to replace rivalry and hostility. The boys learned that their own comfort and pleasure depended on the mutual goodwill of both divisions.

Intergroup conflict, according to the Sherif's findings, will be reduced when both sides recognize a "superordinate goal" and their dependency on each other for reaching that goal. Today, more than ever, it's important that we not pass our hatreds on to our children and that we and our "enemies" recognize our superordinate goals and our mutual dependency.

## Racism

What should parents teach their children about race relations in our country? Racial hatred has been the most destructive and immoral force in our society since its inception. It has divided us as a people and separated us from our highest ideals. Our nation's founding premise was that "all men are created equal," yet our Constitution sanctioned slavery. And even when the Constitution was amended to abolish slavery, Jim Crow laws and brutal discriminatory practices kept African-Americans from enjoying full rights as citizens.

Our children must learn this ignoble history, but we must also teach them that it is not the whole story of race in America. Some say we are a fundamentally racist society. This has become the "politically correct" label. But we question whether it is, in fact, an accurate depiction of our society today, and also whether it is a constructive way to describe our society to our children. Will it help them achieve more just and harmonious racial relations?

We believe that any such global label fails to grasp, and indeed dishonors, the tremendous and sometimes risky efforts of people of good will throughout our nation to fulfill the promise of America as an egalitarian and inclusive society. These ideals, whose roots go back to our very beginnings as a nation, are, we believe, basic guiding principles for a significant proportion of our citizens. Though much remains to be accomplished, we, blacks and whites, can take pride that in the past half-century Jim Crow laws have not only been eliminated but have been replaced by *anti*discrimination laws that bar using race as a criterion for employment, housing, education, political participation, and many other fundamental areas of our communal life (except in "affirmative action" programs which *favor* blacks and other minorities).

For over 150 years we were a racist society *by law*. Those laws have now been turned around. That is not a trivial achievement. Our children need to learn about, and feel a part of, the brave struggle that produced those changes. Children look around today and see black mayors and governors and judges and college presidents and lawyers and military leaders and business executives, and they take it for granted. Just thirty years ago this would have seemed impossible. Without question, we must teach our children that the struggle for racial justice is not over—that discrimination still exists and must be opposed. But we must also let them know that it *is* being opposed, and that when discrimination is exposed it is frequently confronted with widespread condemnation and increasingly with indictments and prosecution.

Racist incidents, like the Rodney King beating and the trial that followed, confirm for some our inherent racism. Yet the very same episode, in which the entire nation, whites as well as blacks, reacted to the beating and jury verdicts with outrage, can be viewed as a sign of how far we have come toward our ideals of justice. Not many years ago, large segments of our society would have dismissed Mr. King as a thug who deserved the beating he received (given his criminal record and the accusation that he was driving recklessly while intoxicated).

The media have become our society's watchdogs against discrimination, exposing and railing against it whenever it surfaces. This is beneficial, but lest we and our children become too pessimistic about the state of race relations, we must remember that the media give us primarily the bad news. Blacks and whites getting along, working together, and assisting each other occurs all around us, but to the media it is not news. For example, a recent article in the *New York Times* described an innovative program, held in a prestigious private school, that was designed to help promising African-American and other minority students prepare for graduate schools. Yet the headline of the story and lead paragraphs focused on the accusations by a few students that their teachers back in their home schools had discouraged them from even considering graduate school (because of their race, they felt). It wasn't until much later in the article that we heard from students who had had the opposite experience and who thanked their teachers for helping and encouraging them (which, we believe, is the more common occurrence). The news item could have emphasized either the positive or the negative aspects of the story. Unfortunately, even though the article was ostensibly about an exciting, new undertaking to help blacks, the negative "racist" elements were given prominence. We need to do our best to inoculate our children against the media's negativity.

Our children also need to learn that white prejudice against blacks is not the only form of racial or ethnic animosity we have in our society. In recent years we've seen an increase in acts of discrimination and violence against Asian- and Hispanic-Americans, and Jews. African-Americans, too, have their racist leaders, inciting hatred of whites in general, or Koreans, Jews, or other groups in particular. (Ironically, neither Koreans nor Jews have a history of oppressing blacks, although certain revisionist "historians" proclaim otherwise.)

Despite the gains of African-Americans, many still live in poverty. Various reasons have been offered to explain the failure of large numbers of black citizens to achieve the "American *economic* dream," as many other groups have done. They range from blaming our society's inherent racism, to blaming the welfare system (it gives too much or too little), to blaming blacks themselves for not working hard enough and squandering the opportunities that have opened up for them. One can find support for all these explanations but we must keep in mind that there is a big difference between assigning blame and finding a solution to the problem. The real issue is how best to achieve an educated, productive, and self-sufficient citizenry comprised of all races and ethnic groups living harmoniously. Unless this becomes everyone's superordinate goal, unless the white population which still owns and controls virtually everything in the country, acknowledges that the blacks are *us* and becomes personally concerned about the quality of *their* lives, all our children will grow up in increasingly squalid and violent communities.

Children who come from turbulent or abusive families, regardless of color, are likely to miss out on the moral and intellectual education they will need to succeed in the mainstream culture. One solution is to have our communities set up splendid day centers (all-day centers) where youngsters could find the nurturance and instruction they are not getting at home.

What options are we giving our children, white and black, if we teach them that they are growing up in a society that is fundamentally and unalterably racist—that all whites, regardless of behavior or conscious intention are racist. For some whites the racist label will be a welcome excuse for their anti-black sentiments ("It's in my nature"). Others will feel so guilty that they will acquiese to any black demands or agenda on the assumption that as whites they are too tainted to make fair and reasonable judgments about black issues, even when they affect not just blacks but the society as a whole. Blacks who come to believe that we are a hopelessly racist society will conclude that no white can be trusted and that they must either accept their second-class status or resort to violence to overthrow an impenetrable class structure. They will also be prone to excuse any immorality among African-Americans as simply a natural reaction to white oppression.

None of these alternatives (stemming from the characterization of our society as inherently racist) will help our children improve their lives, and none are defensible, we believe, given the significant improvements in our society during the past four decades. We need to warn our children against those who prejudge all whites, just as we need to warn them against those who prejudge all blacks. We must certainly give our minority children hope (genuine, we believe) that our society is now open enough so that with discipline and perseverance (and despite the persistence of discrimination) they have a good chance of achieving their highest aspirations. We must also make sure our children understand that without personal responsibility there is no morality, that others are not to blame for one's acts. We should not confuse the contemporary street "hood," wreaking havoc on his community, with Jean Valjean of *Les Misérables,* who had to steal to survive.

During the early years of the school desegregation movement, black parents who sent their children to integrated schools were afraid that they would be harmed by white schoolmates. Today, in many parts of the country, white parents and their children have a similar fear of black classmates because of the high violence rates in black schools and communities. This violence, which has been so devastating to the black communities, remains a major obstacle to overcoming racism in our society at both the institutional and the personal level. All across the country, white parents (and many middle-class black parents as well) have become more protective over their communities, having seen other communities overwhelmed with violence after integrating. And parents in many integrated communities have felt compelled to remove their children from public schools because they fear the violent and disorderly atmospheres there. Even parents who have fought for integration and who abhor racism do not want to subject their children to schools where youngsters have to pass through metal detectors to prevent them from entering with guns.

Indeed, because of this violence, prejudice against blacks has taken some new turns among teenagers that both black and white parents need to be ready for. When American society was highly segregated, white prejudice against blacks was not usually based on negative personal experiences. As we've become increasingly integrated, contacts between white and black children have become common. Just a generation ago few white children had black play-mates or friends. This is no longer so. In fact, in many parts of the country, it occurs so often now that it hardly evokes special notice. But at the same time, crime on the streets and in the schools—a sizable proportion of which is committed by black teenagers—has led many white youngsters to fear and hate blacks in general.

A white mother recently spoke with dismay about her teenage daughter's hatred of blacks. During her own youth the mother had been a strong supporter of the civil rights movement, but now her daughter and her daughter's classmates said they hated blacks be-cause blacks stole money from them in school and a number of them had been mugged by blacks while walking in the neighbor-hood. This mother had thought the battle against racism was being won, she said. Yet here it was again, perhaps even stronger than before. She was confused about what to say to her daughter since she had to agree that as the community became more integrated it became less safe. Because of her own uncertainty she had avoided discussing the issue with her daughter at all.

This youngster's resentment of and desire to protect herself from those who threatened her is natural and understandable. The prob-lem arises when she generalizes her resentment to all blacks. In truth, in a school with hundreds of black students, only a few were dangerous—and they were as likely to victimize other black students as white ones. Similarly, most black families in the community were struggling hard to achieve a better life, just as the majority of white families were. Unfortunately, the black student sitting at home do-ing his homework and black parents going off to work in the morn-ing are not as noticeable—neither to people in the neighborhood nor to the news media—as the black school dropout or street mug-ger.

Parents can take steps to see that community crime doesn't spawn a new generation of racists. This mother needed to assert her feel-ings against racism much more forcefully to her daughter. She needed to make sure that her daughter did not generalize her nega-tive encounters with a handful of blacks to an entire race. We rec-ommended that she take steps to make her daughter "see" the other blacks in the community, to make her notice them as individu-als. She said she could remind her daughter of two black teachers she had liked and respected and the black postman who was always efficient and friendly. Also, the best actor in the school drama club was black, as was the second best chess player in the chess club.

Many other black *individuals* worthy of respect came to mind. She said that she would insist that her daughter take a walking tour of the neighborhood with her in order to "see" blacks living and working side-by-side with whites as law-abiding citizens.

Her daughter also needed a lesson in the history of the black struggle for freedom and a reminder that her own people (Italian-Americans) and almost every other ethnic group had at one time or another been similarly stereotyped (all Italians are gangsters; all Jews are stingy; all Irish are drunks). It was very important that this mother let her daughter know how unfair and destructive she thought it was to stereotype and reject people because their skin color (or last name or the birthplace of their ancestors) is similar to a person who once mistreated you. By avoiding the topic the mother had tacitly condoned her child's attitude. As a way to help her daughter understand the destructive effect of stereotyping and to try to stimulate some empathy for blacks, we suggested that she ask her what a black classmate could do in order to be accepted as an individual by her and other white students—whether, in fact, there was anything at all a black youngster could do to break through the barrier of prejudice and rejection.

Whether or not these lessons would affect her daughter would depend to a great degree on just how emphatically this mother communicated her own real sorrow and disappointment over her youngster's prejudice. Black parents need to provide their children with a similar lesson, helping them see that not all whites are out to hurt them or deny them their rights. Both sets of parents need to stress that racism is a self-fulfilling prophecy: when you expect people to behave in undesirable ways, your own actions toward them will provoke exactly the behavior you predicted.[31]

The goal is to see people as individuals. Yet, sometimes our youngsters will find this difficult to do. A black teenager is not likely to adopt an open-minded attitude upon spotting some young men with shaved heads and Skinhead attire heading his way. Nor should we expect him to, given the Skinheads' record of hatred and violence toward blacks. Similarly, white youths are not likely to feel safe when encountering blacks wearing the typical outfits of urban street toughs. We must work hard to get our children to think about the messages their demeanor and dress send out. If they wear the outfits and adopt the expressions of dangerous people, they should expect to be prejudged and categorized negatively. If they are against racism (and most youngsters are), they need to ask themselves what they are doing to make things better: How are they contributing to their race and to racial harmony in their schools and communities? Our youngsters should not be considered innocent bystanders to our society's racial conflicts. From their earliest ages they should be taught that they have an obligation to make things better.

Different racial groups will continue to live together in our society. Unless all groups recognize a common bond (they are "us"), and we all individually do whatever we can to promote racial equality and compassion, our children will be forced to fight the same ugly battles that have plagued our society for so many generations.

## Sexism

Sexism usually refers to men treating women as inferiors—for example, restricting their access to high status, influential or high-paying positions. Women have had to struggle hard in order to gain the same rights as men, from the suffragette marches for the right to vote to the recent legal battles over the right to become police and fire officers.

On the surface sexism appears to be a simple issue—one segment of the population dominating and suppressing another—clearly a morally reprehensible condition. But there are complications. Many men have defended their so-called sexist acts on the grounds that they are really out to protect women, not harm them. Women are different from men, they say, and need to be treated differently. They argue that women are the "weaker" sex or that by nature they are meant to be subordinate to men. Women have rights, they say, but different rights. For instance, women almost always have the right to keep the children after a divorce, even if the man wants them to live with him. From the perspective of a woman fighting for equal treatment, it's not easy doing battle with people who claim to be your protectors and benefactors.

One might think that no one really argues that women are the "weaker sex" these days, at least not publicly. But in fact, people still do in one form or another. For example, it is still a topic of concern in this country whether a woman is capable of handling the job of president (despite the fact that other major countries, like England, Israel, and India, have had highly respected women prime ministers).

Well, aren't women different from men? They certainly are and attempts to deny those differences only serve to pressure women into trying to act like men, which is, in essence, just another form of sexism. The real issue isn't whether women are different from men, but whether whatever differences do exist should be grounds for placing restrictions on what women can do with their lives. Take the controversy over whether women should be allowed to be police officers. Some people argued that women are not as strong or able to fight as well as men. That may be true in the extreme, but that doesn't mean that with proper training women can't handle virtually any physical altercation that a male officer could handle. Moreover, it may be that women, because of their qualities as women, will be more likely than males to defuse potentially violent situations, making the need for superior fighting skills less important.

The way to avoid the sexist trap with your children is to teach them that everyone has the right to strive to become anything he or she wants. And that no one has the right to "protect" anyone in a way that diminishes that person's options in life. You should expose both your male and female children to people of both sexes who have broken traditional sex-role stereotypes. But be careful not to imply that those who lead traditional lives (a woman who is "only" a wife and mother) are in any way inferior or demeaned because of their choice.

## Sexual Harassment and Abuse

During recent years our children have been exposed to graphic TV news accounts of major public figures accused of sexual harassment and rape. The accused have included judges, senators, and star athletes. While polls have found division among our citizens (both male and female) with regard to the merits of some of these accusations, it is clear that our society is finally acknowledging the demeaning and violent way women have too often been treated by men.

Because of the media attention given these accusations, parents are finding that their children, even their five- and six-year-olds, have serious questions about gender and sexual issues. Just as you teach your children about immorality in other kinds of human interactions, it is important to teach them about immorality in male-female relations—about the disrespect, exploitation, and violence that many women have had to endure. Before their own sexual drives kick in, children have trouble understanding the power of sexual motivation, so it's not always easy to know how a child construes discussions of rape and sexual abuse. But disrespectful behavior between boys and girls begins long before adolescence, and parents should certainly address how their own children and their peers are treating members of the opposite sex. The kind of preadolescent sexual taunting that is so common among youngsters should not be accepted as just natural behavior "at their age." Making others feel bad should never be accepted as natural.

Ultimately, discussions of sexual abuse will need to address the relative political and economic power of men and women in our society, and also what rights women must have in order to transcend their traditional dependency on men (such as the right to membership in various "old boy" clubs). On a much more down-to-earth level, your child is likely to ask questions about how one can tell if a man or woman is lying when a sexual abuse charge has been made, and what laws should be passed to deter abuse or to punish it if it occurs. These are not easy issues, but opening a dialogue with youngsters about them and reading "op ed" articles together that deal with them, should help sensitize children to the pain that sexual abuse causes.

## Religious Bigotry

The old religious hatreds are still with us. In Ireland, India, Yugoslavia, and the Middle East, among other places, people are killed for praying the wrong way or to the wrong God.

Religious tolerance depends on the belief that no matter how sure you are about the truth of your own religion's teachings, you have no right to impose them on anyone else, and no right to injure people or deny them any freedoms because they have a different religion or no religion at all. It's not very difficult to instill these beliefs in children. In fact, religious tolerance is pretty common in America. To be sure there have been numerous incidents of religious bigotry in our history, but thanks to our constitutional separation of church and state, the would-be perpetrators of religious oppression haven't been able to support their hatred with the power of the state—at least not for long.

In the interests of religious tolerance, be careful about giving your child confusing messages. It will be hard for him to uphold the rights of other religions if he is also being taught that people who don't believe in his religion are "evil." If he learns that only his coreligionists are worthy people and the rest of mankind is inferior or even depraved, he is bound to mistrust and dislike anyone with different religious beliefs. He will then be an easy conscript for the next holy war against non-believers. You can avoid this by teaching him not to judge people's moral character on the grounds of whether they agree with his religious beliefs. It will also help if he learns that there have been great moral leaders in every religion, and among atheists as well, and that there are common moral principles like the Golden Rule to be found in all the major religious and ethical systems.

## Homosexual Rights

We have become a more tolerant society in recent decades, at least in our rhetoric. Nowadays, if people loathe a minority group, such as African-Americans, Asian-Americans, Jews, or Latinos, they often hide it or express it cautiously, only when they believe they are with those of like mind. This is especially true for mainstream political leaders. In social and political gatherings it is increasingly unusual to hear public condemnations of minorities.

This was not always the case. Just a few decades ago popular political figures ran for high offices on platforms that promised to keep blacks segregated or to wrest power from Jews. These days it is rare to hear such defamatory oratory except from the most marginal candidates. The law, too, has changed. If an individual can't find any tolerance in his heart, the law says he has to act as if it were there. It is now illegal, under a broad range of circumstances, to discriminate against people for reasons of race, creed, gender, national origin, and even age. Discrimination happens, but because of the law and the widespread acceptance that it is wrong, it is generally kept covert.

One group is an exception to this new norm of tolerance—homosexuals. It is *not* unusual these days to hear mainstream political, religious, and community leaders condemn homosexuals and advocate limiting their access to jobs, housing, and military service, and even their participation in public parades. A few municipalities have passed laws protecting homosexuals from discrimination but these are not nearly as common as sodomy laws which make it a crime to engage in homosexual acts, even for consenting adults.

When members of other groups are the victims of "hate crimes" —violence directed against them because of their group identity— the entire community is likely to express outrage. Not so with hate crimes against homosexuals ("gay bashing"). Attacks on them are often construed as their own fault ("Well, they shouldn't have been walking down the street holding hands").

Homosexuals have suffered greatly in Western civilization, despite the fact that their collective contribution to our culture has been extraordinary. In virtually every intellectual and artistic domain—art, music, literature, dance, theater, film, science, mathematics, philosophy—homosexuals have been among the most distinguished contributors, enriching the communities that treat them as pariahs.

Because many children are taught at a young age to fear and despise homosexuals and because of the magnitude of homosexual suffering at the hands of their fellow citizens, parents need to consider very seriously what to teach their children about homosexuals. Do they want to teach their children that homosexuals deserve the kinds of condemnations and mistreatment they receive? We presume that parents who are trying to raise moral children would not want to contribute to the suffering of so many people without strong justification.

Those who condemn homosexuals usually justify their position on "moral" grounds, asserting that homosexuals deserve isolation and disdain because they are immoral, deviant, unnatural, and dangerous, and also offensive to the sensibilities of heterosexuals. Parents need to consider each of these accusations carefully.

***Are homosexuals immoral?*** Not if one thinks of morality as the inclination to treat others kindly and fairly. Ordinarily we let adults be their own judge of whether they are treated kindly and fairly. But those who say homosexuality is immoral insist that it doesn't matter if two adults of the same sex see nothing unkind or unfair in having sex with each other. And it doesn't matter if the homosexuals treat each other lovingly or stand by each other through life's travails. Those who condemn them say that whether they know it or not, they are harming each other—harming each other morally.

But keep in mind that they don't mean harming in the usual sense of some obvious unkindness or unfairness. They mean that the homosexuals are harming each other by breaking God's rule against homosexuality (as they interpret God's rules), and even if the homosexuals lead happy and successful lives on earth, and even if they are good people in all other ways, they will be punished in the hereafter for their homosexuality. They dismiss the homosexuals' own views of whether they are treating each other kindly and fairly because they claim to know what God has in mind for the homosexuals' eternal souls. As the "Declaration on Certain Questions Concerning Sexual Ethics" of the Sacred Congregation for the Doctrine of the Faith of the Catholic Church expressed it, "In Sacred Scripture they [homosexuals] are condemned as a serious depravity and even presented as the sad consequence of rejecting God."

If the past should have taught us anything it is to be wary of those who tell us it is okay, even desirable, to limit the rights of some group of others because God said so. Our religions, which through the ages have inspired us to so much kindness and fairness, have also justified our cruelest impulses as being in accord with divine schemes. Religious leaders have claimed God's backing for slavery, torture, apartheid, the extermination of Native Americans, the Holocaust against Jews, the slaughter of homosexuals by Nazis, and massacres and wars all over the globe. Of course, other religious leaders have risked their lives opposing all these evils.

When our religious leaders tell us that they have it from God that certain people are "depraved," it is difficult to argue back, even when we, ourselves, have not witnessed them doing anyone any harm. We assume the leaders know God's views better than we do. Homosexuals are on a long list of people who have been marked as vile and deserving of restrictions and expulsion, not because they hurt anybody and are immoral in the usual sense, but because they violate religious doctrine, doctrine that is not designed to make the world—*this* world—more kind and fair.

**Are homosexuals deviant and unnatural?** They are certainly deviant in a statistical sense. There are far fewer homosexuals than heterosexuals, but this isn't the kind of deviance that concerns people. There are far fewer left-handers than right-handers but nobody tries to pass laws to limit left-handers' freedoms. The more serious complaint is that homosexuals are not merely different but that they are psychologically or biologically warped and their inclinations "unnatural"—even that their disinterest in heterosexual intercourse could constitute a threat to our species.

It is important to note that homosexuality is not considered a mental illness by most psychologists and psychiatrists. Homosexuals are no more prone to neuroses, psychoses, or other mental disorders than heterosexuals. The development of homosexual inclinations, like the development of heterosexual inclinations, appears to be biologically based, although there is still great uncertainty about the biological mechanisms for either sexual orientation.

No one knows why homosexuality exists in our species. It existed in antiquity and it appears in every culture today. It has been estimated that one in ten males have homosexual inclinations, although the accuracy of this figure has been questioned (there is even great controversy on how to define homosexuality). Even if that estimate is much too high, there are still millions of homosexuals and it may not make sense to refer to them as unnatural, as if we had some insight into nature's plan for our species.

Within any species there is considerable variability (usually the more the better for the long-term survival of the species). It may be that homosexuals have evolved in our species quite naturally as a way to curb population growth (since overpopulation is now more of a threat than underpopulation). Or it may be that one or more genes that are implicated in the development of homosexuality are also involved in the development of creativity, which could account for why homosexuals generate so much creativity in our society.

Nature's will (like God's) is unknowable and there is no reason to conclude that homosexuals, because their sexual inclinations are different from the majority, are diseased. Even if they were, this still wouldn't justify isolating and restricting them—not unless their disease is catching or contaminating in some way. This gets us into the next question.

*Are homosexuals dangerous?* Here the answer is a straightforward No. The news occasionally contains a story of a homosexual abusing someone, adult or child. But there is no evidence that this occurs any more frequently than similar heterosexual crimes. Nor is there any reason to assume that homosexuals have less control over their sexual urges than heterosexuals. Rape by heterosexuals is far more common than by homosexuals.

Many homosexuals have had exemplary careers as teachers and youth leaders without the slightest hint that they made any sexual advances to their charges. But when one homosexual is caught making such advances, the whole group is condemned and frightened parents sometimes demand that all homosexuals be purged from similar positions. When comparable crimes are perpetrated by heterosexuals the focus remains on the individual accused; all heterosexuals are not automatically held suspect. When we read that a physician or a priest has violated his ethical code and engaged in a sexual seduction, we don't condemn all physicians or priests.

Nor is there evidence that homosexuality is "catching" in the sense that people—young or old—can be induced or seduced into changing their sexual orientation. If sexual orientation were so easily shifted it would be easy to "cure" homosexuals. All we'd have to do is find them suitable heterosexual partners. But this doesn't work. Neither homosexuals nor heterosexuals readily shift sexual orientation. It is widely known that heterosexual prisoners frequently engage in homosexual acts during their incarcerations. But when they leave prison most return to their heterosexuality. Here again, our main point is that justifications for denying homosexuals full rights as citizens are not warranted.

Another argument is that homosexuals should be restricted from certain settings (the military, for instance) because heterosexuals find them offensive and don't want contact with them. This is the same argument that was made to restrict the rights of African-Americans in various settings, including the military and professional sports. In sports it was argued that the white players would be offended if they had to play with blacks.

Fortunately, for the most part, we, as citizens in a democracy, are no longer concerned about the sensibilities of those who would deny to others the rights they claim for themselves. In the military and in sports, whites were told that they had to adjust, and they did. We expect that it will not be long before homosexuals too are afforded their full rights as citizens, and as a society we will look back and wonder why it took us so long.

# 6

# How to Handle Aggression, Stealing, and Other Harmful Behavior

Children are not all good or all bad. What we call good or moral behavior can be broken down into a number of different kinds of behavior, including being helpful, trustworthy, honest, and responsible. Similarly, bad or immoral behavior comes in a variety of forms, including being hurtful, dishonest, and irresponsible. Psychologists have confirmed what most of us observe in our daily experience: people are not always consistent across the categories of moral action. A person can be helpful in certain situations and lie and cheat in others, be scrupulously responsible in one area of living while totally irresponsible in another. A person may, for instance, never even consider stealing from his business partner, but may readily cheat on his spouse. These inconsistencies are also found in children.[1]

To bring up a moral child, you will need to pay attention to each of the main areas of moral and immoral behavior. Aggression and cheating, for example, have different goals—one is to inflict pain, the other is to gain something someone else possesses. You will need to understand these different goals in order to formulate effective strategies for preventing or overcoming each.

## IS THERE AN AGGRESSIVE INSTINCT?

The idea of an aggressive instinct—an inborn need to aggress—reappears periodically in psychology. Sigmund Freud and Konrad

Lorenz[2] are its best-known advocates. But, unfortunately, it doesn't help us understand aggression at all. It doesn't tell us the conditions that lead to aggression, why some people are more aggressive than others, what conditions produce different forms of aggression, or how to reduce aggression. Nor does it tell us anything about the physiological or evolutionary roots of aggression.

To say people are aggressive because they have an instinct to be aggressive is as useful as saying people play games because they have an instinct to play games or bathe because they have an instinct to bathe. Playing games and bathing are as common as aggression, but it's obvious that attributing them to an instinct would tell us nothing about their physiological, environmental, or evolutionary causes.

The idea of an aggressive instinct persists largely because it can't possibly be proved wrong. A theorist who *believes* it exists will always find some behavior that is supposedly an expression of it—and it won't matter to him how different that behavior is from what we ordinarily think of as aggression. You're depressed? It's just your aggressive instinct acting up, said Freud, but now it's turned against yourself. It doesn't matter that depression feels totally different from either the impulse to behave aggressively or from self-hatred (which does feel like aggression turned against oneself). The Freudian believer will not be swayed. No matter what you do or feel or say, "Depression is aggression turned against oneself!"

The reason no evidence will convince him otherwise is because his belief did not arise from evidence in the first place. Ordinarily in science we start with some event or class of events that needs explaining—say, that people harm people. In order to explain why this occurs we need to find some prior event or class of events that consistently leads up to it. But instinct is not an event; it is an invisible spiritlike force that cannot be located at any place or at any time. So when a theorist claims that an aggressive action is caused by an instinct, be aware that he is saying that a real event (the aggression) is caused by a nonevent (the instinct).

The appeal of invisible forces is that they *seem* to make a causal connection between the real event we want to explain and a real prior event. For example, if an economist were to announce that the reason the United States had an economic downturn in the 1970s was because of the Watergate scandal, most of us would wonder how he made that connection. If he explained that it was "God's wrath" over the president's betrayal of the public trust, few of us would be persuaded. But, for many centuries, such explanations have managed to convince people all over the world that totally disconnected events were connected. Such explanations appear quite compelling and logical. A real event (Watergate) leads directly to an invisible event (God's wrath), which in turn leads to another real event (economic downturn).

Instincts and all of psychology's invisible forces and entities (egos, schema, mental structures) work the same way and are compelling for the same reasons. Why did the man kill his wife and children (a real event)? Because of some experience at his mother's breast or with toilet training (other real events that Freudians place great stress on). What's the connection between these seemingly disconnected events that happened, say thirty-five years apart? Here's where the invisible instincts and egos come in. The toilet training experience affected the course of the instincts and the development of the ego, and these in turn caused the man to act violently toward his family many years later. It's not that there can't be connections between events thirty-five years apart. But merely sticking in an invisible connecting link doesn't demonstrate in any way that there really is a connection.

Because instincts and egos sound scientific they are more persuasive nowadays as explanations than God's wrath, but they are no more useful for helping us find effective ways to bring up moral children or improve the human condition. Indeed, these kinds of "explanations" generally have a harmful effect: because they mislead us into believing we understand the causes of people's actions (like acts of violence), we stop looking for the real causes and, as a result, find ourselves unable to cope with real-life problems. As a parent, you are not going to be able to do anything about your child's "instincts." But you most certainly can take effective actions to deal with the real reasons why he or she behaves aggressively and wants to harm someone.

## WHAT MAKES A CHILD WANT TO HARM ANOTHER PERSON?

Here are the main reasons:

- Anger—harming someone who has made him angry is satisfying.
- Harming someone can be a means toward an end, like getting a toy or money. We call this *instrumental aggression*.

- He may harm others as a way to defend himself or get back at them if they've harmed him.
- He may try to harm someone whom he feels inferior to in order to bring the person down to his level. We call this *destructive envy*.
- Harming someone may be a way of proving his courage or virility.
- Harming someone whom his community has labeled an enemy can make him feel virtuous.
- He may experience sadistic or sexual pleasure from inflicting or witnessing pain in others.

We'll look at the circumstances behind all but the last two of these reasons and what parents can do to counter each of them. We have already discussed the next to the last reason in the previous chapter. With regard to the last reason, wanting to harm others for sadistic or sexual pleasure, this is a serious form of psychopathology and parents who suspect that their child is doing harm for such a reason, should consult with a professional psychologist or psychiatrist who treats such patients.

Be assured that how you raise your child will have an effect on his or her aggressiveness. To cite just one study, Joan McCord of Drexell University tracked the lives of over two hundred men over a thirty-year period, starting when they were children, to see what factors contributed to criminal behavior. She found that children were far less likely to turn out to be criminals if they had parents who supervised how they spent their time and insisted that they meet their responsibilities in school and in the family, including caring for younger children, helping with meals, and contributing financially. The noncriminals were also likely to have had affectionate parents who were in agreement about basic values and child-rearing practices. Other recent studies have confirmed McCord's finding of the importance of parental supervision, consistency, and affection on how children turn out.[3]

## WHEN YOUR CHILD IS ANGRY

Anger doesn't automatically lead to aggression. But it does make it more likely to occur. Hurting someone we are angry at feels good. It's very much like eating. Hunger doesn't automatically make us eat. But food does become more desirable, and the likelihood of eating increases. Anger can be thought of as a kind of hunger to do harm.

Like hunger, anger consists of bodily sensations and imagery. When we are angry we might envision ourselves striking others, telling them off, or harming them in some other way. Just like a hungry person who can consciously alter his eating habits and give up tempting foods for the sake of his health or looks, the angry person can find more constructive ways of dealing with his anger than giving in to the temptation to hurt another person.

Contrary to some popular misconceptions, your child will not be doing damage to herself if she learns to keep her anger under control. Anger is not a gas that must be vented lest it do bodily or psychological harm. There is no evidence that choosing to deal with anger in a constructive rather than a violent way leads to ulcers or any other ill effects. True, stewing in one's anger may produce psychological distress (such as depression) or physiological damage (such as ulcers); but not because one hasn't cursed, screamed, or smashed someone in the face. It's not bottled up anger that causes problems; it's feeling helpless to change an enraging situation.[4] Ironically, when we can find no remedy for our dilemma, ventilating our anger only confirms to us how helpless we are.

If you look carefully at what situations make your child angry, you will notice that they have two elements in common:

- He *wanted* something he didn't get.
- He believed that he *should* have gotten it.

For instance, a child will get angry over not getting a toy he was promised or a position on the team he thought he deserved.

A child's beliefs about what he *should* get are based on his understanding of what his "inputs" are worth. A teenager works for a week in anticipation of an agreed-upon salary. If he gets less, he gets mad. A young woman goes to the voting booth and expects to be admitted because she is a citizen. If she is turned away because of her creed or color, she will be outraged. As a child gains experience with people—either from his own interactions or from observing or reading about others—he learns the *value* of both what he does (a week's work) and who he is (a citizen), and if he gets less than he's supposed to, he becomes angry.[5]

Psychologists and sociologists have used this same principle to explain why a worker gets angry when he learns that he is receiving less pay than a co-worker for performing a similar job, why a caged pigeon in a typical psychology experiment starts to squawk and bite when its pecks suddenly no longer produce food, and why a populace rises up against a government that violates its rights.[6] Indeed, it accounts for the anger we feel at being treated unfairly or unjustly in any situation.

You'll also see that your child not only gets angry over his own frustration but also over similar misfortunes when they happen to someone he feels empathy for, for instance, when a friend is cheated out of a prize or harassed on the street. *Empathy-aroused anger* is a common and very powerful experience for children. For instance, a twelve-year-old girl we know became furious recently at two of her friends when she saw them make fun of a crippled child; and the seventeen-year-old son of a friend told us of the anger he felt as he watched a television documentary about the slaughter of elephants for their ivory tusks.

### There Are a Number of Effective Ways to Handle Your Child's Anger

*You can reduce your child's anger by treating him fairly.* Treat your child fairly so that you don't provoke him or her into anger unnecessarily. This means apply rules consistently, keep any promises and agreements you've made, and justify any restrictions you impose, especially if they are not also imposed on siblings, friends, or any others to whom your child compares himself.

Consistency is important because one way children learn what they deserve is through *precedent*. They expect to be treated in the future the way they have been treated in the past. If the same behavior that used to get a child something she wanted (say, turning on the television to watch her favorite Sunday morning show) suddenly, and for no apparent reason, gets her yelled at, she'll feel unjustly treated and will become angry.

Being consistent can be difficult at times, especially when you're tired or frustrated or irritated over something. But do your best to be consistent anyway. Be a good model for your child so she can see that people can control themselves at difficult times in order to be fair to others.

Being consistent does not mean you can never change a rule. Circumstances change and so do children. As a child gets older and her capacities develop, more will be required of her in certain areas and various restrictions will no longer be necessary. When you change a rule or introduce a new one, make sure your child understands your reasons for the change—otherwise any new restriction will appear arbitrary and unfair. For instance, you might appear to be inconsistent if on some occasions you give your child and her friends free run of the house to play in, and on other occasions, when you have guests or work to do or simply need some quiet, you ask her to play in her room. In fact, this isn't a case of inconsistency at all.

The purpose of consistency is to teach your child the relationship between a particular situation, the actions she takes in it, and the consequences she can expect to follow from those actions. You want her to understand that if she does a particular thing at a particular time and place, she can count on a particular outcome to follow. Having guests in the house or work to do or a need for quiet changes the situation.

Even a three-year-old can begin to understand such differences between situations *if* you take the time to explain them to her. If you explain *why* you want your child to play in her room, she is far less likely to feel that you are being inconsistent and unfair than if you simply scream out, "You're driving me crazy. Don't you have any respect for me? Go to your room."

A second way children learn what they *should* receive is through promises and agreements, and any child will feel unfairly treated if his or her parents break their promises or fail to live up to the agreements they've made. Take the case of Hector. His parents promised him money so he could go to a football game with his friends. But then they reneged on the grounds that he dawdled while dressing for school and had been late for the bus. Hector became angry because his parents had never informed him that he would only get the money if he was prompt. As far as he was concerned, they simply broke their promise to him.

A third way we evaluate what we deserve is by comparing ourselves to people we believe we are equal to.[7] "All men are created equal" tells us we have a right to be treated as an equal to *everyone* else—that, for example, we should all receive equal treatment before the law. If an adult or child believes he deserves equal treatment and doesn't get it, he gets angry. Unfortunately, if you convince him that he deserves less than equal treatment—because he belongs to an "inferior" race, sex, or class—then he'll accept far less than you would without getting angry.

A common family squabble based on comparisons is when a

younger child wants the same rights as an older brother or sister. Younger children typically complain about having an earlier curfew than a sibling, or a smaller allowance, or restrictions about where they can go and what they can do. But if you give your younger child a sensible reason for why he's treated differently, he will accept it without too much fuss. If you can't give him reasons that make sense ("Because you're younger" is not too convincing), then reevaluate whether he should be treated differently in the first place.

If you do decide to ease a restriction on a younger child, be aware that your older child might experience this as a loss of her special privileges and status, or she might take the attitude "I suffered, so you have to suffer." But brothers and sisters can learn that while some jealous feelings are natural, it is their responsibility to act in ways that encourage and help each other. "I suffered, so I'm going to try to make it easier for you" is the attitude you want to encourage.

A child will, of course, also compare himself to friends and insist on the same rights that they have and get angry if he can't do what they are doing. At some time or other, most parents are faced with the complaint, "But Johnny's parents are letting him go." If you have misgivings about letting your child do something that other parents seem to be less restrictive about, it's a good idea to talk to them. You might find that they share your misgivings but were hesitant to say no because they too were led to believe that all other parents approved. On the other hand, another parent might have information that makes you realize you were being too cautious and restrictive to begin with.

*You can reduce your child's anger by teaching her to be fair.* Sometimes your child will become angry because she hasn't learned that other people have rights too. Therefore, another way to deal with her anger is to help her redefine both her and other people's rights so that frustrating situations that shouldn't make her angry don't. As you can see we are making a distinction between frustrating situations that *should* and *shouldn't* lead to anger.

Frustrating situations that shouldn't lead to anger are those in which the child has no right to expect people to give him what he wants or to behave as he wants them to. For instance, a youngster might get angry because he has to wait his turn for a swing or give back a toy that doesn't belong to him; or because his parents won't allow him to interrupt their conversation whenever he pleases; or they won't let him stop at every toy counter in the shopping center; or perhaps he gets angry at a friend who disagrees with his choice for team captain. It isn't the simple frustration of not getting what he wants that causes his anger in these circumstances.[8] He'll get angry only if, on the basis of precedent (what he's gotten before), promises made to him, or comparisons with other children, he believes he has a right to these things. He will not get angry in these circumstances if he has learned to respect the rights of others. He may feel disappointed when he can't have what he wants, but he won't get angry.

We are not against anger. Anger is a natural and useful response to injustice. It reminds a child to assert her legitimate rights. We are not suggesting that you suppress your child's anger by making her ashamed or afraid to get angry. As we have already said, children and adults are best able to choose constructive actions when they can label their feelings accurately and are not afraid or ashamed of having them. If we deny our anger to ourselves—because we've learned that it's "bad" to be angry—we will not be equipped to control the aggressive inclinations that ordinarily accompany anger.

What we *are* in favor of is teaching your child at a young age certain realities of everyday life. He needs to understand that people, including his parents, do not exist primarily to satisfy his every whim; that if someone harms him it is important to judge whether it was done intentionally or unintentionally; and that sometimes he can't have what he wants because someone else has an equal claim to it, or because it will infringe on other people's rights or well-being.

For instance, we have said, keep your promises to your child. But children also need to learn that there are times when promises and agreements can't and should not be kept, that sometimes other considerations are more important and must take precedence. Here's an example: Mrs. Dawson promised her eleven-year-old daughter, Nellie, that she would drive her upstate to a camp reunion on Saturday afternoon. It was a two-hour trip and Nellie was excited about getting together with all the camp friends she hadn't seen since the summer. But Friday night Mrs. Dawson got a call from her own mother who asked to be driven on Saturday morning to see her ailing brother in the hospital. His condition had become serious and it was uncertain whether he would live. It was a long trip and it would not be possible to make it back in time to drive Nellie to the reunion.

Mrs. Dawson described the situation to her daughter and said that she was sorry but it couldn't be helped. Nellie's face became flushed and she whined, "But it's been planned for months. And you promised. Why can't you take Grandma on Sunday?" The mother explained patiently, "Because Grandma's afraid that Uncle Paul will be too sick to see her if she waits. So that has to come first." At that point Nellie stormed off, shouting, "You don't care at all about me. And I hate you."

Mrs. Dawson was stunned and hurt. How could her daughter have said that to her? She felt her own anger rising and pictured herself smacking Nellie for being so selfish and unreasonable. She was about to scream at Nellie that because she was so self-centered, all plans for camp next summer were off; but she remembered some advice a couple of psychologist friends had given her. Don't just react when your child does something you don't like. Think about what you want her to learn and then take an action to help her learn it.

Mrs. Dawson realized that she didn't want Nellie simply to feel bad. Nor did she just want to assert her power over her child. She wanted her daughter to learn to recognize when there were more important considerations than her own immediate needs. And she wanted her to be able to empathize with another person's suffering even when that person's plight was the cause of her own disappointment. Children and teenagers *can* learn these things. They can understand that it's easy to be a good person when it doesn't cost us anything, but that the real test of a person's character is his or her willingness to do the right thing even when the price is dear.

Mrs. Dawson told her daughter exactly what she was feeling—sad for her, but also furious over her self-centeredness. She wanted Nellie to know the depth of her dismay over her insensitivity. She explained, "I'm truly upset to think that my daughter is so wrapped up in her own disappointment that she isn't able to think about how her own grandmother must be feeling. You heard what I said about Grandma and Uncle Paul, but you didn't translate the words into pictures of what they must be going through right now. I know you would never have done this if you weren't so disappointed, and I have confidence that once you take the time to think about it you'll understand the difference between your disappointment at missing the party and Grandma's feelings about losing her brother. I also want you to remember that Grandma is my mother and she's very sad right now. I want you to think about how I feel knowing she's so sad. You go into your room now for a few minutes and think about these things. Then we'll talk.''

In a short while Nellie came out of her room with tears in her eyes. Her anger was gone. She apologized to her mother and asked if she could go along the next day to be by her grandmother's side. She said, "I want her to know that whatever happens to Uncle Paul, she'll always have a family that loves her."

In the next example we will see that a child's judgment about what his rights are in a particular situation can be changed by getting him to recognize and respect someone else's rights in the same situation.

Fifteen-year-old Stanley walked into his father's hardware store with an angry scowl on his face, and said, "I'm going to fix that coach. I'm going to file a complaint against him with the principal and get him fired." It was Saturday morning and Stanley should have been at the community league baseball game. He was to be the starting pitcher in the opening game of the season. The conversation went like this:

STANLEY: I hate the coach. I'm not playing on the team any more—not if he's the coach. He can get himself another pitcher.

FATHER: What happened? Why are you back so early?

STANLEY: He took me out in the second inning.

FATHER: Why?

STANLEY: 'Cause he doesn't know what he's doing, that's why.

FATHER: I can see you're feeling really bad. Yesterday you liked him a lot and today you don't, so you must think he was unfair to you. Why'd he take you out?

STANLEY: Because he's stupid.

FATHER: Come on.

STANLEY: I walked in two runs. But it was only the second inning. We could have caught up. I was just beginning to warm up. If he wasn't so dumb he would have known it.

FATHER: How would a smart coach have known it?

STANLEY: 'Cause I told him.

FATHER: And what did he say?

STANLEY: I don't know.

FATHER: Yes, you do.

STANLEY: He said I should warm up before the game—which I did, but sometimes it takes a while. I knew I could get the next batter out. I'm good under pressure.

FATHER: You knew it, but how was the coach to know it?

STANLEY: You sound like you're on his side.

FATHER: No. I know you're unhappy and you have good reason to be. I know how you were looking forward to this game. And I feel very bad for you. But I'm not so sure you were treated unfairly, and your anger may wind up just hurting you more. Doesn't the coach have the right to do what he thinks is best for the team?

STANLEY: Sure, but I was ready.

FATHER: He could only go on what he saw. Didn't he pick you to start over Richie? And didn't Richie feel bad? But the coach thought you were the best and didn't his job as coach give him the right to pick you because he thought you were the best during preseason practice?

STANLEY: I guess so.

FATHER: And doesn't he also have the right to change pitchers during a game if he thinks it's best.

STANLEY: He has the right, but I felt terrible. He should have seen that.

FATHER: He probably did. But should that have made him keep you in if he thought the team was going to lose because of you? Then the whole team would have felt terrible.

STANLEY: I know I could have saved it.

FATHER: Put yourself in his place. What would you have done if you were coach? Come on, think about it and be fair. If you were in his place what would you really have done?

STANLEY: (After a moment) I would have probably taken me out after I walked in the first run. I threw eight straight balls. I guess I shouldn't have gotten upset.

FATHER: It's okay to be hurt. And it's okay to be angry if it's called for. But it's also important to be fair. Feeling bad doesn't mean you have to blame someone for it. What do you think you should do now?

STANLEY: Run back to the ballfield and root for the team for the rest of the game.

Stanley's father felt sympathy for his son's unhappiness and let him know it. But it became clear to him that Stanley felt mistreated only because he was asking for something he didn't have a right to ask for and he was infringing on the rights of the coach. When Stanley acknowledged this, his anger disappeared.

Figuring out what we do and do not have a right to expect from people and what they have a right to expect of us is a process that continues throughout all of our lives in every new situation—in school, at work, in a marriage, and in our communities. Should a teacher be allowed to call you stupid or should you file a protest? Is it all right for the senior members of your fraternity to insist that you do their homework for them? Should a policeman be allowed to search your car if he stops you for speeding? Is it fair to insist that your spouse agree to move to a new locale for the benefit of your career even though his or her career will suffer?

A child who doesn't consider the rights of others is often called "spoiled," and the spoiled youngster is one who expects to get what he wants whenever he wants it, regardless of the consequences to anyone else. When he meets with refusal, he makes sure that those who have denied him suffer.

A good way to teach your child about rights is to discuss his and other people's everyday conflicts in terms of who has a right to expect what. For instance, Suzie got angry at her girlfriend, Angie, and called her stupid when Angie said she didn't like a movie that Suzie had recommended highly. Suzie's mother used this as an opportunity to teach her that:

*Everyone has a right to his or her own opinion.*

Marty got mad at his sister, Ellen, for refusing to drive him to a friend's house on her way to her after-school job. Ellen said he hadn't given her enough notice and it would make her late for work. She also told him that her boss was a stickler for punctuality. Marty got angry anyway. He needed to learn that:

*Just because something is important to you it doesn't automatically mean that others must sacrifice what is important to them.*

We need to give people the right to refuse our requests without their having to worry about our wrath.

Children also need to learn that:

*People have a right to be who they are, even if it's not who we want them to be.*

People have a right to pursue their own goals, develop their own style, spend their money as they choose, and even get tired at times that are inconvenient for us. We may decide we don't enjoy them enough to want to be their friend and spend time with them, but we have no right to be offended if they don't live their lives just to please us.

Sixteen-year-old Rita clearly needed to learn this. Her classmate, Lana, refused to chip in for a class boat-ride that Rita had organized. Lana said that she couldn't afford it since she was saving for a new typewriter. Rita, who was worried about raising enough money for the outing, was annoyed by Lana's refusal and called her cheap.

Another important right to teach your child is that:

*People have the right to make mistakes.*

Twelve-year-old Belinda learned this. She got furious at her brother when he unintentionally overfilled the inner tube of her bicycle, bursting it. As many studies have shown, even three-year-olds can understand the difference between intentional and accidental events and are quite ready to offer up the excuse "not on purpose" in their own defense when they have inadvertently broken a rule or unintentionally caused harm. But, as Piaget observed, they are not nearly as willing to grant this defense to those who have harmed them. Fights between children commonly erupt with accusations like, "She knocked my bike over" or "He stepped on my shoe" or "She ripped my Snoopy." If your child is prone to blame others for their unintentional acts, remind her to ask herself whether or not the person meant to harm her. Ask, "How do you know he (or she) did it on purpose?" Research shows that even children who don't ordinarily think about other people's intentions will learn to do so quickly if you remind them to.[9]

Parents can set a good example for their children in this area by not getting angry at them over honest mistakes. Think about your own reactions to your child's accidents or mistakes. Do you find yourself screaming at him whenever he spills or damages something unintentionally? If so, you're definitely not setting a good example.

***The anger diary.*** If your child has a serious problem with anger and needs some very concentrated lessons about people's rights and intentions, have her keep a diary in which she records every instance of anger. She should record what provoked it, how she handled it, and what consequences followed her actions. Discuss each incident with her at the end of the day. Point out any instances where her anger seems inappropriate. Children often want their parents on their side when they are angry, but be careful not to support her anger when you feel it is unfair. You can give your child sympathy for her disappointment, but if you believe that her judgment is off and she's violated someone else's rights, let her know it.

**Teach your child to express his or her legitimate anger constructively and assertively.** What about those times when your child has good reason to be angry? Aggressive thoughts are natural then. What can you do to keep his or her anger from leading to aggressive action?

• *Institute firm, inviolable rules against hurting others.* If your child does behave aggressively against someone, express shock, disbelief, and horror that he would do such a thing. This is very effective with young children. It communicates to them that aggression is totally unacceptable. Children learn very quickly what they can get away with and where you draw the line. If you equivocate, they will pick it up. There's no way around it. You must let your child know that if he hurts people on purpose he is not fit for human company, and that he has disappointed you.

With a young child who can't be expected to know better, you might say something like, "You have no right to hurt someone to get your way. I know you would never have done that if you thought about how much it would hurt him. Put yourself in his place. Think about how he feels now." Each of these three statements employs a technique from each of our three foundation stones of moral development. The first provides a parental standard, the second uses the "good people" incentive, and the third is designed to induce empathy.

In interview after interview we find that parents who have given their children clear, firm, and forceful messages that they absolutely will not tolerate them hurting people intentionally have children who don't hurt others.

• *Use an "instructive" punishment whenever your child harms someone.* With a young child, sending him to his room for a few minutes (a "time-out" period) should be sufficient punishment. Punishment is useful because it communicates that you are taking his aggression very seriously and that a price must be paid for it. It also provides closure for the incident. When the price has been paid, the incident is over. You can reinforce the instructive message implicit in sending a child to his room if you stress that if he hurts people he must be kept away from them.

With an older child who should know better, a longer period of "docking" may be necessary. Additional restrictions may also have to be imposed. But we do not recommend physical punishment since you would then be giving him an example that is exactly the opposite of what you want him to learn. You would be using aggression to get what you want from him while telling him that using aggression to get what *he* wants is wrong. Whatever punishment you use, it will work best if your child knows in advance what will befall him if he intentionally hurts someone. Try to keep the consequences just severe enough to communicate your unshakable commitment to discouraging any future acts of aggression. We'll have a more extended discussion of punishment later in this chapter.

• *Teach your child to take constructive problem-solving actions when angry.* Just "not harming" someone when feeling legitimate anger at him or her is not enough. If your child is angry there is obviously a problem between her and another person that needs to be solved. You want to teach her to use her anger as a signal to get the problem-solving process started.

Some years ago a client came to us because he claimed he could not control his anger toward his wife and children, and he was afraid of hurting them physically. He explained that he had always had a "short fuse." But it soon became clear that the "short fuse" was in the situation and not in the man. He was a policeman working in a tough precinct. On the job he was a cool and respected professional who never lost his temper or got into fights. Did he get angry on the job? "Sure," he said. We asked him how he was able to control his anger under those tense conditions. All he could say was "It's my profession."

There was an important lesson to learn in his answer. As a policeman he had been *trained* in what to do when he got angry. He had learned to tell himself to keep focused on the problem he was trying to solve and not to let people goad him into arguments. If they did, then they'd be controlling him, which is dangerous for a policeman. Also, there was a strict departmental rule requiring the use of minimal force and he said, with obvious pride, "Professionals can solve most problems without resorting to force." In the family, though, and in certain other personal relationships, he had not had any training on how to handle his anger. In fact, he came from a cultural background in which he was taught that a man is supposed to assert his dominance over his wife and children; otherwise "he isn't a man." "Hitting them once in a while lets them know who is boss," he said. He wasn't uncomfortable about hitting them. He just felt he was going too far.

Clearly this policeman did not know what to do to solve his problems at home. They were too complex for a smack to solve, and when a smack didn't work, all he knew how to do was smack harder. He needed to recognize that he could apply the same kind of problem-solving strategies to his family problems that he used so effectively in his police work. He also needed to understand that the wife he had chosen—"an interesting lady with a good mind who keeps me on my toes," as he put it—was not going to let him dominate her or their children in the way his father had done at home when he was a boy. His power tactics could only be destructive to all of them. If his wife became the subservient woman he said he wanted, she was not likely to remain the "interesting lady" he appreciated so much. If he was going to stay in the marriage and find any happiness there, he would have to question and define what his real values were, including what it means to be a "man."

A child can learn to take constructive action when angry through a series of steps. Since the goal is *self*-control, each step is defined by what the child says to herself. These techniques have been used effectively by aggressive youngsters and adults in a variety of settings.[10]

**STEP 1.** *Acknowledge the signal.* When he's angry your child needs to tell himself something like the following: "I'm angry. It's easy for me to do something destructive now. But I'm going to handle this constructively." In order to control his anger he must first acknowledge it to himself and recognize that he'll be tempted to act aggressively. Only then can he affirm his commitment to self-control and constructive problem-solving.

If your child gets angry a lot and tends to lose control, then whenever he is about to enter a situation in which there is a good chance he'll become angry, rehearse the "be constructive" signal with him. Use the role-playing and guided-imagining procedures for this. You can play the role of someone he usually gets angry at, or simply have him imagine himself being provoked. As he feels his anger rise, he needs to demand of himself to stay calm and *be constructive.*

Psychologists Michael Strober and Alan S. Bellack provide us with a detailed description of how a mother learned to teach her child to acknowledge his anger and calm himself. The child, Brian, was a nine-year-old with a long history of tantrums and aggressive out-bursts. The researchers noticed that before any active outbursts or tantrums, Brian would become progressively more agitated. So they instructed his mother to watch him carefully when he played with his brother or sister. If she saw any signs that he was about to explode, she was to intervene immediately, hold him in her arms, and make him aware that he was becoming upset by calling his attention to such specific behaviors as increased heart rate, breathing, and muscle tension. She was to tell him what she had seen that set him off and the bad effects that would follow his aggressive reaction. Lastly, Brian could continue playing only when he had calmed himself.

Another case study demonstrated that "acknowledging the signal" would work even with an extremely aggressive teenager (a sixteen-year-old boy whose father described him as having been a "problem child" since he was three). He learned to use the signs of impending aggression—cursing under his breath, tension in his body, the tightening of his right arm before striking someone—as a cue to walk away from that person and calm down before continuing to talk to him.[11]

**STEP 2.** *Define the problem.* After your child has acknowledged his anger, he needs to ask himself, "What do we both really need in this situation?" Sometimes the problem is obvious; sometimes not. Let's say your daughter gets upset at her older brother for taking her radio to the beach without permission. Sometimes the issue will be about simple property rights and can be solved by an explicit agreement between the children about who can use what when.

But sometimes the younger child's anger will derive from her feeling that her brother never pays attention to her except when he wants something. This kind of conflict will be more difficult to resolve, particularly if the older child sees his sister as a pest and is too preoccupied with his own life to want to give her more time, or if the younger one refuses to acknowledge any feelings of rejection.

In trying to help a youngster recognize that his or her anger really stems from feelings of rejection, keep in mind that it's not always easy for children (or adults) to admit feeling unloved. Don't push your explanation. You're better off trying to help your child discover her real feelings by asking questions such as "Do you think you'd be as angry about Joey taking the radio if you felt that he was really your friend?"

It's also important to remember and remind your child that "defining the problem" means she has to change her focus from what just happened in the past (which one can't do anything about) to what she can do to improve things in the future. To do that she'll have to try to understand the motives of the person who angered her—not for the purpose of excusing whatever he or she did, but in order to figure out what to do to change the person's behavior in the future. There is nothing wrong with your child saying to herself, "How dare he do that!" as long as it is soon followed by the question "Why did he do that?" or "What did he need?"

A variation on role-exchanging is a useful way to help a child get at the heart of her problem with someone. Have her take the part of her adversary and you play her. This will help her get a better idea of how her adversary sees things; and by enacting *her* role, you can provide her with good examples of what she might say to herself and what questions to ask of herself when she is angry. Some good things to say are, "Stay calm. I won't let him make me lose my temper. Why is he acting that way? I'll think of something constructive to do." Research has shown that youngsters who rehearse these kinds of self-statements do learn to respond to a provocation without becoming aggressive.[12]

**STEP 3.** *Plan a constructive action.* The next questions that your child should ask himself in order to plan out a constructive course of action are, "If I do this, what will happen? What else can I do?" Human consciousness, we assume, has evolved like other characteristics of our species because it has survival value. It has survival value because it allows us to think through various behavioral scenarios and imagine the consequences of various actions before we actually commit ourselves to doing any of them. In this way we can benefit from trial-and-error exploration without actually having to put ourselves at risk; any mistakes we make take place within the safety of our imaginations.

Ask your child to think through what will follow from different ways of dealing with a provocation. You want him to learn that if he responds to a provocation with aggression, he will only compound the original difficulty and launch a cycle of escalating hatred and revenge.

If your child is angry at someone for legitimate reasons—because the person has cheated or maligned him, betrayed a trust, purposely destroyed something of his, infringed on his rights, or tried to hurt him or someone he cares about—what kinds of constructive actions can he take? The guiding principle for thinking about constructive action is *defeat the problem, not the person.* Don't allow someone to harm you, but look for a way to solve the problem between you that doesn't involve doing harm.

For example, imagine the following situation. Sixteen-year-old Frank loans his tennis racket to his friend, Herb. Frank tells Herb that he will need his racket by 1:00 P.M. because he has a tennis match at 2:00. Herb promises to have the racket back on time, but doesn't show. Frank finally tracks him down at the soda shop chatting with a group of friends. Herb apologizes profusely. Frank grabs the racket and runs to the court, but is too late for his match. He loses by a forfeit. He is livid and filled with lots of aggressive fantasies about what he will do and say to Herb when he finally catches up with him.

Let's assume that Frank succeeds at Step 1 and signals himself to calm down and handle the situation constructively. Next, in trying to define the problem, he thinks about what he wants from Herb in the future, and realizes that he would like to remain friends with him because he likes his sense of humor and lively spirit. But if he is going to stay in the friendship, Herb will have to show him that he can care about someone besides himself; and one way he will have to do this is by living up to his promises. When Frank thinks about what Herb needs, he realizes that when Herb is with any of his other friends, he is so concerned about whether they like him that he tends to forget his obligations to anyone else.

How should Frank handle this problem? *By using assertion instead of aggression.* That is, the most constructive thing Frank could do is let Herb know exactly what he is thinking and feeling, which should include telling Herb how angry and hurt he is because he was treated so irresponsibly, making clear that he would like to stay friends, and letting Herb know what he needs from him in the way of friendship to make it worthwhile. By letting Herb know that he does like him, enjoys his company, and wants to remain friends, Frank would be doing more than just criticizing and making demands; he would be giving Herb the reassurance he so badly needs that he is truly liked.

There is a growing body of research on *assertiveness* that shows the positive effects of letting people know in a straightforward way how they are affecting you, what you need from them, and what your goals and limits are in the relationship.[13] If you make clear to people that your goal is not to hurt them or ask for anything you yourself aren't willing to give, but rather that you want to strengthen the bond between you, they are likely to try to meet you halfway. If they refuse, you will have learned that they don't really care that much or are too self-absorbed to respond to your needs. Then it's a lot easier to make a decision about whether to end the relationship or continue it in a more limited form ("We can hang out together, but don't ask me to lend you anything").

Assertive communication makes it easier for a child to control his desire to get back at someone who has angered him because it shifts his emphasis away from the accusing, "He did such and such to me," and focuses him on what he himself requires to make the relationship work. In addition, it is an *active* response, so he won't feel helpless and controlled. If it becomes obvious that through ill intention, irresponsibility, or weakness the person will continue to hurt him, then it is his choice whether or not to break off the relationship. If he still feels some residual desire to get back at the person, remind him of the motto, *Living well is the best revenge,* and that trying to harm someone in a direct way to get even will only distract him from the more productive goals in his life. If, instead, he commits his energies to living the best life that he can, he'll have little time to dwell on others' misdeeds—and perhaps ultimately they'll come to recognize their mistakes.

When you teach your child to use assertion instead of aggression, review past situations in which he's gotten aggressive and work out how he might have handled them assertively. Ask your child to think of someone he admires who knows how to handle provocations constructively. Then ask him to imagine himself in a provocative situation and to imagine that the admired person moves right inside him to guide him toward constructive actions. This should help him get a sense of what it feels like to stay in control and still be effective. Also anticipate future situations in which he is likely to become aggressive, and have him rehearse what he can say to himself and to others to prevent a violent outburst. Children often get flustered when they're angry and can't think of constructive things to say— particularly when talking to people in authority. So rehearsals like this are useful.

In order for your child to assert himself successfully, he or she needs to:

1. Describe to the person what he did that was upsetting: "You promised to have the racket back by 1:00 and you didn't, and because of that I was late and forfeited the match."
2. Express his feelings: "I'm angry at you for breaking your promise and I'm hurt that my feelings weren't very important to you. You know I practiced all week for that match."
3. State his goals: "I want to remain friends with you. I like your sense of humor, and you're fun to be with."
4. State what he needs in the future: "But I have to feel I can trust you and that you find our friendship important enough to keep your promises to me."
5. Show some understanding of the other person's position: "I know you got caught up in a conversation at the soda shop and that you didn't mean to be late."
6. Make the consequences clear: "But if I can't trust you, I won't be your friend anymore."

There are times when direct assertion can be dangerous or inappropriate or more trouble than it's worth. An unfair and authoritarian teacher might, for example, not permit any "back-talk" from students, even if it is polite and reasonable—and the consequences of assertion could be severe. What can be done? What kind of constructive action is possible? Obviously, vandalizing the teacher's car is not a very constructive thing to do, although, if your youngster is angry enough, he might find it very satisfying.

Ask your youngster to think of alternatives: Perhaps a student petition to be given to the principal; perhaps an anonymous letter to the teacher trying to reason with him; perhaps joining together with other students and boycotting the teacher's class; perhaps a request for a transfer to another class; perhaps the teacher can be reinforced for being more reasonable. With a little prompting children will usually be able to come up with some nonaggressive strategy that will either change the way they are treated or allow them to escape an unpleasant situation. Sometimes they'll want to take the risk of confronting the unpleasant situation head-on (for instance, by filing a formal complaint against the teacher). At other times they will decide to just endure it because it will be short-lived. Children do have to learn that not everyone is fair; most will eventually conclude on their own that not every injustice is worthy of a full-fledged battle.

Let your child know that aggression is the least creative reaction to injustice. It may be momentarily satisfying, but there is far more enduring satisfaction to be found in using one's creativity to come up with constructive alternatives. This point cannot be stressed too much because the temptation for revenge and quick and simple solutions is great. Recall that not too many years ago a prominent United States senator talked about dropping atomic bombs on China. Whatever our difficulties with China were at that time, to our knowledge the Chinese fleet had not been sighted speeding toward the coast of California and our cities were not under attack. Fortunately, more creative voices prevailed and now in the travel sections of our newspapers, advertisements bid us to stroll the Great Wall and taste Peking duck *in* Peking; and now Chinese ships *can* be sighted along our coast—merchant ships doing business.

## BULLYING, CHEATING, AND STEALING: WHEN YOUR CHILD USES AGGRESSION TO GET HIS OR HER WAY

Another reason why a child will harm someone is because it serves as a means to an end—to force others to do his bidding or give him something they have or to get them out of his way. We call this *instrumental aggression.*

One form of it involves competition over who has legitimate claim to something, which may be an object ("*I* had it first"), territory ("It's *my* seat"), priority ("It's *my* turn"), people ("*I'm* supposed to bring daddy the mail"), and position ("*I* should play second base"). The child's primary objective in these fights is not to harm his competitor, but to get him to give in or withdraw, and children usually recover from such arguments very quickly.[14]

**Teach your child about rights of ownership.** One way to avoid fights over who has the right to do something or use something is to teach children about rights of ownership and use. Here are some commonly accepted examples:

• The person who owns an object has the right to determine who will use it and for how long.

• When you agree to let someone use something of yours, keep your word.

• When an object is public property, such as a playground swing or a school ball, who uses it is usually determined on a first-come, first-served basis.

• Sometimes, if a lot of children want to use the same thing at the same time, time limits are placed on use so that everyone takes turns and gets a chance to enjoy it.

• Sometimes some special skill or personal characteristic earns one special privileges. For instance, in a game, the previous high scorer (or low scorer) might have the right to go first the second time around.

As your child moves into adolescence she'll become increasingly aware that adults, too, disagree and get into conflicts over rights. For example, rent-control laws, concerned with tenants needs for a stable and safe dwelling, give tenants rights that were previously reserved for landlords; affirmative action programs try to make up to minority groups for rights previously denied them; and unions claim that workers, through their investment of labor, deserve rights previously held only by investors of capital and managers. These are important issues that affect most families in one way or another, and the temptation is strong to teach our children only "our side" of the issue. As your youngster enters adulthood she too will become a participant in these types of controversies, so prepare her for them by exposing her to all points of view.

A second way to help your child avoid getting into fights over competing claims is to teach him that there are legitimate ways to resolve such conflicts, such as through compromise, arbitration, and chance (a coin toss).

Back in the 1940s, Gertrude Chittenden demonstrated that even habitually aggressive children could learn the art of compromising.[15] First, Chittenden had preschoolers watch dolls play-acting everyday conflicts over toys. A typical dialogue between the dolls went like this: "It's mine." "No, it's mine." "I'll hit you hard." "Just hit away. I'm not going to let you have it." Then, either the dolls began to fight or one of them suggested a compromise solution like sharing, dividing, or taking turns with the toy. Chittenden made it a point to say that the dolls were "happy" when they resolved their conflicts without fighting, and they were "unhappy" when their disputes erupted into a fight.

After a child saw a few dolls find happy solutions he or she was presented with additional conflicts between the dolls and asked to advise them on how best to end their disputes. The advice most children gave showed that they had indeed learned the techniques of compromising through sharing, dividing, and taking turns, and believed that these were good ways to resolve conflicts. Of greater importance, they soon began to apply these constructive solutions to their own conflicts in the classroom. In one example, Alice (a four-and-a-half-year-old) was fighting with Dean over a bang-a-bell toy:

> Dean shouts for a turn and grabs again. He gets the hammer with which the bell is pounded. They pull and kick at each other. Alice says, "Well, it won't do you any good to have the hammer because I'll never give you the bell." Then, suddenly, she says to Dean, "Well, Dean, when Sandy and Mandy [the dolls] sometimes got into a fight, they found a way to use it. Let's take turns." Dean agrees and they do take turns. Alice bangs the bell, then Dean has a turn. This kind of play continues for the rest of the period.
>
> At the end of the period Alice says to the nursery school cook as she passes through the kitchen on the way back to the preschool group, "Boy, Mrs. Brown, we had a real fight at first. But we found a way to take turns; then we had a good time."

In general, telling your child stories (with or without the use of dolls) is a good way to teach him or her that there are better ways than fighting to resolve competitive disputes. Effective stories—whether from real life or made up—should present a dilemma (such as one puzzle, two children), and then describe what a person needs to do to make the ending a happy one (taking turns, sharing, or dividing). For contrast, other stories should describe how fighting leads to unhappy endings, such as hurting each other or breaking a toy.

Once children understand these techniques of compromising, it's a good idea to send battling children into a "negotiating room" to work out a mutually acceptable compromise on their own, one that professional negotiators call a "win-win" solution, in which both parties feel that they have gained something.

When children's conflicting claims are very strong they may not be able to reach a compromise or be willing to pin their fate on the toss of a coin. Then, as adults often do, they can turn to an arbitrator to decide whose claim is more valid. Anyone can serve as an arbitrator—a parent, a sibling, a friend—so long as he or she is accepted by both disputants as impartial. The arbitrator's job is to hear both parties' claims, ask questions to get as clear a picture of the dispute as possible, and to try to make a fair decision, including suggesting a compromise. Both parties must be willing to live up to the arbitrator's decision.

Even if the arbitrator picks the other party or a child recognizes on his own that someone else's claim to an object or activity is greater than his, it doesn't mean that there are no legitimate ways for him to get what he wants from the other person. He can try simply asking for it in a nice way (this works surprisingly often), or exchanging something for it ("I'll take your turn washing the dishes if you lend me your bike").

A third way to prevent competition over rights from erupting into aggression is to make sure that aggression doesn't pay. If your child gets something through aggression, she must hand it over. Parents can learn a useful lesson from the provocative research on "interspecies coexistence" by Zin-yang Kuo.[16] As astonishing as it sounds, Kuo brought up dogs, cats, and cockatoos together and trained them to wait their turn to eat at a feeding dish that could accommodate only one animal at a time. One of Kuo's main training techniques was to take any animal that pushed past another and put it at the end of the line. This is a good principle to use with children: *Aggression will not only* not *gain them anything, it will be costly.*

An equally important principle (to borrow from the song) is to *accentuate the positive.* Praise your child when he is cooperative. Let him know you are proud of him when he considers other people's rights. As Nathan Azrin and Ogden Lindsley demonstrated in their classic study on cooperation, children who receive positive reinforcement for cooperating cooperate more.[17]

It's always best to explain cooperative rules to a child before she takes part in an activity for the first time. If she's about to try the sliding pond on her own, tell her that everyone must wait on line for his or her turn without pushing. Give her the reasons for the rule: "So that everyone can have fun and no one gets hurt." The first time she tries to push ahead of another child, simply remind her of the rule. If it happens again, tell her she has to go to the back of the line. Also remind her that when she feels like pushing, she should say to herself, "Mustn't push." If a third pushing incident occurs, give her a time-out from the sliding pond and rehearse the "Mustn't push" sequence with her: first, ask her to imagine wanting to climb up and slide down, and then tell her to say to herself, "Mustn't push, isn't fair, mustn't hurt." Also point out how other children wait their turn. Keep in mind that clear and forceful instructions need not be given in a harsh or frightening manner. Patient teaching doesn't mean humiliating or terrifying a child.

If waiting remains a difficult problem for your child you can teach her how to distract herself by singing a song in her head or playing a finger game. Walter Mischel and his colleagues, in a series of studies on children's ability to wait and "delay gratification," discovered that those who were able to wait the longest used these kinds of self-distracting techniques to take their minds off the thing they were waiting for.[18]

*Predatory aggression.* A more serious form of instrumental aggression occurs when a child begins to think of other people as prey, as when a youngster threatens a schoolmate with harm unless he hands over his lunch money. Here aggression, or the threat of it, is not based on competition, but rather on one child victimizing another. Here there is no uncertainty about rights. When competition leads to aggression, pushing and hitting typically begin as spontaneous attempts to jockey for position or hang on to an object, and the battles are usually filled with emotion. In contrast, a shakedown for money, or what we call "predatory aggression," is premeditated and cool.

Chittenden gives us a clear example of predatory aggression on the part of a boy she calls the "Gangster Leader."

> Paul comes into the playground with a rope in his hand. "Who'll be my horse? I need a horse." No one volunteers. "I'll make somebody my horse 'cause I need one bad." He tries to lasso Jean who is tripped by the rope, falls to the ground and cries.[19]

If parents observe that their child has started to treat people as if they were merely a means to help him achieve his own selfish ends, they must take prompt and decisive action. Predatory behavior takes many forms, including bullying people, stealing from them, and cheating them. Slavery is predatory behavior carried to its ultimate depths.

How can parents guard against predatory aggression? In the broadest sense they should use the basic moral training program: Give your child firm rules *against* doing harm and *for* doing good, provide empathy training, and promote the development of personal moral standards. But beyond this general framework, there are a number of specific procedures that parents can use when a child has begun to steal, cheat, or bully others on a regular basis.

*Try to understand your child's goals.* This cannot be emphasized too strongly. Since predatory aggression is a means to an end, you must try to understand what your child was ultimately after. Only then can you help him learn legitimate ways to reach his goal. A teenager might, for example, steal money because he wants to buy equipment for a hobby or more records or a tape recorder—things you don't mind him having. The issue then is, *How can he get more money in legitimate ways?* This is a question that is bound to come up again and again in your youngster's life and he needs to learn early that the only legitimate way to get money is to provide something of value to someone who has the money to exchange for it. This is the *ethic* part of the "work ethic." Youngsters need to realize that unless they are going to be totally self-sufficient—which is not very likely in today's complex world—the only way they can earn their keep is by doing something that contributes to others.

If money is your youngster's goal, help him explore the various options open to him for earning money. Suggest that he try coming up with creative ideas of his own. If he has no salable skills and isn't acquiring any, that's useful information for him to have. Generations of children have earned money by mowing lawns, raking leaves, and shoveling snow for neighbors, by babysitting, delivering newspapers or groceries, by building or sewing things, and by selling lemonade, homemade cookies, and secondhand books. After his options become clear he must then decide whether the things he wants are worth investing his time and effort to earn the amount of money he needs to purchase them.

Whenever your child uses aggression to get what he wants, try to teach him constructive, nonaggressive ways of getting it. A recent highly successful program to eliminate stealing in youngsters used this as a major part of its retraining strategy. If a child stole to impress friends he was taught constructive ways to win friends. If he stole for "kicks" or adventure, he was steered toward nonaggressive risky activities, like motorcycle riding. Providing training in how to pursue goals through constructive means has also been effective in the rehabilitation of adult criminals. According to recent evaluations, the most promising rehabilitation programs were those that focused on job-skill training.[20] Since recidivism is lowest among prisoners who are able to find and keep jobs, newly released "ex-offenders" were taught how to look for a job, how to behave in an interview, how to schedule themselves to arrive to work on time. These may seem like simple skills, but these men had never learned them before.

*Make "doing good" an assignment.* Whatever the reasons are that led your youngster to be aggressive, don't just give him rules on what he should not do; also give him rules that define positive things that he should do. His job is not just to control his bad impulses, but also to accomplish some good. Controlling the bad will then be much easier.[21]

In the chapter on empathy we described a technique that used charts to spell out what your child could do to make others feel good. These are especially helpful here. Children often resort to bullying when they don't know how to influence peers in any other way. When you give your child the responsibility to treat people well and go over the steps with her on just how to accomplish this, she will learn that being considerate has natural rewards: people will be much more inclined to give her what she wants voluntarily because they like her. And once she and another child exchange a kindness, a bond of friendship will form between them that will work against unkindness in the future.

Keep in mind that your child may really not know how to behave in a friendly and helpful manner with certain people in certain situations. He may not know appropriate ways to get people to respond to his needs or he may never have learned to notice and care about their needs. And, to boot, he may have cultivated a tough-guy image that isn't easy for him to give up. First, you will have to work through the steps of kind behavior very carefully with him.

Let's say you get a report from school that your youngster is bullying her classmates and you decide that she needs to learn how to treat people well.

**STEP 1.** *Provide the assignment.* "Your job when you go to school tomorrow is to be as helpful and kind to your classmates as possible."

**STEP 2.** *Work out a plan with your child to carry this out.* One plan should be, "Let's make a list of all your classmates and figure out what you can do to make each of them feel good." Another plan could start with, "During your free play period tomorrow, I want you to notice what each classmate is doing. If there is someone who seems to need help, ask him or her in a nice way if you can assist. If the classmate lets you help, do it as if you care as much about what that child is trying to accomplish as he or she does."

**STEP 3.** *Rehearse Steps 1 and 2 with your child by having her think up situations that she might actually encounter in class, and what she could do to be helpful.* Don't be surprised to find that she doesn't know how to offer help in a "nice" way. Or she may resist out of fear of appearing "nerdy." Remind her of kind people she knows who aren't nerdy at all and be ready to praise any attempts she makes that are in the right direction. Also let her know that you plan to have daily discussions with the teacher to monitor her progress.

There is a great deal of research evidence that confirms how effective it is to give children assignments to do good or be helpful. In a study of six cultures, Beatrice and John Whiting found that children whose mothers assigned them important responsibilities, such as taking care of babies and tending animals, were more helpful and responsible in general than other children. Ervin Staub demonstrated that when first-graders are put "in charge" of a classroom, they are much more likely to help another child in distress. Bathurst, back in the 1930s, reported that preschoolers who had the responsibility of taking care of pets were more sympathetic to others' feelings than were children without pets. Other studies have shown that when children or adults are given the responsibility to reduce someone else's pain, help others succeed on a task, or protect another's property, they try hard to fulfill their assignment.[22]

Being helpful is deemed so important by society that it recently became law in the state of Minnesota. Prompted by reports that passersby failed to come to the aid of a rape victim, the new law, as described by a staff member of the Minnesota Attorney General's Office, "creates a duty to help someone if a person is exposed to grave physical harm." Thus, being a good samaritan is no longer an option, but now a duty, and there is a heavy fine for failing to help. The law, in a sense, puts everyone "in charge" of protecting everyone else from physical harm. Other states have similar laws, and France and Holland have had laws like this for decades.

*Use instructive punishments.* Make your child give back anything he has gained illegitimately—plus a penalty. As we've stated, it's important that children not only not gain from using and misusing people; they should not even come out even. Remember, we are talking about premeditated behavior, such as stealing and cheating—not the innocent taking of objects by a very young child who doesn't yet know rules of possession, nor the competitive squabbling of older children over possession rights.

As much as possible, make the punishment fit the crime. This means use a punishment that teaches your youngster something about the harm he has caused. One way to do this is to insist that the child give up something of his own that is similar to what he has taken so he understands how it feels to lose something of value. For example, if, through theft or deceit, he has expropriated another child's weekly allowance, have him contribute his own weekly allowance to a good cause in addition to making restitution to his victim. Another useful penalty is to restrict freedom through "grounding." If a child hurts people, he has to be kept from them. When he has to be out of the house, require him to give you a detailed account of where he goes, whom he spends time with, and how he spends his money. And spot check to see if he's truthful. If he can't be trusted to behave well on his own, then he has to be monitored.

Then there is physical punishment. Spankings don't necessarily have a bad effect, unless they are so severe that they terrify a child or make him feel unloved. But they don't teach the child anything specific about what he did, except that he'll get hurt if he does it again. Spankings may be a quick way to "teach the child a lesson," but when adults displease us we don't teach them a lesson by hitting them. Your child deserves more respect also. There is nothing that a spanking accomplishes that won't be accomplished better, even if it takes a bit longer, by the other forms of punishment that are more instructive. Furthermore, severe beatings that physically harm a child (child abuse) appear to make children even more aggressive.[23]

The purpose of punishment is to convey to a child the seriousness of his misdeed and your unshakable commitment to seeing that he doesn't repeat his mean behavior. He needs to know that if he makes someone unhappy for selfish reasons, swift and serious consequences will follow for him. Punishments that are swift, strong, reasonable, and not so severe as to be frightening, are the most instructive and work best.

When a punishment fits the crime, children tend to see it as fair. A punishment that seems unfair will not work as well and may even backfire.[24] Try asking a child to set his own punishment. It will force him to think about and evaluate the harmfulness of what he did, and you'll be surprised to see how hard he will be on himself.

Whatever form of punishment you use, you must make very clear to your youngster exactly what demands and restrictions you are imposing and how long the penalty will last. Once a penalty is fulfilled, it is over. A child needs to believe that he can earn back your trust.

*Arouse empathy for those he would harm.* Remember that punishment alone can never induce kindness. It can only discourage the child from being mean. The bulk of your efforts as moral trainer must always be to promote and reinforce caring and concern for others. So don't just punish. Use the empathy-inducing techniques in Chapter 3 to help your child understand how selfish he has been. He needs to understand that cheating or stealing from people takes away more than just their money or possessions. If he puts himself in their shoes he will realize that they probably feel belittled and betrayed, and may even become distrustful of people in general. You might tell him that you didn't bring him into the world to have him inflict pain on others and that you feel it is your responsibility to make sure that he doesn't become a burden to his fellow human beings.

Try to get him to see and feel what it's like to receive the kind of mistreatment he has inflicted. One mother we know was able to convey her commitment to kindness by sharing an unhappy incident from her own childhood with her youngster. Her teenage son and his friends were plotting to send a taunting letter to a schoolmate whom they considered effeminate and thought was homosexual. This mother was extremely distressed that her son could be so cruel and insensitive.

She had spent part of her childhood in India when it was still a British colony. Her family, upper-middle-class Europeans, lived in the European district and joined a club that only other European families could belong to. She explained to her son that the club members, most of whom were British, felt superior to the Indians. Since she was of Greek origin, with olive skin and dark hair, the British children thought she was half-Indian and half-Caucasian, and made fun of her by calling her a "half-breed." They teased her mercilessly and refused to befriend her. She said that it had hurt her terribly and that she could not stand by and let her son mistreat someone just because he thought the person was different.

This mother was doing more than just stating a rule. By sharing this story she was actually using empathy training in an interesting way. Clearly her son had not empathized with his classmate. But he could empathize easily with his mother's unhappiness. When she pointed out the similarity between the abuse she had received for the way she looked and the abuse he was about to inflict on his schoolmate, he was able to bridge the gap to his schoolmate's perspective and feel the unhappiness that boy would experience if he received such a letter.

*Inspire good will.* A good way to prevent your child from preying on others is to inspire good will toward people. Therefore, don't teach her any of the following: "It's a dog-eat-dog world," "Nice guys finish last," or "Winning is the only thing." Once your child accepts the cynicism expressed in these messages, she will go through life expecting the worst from people and feeling like a fool if she doesn't beat them to the punch. If she treats people poorly, she'll bring out the worst in them and make her (and your) pessimistic prophecies come true.

Certainly the world is dangerous, and a child must be prepared for its hazards. You want him to know that there are people out there who will try to mug him on the street, and false friends who will lie to him or tell lies about him to cheat him out of something he's earned; and there are businessmen who will sell him unsafe cars and drugs, or poison the water supply to make a profit; and there are judges and government agents who will forsake their oaths of office for payoffs. But that's not the whole story. There are also men and women of conscience everywhere. Some lead ordinary lives. Others are our cultural heroes who have earned public recognition for fighting against injustice and corruption.

Inspire your child to turn away from cynicism and egoism by teaching her about people who lead principled lives. Inspire her faith in humanity by teaching her about the moral heroes of the past and present. Teach her that taking other people's needs and feelings into consideration is not a weak or self-defeating strategy. To be sure, cruel people do sometimes rise to the top. But so do principled and kind people. Kindness tends to be reciprocated—not always, but often. We can see this everyday if we take the time to notice. It was demonstrated quite clearly by psychologists Richard Goranson and Leonard Berkowitz, who found that people who volunteered to help another person were later helped by that person when they needed it. Children, also, have been found to be kind to those children who have been spontaneously kind or helpful to them.[25]

Your own attitudes and behavior will have a strong impact on your child. If you put down people who care about and go out of their way for others as being fools or bleeding hearts, your youngster will worry about losing your respect every time he has the urge to be kind. In one recent study, children became less generous after hearing another person's generosity ridiculed. In contrast, children became more generous after hearing generosity praised. Other studies have shown that if you preach generosity and honesty to a child, but he sees you behave selfishly and cheat and lie, he'll learn that when the chips are down morality doesn't really count. What he sees you do will have more of an impact on him than what you say.[26]

A poignant illustration of how powerful a parental example can be was given by a twenty-one-year-old conscientious objector when he was asked what had most influenced his extreme stand against aggression:

> Overall, I believe my way of thinking is attributable to my parents, who by their actions showed me that "reality" and love often collide, and at such times reality must be cast aside and love carried the extra mile. To illustrate, my father, a dentist, has for years taken a month off from his practice—where the reality of having a family to support would dictate otherwise—travelled to Central America, all at his own expense, and set out for places, in the face of physical threats (and in one instance, detainment by the Brazilian police), which would otherwise never have dental services. Thus, when I am confronted by others with the "reality" of Russian aggression, I try to deal with it in the same way my dad deals with what appear to be prohibitive realities—cast them aside and reaffirm a commitment to love.[27]

## Combating Stealing

A child will steal for any number of reasons: she may simply want the money or object, or maybe she wants to prove to her friends that she can take risks. She might be seeking revenge against someone by taking something the person values, or perhaps she wants to provoke her parents into giving her some attention. She could even be after the thrill and sense of power that comes with getting away with a crime.

Whatever the reason, parents are usually shocked and confused when they learn that their child has stolen something and they find little comfort in knowing that it's fairly common for children to try their hand at stealing at least once during childhood. Stealing is, obviously, serious business.

What can parents do about stealing? Some of what they can do should start long before any incident of stealing occurs. By the age of two, children know the difference between "mine" and "not mine."[28] And most know they can do things with their own possessions that aren't allowed with someone else's things. That doesn't mean there aren't temptations. After all, other people sometimes have really neat things.

An anti-stealing campaign can actually begin when you start teaching your youngster rules of possession. Stress that taking something away from people hurts them. Start by stating the basic rules in a clear and calm way: "These things are yours and you can play with them whenever you want. Those are Tommy's things. If you want to play with his things you have to ask him. And he has to ask you if he wants to play with yours."

If your child takes something that's not his (which he more than likely will, at least once), calmly reinforce the lesson: "No, that's Tommy's. You can't take that without asking him. He'll feel bad when he learns that you took it without asking. You have to give it back now. Then you can ask him if you can play with it." Explain that people like to know where their things are so that they can use them when they want, that they feel bad when something is missing, and that they also feel bad because they'll think the person who took their things doesn't like them.

Praise your child when she asks permission to use other people's belongings, regardless of whether she does it on her own or only after you've reminded her. Also tell her that if she is generous with others, they will probably be generous with her. Teach her how to trade, as well.

At first, children take things only for immediate use. Later, they take them for keeps. If your child has taken and kept someone else's belongings, teach him what stealing means: "You can't keep that because it's not yours. When you take things away from someone else to keep, we call it stealing, and stealing is very bad because it hurts people. Good children don't try to hurt people, so you can't be considered good if you are going to steal, and I know you want to be good." Recall from our discussion of personal standards that children take the labels you apply to them and the categories you put them in very seriously.

You can also prevent stealing by arousing empathy in your youngster. Have her put herself in her victim's place by saying: "Think how you would feel if you found that one of your favorite toys was missing; how would you feel if you knew that someone you thought was your friend and invited into your house to play took one of your things on purpose?" Make it clear to her that stealing from people can have bad consequences for herself. Ask her, "How long would it take before *you* would trust that person again? A long time, I'm sure."

To encourage the development of personal standards against stealing, you should ask your child to imagine what kind of world it would be if everybody tried to take each other's possessions, and nobody could trust anyone, and everyone had to sit and guard his things all the time, or hire guards and put in alarms to protect his or her belongings. Show him stores and buildings where this is the case and explain how it makes everyone's life so much harder and unhappier.

Although your message should be firm, if it's a first offense, let her know that you assume she didn't know better. You might tell her, "We believe you didn't know how bad it is to steal and that you won't ever do it again. So after you give it back we won't think of it again." Mean it. And for a first offense, you don't need to embarrass your child by making her confess to her victim. More discreet ways of returning objects can be found—for which she'll be grateful.

But do let your child know that if she takes something again after she's learned how wrong it is, she will have to give the object back on her own to the person she took it from. In addition, she will have to be punished because she intentionally hurt someone. Tell her, "Adults are not allowed to steal and they get punished if they do— and the same goes for children. When an adult steals, people protect themselves by putting her in jail where she can't hurt them. When a child steals she also has to be kept away from people for a while, 'grounded' in her room so she learns that people are there to enjoy things with and not to hurt."

When examples come up of children or adults who have stolen and been punished, point these out. There is evidence that such bad examples reduce misbehavior.[29] But emphasize the feelings of the people involved, how unhappy the thief made everybody—including himself, not just that he was punished.

An instructive punishment for a second offense is to have the child give something of her own that she values to the person she has stolen from. Tell her, "You can say that you are giving it to him because you feel bad that you took something from him, which we hope is true; or you can say that you are giving it to him because your parents made you."

Which brings us to the subject of apologies. One of the silliest things parents can do is demand that their child say she's sorry if she isn't. In essence, they're asking her to lie. Saying "I'm sorry" should be used to let someone know "I regret having hurt you." That often makes the person feel better because it implies "I'll be more considerate about your feelings in the future." Do let your child know that if she truly feels sorry, she should tell the person, but that only her actions in the future will show whether she really is taking the other person's feelings into consideration. Also tell her that if she truly regrets what she's done, she can feel good about herself for having learned an important lesson in how to treat people. It's okay to make mistakes. Everyone does it at one time or another.

It will also help if you make sure she knows that you admire people more for *how* they acquire their money and possessions—through honest and productive efforts—than for how much they possess. If she hears you praise wealth and sees that you envy the wealthy, and you fail to make clear to her that you value honest dealings more, you won't be setting a very good example. Whether one can pursue personal wealth, trying to amass as large a portion of the community's resources for oneself as possible, and still lead a moral life is a question that has long been debated. Without question, though, all societies value behavior that is honest and productive. Let your child know that those are your values, too.

**Stealing to win approval from friends.** What if your child is stealing because it wins him approval from his friends? Maybe they view it as daring or tough or an assertion of independence. If this is the case, you have to ask yourself why he chose those particular friends in the first place. There must be youngsters in the community with other values. All of us, both children and adults, seek out certain kinds of people for friendship, have little interest in some, and shun others entirely. Why did your child seek out an anti-social group?

One answer may be that he felt rejected by the more socially adept youngsters he knew and found camaraderie only with marginal youths who prey on others as a way to offset their sense of inadequacy. If this is the case, then some social-skills training is in order. He needs to be brought together with young people who are engaged in organized, constructive activities. Together, make a list of various organized activities for youngsters his age in the community, including hobby groups, volunteer groups, and work groups. Let him choose which ones he wants to join, but insist that he pick at least one that engages in "prosocial" humanitarian or business activities so he can experience what it's like to give instead of take. Insist also that he participate in the group fully and that he make an effort to make friends there. He will probably crab and resist. Let him know you won't back down. Take him through the steps of researching the groups, joining up, and learning to make friends. Be patient, but firm. Be there for him when he's confused or needs help, but also be forceful. By your instruction and example, help him learn that he can gain people's friendship if he shows an interest in them, gives them support, and develops skills and personal characteristics that they find valuable and attractive.[30]

Perhaps your child has chosen anti-social friends because he values being daring and tough. If so, channel these interests into such constructive activities as community service organizations (rescue squads, neighborhood crime watch teams) or sports. It shouldn't be too hard to find role models who are "macho" *and* moral, and who he won't be able to put down as "squares" or "suckers."

Perhaps your youngster belongs to a group that steals as a way to assert maturity and independence from parents. This could be a sign that he didn't receive enough respect and freedom while growing up or that mature demands weren't placed on him—in other words, that he was brought up under either the laissez-faire or authoritarian family systems that we described earlier. In neither system would he have learned how to assert his rights and appreciate the importance of his obligations to others; nor would either system have made him feel that he was being groomed to take his place as a respected member of the community.

Obviously, it's better to prevent stealing than to have to stop it once it has become a habit. As a child grows older, the influence of peers competes more and more with the influence of parents, and by the time the fourteenth birthday rolls around the influence of peers usually predominates. Starting moral training in adolescence is certainly an uphill battle for parents, but it's still one they can win. There is a growing body of evidence that even adolescents who are already serious delinquents can be turned around.[31]

Telling your youngster which friends he can and can't spend time with will lead to difficulties. It's usually met with a lot of resistance and it's a hard rule to enforce. Nor does it get at the real problem: why he has chosen those particular friends to begin with. But if you channel his free time into organized, constructive, prosocial activities, you will accomplish the same goal, since he'll have little time left for his old friends. Youngsters generally view a parental demand on how they spend their time as more reasonable than restrictions on whom they can have as friends; they accept time demands as more within a parent's rights, and, therefore, less of a violation of their own rights. So they don't fight it as hard.

Whether a child will come to choose more desirable friends in the future will depend on what kinds of experiences he has in the new groups. So do your best to make his new experiences good ones. Monitor how things go for him in the group on a daily basis. Show an interest, insist that he communicate with you. Try making it a policy to discuss his new activities before supper every day. You have to show him how important it is to you that he turns into a kind person.

One other piece of advice: never blame a child's friends for his misbehavior. Children get very insulted when parents do this. In essence it's calling them mindless and spineless, and it also gives them a handy excuse when they try to shift the blame away from themselves. Hold them solely responsible for their actions. This doesn't mean that children are not influenced by their friends; of course they are. This is exactly why you want to steer them toward constructive groups: you want to bring them under the influence of children with more positive values. Since even "problem" children generally *know* which is the "right" or moral way to behave,[32] and peer pressure can just as readily lead them toward moral actions as immoral ones, you want to make sure they have the right kinds of peers.

Recall Stanley Milgram's study in which people were asked to "teach" others a task by punishing them with electric shocks when they made mistakes. Remember that Milgram found that a sizable proportion of subjects were "obedient"; that is, they readily gave the shocks under orders. In one variation on the basic procedure, each subject believed he was part of a team of three teachers. His job was to administer the shocks; another teacher was to read the word list; and the third was to inform the learner whether or not his answers were correct. The two co-teachers were actually working for the experimenter; at certain prearranged points, first one and then the other quit the experiment, saying they would not be involved in giving any more shocks to the learner. The experimenter kept insisting that the training continue.

What did the real subjects do in response? According to Milgram, thirty-six of the forty subjects defied the experimenter. He states, "The effects of peer rebellion are very impressive in undercutting the experimenter's authority."[33] So we see that the right peers can be a force for moral action. That's why it's so important to guide your children toward kind and constructive friends.

**Group treatment.** If your youngster and his friends steal, but it's not practical or possible for you to steer him away from them, a more difficult but nevertheless feasible plan is to try to change the behavior of the entire group of friends, as a collective. You will need the cooperation of each of the children's parents for this, or at least most of them. A number of studies have found that an effective way to change the behavior of members of a group is to reward or punish the group as a whole for the way each of its members behave; this technique was recently used successfully in a school setting to eliminate stealing in second graders.[34]

If you want to try your hand at group treatment, here's how to do it. First, establish a clear definition of stealing and communicate this to each child: "A kid is considered to be stealing if he is caught in the act itself, or has more money than he can account for, or comes home with things that he shouldn't have had the money to purchase and can't explain how he got them."

Let the children know that any suspect explanations ("A kid paid me some money that he owed me") will be checked and, because of their past record of misdeeds, if any of them suddenly acquires anything unusual, he will be presumed guilty until he proves himself innocent. Gather all the parents and children together and explain to the children that since, as a group, they have encouraged each other to hurt people, if any of them is found stealing, the entire group will be penalized. Penalties should include grounding and forfeiting favorite objects and activities. Allow the children to discuss the group treatment and penalties freely and try to include any of their suggestions that will not undermine the purpose of the program.

Remember that it's much easier to reduce bad behavior if you have also set up conditions that promote good behavior. Therefore, it's always a good idea to balance a punishment system with a reward system. So give the children a way, as a group, to earn a reward for being kind and helpful. You can do this by arranging for the group to earn a reward by logging a certain number of hours doing "good works." The number of hours should be more than any individual or even half the number of children, could possibly achieve—but not so high as to be discouraging.

Parents and children can decide together what "good works" they want to pursue (volunteer work in community agencies, tutoring younger children for free, collecting money or supplies for a charity, etc.), as well as how many hours should be volunteered and what would be a fair reward (a trip, a game, horseback riding, etc.). Rewards should be earned weekly.

Try the following reward schedule and communicate it to the group right from the start: For the first two weeks, if the group fulfills its required number of hours of "good works," all group members can share in the reward regardless of anyone's individual contribution. For the next two weeks, the whole group will earn the reward only if the set number of hours have been fulfilled *and* every member of the group has logged at least one hour. After that, the group as a whole must still meet the hour requirement, but only those youngsters who have logged at least one hour can share in the reward. You can use this schedule as a guide, but experiment with it and with the hour requirement and reward, so you can tailor the program to your own circumstances.

Sometimes a youngster will go along with a group's dishonest behavior even though she really doesn't approve of it. This will happen when her loyalty to the group or her fear of being ridiculed and rejected by group members is stronger than her fear of getting caught or her commitment to honesty. We've encountered a similar kind of "going along" in the personal standards chapter, only there it was acquiescence to authority. Here, too, you can bolster your child's moral tendencies by stressing her individual responsibility to live up to her personal values despite group pressure.

You can help your child find the courage to do this by giving her examples of people who stood up to the crowd and followed the dictates of their own conscience. If you suspect that she is succumbing to pressure to do things that she would really rather not do, ask her if she has considered whether or not she truly likes these "friends" whose behavior she disapproves of so strongly. If she really does like them and wants to remain their friend, then tell her that *as a friend* it is her responsibility to dissuade them from doing things that will get them in trouble, and, more importantly, make them less worthwhile people.

Stress that it's important that she be able to respect the values of the groups she chooses to join, and that her real obligation is to be loyal to those values. Teach her that when she's loyal to a group whose values she sees as destructive, whether it's a neighborhood clique or a national government, she is then being disloyal to herself and must share full responsibility for any harm the group does. Group loyalty (called patriotism when the group is one's country) is compatible with moral action when it involves fostering the group's moral ideals and sharing its burdens. But loyalty and patriotism don't serve moral ideals when they are used to justify blind obedience to leaders, jingoism, and the suppression of dissent.

It's usually not easy for children to oppose their peers. They're often afraid they will be ridiculed and become an outcast if they take a moral stand. Unfortunately, in many groups, moral stands are "not cool." So go over with your youngster what she might say to her friends to dissuade them from stealing. Unless she is desperate for friends, she *can* learn to take ridicule in stride. Indeed, she can learn that ridicule from some people is to be expected whenever she or anyone takes a stand in favor of kindness and fairness. Explain to her that if she cares about these friends or about how people in general treat each other, it's worth making the effort to change their minds. Moreover, seeing how your friends treat you when you stand up for what you believe is one way to tell who your real friends are.

**Stealing for attention.** Sometimes children steal to get attention from a parent. These children make sure they get caught. They'll take things from family members that are certain to be noticed missing or they'll hide them in the most obvious places. When they get caught they are suddenly the center of their parents' attention. Sure, they get punished and yelled at, but, oddly enough, it makes them feel loved. Too often when they're not in trouble they get ignored.

Parents who have made their children feel loved and let them know that they enjoy spending time with them are not likely to raise children with this problem. But if you suspect that your child is stealing for attention, then don't give him attention for stealing. Give him lots of attention and affection at other times instead. Note things you like about him—even little things—and let him know what they are. Whenever your child does something you respect, even if it's just a small step in the right direction, tell him so. Curtail criticizing him for all the things he *isn't*. You've probably made this clear enough already. He needs to know that you've noticed the efforts he's made to improve and that it pleases you. Let him know that if he needs you—to discuss something or just to take a walk together—you'll be there for him, patient and interested. Talk to him about yourself and your struggles. Share your confusions and setbacks, not just your accomplishments (you don't want to sound as if you're indirectly criticizing him by setting yourself up as a glowing example).

What should you do if he steals again? Still keep the attention to a minimum. No long harangues. It's sufficient to say something like, "I'm disappointed in you, and I feel sorry for the person you stole from. But I'm determined to find a way to get you to stop hurting people." Then be clear about his punishment: "You have to spend the weekend alone in your room, including meals. If you whine when you're there or leave before 7:00 A.M., Monday morning, we'll have to extend it to the following weekend. I'm upset with you and I will need till Monday to calm down. So I won't talk to you till then unless absolutely necessary. Between now and Monday evening think about what positive things you can do to try to make up for your lack of caring." That's it. No other attention. If the weekend is a few days away and it's not practical to restrict him to his room immediately, don't worry. Delayed punishment will work if you describe it clearly and give a reasonable explanation for it.[35]

It is not uncommon for newly separated or divorced parents to find that their preteen or teenager has begun to steal, often from them or other family members. There are probably a number of reasons at work. The youngster may be seeking revenge for the hurt she feels at the family's breakup. Or she may find that stealing gets her attention from parents who are otherwise preoccupied with putting their own lives in order; suddenly a family meeting is called and *her* problem is the central item on the agenda. She may also be trying to show her parents that she'll "turn bad" unless they patch up the family. She may even be allowing herself to steal out of guilt and self-hatred because she blames herself for her parents' divorce.

Divorcing parents can usually avoid this problem by making sure they give their child a great deal of their time, as difficult as that may be—including spending time talking about and getting her to talk about the divorce. Stress that the family still exists, but in a different form, and make sure she understands that you want her to help determine the new form of the family so that the transition, though inevitably painful for her (and everyone else), is as easy as possible. She should feel confident that if she needs more time or time spent differently, both parents will try to see that her needs are met. Don't forget, it's your child's family too, and she has the right to be more than just a passive victim of her parents' conflicts.

Parents should try to explain that the purpose of the divorce is not to cause unhappiness, but to find relief from unhappiness. That means sharing some of your feelings about the marriage with your child so she can understand the reasons for the divorce. It's very important, though, that neither parent blame the other, and both *must* avoid any attempt to turn their child against the ex-spouse. One way to describe what happened to the marriage in a way a child can understand is that being married is like being "best friends," only stronger, and that sometimes, as with best friends, one realizes that something has changed in oneself or the other person and that one isn't happy being best friends anymore, at least not in the same way. One can still be friends—and it's so important for the sake of the children that the parents try to remain (or become) friends— even if not best friends.

It is also crucial that both parents let the child know that the change in their relationship has nothing to do with anything she did, and that there is nothing she can do to change it back—neither by being very bad nor by being very good. Parents can reassure a child about her importance in their lives by letting her know that they need her to help them get through the difficult transition period. They should also acknowledge her anger and explain that it's understandable for her to be angry at them because their action has hurt her even though they weren't intending to. But they should also explain that being angry doesn't mean you have to try to hurt back and that the most important part of the family—the caring part—can continue if they are all concerned with each other's feelings.

**Stealing for excitement.** Some children say they steal because it's exciting or thrilling, or it gives them a sense of power. Shoplifters often describe their motives in these terms. One man who shoplifted as a teenager said he did it "as a way to even the score. It felt good to know I could get away with it. I was the one in control, not them." These kinds of thieves see themselves in a competition: *It's me against them.*

By *them,* the thrill-stealer doesn't usually mean ordinary individuals. He means the people and institutions with power and money, the ones that control things and make the rules. "Them" is the department store, the rich kids, the big shots, the insurance company, the people who have the upper hand. Typical thrill-stealers are not out to hurt any individual; nor are they likely to be engaged in a political act. They are more interested in beating the system than changing it. They may not even need the things they steal.

The "caper" film dramatizes this competition between the individual and "them" on a grand scale. The "hero" or "heroine" in these films is usually a thief who doesn't really hurt anyone. He or she robs only from banks or the vaults of fancy hotels, pitting cunning and daring against the best security systems that money can buy—and we usually root for the thief. We're so fascinated by his or her ability to outsmart the "establishment" that we don't concern ourselves with the hardworking banker or the security guards who go off to work every day hoping they won't have to face any trouble; nor do we worry about the impact of the theft on insurance rates and banking fees.

Although the thrill-stealer may not see his act as political, it does reflect a deep alienation between himself and other segments of society. That's why he enters a competition with "them" in the first place. He and they are not on the same side. Vandalism often stems from the same sense of alienation. A child doesn't throw a brick through the window of a school that he likes or feels a part of.[36]

What can parents do about thrill-stealing? They can do their best to make sure that their child thinks of himself as a part of his community and society, rather than outside it; that he understands that his actions, even those directed at giant institutions, affect the whole spirit of the community and the individuals living in it. Make sure your youngster understands that when he robs from a store he robs from *people,* not impersonal institutions, and that every institution he deals with is made up of nothing else, just people at work. Somewhere down the line somebody has to pay for what he has stolen.

If you feel that our society's social structure or some of its institutions are unjust, tell your child why you feel that way and guide him toward forthright and constructive ways to change them. There's something pathetic about someone feeling that he is "getting even" with the power structure by ripping off an eighty-dollar pair of sneakers. Once your youngster realizes how impotent and destructive such isolated acts of stealing are—that they will never improve his or anyone else's lot, and that his stealing only adds to a climate of mistrust and alienation—it's highly unlikely that he'll continue to get a thrill from it.

Anyone, adult or child, will become alienated from his society when he believes that it doesn't address itself to his needs, or that he doesn't have a real say in it, or that the payoffs it provides for his efforts seem unfair. Under such circumstances he'll feel indifferent to that society or, more likely, resentful, and he'll work against it. We can prevent this form of alienation among our youth by making sure they recognize how our society serves them, by giving them a genuine say in the institutions that affect their lives, and by assigning them real responsibility for making our communities better places for all of us.

Think about it for a moment. Throughout most of human history what we call an adolescent was once considered a full-fledged member of the community. Yet we give our teenagers virtually no legitimate ways to influence either the schools they spend half their waking lives in, the after-school centers that are built for their recreation, or the community agencies (police departments, job centers) that are there to serve them. Adolescents are simply supposed to show up and do what they're told.

Nor do we provide our youth with experiences designed to teach them about the relationship between the adult world of work and the quality of life in the community. As a result, what adults do often seems pointless to them. No wonder they are alienated. Finally, and most important, we don't provide our youth with meaningful activities through which they are expected to contribute visibly to the quality of life in the community, including projects that are of direct interest to them (such as assisting in the construction of a new sports center). A very good reason to give our youth genuine responsibilities in the community is so that they learn that it's a lot easier to complain about things than to improve them.

One last point about stealing. If your youngster steals because he wants something (or just more of it), it doesn't necessarily mean that you are keeping him deprived. Some children steal even when they have a great deal of money or possessions. And most children with very little don't steal. Whether you are looking at an individual, a whole society, or are comparing different societies, you will find no simple relationship between poverty and stealing—except that poor and rich people steal in different ways. Because "white collar" theft—usually possible only to the relatively more wealthy—doesn't involve direct physical assault, it generally receives less attention and causes less alarm. Nevertheless, its impact on society is enormous, involving the misappropriation of hundreds of millions of dollars.

Whether your child is growing up in relative affluence or poverty, don't be surprised to find that he or she steals—children from all classes do. For your child's sake, and the sake of the community in which he will one day take his place, teach him that no matter what form it takes, stealing harms *people*.

## "MACHO" AGGRESSION: HARMING OTHERS TO PROVE ONE'S TOUGHNESS

Another reason a child might harm others is to prove his courage and virility. He may be trying to prove himself to his parents or his friends, or both. Children try to prove themselves through violence, *when violence earns them approval*. And parents often do, indeed, approve of violence. A Harris poll conducted for the National Commission on the Causes and Prevention of Violence found that seven out of ten American adults believe that it is good for growing boys to have a few fistfights.

That parents encourage their children to be aggressive, and even demand it at times, was demonstrated quite clearly in a study of adolescent aggression by Albert Bandura and Richard H. Walters. They wanted to distinguish between *parental* influences on aggression and the kind of *community* influences that are often found in tough, lower-income neighborhoods, so they focused their study exclusively on intelligent boys from intact middle-class homes where the neighborhood standards of conduct supported law-abiding behavior. They compared the families of highly aggressive adolescents to those of boys who were neither markedly aggressive nor passive. They found that the families differed most strikingly in the extent to which they trained their sons, through precept and example, to be combative.

Parents of *non*aggressive boys encouraged their sons to defend themselves, but did not condone physical aggression as a means of settling disputes. These parents also turned out to be good models of considerate behavior; they relied primarily on reasoning in handling family disputes. By contrast, the parents of the aggressive boys were often combative themselves, and they reinforced aggression in their children; one or the other of the parents almost invariably encouraged fighting, whether with peers, teachers, or other adults outside the family. The boy was expected to use his fists to settle conflicts. In addition, these parents used physical punishment in the home, and thus furnished their sons with vivid examples of how to use aggression to influence and control the behavior of others.

To summarize Bandura and Walters' findings: You get aggressive children when you teach them to be aggressive, reward aggression, model aggression through your own behavior, and praise others who are aggressive. Bandura also cites anthropological evidence to show that societies that actively promote aggression (the Dani of New Guinea, the Comanche and Apache Indians) do, indeed, wind up with aggressive children; while societies that discourage aggression (the Tahitians, the Hopi and Zuni Indians, the Hutterites) wind up with low levels of aggressive behavior: "In cultural settings where interpersonal aggression is discouraged and devalued, people live peaceably. . . . In other societies that provide extensive training in aggression and make it an index of manliness or personal worth, people spend a great deal of time threatening, fighting, maiming, and killing each other.[37]

Of course, parents aren't the only ones who encourage aggression in children. It is all too common in our society for adolescents to reinforce each other for aggressive behavior. Physical toughness is a highly respected quality, particularly in poorer neighborhoods. An interesting demonstration of the impact of peer pressure on aggression was carried out in the mid-1970s by psychologist Richard Borden. He set up one of those shock experiments in which subjects believe they are giving people electric shocks under one guise or another. The special aspect of this study was that an "observer" witnessed the behavior of the subjects. The researchers wanted to determine if different kinds of observers would affect the amount of shock the subject gave. They found it did. Subjects gave stronger shocks when the observer was male rather than female, and more when the observer was described as a member of a karate club than when he was a member of SANE (the activist peace group). Borden concluded that the subjects felt males and karate club members were more likely to approve of aggression than women and members of SANE.

When youngsters encourage and reward each other's toughness, fighting and other destructive actions are seen as fun.[38] Getting drunk and bashing heads becomes a kind of group sport, an evening's entertainment. Even if one acts alone, one can always come back to the group and boast of it. When harming becomes fun, group members, out on an evening prowl, are on the alert for whom they can frighten or beat up or rob, as well as what they can destroy —all in the name of entertainment.

What can parents do to prevent this kind of "macho" aggression? Don't encourage it, don't praise it, don't reward it, and don't be an example of it yourself. Do encourage, praise, and reward kindness and justice, and see that your own behavior serves as a good example of these.

As to peer influence, remember that from a very early age, children can distinguish between people who appear competent and powerful and those who seem ineffectual. Various studies have shown that a child will be impressed by and try to emulate peers and adults who appear to be in control.[39] The tough kids your child comes across will often seem to him to be the ones to copy. They're the ones who appear to be in charge because they seem self-possessed and scary. It is vital to dispel this image. Explain to your child that the local toughs only *look* as if they have control over the way things turn out because they have such limited and meager goals.

Not too many years ago, after centuries of effort, striving, dreaming, and persistence, men walked on the moon for the first time. Suddenly people all over the world had a vastly expanded sense of the universe and their place in it. We're certain that on that very same day some group of neighborhood toughs felt really terrific about themselves because they managed to frighten an old woman and steal ten dollars from her.

It takes a long time to create something of value, whether it's a bridge, a business, a piece of music, or a young man or woman of character. But it takes only a moment to destroy something—which is why destructive people seem to be so powerful. They have the power to mess things up. But if you look more closely, the destroyers turn out to be the trivial, really pathetic people around—temporary big fish in the tiniest of ponds. All they create are enemies.

Your child will be less attracted to destructive people and less susceptible to their influence if you teach him the difference between the power to create and the power to destroy, and point out that the creators are the ones with the real power. Inspire him or her with stories of people whose lives had great and lasting effects. Try Thomas Alva Edison or Eleanor Roosevelt or Pablo Picasso or Marie Curie or Beethoven or Mother Theresa. None of them were violent. But they certainly were powerful. They affected the way millions of people live and think, and the sights and sounds we all see and hear every day.

In the chapter on personal standards we talked about fostering ideals in your child, and we recommended that you teach him about the great human struggles to improve the quality of life. From the beginning of human history individuals have sought to create just societies, to conquer illness, to understand and harness the forces of nature, and to create beauty and share their experiences through art. The toughs on the corner are not going to be part of that history. The torch will not be passed to them. While your children are still young begin teaching them about this history, about the striving and the achievements, about ancient cultures and today's discoveries. Share what you know, and explore together what you don't know. Teach them these things so they'll be inspired to find a place for themselves in these grand struggles. Teach them these things in the hope that if they have reverence for mankind and pride in their own humanity, they'll be less inclined to want to harm their fellow men and women.

Macho aggressors seek confrontations and the escalation of conflict: they send out antagonistic signals. As far as they are concerned, there are only two kinds of people in the world: those who dominate and those who submit. You should oppose these tough-guy characteristics in a direct way. Let your child know that confronting and challenging people has nothing to do with self-assertion or self-defense, and is often just a cover-up for feeling powerless. They are ways of intruding in people's lives and forcing them to acknowledge that you have the power to harm them. They put people on the defensive and bring out their most unpleasant sides; all one sees is their fear and anger.

Set up a program to practice welcoming (as opposed to challenging) behavior, so your child can learn that more pleasant things happen when one treats people in a friendly and polite manner. Take a "good vibe" stroll together. Walk through the neighborhood and give him the assignment to actively try to make people feel comfortable and good. Ask him to look for and describe the sympathetic qualities of the people that you meet as you stroll. Remind him to smile and to give people warm greetings. Treating people with courtesy and warmth is not just a matter of adhering to social conventions. It has serious moral implications because it communicates that you want them to feel comfortable in your presence.

*Teach your child to defeat the problem, not the person.* If your child is well entrenched in the macho role, he'll have to learn new ways to handle conflicts. The macho goal is to subdue "the opposition" without consideration for other people's viewpoints and needs. If someone crosses you, you insult him or threaten him or explode at him. You turn the conflict into a battle of egos in which there can be only one winner. Instead, you want your youngster to practice finding "win-win" solutions in which the goal is to defeat the problem, not the person.

Teach your child to communicate his point of view in ways that don't make people defensive. An important part of the "win-win" conflict resolution strategy is helping your opponents save face. This means not looking for confessions that they were wrong, not insisting on public acknowledgment of their mistakes, and not demanding that all concessions come from them. In other words, the focus is on what to do to make things better in the future, not who did what to whom in the past.

The latest research shows that children acquire aggressive habits when they are very young,[40] and that a large percentage of aggressive children turn into aggressive adults. So we cannot stress enough the importance of teaching your children from a very young age that aggression is wrong and will not be tolerated, and, at the same time, showing them how to use constructive ways to settle disputes and pursue what they want from life.

## WHEN YOUR CHILD HARMS SOMEONE OUT OF ENVY

Another reason children hurt others is out of envy. We've all felt envy at times, wishing we had someone else's qualities or possessions or luck. Merely feeling envy does not cause problems. Other people's achievements can even serve as incentives for us to strive harder to develop better qualities and skills. The trouble begins when the only way we can feel good about ourselves is by bringing down those we envy to our level or by making them feel inferior. So we do things to hurt them and we spread rumors about them to tarnish their image.

People who try to debase others in order to make themselves feel better are commonly said to have an inferiority complex. This term recognizes that the motivating force behind this destructiveness is an ultimate lack of faith in one's own ability to ever get the things one envies so much. It's as if the person were thinking, "If I can drag you down, I won't have to feel so worthless." Sometimes we even drag down people we say we love out of fear that once they gain some confidence in themselves, they'll leave us.

Some examples of destructive envy in children are picking on a smarter classmate, gossiping about an attractive friend, jumping down the throat of a popular youngster whenever he or she makes any kind of mistake, vandalizing a schoolmate's new bicycle, "accidently" destroying a sister's favorite toy, and tattling on one's brother to get him in trouble.

Sometimes an envious youngster will try to hide his destructive intentions under a veneer of concern, such as knowingly giving someone bad advice while appearing to be truly concerned about that person's well-being. For instance, a child who is envious of a friend who was accepted to a special accelerated class while he wasn't might try to dissuade him from entering the class with the argument that "only weirdos are in it."

If you see your child hurting someone out of envy, don't criticize the feeling. In fact, a good first step to help your child overcome destructive envy is to do your best to make her comfortable with her feeling. You might say, "I know you're feeling bad that you weren't accepted for the special class, and when a person feels really bad about things not going her way, it's understandable to want to strike out at someone, especially someone who got what she wanted."

The idea behind telling your child this is not to let her off the hook with regard to her *actions,* but just to let her know that there's nothing unnatural about having mean *thoughts* when feeling hurt. Indeed, psychologists have found with various species that pain can make one more aggressive, and they found with children of various ages that feeling sorry for oneself can make one more selfish.[41]

Next, remind your youngster that it's easy to be kind and generous when things are going your way and you're feeling good, but that the true test of character is to be kind and generous even when you're feeling bad. Morality means feeling pleasure in someone else's pleasure, but not just when that's easy to do. Explain that when she feels sorry for herself and bitter over someone else's good fortune, that's the time to remember that it's really not that person's success that makes her want to hurt him or her. It's her own failure. And hurting someone else won't change that—she can never get what she wants by bringing someone else down. All that will do is make people dislike her for being so selfish.

Teach your child that envy doesn't have to be destructive. She can feel envy and still be glad for other people's joy, if she reminds herself to really "see" them, not as the symbol of her failure, but from *their* perspective—experiencing something good that has happened to them.

Also explain to your child that by trying to hurt others because of their success, she is, in effect, blaming them for something that came either from their own efforts or from luck. In either case, her energies would be better spent on improving her own skills. There is a line of T.S. Eliot's worth recalling: "For us, there is only the trying. The rest is not our business."[42]

There is an important lesson here for children and adults: the world doesn't always reward us as we wish to be rewarded; often we don't even get what we believe we deserve. All we really have control over is our own ability to do our best. If we can find joy in the striving we will never go unrewarded, and we will never be so consumed by bitterness that we seek satisfaction through undermining someone else's pleasure. You can help your child learn this by praising her efforts and not just her achievements; and when she is cursing her fate, remind her of reasons to praise herself. Teaching her the maxim, "Enjoy the process, not just the product," may also help.

**Teach your child to persist in the face of obstacles.** A child can't suffer from an inferiority complex if he doesn't feel inferior. If he has confidence in his ability to make things go his way (in the long run, at least), then other people's successes will serve as an incentive for him rather than as a sign of his worthlessness.

One of the primary indicators of a child's confidence in his abilities is how he handles obstacles and setbacks. The confident child is not thrown by them. In fact, he expects mishaps to occur. But they don't signal failure. They are a cue that more effort or a different strategy is required. The confident child persists. He has developed what psychologists sometimes call "frustration tolerance." The unconfident child gives up at the first sign of trouble. Moreover, the unconfident child's expectations of failure often make it difficult for him to accept criticism; he's not likely to be able to laugh at himself or his foibles. Nor is he likely to be able to accept friendly ribbing from others. His own sense of defeat will make it hard for him to recognize any friendly intentions in humor directed at him and he'll usually react in a defensive, "uptight" manner.

How can we get a child to persist in the face of setbacks? Psychologists have studied this problem extensively.[43] Start by giving your youngster lots of success experiences in his earliest years. Let's say he's trying to put one block on top of another, and he does get it on, but not fully enough to stay on. Don't expect perfection the first time around, and don't focus on the negative. Praise him for his success, even though it was short-lived. You'll see how eager he is to try again. Then, little by little, raise the requirement for praise. Help him bridge the gap between one success and the next by giving him encouragement and instruction, such as, "Good try. You almost got it. Relax for a second, then try again. Line up all four edges of the blocks before letting go. You can do it." Then, gradually fade out your reminders. "Line up all four edges" can be reduced to the simple one word reminder, "Edges," and this can then be replaced by the general reminder, "Careful." Finally, your child should be able to give all necessary reminders to himself.

The keys, then, to training for persistence are making sure your child experiences lots of success, gradually letting him get used to longer tasks and occasional setbacks, and teaching him what to say to himself that is both encouraging and instructive.

A few years ago, psychologists Donald Meichenbaum and Joseph Goodman worked out a detailed self-instructional "persistence" program for children who were labeled impulsive.[44] These children lost concentration easily and their work deteriorated as soon as they made an error. They had not learned how to persist with care when faced with an obstacle. The technique is highly effective and can be used easily by parents. One of the experimenters worked through each of the series of tasks for the children (who were five to seven years old), and spoke his thoughts aloud as he did so. This enabled the children to hear what he said to himself each step of the way.

> Okay, what is it I have to do? You want me to copy the picture with the different lines. I have to go slow and be careful. Okay, draw the line down, down, good; then to the right, that's it; now down some more and to the left. Good, I'm doing fine so far. Remember, go slow. Now back up again. No, I was supposed to go down. That's okay. Just erase the line carefully . . . Good. Even if I make an error I can go on slowly and carefully. Okay, I have to go down now. Finished. I did it.

Notice that in his "self-instruction" the experimenter included a) defining the task, b) planning each step, c) calming himself, and d) praising himself. After hearing the experimenter go through these steps, the children did the same task three times. The first time they spoke out loud just as the experimenter had done; the second time they whispered the self-instructions; and the third time they went through the self-instructions silently. The children's performance improved markedly.

Meichenbaum and Goodman's research doesn't deal directly with moral behavior, and, to be sure, a youngster with faith in her ability to reach her goals and with confidence to persist despite setbacks won't automatically be a moral child concerned about kindness and justice. But if she is concerned about kindness and justice, self-confidence will make it easier for her to live up to her personal standards. Temptations to be devious and destructive are so much harder to resist when you believe that they are the only means through which you are ever going to get the things you want. This relationship between a child's ability to persist in the face of difficulties and the likelihood that she will behave morally was confirmed in a recent study that found that once children had learned to persist through a set of difficult puzzles, they were less likely to cheat on a new, even harder set.[45]

**WARNING: *Pity can lead to permissiveness.*** Sometimes parents unwittingly foster their child's destructive envy. They see full well that his sense of inferiority leads him to be harmful to others. He may put on a haughty facade, but they know he doesn't really have the friends he'd like and can't manage to get what he wants from life. So out of compassion or pity for him, or their own guilt (perhaps they are somehow to blame for his poor self-image, perhaps they favored one of their other children, perhaps they weren't encouraging enough), they tolerate his meanness and permit him to get away with things that they would never allow another child to do. They're afraid that if they come down hard on him, they'll only make him feel worse about himself.

At first their thinking may be along the lines of, "He's only a child now. He'll learn to be nicer when he gets older." This is wishful thinking. Parents who ignore destructive envy out of what they believe is compassion are doing their youngsters a tremendous disservice. By accepting harmful behavior they are tacitly condoning it, and, in effect, reinforcing exactly the opposite of the skills their children need to overcome their feelings of inferiority. Harmful children are the least liked by peers and the most often rejected.[46] And being rejected by others will obviously only make a child feel worse about himself—in turn making him more inclined to bring others down.

A particularly destructive side-effect of letting your child get away with aggression and other nasty behaviors is that, without realizing it, you will be communicating that you believe he is in fact inferior— that he is incapable of learning normal social behavior and cannot be held responsible for his actions like other children; in effect, that he is "sick" and needs special treatment. A child knows when he isn't treated like other children. He realizes that the people who care the most about him really don't expect very much from him. Typically, he loses the little faith he had in himself, and often he learns to play the role of the special or sick child, using the incapacity that everybody agrees he has as an excuse for being rude or cruel or irresponsible. Remember, a child is never too young to be taught not to harm someone else just because he feels bad, and never too young to be corrected and held responsible for being hurtful.

## WHEN YOUR CHILD USES AGGRESSION IN SELF-DEFENSE OR FOR REVENGE

At a parent counseling seminar a father complained that his six-year-old son was too gentle, too *un*aggressive. "If another kid in school or in the playground pushes him or takes something from him, he doesn't defend himself." "What does he do?" we asked. "He tells the teacher or a nearby parent," the father answered. We asked if he thought his son was afraid to hit back or confront another child. The father said that he didn't think so. "He's always been very gentle and sensitive to people's feelings, and I don't want that to change. I don't ever want him to start fights or hurt anyone first. But if someone hurts him, I want him to give it back to them so they know not to do it again." We were reminded of Polonius's advice to his son, Laertes, in *Hamlet:*

> Beware
> Of entrance to a quarrel; but being in,
> Bear't that th' opposed may beware
> Of thee.

We then asked this father, "Isn't your son doing just what you'd want an adult to do? He's not just giving in. He's going to the authorities." And another seminar participant added, "I'm a teacher and I want a child to tell me if someone hits him or takes something from him. You can't just have all the children hitting and grabbing, and then screaming, 'He did it first.' "

But this father had very little confidence in the ability of authorities to protect the innocent. "There's a kid in my son's first-grade class who picks on everyone. The teacher reprimands this kid every day, but it doesn't do any good. And it's the same for adults." He reminded the group of a news report that had made headlines earlier in the week about a Buffalo man who had raped a young girl while out on bail awaiting trial for a sex crime. According to *Time* magazine, the man was a "twice-convicted felon with a total of twenty-eight arrests since 1970, some for robbery and rape."[47] "Where were the authorities who are supposed to protect our children from people like this?" the father asked. "The girl's father and his friends went after the guy with a knife and had a right to, I believe."

"But the guy denied doing it," another parent reminded him. "What if the little girl gave a wrong description or lied for some reason and they just went after this guy because of his past record? Wouldn't it have been better to take the man into custody and give him a fair trial?" "It just doesn't seem to work," he replied. "You have to stand up for yourself or people take advantage of you."

He then told us an incident from his childhood.

> When I was a kid I had a dog named Thunder. He was a German shepherd and the sweetest dog in the world. He liked everybody, including other dogs. But every once in a while some new dog would come by and charge at him. Thunder would stand up—and he was a real big dog. If they ran away that was the end of it. If they smiled at him and said they were only kidding, he'd be their buddy. But sometimes they'd attack him and every one of them wound up at the vet's. The next time they saw Thunder, they knew to keep their distance. That's how I'd like my kid to be: loving and gentle to everyone—except the people who try to hurt him.

How *should* children defend themselves? Parents obviously do not want their children to be victimized by others. What should they teach their boys and girls to do when another child hits them or tries to take something from them? What would be effective? What would be moral?

Self-defense is not a moral issue. A child can still be considered kind and just if all he does is defend himself. But in most cases, he will not be able to defend himself without using physical force against his attacker. That's when the moral question arises: Should he ever hurt another human being—even one who is attacking him? Gandhi said no, and he certainly received his share of beatings, but he would never let anyone provoke him into violating *his* choice against using violence.

But you must ask yourself, "Do I believe my child has any moral obligation to someone who is trying to hurt her?" Most parents would say yes. If a classmate pushed their child out of a seat, they would not want her to respond by smashing open the child's head with a baseball bat. So the question becomes, How much force is the right amount to use in defending yourself? Do you do to them what they did to you—no more, no less? That might seem just, but it might not be enough to prevent future attacks. Then is the "right" amount the minimum force needed to prevent future attacks? Obviously, one can only guess at the minimum force needed.

There are certainly no universally accepted answers to the question of whether or not to use force, how much of it, and when (only after you've been attacked, or "preventively" in anticipation of an attack?). There are no mathematical formulas that will help you weigh your moral commitment to kindness and justice against your concern for your own and your family's safety. But here are some recommendations that we think make sense, and why we think so:

*Teach your children that whenever possible they should rely on legitimate authorities to protect them and their rights.*

A system based on the rule of law is very precious and very fragile. Taking the law into your own hands often leads to the opposite of what you want. Fights escalate. The child who pushed first and is pushed back suddenly feels moral outrage or humiliation because the push he received is harder than the one he gave. So he now looks for a way to get even and may seek the aid of his big brother or friends.

A great deal of bloody human history has followed this lawless scenario of attack and counterattack. It's worth remembering and telling your children about the notorious blood feud between the Hatfield clan of West Virginia and the McCoys from nearby Kentucky. For thirty years these two families tried to kill each other off, and each killing was justified as an act of revenge for a previous murder by the other side. Open your newspapers any day of the week for similar, even more bloody incidents. We have all seen that, as soon as Communist domination was lifted in Eastern Europe, violent ethnic rivalries erupted and people started killing each other under the pretext of avenging atrocities inflicted on their group decades (and even centuries) earlier.

Sometimes children develop an unwritten code against going to authorities. To do so is looked on as tattling or cowardice—getting the teacher to fight your battles for you. This places a child who doesn't want to be drawn into a battle in an awkward position. But children will show unexpected reserves of courage and will be able to stand up to peer pressure if they are clear about their own commitment to rule by law. A child who tattles will be disliked by other children only if they believe his goal is to harm the person he is tattling on. We believe a child *can* earn respect from his peers if he makes it clear to an opponent that he will neither be goaded into a fight *nor* allow himself to be abused—that he chooses to tell the teacher when that's the only sensible way to resolve a dispute.

It will be easier for your youngster to take this kind of stand if you have taught him something about the on-going human struggle, from the dawn of civilization and continuing all over the world today, to establish societies that are governed by law, from village tribal councils to the United Nations and the World Court. It will put his own current confrontations in an idealistic context and make him feel that by upholding rule by law he is part of a rich tradition.

Almost every child gets picked on at one time or another, and studies do confirm that bullies are reinforced when they get what they want. The child who gives in to a bully generally gets picked on again.[48] Therefore, it's important that a child who intends to bring his case to an authority also lets the youngster who is picking on him know that he is doing so because of his strength of character, and not because he is intimidated. One way or another he should communicate that he will not allow anyone to hit him, take his belongings or trample on his rights.

How a youngster should convey this depends on his age and temperament and the circumstances. Some children, for example, can defuse a confrontation through humor while still standing up for themselves. Others will be so busy trying to keep their urge to counterattack in check, or so frightened, that their reaction will probably be more sober and measured. Whatever form it takes, your child should:

1. Let the bully know that he will not go unchallenged anymore ("You can't take any more things from me and you have to give me back what you took").
2. Suggest that it will be in both their interests if they become friends ("I don't mind loaning you something of mine as long as I know I can trust you with it and that I can borrow your things too").
3. Make it clear that if he's forced to defend himself, his *first* choice is to work within the rules and seek the help of an authority ("I think it's dumb for us to start hitting each other over this; that's not why I'm here. So if you keep acting that way, the first thing I'll try is to get the teacher to stop you").

*Children should learn how to defend themselves if necessary*

A youngster should first seek the help of authorities. But sometimes authorities are unavailable, or inept, or corrupt. What, for example, does a child at camp do if he complains to his counselor about a bully and is told to fight his own battles? We assume that most parents don't want their child to be an easy mark.

Since children who defend themselves don't usually get attacked again, it's a good idea to have your child take a self-defense course—one that emphasizes defense. As researchers on street gangs have found, tough kids prefer to pick on easy targets.[49]

If the bully who picks on your child is a lot older and stronger and self-defense is out of the question, or if your child is too frightened or sensitive to hit back, you may have to intervene. Sometimes simply talking to the bully and asking him to stop frightening your child will be sufficient. You might even try asking the bully to become your child's friend and protector. Sometimes you may have to talk to the aggressive child's parents or may have to consult with authorities, or take stronger action yourself.

Besides the plain old-fashioned bullies that have always been around, our children nowadays are often confronted by other children who are truly dangerous, children who carry weapons and who have been in and out of various penal institutions. It is one of the unfortunate aspects of our society that it fails to isolate these dangerous youngsters from the community, often even after they have been convicted of serious crimes. As a consequence, we have subjected ourselves and our families to an epidemic of crime in the streets and schools, and our children (especially if they live in poor, high-crime neighborhoods) grow up frightened and demoralized because they know that the adults they look to for protection aren't really protecting them.

*A reminder:* If you only see to it that your child learns fighting skills, he may get the message that you'll be proud of him if he comes home and tells you about the kids he's beaten up. Make sure he understands that it's more important to you that he learn to avoid fights and defuse confrontations. And don't wait for an incident to occur to teach him this. Spend some time with him sharing ideas about how fights can be avoided so he won't be unprepared if he is bullied.

Children *can* learn to avoid fights in a constructive way. Some friends of ours live in a garden apartment complex with their eleven-year-old daughter, Jessie. A new boy moved into the complex and right from the start began fighting with the other children. After a week of having their games interrupted by this belligerent newcomer, a few of the children decided they would band together and give him a beating. Jessie, whose parents had always stressed that most fights could be avoided if people worked at it, took the initiative to approach the new boy and talk to him privately. She explained that the kids really wanted to be his friend and that she was sure he'd like them if he gave them a chance. She said she understood how hard it is to make friends when you first move into a new place; that it had been hard for her, too. So if he wanted, she would be his first friend and try to help him get to know the rest of the kids. It was an offer he couldn't refuse.

Getting back at someone who has hurt you can be very satisfying. As many writers have pointed out, revenge is sweet. And sometimes it will prevent a person from attacking you again. But revenge tends to go beyond the needs of self-defense and rather than putting an end to the fighting, it sparks an endless cycle of hostilities. It's easy to become obsessed with the goal of getting back at someone. But children *can* learn that revenge-seeking will only bind their lives more tightly to the person they dislike and want to get even with. It is possible, as a recent *New York Times* story shows, to help children develop a perspective that can overcome this knee-jerk impulse for revenge.[50]

On June 7, 1983, a sixth-grade teacher took a group of mostly black and hispanic sixth-grade students from Brooklyn to a Staten Island park for their graduation picnic. One black boy was stopped by two local teenagers as he walked alone on a pathway from the water fountain to the playing field. "This field is for white people only," they said. Soon other neighborhood teenagers—all white—joined the first two to chase the black sixth-graders off the field. "Go back to where you belong," they shouted, throwing rocks and shouting racial slurs at the retreating twelve-year-olds and their teacher.

Six of the schoolchildren received minor injuries. The police arrested a couple of the white teenagers and recorded the episode as a "confirmed bias incident." The parents of the white youngsters were afraid of revenge. As one put it, "If our name is in the paper, they'll come back here to rob us. Those kids from Brooklyn have relatives, uncles, brothers. What if those people from Brooklyn come after us?" And perhaps there was some reason to fear retaliation. The Brooklyn children came from a high-crime area in which 3,534 burglaries had been recorded in 1982, and many Staten Island whites had fled areas like that in order to bring their children up in safe surroundings.

Yet something else was happening back in Brooklyn. It would have been so easy for the sixth-graders to come away from this incident feeling only rejected, defeated, and angry. But the school and the children's parents were taking steps to make these eleven- and twelve-year-olds feel proud of their own "mixed" school and neighborhood, reminding them that theirs was a community in which people of all races were striving against considerable obstacles to live together in harmony. They were also teaching their children to be proud of themselves for not being racists. As one parent expressed it, "Part of the strength of [our school] is that it reflects the racial mix of the real world. And it would be wrong for our children to simply forget what happened that day. They should remember so that they can someday do something about the hatred which exists in this very imperfect, but very real world."

The lessons seemed to be working. A twelve-year-old youngster expressed his growing pride in his own community in this way: "They could come here if they want. Maybe they should. Those kids from Staten Island in their Punk-Rock T-shirts should see that all kinds of kids can get along out here." Another youngster, an eleven-year-old boy, reflecting on his feelings during the attack, said, "I was scared, but I'd rather be scared than a racist." We find that an extraordinary sentiment for a youngster to express. He's saying that he'd rather receive pain than inflict it. Moral leaders from Socrates to Martin Luther King would have been proud of him.

# Part Three

# Moral Development Through the Ages of Childhood

# 7

# Moral Development and Training in Early Childhood: Birth to Age Five

We call this part of the book "Moral Development Through the *Ages* of Childhood" rather than through the *stages* of childhood because, unlike Piaget, Kohlberg, and other stage theorists, we don't believe it is accurate or helpful to break down the developmental changes a child goes through into discrete stages. Stage theories are based more on the philosophical presuppositions of their creators than on controlled observations of children. Indeed, many of the central notions of stage theories, such as Piaget's assertion that infants can't tell the difference between themselves and their environments, cannot possibly be tested even if one wanted to.

One of our favorite illustrations of the problem with stage theories is the study by Jacques Mehler and Thomas Bever on one aspect of Piaget's theory. Piaget believed that children's mental abilities develop through clearly defined stages and that a child is incapable of certain tasks before reaching a certain age. To test this, Mehler and Bever used a standard Piaget task. They placed four stones in a row, spaced widely apart; next to this row they lined up a shorter row of six tightly spaced stones. They then asked four-year-olds to choose which row had more. As Piaget had predicted, the children had difficulty doing this. But when chocolate candies were used instead of stones and the children were asked to "take the row you want to eat," very few of them had any difficulty picking the row with six candies rather than four. From Piaget's point of view, these children were doing the impossible—yet they were doing it very reliably. As we see it, they were, for the first time, being asked to make judgments of "more" in a way that made sense to them, and getting the right answer wasn't hard at all.

In another part of the Mehler and Bever study, contrary to stage-theory prediction, two-year-olds performed better on one of Piaget's standard tasks than three-year-olds, and just as well as four-and-a-half-year-olds. Piaget didn't discover this in his original research because when he found that three-year-olds had problems on the task, he didn't bother to test two-year-olds, *on the assumption* that intellectual development always progresses with age.[1]

Children can understand much more than we give them credit for—as long as what we ask them and tell them makes sense within a framework with which they have some experience. In moral education or any other kind of education it is self-defeating to start out with assumptions about what children are *in*capable of learning. A little more ingenuity on our part might just do the trick.

For instance, not too long ago we were at a small dinner party in Boston when the host's three-year-old daughter asked one of the adult guests where he lived. He promptly replied, "Albany." She asked, "Where's that?" He began to answer, "It's . . ." but stopped short and looked confused. "How do you explain where Albany is to a three-year-old?" he muttered out of the side of his mouth. "Would she understand?" he asked his hostess. "Sure," she said, and proceeded to answer her daughter's question like this: "If we got in the car right after breakfast, and drove out past the supermarket, and then drove and drove all morning, we'd get to Albany just when it was time to have lunch." "Oh," said the little girl, and nodded. Then she turned back to the guest from Albany and said, "So that's why you don't come here a lot."

We don't need a stage theory to recognize that older children know more and have more skills, and can attend to a broader array of stimuli than younger children. Nor do we need stage theories to tell us that all good teaching builds upon what a child can already do. But when parents or teachers start out already convinced of what a child is *not* capable of learning, there is no question that their expectations will be fulfilled.

Although they have been around for years, stage theories have never provided parents and teachers with formats for better teaching. No successful educational program has emerged from them. In fact, even when research has shown that stage theories are not accurate, as when Arthur Staats taught two-year-olds mathematical skills that only five-year-olds were supposed to be able to learn, stage psychologists continued to cling to their positions by claiming that only the "surface behavior" of the children in the study was changed; the inner schemas or mental structures (which, of course, are invisible) were not touched.[2]

In general, there has been much too much disconfirming experimental evidence to base child-rearing programs on stage theories. Piaget's has been the most influential developmental stage theory, and most similar theories, like Kohlberg's, derive from his. But when researchers try to replicate Piaget's findings they usually can't, especially if, like Mehler and Bever, they vary his procedures even slightly. Children are not egocentric in the way he described (even two-year-olds can understand other people's feelings and empathize with them); they also understand causal relationships at a much earlier age than he predicted (they talk about causes before the age of two; not when they reach seven); and they *do* base moral judgments on intentions—to name just a few of the areas in which experimental findings contradict his theory.

Kohlberg, too, clung to his theories regardless of data. For example, in an article that he co-authored with June Tapp he asserted the standard stage-theory position that it is impossible for children below the age of seven to understand that rules may be changed or broken for good reason. He said this despite the fact that in the very same article June Tapp, in a section that she wrote independently, pointed out that her research shows clearly that even five-year-olds understand these things.[3]

For decades now, researchers have been nitpicking endlessly about the fine points of Piaget's and Kohlberg's stage theories, while they've neglected such basic questions as how parents teach their children to respond to the instruction "Be fair," and which ways of teaching fairness are most effective at different ages. Theories of moral development that aren't interested in questions like these are, to say the least, of little practical value.

In this and the chapters that follow we will cover a number of everyday problems in the areas of moral training and development and offer practical solutions based on our "three foundation stones" theory. We cover many of the major moral dilemmas that parents and children face. But, without question, each family will encounter moral challenges that vary from those we discuss. When you try to deal with moral issues in your own family, you will find it helpful to keep going back to the foundation stones and ask yourself the following questions:

- How can I get my children to *want to* follow moral rules?
- How can I arouse their empathic and affectionate feelings?
- How can I get them to want to think of themselves as moral people?

## WHEN MORAL TRAINING BEGINS

We have already discussed the overriding importance of making your child feel loved. This is crucial for moral development since children who feel secure in their parents' love tend to give love back and have an easier time developing friendships—they are more inclined to like people and people usually like them. Three recent studies with preschoolers confirmed that children who were secure in their parents' love were the most socially accepted and self-confident.[4] Securely loved children have an easier time liking and loving because 1) their parents have provided them with good role models on how to express love; and 2) they have not had to develop the kinds of unpleasant strategies that unloved children develop in their desperate attempts to get some attention and affection from unresponsive parents.

Since making a child feel loved has such a profound and enduring effect on his or her feelings for others, moral training can and should begin the very first time you and your child set eyes on each other. Communicate your love right from the start. We've said that moral behavior involves taking pleasure in someone else's pleasure. Remember, then, that the very first experience of moral behavior that your child can have is the awareness of *you* taking pleasure in his pleasure. Unloved children have a hard time learning that such a thing is possible.

You're all your newborn has. She must get you to meet her needs or perish. And she'll sense pretty quickly whether you enjoy being there for her or whether she's mostly a chore for you to deal with. If you are slow to respond to her, she'll scream until you do. If she has to make you miserable in order to get you to attend to her, then that's what she'll do. She has no choice. Taking care of an infant is, unquestionably, taxing. But keep in mind that how she learns to make you attend to her will be the template for all her future exchanges with people. You don't want to teach her that the only way she can get what she needs from people is to irritate them. That would not be a promising beginning for a moral training program.

Your newborn's entire body needs nourishment—his entire body. He needs you to feed him, of course. But his eyes also need to be filled up with smiles from you. His skin needs your caresses. His ears need to hear sweet sounds. If, during his first months and years, he gets these things from you willingly and in abundance then, when he's a little older and beginning to get about and socialize, he'll be able to tell easily and quickly by changes in your expression and tone of voice that he's behaved toward someone in a manner that you disapprove of. And it will be important to him to bring back those smiles and sweet sounds. On the other hand, the less pleasure and more frustration he's received from you, the more important other sources of pleasure will become, and the more willing he will be to risk your anger by doing things that *he* likes, but you don't.

Making your child feel loved is just as important when she's in her second year and her greatest pleasures come from exploring places and things. If she knows that *you* take pleasure in her explorations, she'll be far more willing to accept the limitations that you'll invariably have to impose on her. If she's faced with the hard fact that what is so important and natural to her is just an enormous burden to you and that you aren't really on her side, she'll know she'll have to fight you and badger you to gain any satisfactions in life. Your options then, unfortunately, will be to either suppress her spirit by severe punishment or to eventually give in to her if she manages to pester you long enough or has a big enough tantrum. In either case, moral training won't get off to a good start. Again, you don't want her to learn that the way to get people to give her what she wants is to become sufficiently annoying.

Our point is that if you are caring and sensitive to your infant during her earliest years, she'll be inclined to do what you ask, to respect your wishes, and do her best to be cooperative.

A study demonstrating exactly this was carried out about a dozen years ago by Donelda Stayton, Robert Hogan, and Mary Salter-Ainsworth. They observed nine- to twelve-month-old boys and girls interacting with their mothers in their homes. They found that mothers who were sensitive, accepting, and cooperative had children who generally obeyed them and did what they asked. These mothers did not have to use force to get their children to cooperate, nor did they have to give a lot of orders. By and large, the children went along without conflict. In other words, children who were treated with sensitivity and cooperation tended to be sensitive and cooperative in turn.

Exactly what does it mean to be a sensitive, accepting, and cooperative parent to a one-year-old child? Stayton and her colleagues gave these definitions:

**Sensitive:** "finely attuned to the baby's signals and communications and able to see things from his point of view . . . [responding] promptly and appropriately"

**Accepting:** "accept[s] almost all aspects of the baby's behavior . . . and . . . the responsibility of caring for him without chafing at the temporary restrictions of her usual activities"

**Cooperative:** "avoids imposing her will on the baby, but, rather, arranges the environment and her schedule so as to minimize any need to interrupt or to control him . . . helps him to accept her wishes or controls as something congenial to him"

Of great importance was the finding that the children of sensitive, accepting, and cooperative mothers were already beginning to show signs of "internalized controls"; they "were observed to initiate and then spontaneously arrest any act which had been forbidden or punished in the . . . past." These researchers propose that when parents are sensitive, accepting, and cooperative it not only fosters simple compliance in the child's first year but it also seems to promote internalized controls in the second year. This suggestion has now been confirmed by other investigators studying children who were approaching two years of age. Among the details added by the new study were the findings that mothers who gave their children directives in a warm tone of voice and who handled them affectionately when physically guiding their behavior, had the most cooperative and self-controlled youngsters.[5]

So giving your child lots of love (otherwise known as being sensitive, accepting, cooperative, warm, and affectionate) not only fosters her attachment to you, but also primes her to obey and internalize your instructions. By the time she starts her third year, many of your directives will be about how she treats people. By then she'll be a social—and therefore, a moral—being and will be able to be both hurtful and kind to others. She will learn the moral lessons you teach her much more quickly if, because of the love you've given her, she's already disposed to do what you ask and to internalize the rules you set.

Formal moral instruction can actually begin even before your child has reached her tenth month. When your child is too rough with other children, pets, or with you, teach her to "make nice" or "be gentle." This is a very important lesson and many parents do it naturally. Say your baby daughter investigates the family dog the same way she investigates any interesting object—by banging or pulling on it. Take her hand and say no. Say it firmly but not harshly. Then say "Make nice" or "Be gentle" and move her hand gently through the dog's fur. Repeat the word *nice* or *gentle*. And repeat it again as you pet the dog, providing a model of gentleness. Then pet your child gently on her cheek or forehead while saying "nice" or "gentle" so she understands how nice or gentle feels. Even a ten-month-old can learn to behave more gently this way. After a while, just the reminders "gentle" or "nice" will affect how she behaves. This is her very first lesson in modifying her behavior according to what or whom she is dealing with. It is a first step toward sensitivity to others.

You can add another lesson a short while later by teaching her the word *ouch*. Whenever she hurts herself, say the word *ouch* and point to the spot she hurt. Soon she'll make the connection between the word and the feeling (and when she starts to speak she'll actually say "Ouch" whenever she hurts herself). Then when she does something that hurts someone else, point to the hurt spot (the dog's tail) and say "Ouch." This will help her understand that her actions can hurt others, and it's often all that is needed to get a child to refrain from acting that way again.

On about his first birthday, your toddler will start to give you things. He'll hand you toys, objects, and food (often right from his mouth). Be very appreciative. He will enjoy seeing you smile and hearing your "Thank you." In this way he will learn that giving makes others feel good and that, in turn, it makes one feel good oneself. You can encourage this giving by asking your child when he is handling an object, "May I have that?" and putting your hand out. If he places the object in your hand, express your delight. He will often want what he has given you right back. Express delight on giving it back to him so he sees that you find giving a pleasure. If he refuses to give you something, don't criticize him. Just try again later.

If your nine- or ten-month-old is becoming too whiny and fussy, complaining loudly over every inconvenience, such as diapering or dressing, or when you take an extra few seconds preparing her food, you can ask for and insist on some self-control and cooperation. You can cut off her fussiness with a sharp "Uh uh" or "Hey" or "No whining." This will draw her attention momentarily away from her own discomfort to yours—as long as your tone isn't so sharp that it frightens her. Then explain in firm but affectionate tones that you need some cooperation from her. She won't understand your words, but will attend to your communication, at least briefly. When the whining starts up again, remind her firmly, "No whining." This will extend a child's ability to tolerate the inevitable delays and frustrations of daily activities. But you will have to be sensitive to occasions when it is inappropriate to ask a young child for self-control, such as when she is very hungry or bored, overly tired, in pain, or frightened. You can also avoid many frustrations by anticipating times when your child gets fussy and having interesting objects handy to distract her and by turning routine activities into games or occasions for songs, and by labeling and explaining what you are doing. Still, no matter how hard you try to anticipate her needs, some frustration for her is inevitable and you'll have to insist that she learn patience.

Also, be as sparing as possible with your *no*'s. If, for example, your child is banging a toy on a piece of furniture that you're afraid he'll damage, a clear but good-humored "Uh-uh" or "No," followed by shifting his attention toward another object that he can explore, should be sufficient to teach him that he is not supposed to bang there. But expect to have to repeat the lesson a few times. If you accept and enjoy his delight in exploring objects by banging them together you won't find the repetition too burdensome. On the other hand, a harsh reprimand may very well make him fear the piece of furniture or the part of the room it is in, and may also make him afraid to explore in your presence. Save the firm, alarmed uh-uhs and no's for actions that must be stopped immediately and never repeated—that is, those that may harm him or others, such as chewing on an electric wire or poking at a sibling's eyes. The alarm in your voice is all that is needed to convey your message. Don't tell a child he is bad for doing something that comes naturally to him when he could not possibly have understood the danger he put himself or someone else in.

Remember also that unless you are consistent in your reactions your child will be confused about your rules. We recently saw a parent enjoy chaperoning her toddler on her climbs up and down the staircase in their home. A few minutes later, just after the parent had sat down with a cup of coffee and a snack, the toddler headed for the staircase again. The weary mother shouted out a harsh, "No. No." Unfortunately, there was no way her eleven-month-old could learn the lesson that it is all right to climb the stairs when mother is feeling energetic, but not when she is resting on a coffee break. The incident would have had a happier ending if the mother had placed a gate in front of the staircase or had provided the child with an alternate activity that was engaging enough to occupy her throughout the much needed coffee break.

## RESPONDING TO AN INFANT'S CRY

Some parents are afraid of being *too* responsive to their child. For instance, they ask, "If I pick up my child whenever he cries, won't I be reinforcing crying and won't he cry more?" Yes, you can reinforce crying. If you don't give your baby much stimulation and affection except when he's crying, then he is certainly likely to cry more often for you. On the other hand, you can reduce this kind of demanding crying if, as psychologists Barbara Etzel and Jacob Gewirtz demonstrated with both a six-week-old and a twenty-week-old infant, you give your child pleasurable stimulation and affection when he's not crying. If you're generous with your affection, he won't need to cry for it. Then when he does cry you can feel pretty certain it's because he's uncomfortable in some way.

In fact, *do* pick your infant up when he cries. Comforting a crying newborn doesn't produce more crying; it produces less. Sylvia Bell and Mary Salter-Ainsworth confirmed this by tracing the relationship between infant crying and maternal comforting during the first year of life. They found that "Mothers who ignore and delay in responding to the crying of an infant when he is tiny have babies who cry more frequently and persistently later on, which in turn further discourages the mother from responding promptly and results in a further increase of infant irritability."[6]

When you respond to your infant's crying quickly, she won't have to acquire the habit of badgering you to get you to attend to her. She'll only cry when she's uncomfortable and it won't take her long to learn that she can count on you to be there when she feels bad. She'll see that you are responsive to her signals, and that badgering is unnecessary. When in her second year she can begin to use words and gestures to signal her needs to you, she will. She'll have learned that simple signals are all that are necessary to get your attention—

prolonged crying isn't needed. And since she'll feel secure that you are on her side, she'll accept your rules and restrictions with far less fuss than a child who has learned that she has to make trouble for you before you respond to her needs.

By teaching your infant that she can get people to respond to her needs without her having to use coercion, you are, in effect, setting the stage for all later moral development. And she'll want to reciprocate your affection. For instance, you'll find that she's likely to begin to share her things with you on her own initiative. In a study of nineteen-month-old children, Robert Klein and Leon Yarrow found that the children of affectionate mothers were much more likely to show and give things and exchange smiles with them.[7]

But what if your child is already a marathon crier? What should you do, for example, if he shrieks endlessly at bedtime? What if you've already established a pattern in which he cries, you hold out for a while but then give in and come back into the room and pick him up? More than likely you've inadvertently shaped his long-distance crying abilities by holding out a bit longer and longer on successive nights. Some psychologists suggest one way you break your child of this is by holding out for as long as it takes, which may be a couple of hours.[8]

But we recommend a different approach—one that doesn't pit your will against your child's in such a cut-and-dried way. Get him good and tired and do your best to keep the mood pleasant and calm as you prepare him for bed. Sing to him or tell him a story. Be affectionate even if he starts to fuss. Caress him, kiss him, then say goodnight, dim the lights, and leave. After you leave him alone and he starts to cry, wait for two minutes. Then go to him. Calmly and pleasantly say, "No, no. It's time for sleep." Stroke his head with your hand—and leave quickly. If the crying continues (expect it to), wait two minutes and do the same thing. Then leave again. Repeat this sequence until he falls asleep. And repeat it for the next few nights if necessary.

You want him to know that you are nearby if he needs you, but beyond that you want to keep all stimulation to a minimum. Your very regular entrances should make him feel secure about your presence. But once he apprehends that your appearances are certain, dull, and unvarying, he'll get bored and fall asleep. It shouldn't take more than a few nights of this for him to accept his bedtime more peacefully.

Whatever technique you try with your child, remember that your love for him is communicated by the entire pattern of your behavior toward him, and not by any single incident or over any single issue (like bedtime). Any technique has to be adapted to the child, and every child is different. Some come into the world relatively placid and easy to comfort, while others scream for hours for no discernible reason and nothing calms them for very long. Also, every family is different. Some parents are able to devote their entire day to their child. Others have obligations that simply cannot be neglected— other children or jobs—so that even if they want to attend to his every whimper, they simply aren't able to. A child can feel loved growing up in many different kinds of family circumstances.

We've recommended comforting your child as much as possible, but sometimes parents find that they need to put a crying and inconsolable baby in another room to just cry it out. They may need to do this because other work *must* be done or because they simply can't bear another moment of screaming, and nothing they are doing is comforting him anyway. There's no evidence that letting a baby cry himself to sleep once in a while does any harm.

Living happily with a child, like living happily with anyone, depends on balancing everyone's needs and learning to compromise. A newborn obviously cannot compromise at all. She has a few pressing needs that want immediate satisfaction and she can't recognize that you're tired today or have soup boiling over on the stove. When she wants food that's all she knows. You might distract her for a short while with a pacifier or some rocking, but not for very long.

Little by little your baby will be capable of some self-control and will be able to engage in some give and take. But it's not easy for parents to tell what kind of self-control their child is capable of. For instance, does a two-month-old have any control over his crying for food, or is he just helplessly responding as his system dictates? If you give in are you reinforcing his crying? Or is the crying simply a reflex that's going to follow its natural course whenever he's hungry, no matter what you do?

Although research on infant feeding is shockingly rare ("feeding" is not even listed in the index of most child psychology texts), pediatricians nowadays generally recommend demand feeding in the belief that an infant's system can't really adapt to a schedule; that she doesn't have much control when it comes to hunger. If you put your infant on a four-hour schedule, she'll probably cry for hours until she's fed (or falls asleep from exhaustion). Then, some time between her second and fifth months, she'll start to adapt to the schedule, eating every four hours or so without long bouts of crying beforehand. But the schedule you imposed may not have had anything to do with her new cycle since demand-fed babies arrive at pretty much the same schedule at about the same time—but with a lot less suffering along the way.[9]

The question of how much you can reasonably demand from your child will come up many times during his upbringing. It's not always an easy question to answer, particularly for parents who want to be sensitive to their child's needs and fears and emotional states. For instance, if your child develops a phobia and won't leave the house, should you push him to confront whatever is frightening him or allow him to avoid facing it and stay home? You can often find good compromises—such as helping a phobic child learn how to overcome fears (perhaps through the confidence procedures described earlier).

But sometimes you'll push your child too hard or not hard enough. Don't agonize over your mistakes. Talk about them together, explaining why you did what you did. The important thing is that your child recognizes that you truly want to be sensitive to her. You may not always succeed and her needs can't always come first, but if she's secure about your love and knows that her pleasure is your pleasure, then she'll be okay and won't resent you (for long) for your mistakes. She'll trust you and want to be sensitive to you, too. When this happens, you and she will have developed a moral relationship that will give her a solid model for all her future relationships.

## COPING WITH OPPOSITIONAL TODDLERS AND PRESCHOOLERS

We've seen that children who are brought up with affection tend to be responsive to their parents' instructions. But what should you do if your child has turned out to be difficult—if he's often disobedient or, as these children are sometimes called, "oppositional"?

### Anticipate Your Child's Needs and Prepare Him or Her for Problem Areas

First, make sure *you* are being responsive to your child's needs. Sometimes children are difficult because we put them in unnecessarily difficult situations. Some years ago on a seven-hour flight to

Europe, we were sitting across the aisle from a mother and her four-year-old son. About an hour after takeoff, the boy became fussy and cranky. First, he began banging seat belts together. Soon he was storming down the aisle, kicking the seats and making a general nuisance of himself. It was very unpleasant for everyone around, especially his mother. She kept retrieving him, putting him back in his seat, and telling him to quiet down—which he did for about five minutes, after which the bothersome activity began again.

The problem was that this little boy was doing just what a normal, healthy, totally bored child should be expected to do. He was seeking some stimulation. His mother had brought magazines along for herself, and she listened to music on the rented earphones, and she watched the movie when she wasn't fetching the boy back to his seat. But she had not brought anything along to amuse or occupy her son. When he quietly sat down next to her, she did not talk to him, except for occasional "business" talks about food and bathrooms. Most four-year-olds cannot stimulate themselves for seven hours by quiet contemplation. Most adults can't, either.

You can see this same kind of unresponsive parental behavior any day of the week in your local supermarket. Too often parents expect their children to sit in the shopping cart, unmoving and obedient, for up to forty-five minutes as they are wheeled past a dazzling array of colors and shapes and other people with their children. Not likely.

Recognizing that not all parents have the same kind of difficulty with their children in supermarkets, psychologist George Holden decided to investigate why. He observed twenty-four mothers and their two-and-a-half-year-old children on two separate shopping trips and discovered that the mothers who had fewer problems with their children were those who anticipated the child's needs. They initiated conversations with them and provided them with objects and food without always waiting to be asked. As one mother put it, "I try to anticipate and structure the environment so we don't run into problems." Another said, "You have to carry on a toddler-level conversation." Some mothers, who had problems with their toddlers had, unfortunately, come to see shopping trips as a testing of wills.

Shopping is such a common area of parent-child conflict that psychologists at the University of Kansas went so far as to devise a "Parent Advice Package for Family Shopping Trips." This was designed to help parents teach "good shopping" behavior to children of grade-school age who often see supermarkets as great play-

grounds. Some of their recommendations include giving clear behavioral guidelines in advance, such as "Stay close enough to reach
out our arms and touch hands—this means we will be close enough
to talk to one another and please do not roughhouse, run, yell,
fight, or hang on other children in the store because this will slow
up our shopping and bother other people in the store."

These researchers made two other recommendations that we particularly like because each recognizes and respects the needs of the
child. They suggested that the last few minutes of the shopping trip
be set aside for the child to shop so that it is her shopping trip, too.
At that point she can spend part of her allowance on things that *she*
wants (although for every violation of one of the good-shopper rules
they suggest making a nickel deduction).

They also recommended that parents talk to their children about
the shopping they were doing, about interesting items, and where
things could be found.

Parents should make it a practice to anticipate and prepare their
children for the times and places where problem behavior is likely
to occur. Depending on the child, this may be at mealtimes, or
during the mornings while getting ready for school, or at the community center. Psychologists Matthew Sanders and Mark Dadds set
up just such a program. First they had parents identify their child's
"high risk" settings—those in which he was likely to get into trouble. Parents then prepared their children in advance for these settings by discussing specific rules with them, outlining acceptable
activities (finding items on a shopping list, playing quiet games in
the car), and, when necessary, had the child practice the desired
behaviors. The programs turned out to be highly effective.[10]

## Be a Respectful and Cooperative Parent

You might ask, Does a child's behavior in the supermarket or at
mealtimes really have anything to do with morality? The answer is
yes, because his behavior in these places affects you and other people. He can be a terrible pest or a respectful and cooperative companion. But remember that in order for him to be respectful, he has
to be treated with respect. And that means that you, too, have to be
a respectful companion, and respect his right to be a child with a
child's curiosity, enthusiasms, and short attention span, as well as a
child's lack of knowledge about how to behave properly until someone teaches this to him. Similarly, if you want him to be cooperative,

you'll have to give *him* cooperation. You'll have to make his goals important to you. Most children will be very eager to meet you halfway. If you respect and cooperate with them, they'll respect and cooperate with you.

Keep in mind that the opposite of an oppositional child is not an obedient one. It is a respectful and cooperative one. If your youngster respects you, she will *give* you authority over her. You won't have to drag it out of her. On the other hand, if you demand unquestioning obedience from her, the only way to get it is by making sure she fears you and has no confidence in herself. Cooperation is a two-way street.

You'll find it a lot easier to give your child respect and cooperation if you recognize the following:

***Recognize that his activities and interests are truly important to him.*** Respecting your child's interests means, for one thing, that you never ridicule his activities or goals. Maybe he likes to play checkers a lot, and you find this a foolish waste of time and energy. While it *is* your responsibility to guide his activities and extend his interests, and that may mean making demands on how he spends his time, there is never any reason to make him feel bad for what he enjoys, so long as he's not harming anyone.

Respecting his interests also means that, whenever possible, you will give him some advance notice before changing his activities. Try to avoid just springing orders on him when he is in the middle of a game or project or a conversation that he is enjoying. Don't just intrude with "Come on, we're going," or "Bring it immediately." Give him some time to finish, or at least wind down from whatever he was doing. You'd want the same consideration for yourself, and research shows that advance notice leads to much less resistance and conflict.[11] Set up a signal so that he knows that when you do say "immediately," you have good reason to and an immediate response on his part is necessary.

***Recognize and respect your child's style of loving.*** Children differ in the degree to which they enjoy physical contact, like hugs, kisses, and being held, and many go through phases when they want more or less physical contact with their parents. The eleven-year-old son of a friend of ours asked his father not to put his arm around him when he was with his schoolmates. The boy said, "I like it when you put your arm around me at home, but it makes me feel funny if you do it in front of the kids."

Don't make overt affection a test of your child's love, and don't make him feel guilty because he doesn't spontaneously express his love in a form that pleases you. If you want more physical contact, ask for it. There's nothing wrong with teaching your child *how* you need to be loved, as long as you're not also saying, "You don't love me enough. I need more."

Here's an example of a father doing what we thought was a pretty good job of expressing his need for physical contact to his six-year-old daughter, who wasn't very keen on hugging. He didn't criticize her for not hugging him more or make her feel guilty. He communicated *his* need: "I know you don't like a lot of hugging, but sometimes a hug from you is exactly what I need to make me feel good. So once in a while, when I ask you for a hug, I'd like you not to think about whether you want to or not but just to think, 'Daddy really needs a hug now,' and come over and give me a nice big one."

In every relationship people need adjustments from each other; a little more of this and less of that. To one degree or another, we all have to teach the people we love how we need to express and receive love. There's no better way than telling them directly. As long as it isn't our insecurities that compel us to ask for affection as proof that the other person really loves us, we shouldn't have trouble keeping our requests within a range that takes into consideration his or her needs as well as our own.

***Recognize that she has a right to her own tastes and preferences.*** When your youngster voices a preference, unless there's some strong reason to say no, *say yes*. One afternoon we were in a sandwich shop with a friend of ours, his new fiancée, and his two children, ages seven and nine, from a previous marriage. All kinds of meats and cheeses were on display at the counter. The youngsters looked them over carefully, consulted together, and then asked for two brie-and-baloney sandwiches. The fiancée grimaced, "Ugh, that's awful. You're not going to let them have that, are you?" she asked. "Why not?" the father replied. "They like brie and they like baloney. Maybe they'll like them together. If they want to try it, it's all right with me." He told his children to share one sandwich first to see if they liked it. If they didn't, they were to get a more traditional combination for their second choice. As it turned out, the children did like the sandwich, but from the fiancée's comments and grimaces it was clear that she still did not approve.

Without question, we feel the father did well. He was respecting his children's preferences and there was no reason to do otherwise. He gave them the same freedom he would have demanded for himself. And he didn't do anything to turn their little taste odyssey into a tense event with threats like "Okay, but you'd better eat every bit of it." He respected their interest in trying new foods. Of course, once in a while they tried something they didn't like and it ended up costing him an extra few dollars. But that was okay, he felt. He said that he would impose a limit on what they could try if it got too costly, but this wasn't necessary. His youngsters didn't pick foods randomly or frivolously; they tried what they thought they would like and usually they were right.

One would think from the fiancée's reaction that brie-and-baloney was an *indecent* combination, that in some way it was wrong to eat those foods together. Obviously, what foods most of us think go well together is based totally on the conventions of our culture. Just as obviously, every culture has different tastes. Respecting your child's preferences means that you don't turn matters of taste, custom, and convention into moral issues of right and wrong. Parents who do this have endless conflicts with their children. What's more, even if you do treat a conventional issue, such as a dress code or bedtime, as a moral issue, your children are going to be able to tell the difference.

Research confirms this. One group of psychologists that observed hundreds of children in preschool and school settings found that children of all ages, from two-and-a-half-year-olds to adolescents, know the difference between breaking a moral rule and a conventional one.[12] Moreover, children take moral rules (rules against hurting and being unfair) far more seriously than conventional rules (say, school rules about what part of the lunchroom to eat in or where class assignments should be done). They said that harming a classmate was wrong even if the school had no rule against it; but when it came to practical behavior such as where you are supposed to eat or do your work, right and wrong depended totally on what rules the school had made up. This finding is particularly important because it helps explain why children don't usually resist moral rules while they often fight conventional ones with all their strength.

Moral rules seem reasonable to them because they know that unkindness and injustice hurt. Youngsters may not always want to live up to moral rules, but they don't usually question that they are reasonable (that is, until they get to college and study philosophy).

On the other hand, children recognize that social conventions are based on habit, taste, and convenience (although not usually *their* convenience), and they are quite ready to resist adult-imposed conventions and find ones that are more to their liking.

The cultural forces that shape social conventions evolve and change over time. As a result parents may find that their children's tastes are very different from the ones they themselves acquired twenty or more years earlier. Moreover, even when children adopt their parents' basic values, they may apply them in unexpected ways. For example, parents who bring up their children to value independence and self-expression are often surprised and dismayed when their youngsters apply these same values to what they wear or how they cut their hair. Similarly, parents who bring up children to value social equality and scientific achievement may not anticipate that this might lead their youngsters to question their religion's rituals or its marital, sexual, and dietary codes.

We cannot stress enough the importance of keeping moral and conventional issues separate. Just because your child resists you in matters of taste and social convention doesn't mean she'll resist your moral training. Young children *do* understand and care about morality and they expect and want parents to take a stand against moral transgressions. If you tell children, even four-year-olds, a story about a mother who let her child refuse to give a toy back, or permitted her to throw sand at other children, or hurt a puppy, or be rude or destructive, most children would say when questioned that she was not a good mother. In contrast, if this hypothetical mother did try to stop her child from doing these things, almost all children would judge her as good. This is exactly what psychologists Michael Siegal and Jackie Rablin asked youngsters between the ages of four and eight, and this is exactly what they found. They report that "a large majority of all children, regardless of age, sex, or social class, preferred the interventionist mother and responded that misbehavior is naughty regardless of whether mothers care to intervene.[13]

Giving children choices respects the fact that they have preferences. But sometimes giving a child a choice is inappropriate. If you are taking your two-year-old on a boat and he protests about wearing a life jacket, you're obviously not going to let him have his way. You're not going to let him make choices when he doesn't have the information or experience to make competent judgments. You are not going to let him harm himself or someone else.

When you do give your child a choice, be patient about how long she takes to make a decision. Some children, like some adults, weigh alternatives very carefully, and with their limited experience it's not easy for them to figure out which of two possible future events they would enjoy. For many children it takes a lot of thought to answer a question like, "Would you rather go to the circus or the zoo?" Ask yourself right now, "Would I rather go to Paris or Rome?" Lots of images related to these cities will pass through your thoughts. For most of you it will take a bit of time to work your way through what you know about these cities and decide which is more appealing. Children have the same difficulty; and since they aren't very practiced in comparing things in a systematic way, they often need some time and perhaps a little prompting. You might ask, "Would you rather look at an elephant doing tricks or would you rather ride on one at the zoo?"

**Negativism.** Sometimes parents find that when they give their two-year-olds choices, they just feed into their child's growing negativism. Two-year-olds are beginning to learn that they have some real power in the family. When a parent or sibling wants something from them, they can say yes or no, and sometimes saying no has a much greater impact on everyone. So they say no a lot. One way around this is to avoid presenting options in a way that calls for a yes or no reply.

Thus, if your daughter is going through a negative phase, don't ask her, "Would you like to share one of your cookies with Katie?" You're likely to get an abrupt "No." You'll do better if you phrase your question like this: "Which of your cookies would you like to share with Katie?" That's far more likely to lead to actual sharing, particularly if you follow up the question with a hint that makes her think about Katie's pleasure rather than her own loss. For example, you might say, "Try to remember which kind of cookie Katie likes best. She'll be pleased that you cared enough to pick her favorite."

When a child has a bad case of the no's, it's a good idea to point out how all those no's affect other people. For example, if your youngster habitually refuses requests, tell him it makes people think that he doesn't like them and their feelings get hurt when he doesn't even consider giving them what they asked for. Remind him of how good he feels when people give him something he has asked for and that it makes him feel loved and important. If necessary, give him a taste of his own medicine by refusing a request "on principle."

*Recognize and respect the fact that your young child must first be taught the rules of "good" behavior before he or she can be expected to follow them.* How should a child know what is the courteous way to behave in a supermarket or what you mean by "Be polite" when you have friends visiting? "Respectful" behavior in most situations seems so natural to us as adults that it's easy to forget that we once had to learn it. Those of you that have visited exotic places like Japan (or even formal Japanese restaurants) have probably had a refresher course in how awkward one can feel when one is uncertain about social rules. You need to teach your child not only that being kind and respectful is good, but *how to be* kind and respectful. Direct instruction, stories, modeling, and role-playing are all ways to do this.

Ruth Sidel described an interesting example of such direct moral training as she observed it in a Chinese nursery:

> [The children] learn to "care for each other, love and help each other," through stories, pictures, and lantern slides, but most important they learn through actual activities. We were told repeatedly that if a child falls down, other children are taught to help him up. The teacher does not run to him but encourages the other children to go to him and help him. At the moment the child falls, the teacher says to the other children, "We have to help each other," and encourages them to do so right then. When I asked in some disbelief at what age the children would "help" each other, she said that by three they were doing it. "At the beginning it is under the instruction of the teacher; but then it gets to be a habit. In the winter the children wear jackets with buttons up the back; since they cannot reach their own buttons, they button each other up; again, they are encouraged to help each other."[14]

Direct instruction is only one way to teach children. They also learn a great deal by simply observing how others behave. That's why it's so important to set a good example for your child and to point out other role models. In research done in the early 1970s psychologists Elizabeth Midlarsky and James Bryan confirmed that children will become more generous by simply observing someone else's generosity. What's more, they also found two ways to make the role model's influence even stronger, and these techniques can be used easily by parents.

One is to explain to your child the specific way his act of kindness will benefit someone. The children in the study could win money playing a game, and they were free to donate some of their winnings to a "needy children's" charity. But first the youngsters watched someone else play the game. This person began by saying, "I think that I'll like this game. It seems like fun. I hope that I'll win some money because I'd really like to give some to the needy children . . . if I were a needy child, I would feel important just knowing that other(s) cared about me enough to leave money for me." The children who heard this kind of "exhortation" describing how the needy children would feel gave more money when it was their turn.[15]

The second technique Midlarsky and Bryan used was having the role model express how good he felt after donating. He said things like, "Giving to the poor makes me feel good," and "Giving is really fun." Whatever the nature of the feeling ("fun" may not be the best description), it's worth letting your children know when you feel good about something you've done for others. Of course, you don't want to sound as if you are boasting about your generosity. You can avoid this by stressing that what made you feel good was strengthening a bond with, and meeting your responsibility to, your fellow human beings, rather than that what you did was out of the ordinary or remarkable.

### Use Rewards and Punishment Wisely

Observations of over 100 two-year-olds and their parents in the home confirmed that a good way to get your child to do what you ask is to ask him or her in a nice way. How obvious; yet how easy to forget. But what can you do when your child remains resistant and stubborn? You can increase his or her compliance and cooperativeness by using reward and punishment wisely.

Among the best-established principles in psychology are that you can increase the frequency of behavior by rewarding (or reinforcing) it, and decrease the frequency of behavior both by making sure it goes unrewarded or by punishing it.

***Rewards.*** Research shows that you can get your toddler to be more cooperative and less resistant by giving him rewards, like hugs and praise, when he follows directives.[16] Many parents do this naturally. When they first teach their child the meaning of simple directives like *come, give,* and *bring,* they lavish lots of praise on him when he does the right thing. Then they gradually get him used to receiving rewards only once in a while, saying things like, "You're a good boy" and "You're nice to have around," only every so often.

As your child gets a bit older and you stop making a fuss over him every time he does something you ask, don't fall into the trap of neglecting to show any appreciation at all when he complies. You don't want him to feel taken for granted. Praise ("You're a good boy and nice to have around") and affection (smiles and hugs) are the best kinds of rewards to use because they not only make him feel good, they also indicate that his actions made you feel good. It's important for him to know that he has the power to make you feel good. On the other hand, if you tell him that you'll buy him a toy or let him watch television if he's good, your feelings only become worth considering because they are the means to a totally selfish end (the toy or TV).

If you and your child have gotten off to a bad start and your praise and affection don't have much value for him, you may have to rely temporarily on material reinforcers like toys and television time. A reinforcer can be anything your child would, if he could, have more of (praise from you, an ice cream cone), or *do* more of (talk to you, go horseback riding).[17]

To insure that you won't always have to use material rewards, don't just "do business" with your child, exchanging so many hours of television time for so much good behavior (such as hours without fighting). This only teaches her that her bad behavior annoys you enough to pay to get her to stop. It teaches her nothing about exchanging affection. Therefore, make sure to tell her that the reason you are arranging to give her a toy or more television time when she's good is because when she's good, you feel good about her and you enjoy giving her things she likes. You want her to experience your affection and associate it with the pleasant feelings she gets from receiving the toy or whatever material reward you give her. Before long your affection should become important to her in its own right. At that point you won't have to use material rewards to get her to live up to the rules you set for her.

**Punishment.** There are times when rewarding good behavior isn't enough. Sometimes a child's misbehavior must be stopped quickly, particularly when he behaves in ways that put him or someone else in danger. At such times you may not be able to wait for a reward program to take effect. In addition, there are times when rewards aren't working because your child has access to other, more powerful, rewards that you have little control over, for instance, from friends who give him attention when he misbehaves.

Research on children in the home and in school shows that punishments in the form of *forceful reprimands* and *time out* will often work quickly to stop misbehavior. A forceful reprimand is one that you deliver promptly, making eye contact while standing near your child, and, if necessary, holding her in place with a firm grasp on her shoulder. This will be more effective than reprimands that are delivered in an offhand or casual way. You want your child to know that you mean business, that the issue is of such concern to you that you are willing to stop what you are doing to make sure she won't continue her misbehavior. And it's always important to give your child an explanation of why you are taking such a firm stand so she understands the harmful consequences of her actions and that you are not being arbitrarily harsh with her.

*Time out* can take various forms. The purpose of this technique is to make sure the child can't engage in or enjoy her misbehavior. One form of time out is to take objects away: "You can't play with that toy for a half-hour because you hit people with it." Other forms include sending a child to her room for a specified period of time or demanding that she sit by herself for a while.

Time out works best when: **1)** it is instituted promptly; **2)** you make clear why you are using it; **3)** you add penalty time if your child causes a disturbance during time out; and **4)** you state what behavior would have been appropriate in that situation. An explanation doesn't just inform a child, "You disobeyed me, therefore go to your room." You have to let her know exactly why it is important to you that she stop what she's doing.[18]

As a general principle, discipline techniques like reprimands and time out work best when you give your child lots of positive attention. If you only give her attention when you discipline her, discipline can turn into a perverse kind of reward; she'll misbehave just to get you to notice and spend time with her.

## TEACHING PROSOCIAL BEHAVIOR

In the past few decades psychologists have begun to use the word *prosocial* to refer to any action that a person takes in order to benefit someone else. It is synonymous with the word *kind*. It includes sharing, helping, protecting, giving aid and comfort, befriending, showing affection, and giving encouragement.

As most parents know, preschoolers are capable of every one of these behaviors. You might want to make a list of them as a reminder to yourself to make sure that your child is learning each of them. Then make a note on the list whenever you see her act in a kind way and also note whenever you do anything to teach or encourage her to behave kindly. The list will then serve as a chart of her prosocial lessons and provide you with an ongoing record to see if the lessons are working. You can reinforce prosocial behavior even if it occurs infrequently. You will find that even a generally self-centered youngster will act kindly once in a while. Your job is to *catch him in the act of being good* and then reinforce it. You might say, "I saw you share your toy with the boy in the playground. That was very kind of you and it made me feel proud of you."

If by your child's early or middle school years treating others kindly has become a personal standard for him, you may sense that he would rather not have you comment every time he behaves kindly. One reason for this is that he may not want you to think he does nice things as a way to get your approval—although he may still be pleased that you notice and feel proud of him. At these times a simple smile is sufficient.

It's worth remembering that praise is not an automatic reinforcer. In fact, if your child thinks you are trying to manipulate her through praise, then praising something she does may make her think twice before she ever does it again. Let's say you heap compliments on her for being kind, yet she suspects that you don't *really* care whether or not she treats people kindly but are only interested in impressing the neighbors by boasting about her or in using the incident as a way to reopen your case against her spending time with certain friends ("Why's a nice kid like you hanging around with friends like that?"). Praising her can then have the opposite effect of the one you want.

Reinforcing prosocial or kind behavior is good, but if that's all you do—wait for your youngster to act kindly and then reinforce her for it—learning will be unnecessarily slow. You should also give her prosocial assignments ("Be helpful"), instruct her on how to carry them out, stimulate her empathy for others, serve as a prosocial model yourself, point out other good models, and help her develop prosocial values.

To act kindly, a child must first recognize other people's needs and then want to meet them. But her kind intentions can only be helpful if she knows what to do to help. Take comforting, for example. If after recognizing that someone is in pain, a child wants to ease that person's pain, she must know how to give comfort, the first step of which is trying to understand what led to the person's unhappiness. Fortunately, even two-year-olds are already pretty good at connecting people's happy and unhappy states to the circumstances that gave rise to them. Psychologists Inge Bretherton and Marjorie Beeghly recorded children's "causal utterances" to illustrate this ability. Some of their examples are: "You better get shirt so you won't freeze," "I'm hurting your feelings cause I was mean to you," "Grandma mad. I wrote on wall," and "You sad, mommy. What daddy do?"

These researchers also recorded statements that showed that two-year-olds are already developing comforting skills. For example: "Take bubble bath, mom, to get warm," "I give a hug. Baby be happy," "No cry, mamma. It will be all right," and "Don't feel bad, Bob."

By the time children are about five most have had enough experience to know the kinds of things that generally bother and please people, and that to help someone who is unhappy, it's useful to know what caused his or her unhappiness.[19]

In teaching a child about comforting, keep in mind that giving comfort can take many forms. These include:

- letting the person know that you care that he feels bad and that you will do whatever you can to ease his unhappiness
- giving him something or saying something to cheer him up
- reminding him of the good things in his life and that pain passes in time
- hugging him
- listening without judging if he wants to talk about what's bothering him
- reassuring him that it's all right to feel bad and to express emotions
- bolstering his faith in his ability to endure the pain or overcome a setback
- helping him gain a different, less painful perspective on the situation
- helping him figure out what to do to make the situation better

Which of these actions will actually provide comfort depends on the person who is hurt, his particular need, and your child's relationship to him. Some ways of comforting are obviously more sophisticated than others and what kinds of comfort a child can give will change as he grows up. But it's not uncommon for two- and three-year-olds to comfort a parent, sibling, or playmate with a hug, or by giving the person something that they think will cheer him or her up, or by saying comforting words like "No cry." Children this young aren't likely, though, to talk about how pain passes in time. It will be a while before they accumulate enough experience to know this.

While it's important to recognize that the form that comforting can take will change as a child gets older, don't underestimate the very young child's ability and interest in comforting. In a recent laboratory study of 18-to-24-month-old infants, they and their mothers were each given a doll to play with. After a short while an adult came over to the mother and tried to pull her doll out of her hands. She struggled, but he won and walked away with the doll, dropping it on the way out. The mother then put her hands to her eyes and feigned crying. A majority of the infants either retrieved their mother's doll or gave her their doll, and many tried to comfort her physically.

In another part of the same study the mothers spent two weeks recording their children's reactions to seeing other people in distress in everyday settings (in the home, in stores, at the park). During those two weeks, three-quarters of the children tried to help or to summon help for a person who seemed upset, including their parents, siblings, and other children. Remember, these helpers were not yet two years old.[20]

In teaching your child how to give comfort make sure you cover all the steps: He needs to recognize when someone is unhappy, he must want to help him or her, and must know what steps to take to help. For example, if your child's playmate feels bad because her toy broke, but he doesn't seem to notice or care, first draw his attention to the fact that someone needs help and then prompt him to think about what caused his companion's unhappiness. You might say, "It looks to me like Florence feels really bad. What do *you* think? Any idea why?" If he says he doesn't know why, point out her broken toy and suggest to him how he might comfort her: "I bet you could make her feel better by inviting her to play with you and your toy." If he is resistant, try to arouse his empathic feelings so he'll want to help. Ask him to put himself in her place: "Imagine how bad you'd feel if your toy broke and you had nothing to play with. Wouldn't you feel better if someone saw that you were unhappy and offered to share his toy with you?" Also give him a rule about comforting: "When we see that someone feels bad, we should do our best to help."

As your child comes to understand comforting, have him figure out what to do to help. You might say, "Florence seems to feel bad. What do you think you can do to make her feel better?" If necessary, let him know that he can ask people directly about their feelings. You might suggest, "Why don't you ask Florence what's wrong and whether there's anything you can do for her?"

There will be times when your youngster wants to comfort someone, but doesn't know what to do or does the wrong thing. Suggest what she might do and why you think it would be helpful. For instance, if she's confused about how to comfort a friend who is crying because his dog died, you might explain that the friend has to cry for a while because he loved his dog; but that he might be comforted if she just sat near him and held his hand and listened to him talk about his dog if he wants to.

Even as an adult one is not always certain about what to do or say to give someone comfort. In teaching your child to give comfort, make him aware that he needs to be observant, to see what seems to help the person and what doesn't.

All prosocial behavior involves some type of giving or sacrificing of something of one's own—money, time, safety—for the good of someone else. If you teach your child to be kind, she will inevitably be faced with the question of how much she should give. In making moral decisions we all are faced with this and similar questions: How much of our money and possessions and time *should* we give away to people in need? How much risk should we take to protect others? To what degree should we neglect our own interests in order to help someone else? As your child becomes more committed to treating people kindly, these kinds of moral dilemmas will grow in importance to her and they will remain of concern for the rest of her life.

There is no objective way to answer questions like how much should we give or how kind should we be. We often honor people who give up all their worldly possessions for the sake of others; we call them saints. But we don't necessarily condemn others for being less generous. Our society honored the man who, as many saw on television a few years ago, jumped into the icy Potomac to rescue passengers from a plane crash. But no one pointed a finger of blame at those who saw the crash and didn't plunge in. There is no generally accepted standard of charitability or selflessness, no universal criterion by which to make judgments on how giving people should be.

So, as your child's moral teacher, you will have to think carefully about how much giving you want to encourage. You'll find that it's a lot easier to decide that you don't want your child to harm people than it is to decide on how much good you want to encourage him to do, or what degree of danger he should put himself in for others.

It's worth remembering that many people have found that the greater the act of giving, the more one's own life is enhanced by it. A dramatic example of how extreme generosity can enrich a life is found in a study of people who voluntarily gave one of their kidneys to someone—often a relative but sometimes not—in order to save the person's life. Almost all kidney donors felt that their own lives had been enriched by their act. As one researcher expressed it:

> . . . the act of making such a gift becomes a transcendent experience, akin to a religious one. Many donors testify that giving an organ was the most important, meaningful, and satisfying act of their lives: one that increased their self-knowledge, enhanced their feeling of self-worth, gave them a sense of "totality," belief and commitment, and increased their sense of unity with the recipient, people in general, and with humanity.[21]

Once your child becomes concerned with being helpful, generous, and comforting, the next question is, Should she help some people more readily than others? Is it right to be more helpful and giving to friends, family, countrymen, co-religionists, fellow lodgemembers, than to others? What if a classmate whom she doesn't really like feels bad, for example, at not being invited to a party? Is she obliged to aid or comfort her? If she'd loan money to a close friend, should she feel obliged to loan money to a mere acquaintance?

Nancy Eisenberg asked both elementary and high-school-age children about their sense of obligation to others, and not surprisingly, she found that they'd be more willing to help and sacrifice for family, friends, and countrymen than people they were less close to. They also said they'd be less willing to put themselves out for people they dislike.[22]

This finding is to be expected since, by definition, relationships such as family, friend, and countryman imply mutual obligations. Being a friend means giving help when needed. Also, family members, friends, and countrymen are *us*. It's easy to empathize with their plight. What you teach your child about the boundaries of *us* will affect whom she feels she is morally obliged to help. This is a difficult question. And don't feel bad if you can't give her pat answers. But do discuss her prosocial dilemmas with her *(how much* and *whom* to help) because she will face similar issues for the rest of her life. Someday it will be her turn to wonder whether in a world with millions of starving people we should pay our farmers *not* to plant crops.

The fact that prosocial (or altruistic) behavior involves some degree of self-sacrifice, at times to the point of considerable risk to oneself, has caused some theorists to wonder how such behavior could have evolved. Behavior that benefits others at one's own expense would seem to have less survival value than selfish behavior, and therefore should presumably have dropped out of our species long ago. Because it obviously hasn't, sociobiologists have come up with some complex twists on evolutionary theory to try to explain why (for example, if we help our kin survive, some of the genes that they pass on will be identical to our own).[23]

We don't believe there really is any need for such exotic theories. Under most conditions throughout our evolutionary history (including today), the survival of an individual depended on the survival of his group (his band, tribe, city-state, etc.). Therefore, altruistic behavior paid off directly for the individual who engaged in it— most of the time. By helping and protecting members of his group, he kept his group intact, thus making it easier for him to meet virtually all challenges to his own survival, including hunting and gathering food, fighting predators and enemies, and building shelters. Isolation is far more dangerous than altruism.

Sometimes people do die protecting others, but so do people who engage in daredevil behavior. If dangerous behavior of any kind contributes more frequently to the survival of the people who engage in it than it kills them off, then the risky aspects of the behavior require no special evolutionary theories.

## TEACHING FAIRNESS

When does a child begin to respond to the instruction "Be fair"? Experimental research shows that by the age of four, children can and will follow an instruction to be fair. In one study, psychologists Sharon Nelson and Carol Dweck gave four-year-olds a task and asked each to divide a bunch of candies between himself and another child based on the amount of work each did. Almost all children who were told to give out the "right amount" divided the candies perfectly equitably. The number each took for himself was based on how much work he completed in comparison to the other child, even when it meant giving himself only three candies and the other nine.[24]

Many parents report that their children become concerned with fairness during their second or third year of life, although their initial concern is with being treated fairly. They want to do what they see other children doing—say, climbing after an older sibling on a jungle gym—and they protest if they are restricted while the other child is not. Research shows that this kind of imitative behavior and protesting can be seen in children as young as one, but more often in two-year-olds.

Once your child asks to be treated fairly she will then be able to respond to your requests to treat others the same way. If you see her treating another child unfairly, tell her so and point out that that child feels just as badly as she did when she was receiving the same treatment. Ask her to put herself in the other child's place. Even if her desires sometimes get the best of her and she continues to behave in unfair ways, like taking too large a share of something or always demanding to go first, your insistence on fairness, even to the point of punishing her if necessary, will usually be met with respect. Children as young as three have a surprisingly keen sense of right and wrong, which includes an awareness of what is just. As researchers D. Michelle Irwin and Shirley Moore have found, children this young can recognize that selfish and unfair behavior, like taking a toy away from one's sister or friend, is bad; and they understand that people have a right to get angry at those who are unfair to them.[25]

When can you begin to teach your child about fairness? Our recommendation, based on the research evidence as well as our own interviews, observations, and work with parents and children is that you begin during your child's earliest social interactions, during his second year of life. Telling a child "That's not fair," not only communicates "Don't do that again." It says, "Consider the other person's rights, recognize his or her similarity to you, and treat everyone as you want to be treated." If you start reminding your child of this before he's two, by the time he's four or five you'll find that treating people fairly will be important to him.

Of course there will be times when your youngster will want something so much that her sense of fairness will get overwhelmed. This is particularly likely to happen if you break your promises to her often and subject her to a lot of uncertainty about what she can expect to get and when she'll get it. For example, if you often respond to her requests with an offhand, "Yes, later"—but "later" never comes, then when something she really wants is virtually within reach, she'll be tempted to grab for it without stopping to consider whether she is being fair to others. On the other hand, the more fairly and less capriciously you treat her, the more likely she will be to heed your reminders to be fair.

## HELPING CHILD-CARE WORKERS PROMOTE YOUR VALUES

Many mothers these days return to work sometime during their child's first years, either to continue careers or simply because they need the income. Sometimes fathers are able to stay home to care for their children, but usually child-care help must be sought. That means finding someone who will in effect be responsible for bringing up one's child during a large part of the Monday-through-Friday workweek.

Parents, of course, try to find someone who is experienced, trustworthy, and kind, and who likes being with children. Many are also concerned about the kind of moral training their youngster will receive from this person. If you teach your child to be sensitive to people, you're not going to be happy with a caregiver who, when the child asks her about someone who seems hurt, tells him brusquely, "Just watch out for yourself. Don't worry about anyone else."

Here are some suggestions for working with a caregiver in order to see that her (most are women) manner of handling and instructing your child supports your efforts in moral training:

• In your initial interview ask questions that will give you an idea of her approach to child-rearing. Ask her if she has any pet peeves about the way people bring up children, things she's seen that really bother her. Also ask if she thinks you can really "spoil" a child. If she does, ask how and how it can be avoided. Does she think boys need to be treated differently from girls, and are there times when it's all right to hit a child?

In the interview make it clear that you are trying to bring up a child who treats people kindly and fairly, who likes people and is sensitive to their feelings. Ask her if she has any ideas about what influences children to become good-natured, and what makes them mean and selfish.

Don't expect her to say all the right things. Use the discussion to get an idea of what her values are, and whether she seems to be a compassionate and sensible person. You also should get an indication of how dogmatically she holds her views, how harshly she is likely to treat misbehavior, and whether you like dealing with her.

In the discussions, be careful about using the word *morals* since she may misunderstand your meaning and think you want strict discipline about things like saying Grace before meals and addressing adults as Sir or Ma'am. If you aren't basing your moral training on a belief in God, mention this and see how she feels about it. You might tell her that you want your child to treat people well because he cares about their feelings and not because he is concerned about God punishing or rewarding him. If you are using religion in moral training, discuss that too to make sure she's not going to teach your child about religion in ways you disapprove of (say, by stressing the fear of God rather than love of God).

• Before hiring anyone permanently, have her spend a few days taking care of your children while you are home. You want to see if you like the way she handles them, whether she seems to enjoy them, and whether she is responding to your wishes—and if you like having her around. You also need to know whether your children like her. That's a must.

• Once she's hired, try to give her as clear a framework as you can on how to treat your children. Explain house rules to her ("We eat in here but not in there"), and how you discipline ("If the children fight, the first thing I do is send them to separate rooms for a half-hour. If I have questions or they want to discuss what happened, we talk about it after the half-hour is up. I don't hit them"). Let her know that you'd like her to handle rules and discipline the same way you do so the children have a consistent set of standards.

• Although rules and discipline are important, place the emphasis on what she will do so your children enjoy their days and get the experiences you want them to have. Set up a "lesson plan" with her that focuses on their fun and development. Discuss opportunities for moral training that might come up during the day: In the playground—taking turns. At the supermarket—helping carry. In the library—observing "no talking" rules. Make sure she understands how you want rules explained to your child.

• Be a good supervisor, just the way you want her to be with your children. Treat her with respect. Remember to tell her when you are pleased with what she's doing. Be open to her suggestions. She may have a lot of experience with children and there may be a great deal you can learn from her. She may not be able to use fancy language to describe what she knows, but her intuition and insights may be worth a dozen child-rearing manuals.

If you want her to handle something differently, don't just criticize her; patiently explain your goals and why you want the change. For instance, you might find that she handles your son too severely and not instructively enough when she finds him taking another child's belongings. You might explain your position this way: "That's still a problem area for him. He needs to know that the rule against taking other children's possessions is going to be enforced and that he'll be punished if he breaks it. But I try to suit the punishment to the crime by removing one of his favorite toys for a while. Then I restate the rule firmly, but there's a reason why I don't yell or get too rough with him. I don't want to just frighten him into being good. I'm trying to teach him to think about the feelings of the child whose toy he's taken so he'll *choose* not to take things from people even when no one's around to punish him. One way I do this is by reminding him before a play session how to ask for something he wants. Another way is to try to catch him just before he is about to grab something from his sister or a playmate. I ask him to imagine how she will feel if her toy is pulled away. That way I get him to focus on the other child's feelings rather than his own desire at that moment, and I do it at a time when he's not worried about being punished since he hasn't done anything wrong yet. It's important that you and I coordinate tactics."

Ask for her ideas and be open to them. She will have her own style of handling things, and in areas that aren't really that important, it's best to give her the room to do things her way. When you disagree over matters that you feel truly affect your child's well-being and character, you *must* have the final say.

• Ask her to keep a diary for you entitled *My Child's Day* so you can get a detailed report from her when you return from work on how the day went. The diary can be written (a desk diary is handy) or spoken into a tape recorder. Set up regular time periods—four times a day should suffice—and ask her to make a few notes on what happened during the previous few hours. Since she may find this inconvenient, emphasize that her reports can be very brief, that they are really just reminders for her so she's able to fill you in on your child's activities and experiences. She should understand that you feel you are missing out on part of your child's life and feel a need to be filled in on as much of his day as possible. If she's really uncomfortable with the diary, don't make a fuss. The goal is to get details on your child's day. The diary is only one way to accomplish this.

The daily discussions and the diary should help you become aware if your youngster is having any problems or the caregiver is handling anything in a questionable way. Your own authority over your child will also be bolstered by the fact that you know all about his activities. You want him to know that you're concerned and informed. He'll appreciate your interest.

Let the caregiver know that you are interested in minor events as well, but particularly in how your child gets along with others—whether he shares, fights, makes fun of children—and whether he's cooperative with her. If you want her to be detailed and frank with you, don't attack her when she tells you something that bothers you. Don't just blame. Talk about how the situation might be handled in the future.

• Help the caregiver establish her authority by giving your child firm instructions that he is to listen to her, treat her kindly and respectfully, and cooperate with her. Make sure he knows that you've worked out the lesson plan for the day with her, and that you'll get a report at the end of the day.

You might go over some house rules with him in front of the caregiver so he knows that she's aware of the rules and that she has your full authority behind her. Go over some discipline techniques too ("If you do that, Mary will put you in your room for a half-hour. We've made that arrangement").

You can also support the caregiver by expressing affection for her in front of your child, and by giving him some explicit responsibilities to help her: "Today I want you to help Mary with the laundry. You carry the soap for her and help her fold things."

• Make sure your child knows that you are still in charge, that you still set the rules. One way to do this is to give the caregiver an instruction in front of your child. Make sure there is no criticism implied in the instruction that might embarrass her and undermine her authority. Something like, "The zoo is having a special tour for children today at noon. I think Andy would like that, so why don't you two go?"

• Communicate to the caregiver that you truly want her to enjoy her job and that you are open to discussing any adjustments she might need in the work arrangements. Try to accommodate her as much as possible, so long as your basic requirements are met.

• Keep tabs on your child's feelings about her. Of course, you want him to like her, but don't take a single complaint too seriously. He might tell you that the caregiver was mean to him, when all that will have occurred is that she enforced a rule as you would have done. Make sure that your youngster feels he can talk to the caregiver about things she does that he feels are unfair. He needs to feel he can trust her, even if she may not always be endlessly patient or be totally consistent. In other words, he needs to recognize that like parents, she's a human being with flaws. He'll adjust to this knowledge without much difficulty as long as he feels she's sincerely interested in his happiness.

• If the caregiver does her job well, your children are bound to get very attached to her and you may find yourself feeling jealous and saddened by the thought that your very own little ones have become less dependent on you. That's natural. That's also the time to make sure you don't say or do anything to undermine her authority over your children or their affection for her.

# 8

# Middle Childhood, Five to Twelve: Joining the Community of Children

During the middle childhood years your child will be developing into an increasingly social and independent person. She will be spending more time with nonfamily members; become increasingly subject to the influence of television, books, and movies; and will start to acquire interests—whether in sports, science, or stamp-collecting—that will affect how she spends her time and who she spends it with. Your approval will still be important to her, but she will no longer be completely dependent on it, particularly as she approaches her teens. The approval of friends, teachers, and other adults will have a greater and greater impact on her.

As she moves through middle childhood, she will begin to form intense friendships and become embroiled in conflicts. Thus, two of the most important things she will need to learn are how to be a friend and how to resolve conflicts constructively.

During these middle childhood years your youngster will also begin to define the kind of person she wants to be and how she wants to be seen by others (as smart, honest, tough). She'll form her religious, ethnic and national identities, and judge these as either compatible or at odds with other religious, ethnic, and national identities. She will also encounter her first moral dilemmas ("Should I stick up for a friend who is wrong?") and discover that lying and cheating are handy ways to get what she wants or avoid punishment. She will begin to develop her attitude toward money and responsibility, and will be shocked to learn that grown-ups don't always know what's best, that they themselves often lie and cheat (as one child said in self-defense, "Even the president lies"), and that adults are capable of being horribly cruel to other people and animals. She will also learn about death.

## FRIENDSHIP

For the six-year-old a friend is someone you play games with. Although attachments between friends at this age can be strong, they are not nearly as intense as they will be in the preteen and teenage years. By the time your child is ten, friendship will not only involve having fun but also feelings of solidarity and loyalty. The ten-year-old has "best friends." At that age friendships become like marriages, with formal declarations ("You're my best friend") and divorces ("You're not my best friend anymore"). As children grow older, their friendships become increasingly intimate; they reveal secrets and dreams to each other that no one else knows. Trust now becomes an important part of friendship.

The relationship of friendship to moral behavior is summed up in the old adage, "To have a friend, be a friend." Research confirms this as good psychological sense. In a recent study of close friendships among ten- and eleven-year-olds, researchers at the University of North Carolina found that the children who were most often chosen by their classmates to be "best friends" were generally both more altruistic and sensitive to what others were feeling. Other studies have found that children want their friends to be truthful, cooperative, helpful, trustworthy, and fun; and that they don't want them to be touchy, sarcastic, or aggressive. In general, popular children are more helpful, encouraging, and generous. Disliked children are those who start fights, gossip, lie, cheat, or demand unfair privileges. The findings have been quite consistent: Treat people well and there's a good chance they'll want to be your friend.[1]

Since most children want friends, this is an important lesson for them to learn. Keep in mind, though, that there's a difference between the child who has trouble making friends because he is shy or lacks basic social skills and the one who winds up ignored or actively disliked by others. The ignored or disliked youngster may be highly social and desire close friends, but may be doing things that make people avoid his company.

Over the years there are likely to be many emotional scenes over issues of friendship. On one occasion, your child may feel hurt and rejected by a popular classmate whom she would like as a friend. At another time she may react with rage when she discovers that her best friend went on an outing with other friends and didn't invite her. Children have to learn about friendship, including how to attract friends and what friends have a right to expect of each other. They also need to learn that friendship can't be demanded. You can't insist that someone become your friend. Friendship has to be earned.

We want to be someone's friend and spend time with that person because we value certain of his or her qualities. These might be the person's intelligence or physical attractiveness, or his or her energy or enthusiasm, or sense of humor or curiosity. We also want our friends to possess various moral attributes, such as trustworthiness, a sense of fairness, and sensitivity to the feelings of others. In addition, we look for friends who know how to reciprocate friendship, who know how to be a friend.

Here are some lessons you may at one time or another have to teach your child about being a friend.

Being someone's friend means:

• helping her reach her goals (unless you firmly believe she is doing something self-destructive or harmful to others).

• being available when she needs you, even when it's inconvenient.

• sharing your possessions with her.

• keeping her secrets.

• keeping your promises to her.

• not allowing jealous feelings to make you possessive. If your friend is really a worthwhile person, other people will like her too and she will like them.

• recognizing that there will be times when what she needs from you should take precedence over what you need from her—for example, when she has either serious troubles or great joys that she wants to share.

• never making her regret having told you something personal by embarrassing her or using it against her.

• not trying to gain her friendship or get her to spend more time with you by making her feel guilty or sorry for you.

• enjoying and showing enthusiasm at her successes.

• comforting her when she's sad or frightened.

• encouraging her when she is discouraged.

- helping her face the truth when she is deceiving herself.
- respecting her independence as well as your own. If a friend disagrees with you it should not be taken as a betrayal of the friendship. On the other hand, agreeing with her just to win her friendship is a betrayal of oneself, and in the long run you'll lose the respect of the person you want to have as a friend.

## RESOLVING CONFLICTS

During middle childhood, children's conflicts start to become complex. Youngsters no longer just yank each other's toys away. By six they have a pretty good understanding of possession rules and generally live up to them. More and more their disputes arise over conflicting interpretations of rules, obligations, agreements, and loyalties.

In earlier sections we recommended that you teach your children to strive for "win-win" solutions to conflicts so that both parties come out ahead. You can motivate your youngster to seek these kinds of cooperative solutions 1) by stressing that they are kind solutions and that concerns about kindness are not to be abandoned even during conflicts with people; 2) by teaching him that more often than not they are the most practical solutions in the long run; and 3) by helping him develop a long-term perspective and sense of humor about his immediate needs and pursuits.

### Cooperative Solutions Are Kind

The following argument took place between Barney, a nine-year-old, and Ken, his ten-and-a-half-year-old brother.

BARNEY: Can I use your bike now?
KEN: No.
BARNEY: But when I loaned you my dart set you said I could use your bike.
KEN: I said you could use it if I wasn't using it.
BARNEY: But you're not using it.
KEN: (Gets on bike. As he rides off) I am now.

If the issue between Barney and Ken is who is right and who's wrong, no resolution is possible. The real issue here is *kindness*. Does Ken want to treat his brother kindly, or is he just "doing business" with him, looking for a loophole in their agreement so he can get out of lending him his bike? If he's just doing business, his obligations will be fulfilled as long as he meets the letter of their agreement. That's all that business ethics require. In the adult world, one hires lawyers to make sure the wording of the agreement is as much in one's favor as possible. If loopholes can be inserted without the other party noticing, so much the better. In *A Christmas Carol,* Scrooge was not unethical, just unkind. In business, kindness is not a requirement, although many businessmen find that the old maxim, "A little kindness goes a long way," makes as much sense in business as in any other area of life.

If you find that your child's conflicts grow out of her selfishness, do your best to keep her focused on the question of whether she is treating people kindly rather than on whether she has met her "contractual" obligations to them. There are two things at stake in a conflict between children (and adults too). One is the objective item or issue that both sides are fighting over, such as a toy, money, a desirable position, or simply being right. The second concern to each party is pride (also called ego or self-esteem). Some people's pride in themselves is tied to winning, and it matters little what the contest is about. They see the world in terms of winners and losers, the powerful and the powerless, and their primary goal—often based on their fear of being a loser—is to come out on top.

But there is a different type of pride that you can nurture in your child—pride in finding amicable settlements to conflicts, solutions that benefit everyone fairly. Teach him that power doesn't always come from overpowering others. It can come just as readily from mastering one's own self-centeredness and from devising and implementing harmonious ways of living with others.

There will be people who will tell your child that to compromise is weak. They're the power-seekers, those who grab up the latest books on how to intimidate and overpower others, the hot-warriors and the cold-warriors, those who always seek an advantage and who refuse to negotiate if they can't do so from strength. They're out there huffing and puffing and toughing it out and threatening to blow everyone's house down if they can't have their way.

Prepare your child for their arguments. Teach him or her that there is nothing weak about trying to understand and satisfy your opponent's interests, not if your goal is to live harmoniously with others and not if you can take pleasure in seeing other people happy. Searching for a solution to a conflict that will benefit everyone is only seen as weak by people who demand everything for themselves, for whom a human relationship based on caring about what happens to others is not as important as winning.

On the other hand, compromising doesn't mean letting yourself be bullied. Surely parents don't want their child to placate bullies since bullies always come back for more. But just as surely a child can assert and defend his own interests without becoming a bully himself. Looking out for your own interests doesn't mean you have to be hard-hearted. To be resolute doesn't mean you can't also be sensitive to others.

A child's own weakness and confusion can make people who seem self-assured and powerful particularly appealing. But sometimes youngsters mistake defensiveness and short temper for confidence and strength. So don't be surprised if you notice that your child admires someone whom you consider abusive and shallow. Make your child aware that the "powerful" personalities she may admire often have little substance beneath their tough exteriors.

For instance, we know a teacher who can't bear it when a student disagrees with him. He becomes insulting and will twist his reasoning in any way he can in order to cover up any weakness in his argument and make the student appear foolish. Students talk admiringly of his ability to "put down" any opponent—but it's only the frightened and less talented ones who talk this way. The bolder, brighter students—the ones who are not about to be intimidated by the teacher's sarcasm and bravado—quickly spot the flaws in his reasoning and recognize his insecurity. These students stay with him only a short while. So this powerful teacher, who once did some worthwhile work in his field, now simply protects his territory, surrounded and admired by a lackluster bunch of sycophants.

## Cooperative Solutions Are Practical

An "I win, you lose" attitude may be appropriate in sports, but in most other areas of human conduct it is, in the long run, self-defeating. In essence, it is a declaration of war, and usually your opponent fortifies his position and sets out to defeat you with as much vigor as you have mustered against him.

Children are no more combative and competitive by nature than they are cooperative. In fact, by the age of eighteen months, children are already cooperating with other children as well as adults on joint activities. And three-year-olds are able to work together cooperatively to solve tasks that require coordinated effort (such as placing objects on two sides of a scale to balance it). Many are also getting pretty good at finding mutually beneficial solutions to their disputes.[2]

Various studies show that whether children adopt competitive or cooperative strategies depends on how the payoffs are arranged. When they are encouraged to think only of themselves, that's what they'll generally do. But they can just as easily be encouraged to care about what happens to the other person too, to take his or her feelings into account.

One of these studies, carried out by psychologists Linden Nelson and Millard Madsen, provides us with a particularly important lesson. Two four-year-old children played a board game that had a pointer and two targets. In order to land the pointer on a target, both children had to cooperate and coordinate pulling strings attached to it; neither of them could accomplish it alone. First, the children were told that both of them would get a prize if they moved the pointer to either target within thirty seconds. They immediately began to cooperate and quickly started to win prizes. Then each child was assigned one of the targets as his own and told he would win only if he managed to get the pointer on his own target; the other player would then get nothing. The children immediately began to pull against each other, trying to beat each other. While they were cooperating, they rarely failed to get a prize. But when they started to compete, fifty-four trials went by without either child winning a prize.

What makes this study particularly interesting (and sad) is that by simply taking turns—first you win, then I win—the children could have easily continued to earn prizes in the competitive condition. But only a few of them came up with this solution. The payoff for cooperating was there, but the children didn't recognize it. Most were too caught up in their pursuit of an immediate prize for themselves.[3]

Sounds like a lot of adult interactions, doesn't it? Sometimes out of greed, sometimes out of pride, and always out of shortsightedness, we humans have managed to acquire a long history of embarking on battles with our "opponents" that has cost us more in the long run than whatever it was we were fighting over in the first place. As someone once said, only the lawyers, the arms makers, and the undertakers come out ahead. Shakespeare gives us a vivid description of just how absurd our competitions can become. Hamlet comments on a passing army going off to do battle over a piece of land not large enough to hold the armies that will fight for it; not even large enough to hold the bodies that will die there:

> I see
> The imminent death of twenty thousand men,
> That for a fantasy and trick of fame
> Go to their graves like beds, fight for a plot
> Whereon the numbers cannot try the cause,
> Which is not tomb enough and continent
> To hide the slain

The children in the Nelson and Madsen study could easily have been taught the benefits of cooperation—in their case, of taking turns. Your own children can be taught this same lesson: cooperation generally pays off. When they are confronted with what seems like an irreconcilable conflict, remind them to look hard at the long-term prospects, to put themselves in their opponent's place in order to understand how he or she views the conflict, and to try to come up with a way in which both sides can come out ahead.

But cooperation doesn't mean capitulation. Opponents can certainly be unreasonable. Being unreasonable as well won't change them, but neither will simply giving in. That wouldn't be fair to oneself. In the Nelson and Madsen study some children gave in to their partners on almost all contests. They were never willing to hold out long enough to force them to see that cooperation was in their interest too. Your child's best bet for getting an unreasonable opponent to change is a steadfast commitment to finding a cooperative solution that is fair to both parties.

### Making Molehills Out of Mountains—Rx: A Sense of Humor

In the heat of confrontation, the issue we are doing battle over seems so crucial and our own position so justified. Later, when we calmly think it over and weigh what really is important to us, we often recognize the folly—even the humor—of our puffed-up ire and righteous indignation. It's easier then to opt for a cooperative solution. The trick, though, is to be able to take a moment's pause while we're still embroiled in combat or competition and ask ourselves, "What am I really fighting for? Is this really important enough to warrant this amount of energy or risk or self-humiliation?"

A junior high school teacher described an incident she witnessed on a staircase of the inner-city school in which she taught. One boy was coming up the Down staircase. Another boy, on his way down the same narrow steps, wouldn't make room for him. "I'm not stepping aside. You step aside or go to the other staircase where you're supposed to be," the boy on the way down said as he barred the way. The other boy cursed at him and said, "Get out of my way." Some more curses were exchanged, then some threats, and within a few seconds, both boys had knives drawn, threatening to kill each other. *To kill each other.*

Fortunately, a school guard was nearby and intervened. Later, in the principal's office, as one of the boys was describing what happened, he started to laugh. "What's funny?" the principal asked. "I must have been nuts," the boy said. "I could have been killed over nothing or gone to jail if I killed him." "Do you want to kill him?" the teacher asked. "I did then," he answered. "But that's stupid—to kill someone over who's going to move out of the way. I should have stayed cool."

If only he could have seen the foolishness of it as it was happening! Most of us have had occasion to laugh at ourselves—at our ambitions, our self-delusions, our pettinesses, our anxieties, and our manias—when we suddenly realize that we've blown something out of all proportion to what it's worth.

Children need to be reminded to keep their conflicts and frustrations in perspective. This can be done even before a child turns six. Helping your youngster recognize that he is overreacting (sometimes called making a mountain out of a molehill), doesn't mean belittling his feelings. He'll resent you if you do that. Try instead to help him recognize on his own that, given his values and long-term goals, the intensity of his reaction is unwarranted and self-defeating. You can do this by asking him leading questions and by suggesting solutions so absurdly extreme that he'll get the point.

Here's an example. Belinda, age eleven, was angry when she came home from the gym:

**BELINDA:** I hate Marcy. I'm not speaking to her for a year.

**MOTHER:** A whole year? She was your best friend. What did she do that was so terrible?

**BELINDA:** She laughed when Brian said I looked like a sick fish when I swim.

**MOTHER:** She laughed at that? Oh, dear. What does a sick fish look like when it swims?

**BELINDA:** I don't know.

**MOTHER:** Like this? (Moving her arms and mouth.)

**BELINDA:** (Starting to smile.) No, like this.

**MOTHER:** Oh, then I wouldn't talk to her for five years if she laughed at that.

**BELINDA:** (Laughing): Twenty-five years.

**MOTHER:** What does Marcy look like when she swims?

**BELINDA:** A frightened puppy. (Imitating movements. They both laugh.)

**MOTHER:** Sometimes you just have to laugh about things. Even your best friends can look funny sometimes. It doesn't mean you don't like them.

**BELINDA:** Well, tomorrow they'll see I can swim differently.

**MOTHER:** How are you going to swim tomorrow?

**BELINDA:** Like a sick camel, like this. (She demonstrates and they both laugh.)

A sense of humor will not only help your child keep his conflicts and strivings in their proper perspective, but will also help him handle many of the shocks and disappointments that life may send his way. Psychologists Rod Martin and Herbert Lefcourt recently gathered evidence for what they refer to as the stress-buffering role of humor. They found that people with a good sense of humor were not as crushed by "negative life events."[4] There's little of greater value that you can foster in your child than the ability to laugh at himself and at this often absurd world we live in.

### Fair Fights

Children often evolve their own rules on how to resolve conflicts. For instance, they might have an unwritten rule against seeking the aid of parents or other adults. If they've formed a club, as children often do, they may even set up formal "judicial" proceedings for settling disputes. They may also have rules about fair fights.

Most youngsters accept that physical confrontations are bound to occur, but they usually place limits on what is allowed in a fight. And they take these limits seriously. An unfair fighter may be ostracized or even challenged by the group as a whole. Typical fair-fight rules among preadolescents forbid hitting below the waist, kicking, biting, pulling hair, eye-poking, and using weapons. Other common rules that most youngsters will agree on state that when your opponent says "I give" you stop the fight, and that you never say "I give" to trick your opponent into releasing you.

Fair fights are very much like jousts. The goal is to defeat your opponent—to prove your point or strength or valor—and not to seriously harm him or her. If the idea of a fair fight has any moral standing it is because it limits the amount of damage one child can do to another. But fighting fairly can also be risky because one's opponent may not honor the rules and suddenly launch a "dirty" attack. Therefore, a child's peers will not necessarily expect him to fight fairly if he is attacked by an outsider who can't be trusted to adhere to the rules.

There may be a time when your youngster decides that there is no reasonable way to resolve a conflict with someone, that his opponent is dead-set on an altercation, and a fight is unavoidable. In the chapter on aggression we suggested that your child learn self-defense skills for just such cases. Also make sure that he understands his peer group's rules about fair fights. Self-defense and fair fights are compatible if the goal of both is primarily to protect oneself while doing as little harm as possible to one's opponent.

Ethical questions about how fighting should be conducted are likely to come up a number of times in your child's life. Many communities and their police departments have struggled with the issue of when policemen and citizens can use "deadly force" to protect themselves. Even warfare is covered by various codes of conduct, including restrictions on certain kinds of weapons and rules about the treatment of civilians and prisoners (the Geneva Convention rules). Although discussions about the ethical standing of different techniques of mass annihilation can sound quite absurd sometimes, these concerns are taken seriously, as witnessed by the recent controversies over the ethics of killing people with napalm, poison gas, and neutron bombs.

## PLAYING WITH TOY GUNS

Many parents are worried about the effect that playing with toy guns might have on their children. Will it make them more violent? Will they value life less? This is a fairly new concern. Not too long ago virtually every boy was given a toy gun without his parents thinking twice about it, and when he got older, he got his first real gun, usually a BB gun. Real guns are an important item in American life. We have more guns and easier access to them, as well as more murders with them, than any other nation. Millions of American sportsmen eagerly await hunting season every year with guns, telescopic eyesights, and cases of beer ready so they can go out and brave the dangers of stalking deer and ducks.

But many people nowadays worry about the proliferation of guns in our society, even among our children. Some school systems have even begun using metal detectors to spot concealed weapons as youngsters enter school. The mounting fear of being assaulted by an armed adult or child has led to more concern and more confusion about what to do about guns in our society. Public opinion polls find that a majority of citizens want stricter gun registration laws. Yet more people, many of whom never imagined they would ever own a pistol, are applying for licenses and enrolling in courses on how to use handguns to protect themselves and their families.

As far as toy guns go, we know of no evidence that shows that playing with toy guns makes children more violent. Nor is there evidence that it makes them less violent, as proposed by ethologist Konrad Lorenz and some psychologists who maintain that we all have aggressive energy that must be channeled into socially acceptable outlets like aggressive play.[5]

For most youngsters pointing a toy gun and saying, "Bang, bang, you're dead" isn't very different from touching a playmate in a game of tag and saying, "I got you. You're It." The goal in both is to win the point. Taking a life has nothing to do with it. If you were to tell your child you don't want him to kill people, even in make-believe, he'd probably say, "Oh, Mom, we're only playing." And that's really all he'd be doing. We know some very kindhearted boys who play with guns. Their fantasy play is about defeating the bad guys. We also know boys who, in play, turn their fingers into guns when store-bought ones aren't available. Most boys (but few girls) have strong inclinations toward violent fantasy enactments. Heroic fantasies (vanquishing the bad guys) as opposed to destructive ones (such as blowing up the school) are not a sign of future anti-social behavior.

We are definitely not arguing that you should let your child play with guns. The ready acceptance of guns in our society—toy or real—may offend you; and you may also be offended by the fact that children aren't actively discouraged from playing with them, that they aren't taught to shun guns since their only purpose is to hurt people and animals. During the Vietnam War, "anti-war-toy" groups tried to convince toy manufacturers to "demilitarize" the nursery and playroom on the grounds that guns and war toys promote and perpetuate America's "culture of violence." They asked for a switch to constructive playthings that train children for peace. Some companies agreed; others said they were only giving the public what it wanted. An editorial in a toy manufacturers trade magazine responded to this argument with some ideas worth thinking about when you consider buying your children guns and war toys:

> Profit is, of course, the businessman's legitimate major concern . . . but it must not be his only concern. We often hear: "If they wouldn't buy it I wouldn't make it." Does this also mean: "I'll make anything that will sell," or are there other considerations?
>
> What, after all, do toys really stand for? Diversion and entertainment for the child, to be sure, but much more importantly they indicate what skills we, society, think he should develop, what activities of life he should be concerned with, what vocations or attitudes or heroes he should glamorize. No one, I think, would give a child a game based on the activities of the Ku Klux Klan, for example, although this is certainly a very real part of life; or how about a miniature Nazi concentration camp complete with crematoriums for turning tiny figures of Jews into soap. No one would make items like that because they go so obviously beyond the bounds of good taste . . . no matter how well they might sell.[6]

The anti-war-toy movement claimed that its efforts did reduce war-toy buying by American families. In a survey that covered the years from 1964 to 1967, the proportion of parents who said they didn't buy war toys increased from 15 to 32 percent. Also, 21 percent of parents in 1964 rated war toys high on a list of playthings they liked, while in 1967, *none* gave war toys a high rating.

Despite all the violence in our society, or probably because of it, there is, we observe, less interest in and tolerance for the symbols of violence. We are a society with few military heroes—and that's very unusual. Ask an American who he thinks of as a modern hero and he's more likely to name Martin Luther King than any military figure.

Whatever the reason, a lot of people nowadays don't want their children playing with war toys and guns of any kind. If that's your decision, be prepared to explain your reasons clearly to your child. That will mean telling him about the suffering that people inflict on each other with guns. Teach him that real guns kill. What he makes of this information will, of course, depend on his understanding of death. Sometime during his middle childhood years—often around the age of six—your youngster will come to understand that death is permanent and universal.[7] He may learn this through the death of a relative or a pet. Even if he doesn't have any direct experience of the loss of someone he loves, you can teach him about the impact of a person's death on those who loved him. Also teach him what a miracle each human life is—totally unique, infinitely complex, imbued with so much potential for love and creativity.

If you do decide to ban guns, we suggest you discuss your reasons with the parents of your child's friends. Since children, especially boys, play with guns a lot, your child might miss out on some playtime if he's the only one who doesn't play with guns. You may find other parents quite happy to ban guns too.

## TELEVISION

Another common concern of parents is the effect of television violence on children's aggressiveness. There are estimates that from the ages of five to eighteen, children see approximately 20,000 murders and over 100,000 total acts of violence on television. In recent decades there has been extensive research on the effect all this observed aggression has on children's behavior. The findings are not consistent and even when researchers do find positive correlations between TV watching and aggressive behavior, they are quite small. Still, most psychologists regard a steady diet of violent programs as harmful. But, frankly, it's hard to sort out the specific effects of television from other factors in a child's life that may also contribute to his or her aggressiveness.

There's no evidence that television can make a kind child mean or a mean child kind. It's impact will, rather, depend on the child's already-established orientation toward people. For instance, there is some evidence that children who are already aggressive become more so or learn new forms of aggression from watching violence on TV. Shortly after a television drama depicted the killing of a derelict by setting him on fire, groups of adolescents in Boston and Miami carried out similar acts. Many other examples of such "imitation learning" of aggression have been reported.[8]

But there is also evidence that television can have a positive effect. Most television dramas do take a moral stand. People who intentionally hurt others are generally portrayed in an unfavorable light and are usually opposed by "heroes" who are caring and incorruptible (although often highly violent). The central characters on TV shows are, for the most part, struggling to be kind, fair, and responsible, and research shows that children do imitate acts of kindness that they've seen on television. Kindergartners were regularly shown "prosocial" television shows, including "Lassie," "The Brady Bunch," and "Father Knows Best," during a four-week period. Another group was shown "neutral" programs that had no moral content. Children who saw the prosocial programs became more helpful and cooperative on various measures. Other researchers report that children displayed less racial discrimination after watching "Sesame Street" or "prosocial cartoons."[9]

If your child seeks out a steady diet of violent programs—which has been found to be associated with high aggression in children and teenagers—or if she identifies with the villain instead of the hero, then there is certainly reason for concern about whether her feelings and intentions toward others are developing in a moral direction. Also, the more a child believes that television violence represents real life, the more aggressive she's likely to be.

It's important that children, regardless of whom they identify with, understand that in real life people generally don't resolve their conflicts or right wrongs in the simpleminded ways depicted on many television adventure shows—by smashing people in the face or shooting them. Such acts, of course, occur in life and receive a lot of attention when they do, but they really are the exception rather than the rule. Contrary to what television would have children believe, admiration and success in our society is not earned with either a right to the jaw or a quick draw. That's not what American values are about.

Violence in children's stories is not new with television. Fairy tales are filled with acts of cruelty and aggression, as are a great many traditional children's stories, as well as bible stories. Radio programs were violent, and comic books still are. Seeing violence enacted right before your eyes on a video screen may give TV violence a greater degree of reality and, hence, more influence than other forms of fiction. But this turns out not to be the case for most children. Recent research with first- and third-graders found that even children this young don't believe that the popular television adventure shows depict the way things really happen in real life.

Television stories, like most fiction, highlight the drama of life. Violent events have obvious dramatic value that can be exploited without a great deal of creative talent. Contrary to popular belief, violent shows don't attract the largest audience;[10] they're just the easiest for TV writers to create. So the world that television depicts tends to have more killing and crime than the real world. And, whereas most real-life violence takes place between friends and family members, most television violence is committed by strangers—probably so that characters can more easily fit the good guy/bad guy format. Even the acts of violence portrayed don't depict reality. In real life the force and quantity of the punches TV characters give and receive would have to leave them with broken jaws, concussions, smashed hands, toothless smiles, and long recovery periods in traction. Not so in TV-land. At most the hero will have a mild bruise for his girl friend to nurse in the closing scene.

Television violence should not be a problem if you make sure that your child understands the unreality of the stories he sees on the screen. Discuss how television fights and stunts are staged with choreographed punches, breakaway props, fortified automobiles, and trick camera shots. If possible, take your child to a television studio so he can actually see how programs are filmed.

Discuss the moral implications of programs with your child, such as the intentions behind a character's actions. Talk about why a character got angry and wanted to hurt someone. Even five-year-olds are able to make connections between people's feelings and what someone else did to make them feel that way. Ask your child to suggest other ways characters might have resolved their conflicts without resorting to violence. Television stories, when they're well done, can actually provide a great deal of insight into people's feelings and motivation. Indeed, that's one of the reasons we turn to any kind of good fiction. You can use television for teaching about feelings and motives. In a study of third- and fifth-graders, children who had the most insight into the emotions and motives of characters that actors portrayed were ranked high by their teacher and classmates on leadership, friendliness, sensitivity, and interest in others, and low on cruelty.[11]

If TV stories are simpleminded or if they distort reality, help your child understand in which ways. But be careful. Children—and adults—enjoy fantasy, adventure, and even foolishness. Don't assume that they can't tell the difference between what's real and what isn't. Children who love to watch "Superman" don't believe that people can really fly. Don't spoil your child's pleasure in fantasy by comparing every program he watches and book he reads to real-life. Don't assume because he sometimes enjoys seeing the "bad" guy get blown away that he'll turn into a mass murderer. Help him learn to appreciate programs that portray human events more realistically and artistically, and you'll find he'll soon lose interest in the more simpleminded TV fare.

You won't be able to understand the influence and effect television has on your child unless you spend some time watching it with her. If she's like most other American children, she's spending more time in front of the TV than in any other pastime. Therefore, it's essential that you know what information she's getting and how she's perceiving it. You want her to learn her values from you, not from the networks.

***Should you censor what your child watches?*** Some parents only let their children watch what they've selected for them rather than keeping the TV on all the time as an all-purpose distractor and babysitter. In that way they guide their children to shows they approve of. But however you handle television viewing, inevitably your child will want to watch a show that you would rather he didn't see. Perhaps the violence is excessive or too frightening, or nationalities and racial groups are stereotyped unfavorably, or the sex scenes are explicit. One problem with censorship is that it often backfires and makes the program you've banned all the more enticing. Your child may have heard about a program from friends, or seen an episode at a friend's home, or read about it in the newspapers. When you say no, you won't extinguish his interest; on the contrary, you'll more than likely fan it.

At what age should a child be able to watch what he wants? It's hard to tell what children are ready for. Often parents restrict what their child can watch until he protests strongly enough—which isn't a very good reason to change your mind about what's good or bad for him. Sometimes parents say no and assume he'll find a way to watch the program anyway—but at least they've done their duty. This isn't very sensible either. In neither case are parents helping their child develop the more mature perspective they want him to have.

Children can handle most things that they are truly interested in, and no program is going to be powerful enough to alter your child's basic values. How a program affects him will depend very much on the kind of person he was when he first sat down to watch it. If he cares about people, he'll dislike a program that promotes questionable morals as much as you will.

Telling a child "You're too young" doesn't help him grow. Before you censor a program, ask yourself what your youngster needs to understand in order to appreciate its content in a mature way. Then, if possible, help him understand it. That means watching the show together and talking about it. In these talks, be open to your child's point of view. He may see redeeming aspects of the program that you—so focused on protecting him from harm—may have missed.

Keep in mind that many of man's greatest achievements in literature and theater have been banned and burned at one time or another. Even today, in our own country, there are self-declared literary "watchdogs" doing their best to purge from public libraries and schools books they feel our children shouldn't read, including such classics as *The Grapes of Wrath* and *Huckleberry Finn*. Whether your concern is nurturing a child with moral values and an independent mind, or promoting a free society, it's always better to oppose a bad idea with a good one than to prevent an idea you don't like from being heard at all.

By suggesting that censorship creates more problems than it cures, we are not recommending that you expose your child, regardless of age, to any and all material that TV has to offer. For example, your seven-year-old is not likely to benefit from watching a story about rape (nor is he likely to be interested in it). At seven a child does not yet understand adult sexuality, and certainly won't be helped to understand it by witnessing sex as a brutal and terrifying act. If you want to watch an adult program, but your TV set is in the family room and your seven-year-old would normally be up and around at the time of the broadcast, there is nothing wrong with asking him to play somewhere else in the house. Most children won't fuss if you ask for privacy as long as you help them find an interesting activity for themselves. Whether it's for a television program or a bridge game, you have a right to "adult time" and it's worth establishing this with your child at a young age.

When it comes to television viewing, the best lessons come not from imposing upon the child a list of tabooed shows, but from teaching her criteria for judging the truthfulness and artfulness of programs. Moreover, any show, regardless of how offensive parents find its content, can be used as a touchstone for a moral lesson. A child who has been taught to enjoy great art is not likely to be titillated for long by the simpleminded offerings on TV. A child who has been taught to consider the moral implications of actions is not likely to want to recreate in her own life the mindless brutality and exploitation that she might see on a program.

## LYING

Almost all children lie at one time or another. The first time parents find out that their child has lied to them, they usually become both angry and hurt. "How dare she lie to me"; "How dare she think she could put one over on me." Your child lies to you and suddenly you realize she is seeing you simply as an obstacle to get around—and that hurts.

Perhaps she lies to prevent you from keeping her from something she wants, or perhaps to keep you from punishing her for doing something she knows you disapprove of. In either case, what should you do about it? And what should you do if she's also lying to her friends or teachers?

In discussions with parents we find two opposite viewpoints (along with a lot of uncertainty) about what should be done when you catch your child in a lie. Some parents feel that children have to learn that lying produces a serious breach of trust and that, therefore, they should be punished for it. These parents believe that in most cases, telling the lie was far worse than the act their child was trying to cover up. Other parents feel that their youngster would be a fool to tell the truth after doing something she knew she wasn't supposed to do and could be punished for. They believe the real problem is the initial act of disobedience. They view the lie as a natural act of self-protection.

Lies do produce serious breaches of trust and no parent likes to be lied to or discover that his or her child is lying to others. But we agree that lying is a symptom of a more basic difficulty: the child's unwillingness to accept the rules that have been established for her. The best remedy for lying is, therefore, to get your child to agree that your rules are reasonable and that she has an obligation to obey them. Without her cooperation, the only way to get her to follow rules and tell the truth, is to keep the threat of punishment constantly hanging over her head.

If your child commits an ill-intentioned act, for example, stealing, and tries to hide it through a lie, you'll find that what you primarily mistrust are her intentions toward others. Your main concern will be whether she'll steal again—not whether she'll tell you about it if she does. You certainly won't be content if she walks into the house, asks what's for dinner, and calmly announces, "Oh, by the way, I stole twenty dollars today." You'll rest easy only when you know that your youngster wants to do the right thing. At that point, she won't need to lie because there will be nothing to cover up.

A youngster might lie to her parents for a variety of reasons. She may not like a rule they've imposed (such as, "You can't spend time with those friends anymore") and doesn't accept their right to have the final say over what rules she must follow. So she breaks the rule —sometimes feeling guilty, sometimes self-righteous, often both— and lies to avoid punishment. Or she might lie to manipulate her parents, to get a brother or sister in trouble, or wheedle money from them, or get out of doing chores.

Children also lie to avoid being punished for an accident, say, breaking a vase. Some parents are unreasonable enough to punish for accidents. But even when parents are understanding about mishaps, a child—knowing how much they valued the broken object— may lie anyway to disassociate herself from anything that causes them pain. Some children also tell tall tales ("Superman took me for a ride this morning"). These innocuous but often annoying lies —*fabrications* is a better term—are a way to make them feel more important.

Children will lie to friends for many of the same reasons that they lie to parents: to manipulate their feelings and allegiances, to con them out of money or belongings, to avoid meeting an obligation, or to enhance their own status.

## What to Do About Lying

There are some questions you should ask yourself to help you decide on the best way to handle your child when you catch him in a lie. The first is, *Was the lie told to cover up a violation of a moral or conventional rule?* Moral rules, of course, are those against hurting people. Conventional rules are about such matters as doing homework, attending classes, whom a child spends time with and where he goes. The latter aren't about behavior directed at harming others, but they might involve doing something that could put a child in danger, such as "hanging out" in a dangerous part of town.

When you catch your child in a lie about breaking a moral rule (say he's picked on other children and lied about it), your primary focus should be on his intentions toward others. In other words, it's time for some moral training. Although the need for the truth is important, it is obviously secondary to attacking others or stealing from them. Let your child know that you want him to work with you in trying to change. This means that when he breaks a rule you want him to tell you what he's done and why he's done it so you can work out together how else he might have behaved in that situation. For example, if he does pick on other children, it may be because he felt rejected by them or didn't know how to influence them in acceptable ways.

Explain to your child that you want to work on these difficulties with him, but in order to do that, you need to know what provoked him into attacking. If he does try to hurt someone in any way, he should expect to be punished. If he then lies about it and you have to hear of it from someone else, he should know that his punishment will be more severe because it shows that he's not trying to change. Also explain that you need to trust what he tells you in order to be able to take his side in case someone accuses him falsely of a misdeed.

Your youngster will lie to you about breaking a conventional rule when he doesn't accept the rule and doesn't acknowledge that you, as his parent, have a right to have the final say on what the rules are. Let's say your child tells you he was working at his friend's house on a joint homework project and you learn that he went to the playground instead. A breach of trust is certainly at hand, but you'll be making a mistake if you focus only on punishing him for lying.

You need to ask yourself why he felt a need to lie about going to the playground. Why couldn't he just tell you he was going and that he'd do his homework later? The answer may be that you are too inflexible about how he apportions his work and playtime. Or perhaps he hasn't learned to take his school responsibilities seriously enough. Whatever the reason, it's obvious that he hasn't made your rule about homework his rule too. You can overcome this conflict if the two of you work out a mutually acceptable rule together, one that gives him the flexibility he wants as long as he demonstrates to your satisfaction that he is taking care of his schoolwork.

Children are likely to reject a conventional rule when they think it is unfair—for instance, when they believe parents have instituted the rule on the basis of misinformation. Many parents have heard something like the following: "There's no reason for me not to go there. Those kids may look rough to you, but I know them. They wouldn't hurt anyone."

If your child balks at observing a conventional rule, remember, there are no absolutes of right and wrong in this category. For instance, there is no objectively "correct" curfew time for children. Each family has to work this out by balancing such factors as the child's desire to be with friends, how much time he or she needs for homework and other responsibilities, and the parents' concern for their child's safety.

If your child lies to you about breaking a conventional rule, you may want to punish him for both the infraction and the lie so that he knows you intend to see that your rules are followed and that it's not in his interest to hide violations from you. At the same time, though, make sure you open up a discussion about why you think the rule is a good one and why he thinks it's bad. You might start with something like the following: "We have to find a way to come to an agreement about what the rule in this situation is so I don't wind up mistrusting and resenting you and you don't wind up thinking of me as your jailor." Then *negotiate*. Both of you state the reasons for your positions, and then look for a way to resolve your conflict, perhaps by devising a mutually acceptable compromise ("It's all right for you to change your plans as long as you telephone me before you do so I know where you are"), perhaps by giving him more freedom for a trial period to see if he can still meet his other responsibilities.

Once your youngster agrees to a rule that you've hammered out together, he's more likely to uphold it. He'll also appreciate your respect for him and be inclined to give you respect in return. Various studies have shown that formal negotiations between parents and children go a long way toward reducing family conflicts.[12]

What should you do if you can't reach an agreement? Sometimes you may decide to let your child do it his way so he can learn from experience. But sometimes you may feel that the lesson will be too costly or dangerous for him (like getting expelled from school). Whatever you decide to do, you need to insist that the final decision is yours, that it is your right and responsibility as a parent. If you've generally shown him that you are on his side, that you respect his feelings and desires, and that you only clamp down when absolutely necessary, it's a pretty safe bet that he'll respect your right to have the final say over rules. If not, you should be able to gain compliance by setting up a system that rewards him for upholding the rule and punishes him for violating it.

The moral-conventional distinction is also important when your youngster lies to peers, teachers, or other adults. An example of lying to others to cover up breaking a conventional rule would be making up a false excuse to a teacher: "I couldn't finish my paper because my dog was sick." A lie in the moral domain would be to mislead someone in order to con him or her out of money.

When lies to others involve moral infractions, empathy and personal standards training are in order. In the present example, you might start by asking your child to put herself in the place of the person whose trust she betrayed: "Think how he must feel now knowing that everything you said was a lie just calculated to hurt him." Personal standards training should be geared toward developing her pride in striving to be an honest person. Stress how good the honest person feels about herself and how lying destroys any bond between people, whether in a friendship, a family, a business enterprise, or among citizens in the community at large.

You may also find that your child lies to boost his status with peers, say by telling a classmate, "My father was an astronaut." Even though these kinds of fabrications don't hurt anyone, they may get him into the habit of lying as a convenient way to manipulate others. If you wish to convey to him the importance of honesty, you'll let him know that you disapprove of these lies also.

Another question to ask in deciding how to handle a lie is: *Was the lie premeditated?* Let's look again at the situation in which a child went to a playground when he was supposed to be doing homework at his friend's house. Many parents would consider it a greater breach of trust if their youngster planned to lie to them in advance —if he was planning to go to the playground all along—than if he lied to cover up an unexpected circumstance or momentary impulse (for instance, if he said he and his friend were talking about next Saturday's game and suddenly realized they needed more practice on the double play).

In our families, and our legal system as well, we judge planned acts more harshly because the premeditated rule-breaker is telling us, in essence, "I don't accept the rule or your right to impose it on me." Therefore, if your child tells you a premeditated lie, he has clearly defined you as the enemy, at least in that specific situation. Explain to him that you don't want to be his enemy, but you can't let him intentionally hurt people (if his lie was to hide a moral transgression) or you can't let him jeopardize his health or his future (if his lie was to hide a conventional transgression). He's more likely to believe that you don't want to be his enemy if, besides holding firm to your rules, you try to understand and sensitively help him overcome any insecurities and inadequacies that may have prompted an immoral action (such as fighting with schoolmates because he doesn't know how to make friends or settle differences constructively), and if you remain flexible in negotiating conventional rules.

In deciding how to respond to your child's lying you will also want to ask: *Are the consequences of the lie serious or minor?* As we said earlier, no parent likes to be lied to, but some lies have more serious consequences than others. Lies made to cover up moral infractions and hide intentionally harmful acts are obviously the most serious. Lies made to cover up conventional rule violations may or may not have serious consequences for anyone. It's unlikely, for instance, that a child with good grades and study habits will be harmed if he says he's finished all his homework when, in fact, he still has some left. On the other hand, his very life may be in jeopardy if he lies to his parents about his whereabouts and goes with friends into dangerous neighborhoods. There are other kinds of lies that ordinarily do little or no harm at all, and some are well-intentioned. "White" lies, for example, are actually told to make people feel better or to spare them pain. Even five-year-olds recognize that there are different kinds of lies, and rate some as worse than others.[13]

You need to decide whether you want to take a strong stand against all forms of lying regardless of their consequences or whether you want to let "white" or minor ones pass without comment. Whichever you decide, make sure your children understand which lies you take seriously and that you expect the truth at all times in those areas.

Two other recommendations: Don't make the act of lying more important than the infraction behind it. Remember, a child lies for a reason. If you make the act of lying the most important thing, then those reasons might get overlooked.

Also, don't try to entrap your child to test her truthfulness. If you already know that she broke a rule (you saw her at the playground when she was supposed to be doing homework), don't ask her where she was and then dramatically accuse her of lying if you don't get the truth. Tell her immediately (but privately) that you saw her there and let her know what the consequences will be. As quickly as possible, open up a dialogue. Ask her why she disobeyed and remind her of your reasons for the rule. Place your emphasis on overcoming the difficulty behind the lie.

## MONEY: ALLOWANCES AND OTHER "FINANCIAL TRANSACTIONS" WITH YOUR CHILD

Sometime during his early middle childhood your child will discover money. He'll learn that he needs money in order to get some of the things he wants. And it won't take him long to find out that money is a scarce item; there won't be as much of it around as he'd like. He'll also learn that most people get money by doing things for, and selling things to, other people.

Sometime during these years he'll also discover that money places limits on how kind people are to each other—that they *compete* for money, that when it comes to money, people try to gain at each other's expense by charging as high a price as possible for their own goods and services and paying as little as possible for the goods and services of others. He'll also notice that some people have a great deal of money, enough to indulge every whim and fancy, while others have little, many with barely enough to survive on.

An eleven-year-old boy from an upper-middle-class family overheard a conversation between his father and their housekeeper, Bea. His father was refusing Bea's request for a 50¢-an-hour raise in salary. Later, the boy asked his father why he had said no. He knew the $20 a week wouldn't affect what his family could afford to buy or do, and he knew that Bea was worried about whether she could afford to keep her own son in college.

The boy's father said, "That's not our problem. She's getting paid what housekeepers get paid, plus some extras that not everyone gives. I like Bea, but feelings have nothing to do with this. If she doesn't like her salary, she's free to quit and go find another job." "But what if there are no other jobs?" the boy questioned. "And what difference would it make since everyone else is paying housekeepers the same thing?" The boy's mother agreed with her husband. "Don't worry," she said. "Bea's good at working things out."

The boy, who is now a man, never forgot this incident. Bea had been with the family a long time. He had even heard his mother tell friends, "Oh, Bea—she's just like one of the family." His parents had taught him to treat Bea with respect and kindness. "When we're not home," they would say, "you listen to her as if she were your mother."

But now he was getting a different message. Bea's troubles, if they involve money, are not "our problem." We don't want to see her anxious or worried, but *the market* determines what we pay her, not our feelings. This made the boy feel ashamed and angry at his parents.

What should his parents have done? Should they have given Bea the raise? As with all moral dilemmas, your answer will depend on how you think people should live with each other and what values you believe deserve priority.

Answers are never easy when it comes to money. Let's say your eight-year-old daughter comes to you on a hot summer day and says she wants to open a lemonade stand. She asks you how much she should charge. "How much do the other stands charge?" you might ask. "But what's a *fair* price?" she might wonder. She has other questions too. "Should I use the best ingredients? And what if someone says he's really thirsty but doesn't have enough money to pay? Should I give him lemonade anyway?" What do you say? Do feelings count in the lemonade business? Do you give drinks to the thirsty regardless of their ability to pay? Or does it matter why they can't pay? Are they temporarily down on their luck or chronically trapped in poverty, or have they spent their money on frivolities or are they lazy and refuse to work, hoping to play on people's sympathies?

Competition for money has created problems for humankind from the beginning of civilization. Money is not the only thing individuals kill each other over or countries go to war for, but it surely ranks high on the list of reasons. Competition over money raises moral conflicts because, as the story of the housekeeper illustrates, in trying to make ourselves richer we often make others poorer. When we are competing with people for money, it's hard to have empathy for them.

## Allowances

Your child's first relationship to be strained by money will probably be with you. You control his access to money, and when he wants more than you're willing to give him don't be surprised if he tries all kinds of annoying tactics to extract a few more farthings from you. He'll nag and cajole, have tantrums, and try to make you feel guilty; he may even steal from you. Many children do.

All parents must face the question, how much should I give my child? First there is the issue of how large an allowance. But you will also have to decide how much to spend on toys and clothing—and with children's stores now stocked with computer games, mini-bikes,

and designer clothes, the expenses can be exorbitant. Just as sometimes happens between husbands and wives, the relationship between parents and children can become dominated by conflicts over
money.

When you think about moral training, one important question
with regard to money is, how do you want your child to behave
toward you when she wants more money or more of the things that
money can buy? Nagging you or stealing from you are obviously not
moral solutions. The best alternative is to set up a system for determining your child's "income" that seems reasonable to both of you.

There is obviously no right or wrong amount of money to give
your youngster as an allowance. In coming up with a figure, parents
usually take into account what they can afford, what their child's
reasonable expenses are, and what other children his age are getting. Many families are also influenced by their belief about what is
good for their child's character. Some feel a youngster on a tight
budget learns the "value of a dollar" and to be disciplined in
money matters. Other parents want their child to have all the good
things in life. They believe that if they give him everything they can
afford to, he'll be happier for it. These points of view are not incompatible. You can be very generous and still set up limitations that
teach your youngster to select the things he wants carefully and
require him to save up for particularly expensive items that he wants
badly.

The best way to arrive at an amount is through an open discussion
of all the factors that both you and your youngster believe should
affect his income, including teaching him how to budget and save
and use money responsibly. Try to come up with an agreement that
both of you feel is reasonable. Make the agreement temporary, say
for two weeks, and then reassess it in the light of what you have both
learned during that period. Since your youngster's money needs will
change from time to time and will certainly increase as he grows
older, set up regular time intervals to re-evaluate the agreement.

The purpose of the discussion and agreement is to substitute reason for power tactics on both your parts. Some parents keep tight
control over the purse strings, forcing their children to come to
them every time a money need arises and never giving them a lump
sum to use as they want to or an adequate and reliable allowance.
They want to make sure their child knows who the boss is. Children
have their own power tactics. Use reason so that money conflicts

don't drive a wedge between you and your child and turn you into enemies.

On your part, you need to appreciate that your youngster needs a predictable and sensible income, just as you do—one that he doesn't have to come begging or nagging for. For your child's part, he needs to understand that there are good reasons why he can't have as much money as he wants.

Don't expect your child to become the perfect money manager instantly. One week she may spend all her money in the first few days. Part of learning to be responsible is learning the consequences of being irresponsible. Her own discomfort at getting through the rest of the week without money is sufficient punishment and there's no need to scold her on top of that—although, if you have some good advice to help her budget more carefully, provide it. Also consider offering her a loan to ease her burden a bit by spreading it out over a few weeks. Instead of having no money for almost an entire week, she can have her allowance reduced for two or three weeks until the loan is paid back. She's still likely to learn the budgeting lesson, but without quite as much discomfort.

Work out an agreement on how to handle the many unexpected expenses that will come up. Your youngster and his friends may plan an outing of some kind—one that you want him to go on—but that his allowance can't cover; or his baseball glove may tear in mid-season. Most parents handle such unexpected circumstances informally: their child lets them know what he needs and they decide yes or no. There is nothing wrong with this approach, as long as he doesn't badger you when you say no and you give him a good reason for saying no. Children generally accept good reasons.

A more formal way of handling unexpected expenses—a way that gives a child both more responsibility and more freedom—is to establish a "savings box" or to open a bank account in his name with funds to meet extra expenses. This will give him some flexibility on how much he can spend and clearly define the limits of his budget. You can use this contingency account to teach fiscal responsibility if you open it with an initial contribution, and then match any money your child saves from either his allowance or a part-time job. You can match him dollar for dollar, or two for every one he saves, or any amount you want. You might even let him borrow against future savings if a special expense comes up that he can't cover.

**Should Money Be Used as a Reward or Punishment?**

We are against using money to reward your child for doing household chores, homework, or anything else that simply fulfills her responsibilities to herself and others—and that includes asking her to do you a favor. If you pay her for doing her share and for preparing for her future, you won't be teaching her to accept *her* responsibilities and take pride in fulfilling them. Getting some immediate cash will be her only goal. The only payoff a child should expect for contributing to the daily maintenance of her family is the satisfaction that she has met her responsibility well.

Paying a child money can also undermine her bond to family members. Sensitivity to others will become merely an expedient way to earn money for herself. Recent research shows that a youngster's "moral motivation"—her sense of obligation to help others in need—can be undermined by paying her to help. Once you pay a child to do something, she may not want to do it for any other reason but money.[14]

A child *earns* his income—including his allowance and the things you purchase specifically for him—simply by being a member of the family in good standing. "In good standing" means that he meets his responsibilities as a family member voluntarily, and not because you pay him on a per-item basis. Husbands and wives don't pay each other for each service rendered—so much for cooking, so much for taking out the garbage; they share incomes and responsibilities. Your child should be treated the same way.

One mother we recently spoke with confirmed that even very young children can understand and accept important family responsibilities. She asked her five-year-old son to let his ten-year-old brother read stories to him three nights a week after supper. The older boy had a reading problem and his teacher recommended that he read aloud regularly. The younger child protested. He wanted his parents to read to him, not his brother. He didn't like the way the older boy read. But once his mother explained the true purpose behind the reading sessions and asked him to help his brother out, he did so without another protest.

If she had offered him money to get him to comply, she would have undermined his pleasure in giving to his brother, his self-esteem over his generosity, and his pride in knowing that his mother was pleased by his kindhearted action. If you teach your children when they are young that the happiness of the family depends on everyone fulfilling his or her fair share of responsibilities (without moans and groans), you'll find that family camaraderie will be more important to them than cash.

Should parents punish their child by taking money away when she is "bad" or doesn't fulfill her obligations? Only under certain conditions. Remember, a child makes plans around how much money she anticipates having, so it's important for her to be able to rely on a steady income. But if you feel she is misusing her money, say by buying drugs, then there is good reason to cut back on her funds.

Also, if she loses her good standing as a member of the family because she fails to meet responsibilities, you may not want to share with her. Explain your feelings carefully to her so she understands that you aren't just in a bad mood or handling her money in a capricious way. Let her know that you enjoy sharing with her, but not when you see that she doesn't want to do her share. Give her some forewarning about where your feelings are headed so she has time to alter her behavior. Keep the emphasis on your feelings toward her, and not on rewards and punishments, and be very specific about what she needs to do to make you feel like sharing with her again.

It's also best to avoid withholding money every time your youngster misbehaves ("You hit your sister—so you can't have your allowance next week"). Since you're not likely to be totally consistent if you try to do this, he'll probably wind up thinking that you're unfair, and he'll always be uncertain about his income.

You can, though, set up a contract in advance that states clearly what misbehavior will cause him to lose part or all of his allowance. Discuss your reasons with him and why you are using money as a reward or penalty. You might, for instance, say, "I don't want you hitting your sister. Right now you don't care if you hurt her, but I know you do care about money. I can't allow you to go on hitting her, so while we work on the problem between the two of you and your feelings toward each other, you're going to lose (some specific amount of money) every time you raise your hand to her." As usual, be open to his point of view and suggestions.

If it's clear that his sister is baiting him, set up a similar penalty for her in order to be fair. If you find that he stops hitting soon after you set up the penalty, don't make the mistake of thinking your job is over. Research shows that when a material reward or penalty is withdrawn, the unwanted behavior comes right back.[15] Material rewards and penalties can be useful, but they are no substitute for moral training. They will not help your child develop empathy, get him to care about resolving conflicts constructively, or help him acquire personal moral standards.

Researchers have found that an effective way to use material rewards and penalties is to let the child evaluate, on his own, whether his behavior has met some prearranged criterion. You can use such self-evaluation in a way that incorporates our suggestion to make your child feel that he is a shareholder in the family enterprise. Instead of giving him money (say, portions of his allowance) when he behaves properly, or subtracting money from next week's allowance when he misbehaves, give him his whole allowance in advance in an envelope. Tell him that he will monitor his own behavior. If he meets the daily criterion (say, no fights that day), he can withdraw one day's allowance from the envelope.

Stress that he's not *earning* money. It's his share and set aside for him. But he has to deserve it in order to use it for himself. If there is money left over at the end of the week, it goes to a charity he has chosen (with your approval). Let him know that if you find him cheating, you will have to take over the daily evaluations. Youngsters generally prefer self-evaluation and the "honor system" and it tends to make them take responsibility for their own actions.[16] When parents do the monitoring, it's easy for a child to focus on what he can get away with. This arrangement also allows you to communicate more in terms of feelings than exchanges of cash.

### Coping with Your Child the Consumer

Children's desires for things tend to be impulsive and intense. Getting what they want, whether it's a bike, a chemistry set, a dress, or a video game, can seem like a matter of life and death. And children are very adept at convincing parents that their whole future and psychological well-being depend on getting the particular thing they want. A couple of years ago a father told us that he was surprised at what an easy pushover he had become for his child. He had just bought his son an expensive video game that had become the rage in his community, but which he really couldn't afford. Why had he done it? His son used the old ploy that all his friends had the game, then added, "They can practice all they want, so they all beat me"—stressing *beat*, of course. That did it. Good Old Dad bought the game that afternoon.

There is nothing more frustrating than buying a youngster something she desperately wants, only to find that she has become totally bored with it a few days later. At those times it's worth remembering that it takes a child time to learn about her own interests—which ones will pass and which will last. As long as she's investigating her world and developing some serious interests, there's really nothing wrong with her having a string of intense but passing interests— except that it can be expensive.

If your child has become overly demanding because she gets bored quickly, rather than scolding her for not knowing in advance which activities she will continue to enjoy, you'd be better off giving her a budget. If she knows she can only spend so much money over a given period of time, she'll evaluate the objects of her desires more carefully—just as she'll have to do as an adult. The lesson you want her to learn is that money is limited and has to be allocated carefully. Scolding her won't give her practice in apportioning her funds. It will only teach her that she's displeased you.

*Once you've decided to buy something for your child, don't let your money worries overshadow your pleasure in giving and his pleasure in receiving.* Not long ago we were waiting on the checkout line in the toy section of a department store. In front of us was a woman and her eleven- and twelve-year-old sons. Both boys were caressing brand new mini-bikes their mother was about to purchase for them. As the mother was counting out her money, all in small bills, she was scolding the boys about taking good care of the bikes and not losing them, and she warned them that she could not afford to replace them if they were broken or lost. It was a tense time for her. Clearly this was a lot of money for her to be spending. But she *was* spending it, and instead of finding joy in her sons' excitement, she was overwhelmed by her own money worries. Only after one of us commented on how happy her sons seemed did she turn to look at their joyful faces and relax for a moment.

*Shopping trips.* Some children can make trips to the supermarket or department store a misery. They want everything in sight and they'll nag and whine till they get what they want. One effective way to deal with this is to tell a child before you go shopping that as you pass down the aisles together she can make up a list of up to five things that she thinks she might want. But she'll have to hold off on choosing one until all the shopping is done. Then she can evaluate them all carefully and decide which *one* she wants most. Whichever she decides on she can have (within some price range, of course).

This strategy will keep her occupied and help her learn to tailor her desires to clear and firm limits rather than to how much wheedling Mommy can endure; and it'll give her the security that she is definitely going to get something on the trip without having to battle for it. Most children find the deliberation fun.

If your youngster still nags and whines, make sure you don't reinforce this by giving in. Take her home immediately and put her in her room as soon as she starts to become demanding. You may have to waste a trip or two, but it's worth it. If necessary, have a babysitter or friend stay with her while you go out to "have fun" shopping. Make sure she understands that she's missing out on the fun because the shopping trips are not fun for you when she tries to bully you into buying her things. The babysitter should keep her in her room and not try to make her stay at home enjoyable. That way she is more likely to behave herself on your next shopping trip.

### Your Child the Philanthropist

An important lesson to teach your youngster is that money need not only be used selfishly. It can also be spent to benefit others by giving presents or donating to charity. If you've already encouraged him to share his possessions and to think about other people's needs, then it won't be difficult to get him to share his cash. Why not make his allowance large enough to include a gift and charity fund that he can spend on presents and donations? That way he'll feel that he's giving *his* money and he'll learn that giving isn't something you think about only during holidays or other special occasions. You might also set up a matching fund so that any week that he contributes more than the standard amount to the gift and charity fund, you'll add an equal amount also.

*Gifts.* When you teach your youngster how to give appropriate gifts you're also teaching him to be more observant of and sensitive to the people around him. He'll have to notice and remember what they like and don't like. The whole process of giving gifts can be very exciting for children—from planning, to buying, to hiding, to giving and watching the recipient tear through the wrapping.

The adventure of it all and his awareness that he's been given an "adult" responsibility will help him discover that giving can be joyful. Guide him through each phase. He'll be happy to have you as his confidant, but do more prompting than suggesting ("Try to notice what she likes" is better than "I think she would like a new scarf"). Let him decide what to give.

**Charities.** When you explain to your child about charities you'll be teaching him that people's (and animal's) fortunes differ vastly, often due to forces totally beyond their control. One child contracts a debilitating illness, another becomes an orphan; one puppy becomes a pampered pet while it's littermate becomes a subject in an experiment on electric shock. You'll also be communicating that we share a bond with other people and animals—perhaps because we can understand their suffering even if our own lives are happy—that makes us capable of wanting to ease their pain.

Introduce your child to three or four charities that you think she'd be interested in. Give her the option of selecting one or several to donate to. Teach her what you think is appropriate and what you think she's capable of understanding about the human, animal, or environmental conditions that a charity is designed to serve. The average seven-year-old is obviously not as likely to understand a charity for political refugees as one for orphaned children or homeless animals.

As with giving gifts, children can get very involved in giving to a charity, particularly if they are well informed about the needs of the recipients. Your youngster will have more of an incentive to be charitable if she knows that you are. If you give money or time to help others, share your feelings with your child; explain to her what motivates you. You might give because of empathy or out of a sense of duty, or both. Talking to her about it will help arouse similar feelings in her and teach her that they are feelings to be acted upon.

One note of caution: Some researchers have found that some children believe people wouldn't be suffering unless they deserved it or that the unlucky are inferior in some way.[17] They want to believe that the world is just. If you find that your child thinks this way, it's important that you correct her misconception. It's so easy not to help when we believe that the unfortunate deserve their misery. Illusions like this aren't worth preserving; they are self-righteous and self-congratulatory. The implication is that they deserve their miserable fate; therefore I must deserve my good fortune. Children aren't the only ones that show this tendency to blame the sufferer, as evidenced by the "You're getting what you deserve" attitude of some religious groups toward homosexual sufferers of auto-immune deficiency syndrome (AIDS). Given the incredible horrors that people inflict on each other without ever being visited by heavensent plagues, it would be a very vicious God indeed, and one with a baffling value system, if he concocted such a horrible disease just to punish adult males for having sex with each other.

## CHILDREN AND ANIMALS

Most children start out liking animals and attributing human qualities to them. Children's stories, cartoons, and films are filled with sympathetic animal characters, from Lassie to Bambi. Their clothing and wall decorations generally have animal designs on them. We take our children to zoos to pet and feed newborn animals. Then a child learns that he and his family eat cows ("Oh, Elsie"), and wear shoes and gloves made out of their skins. He learns that the soft pretty coat his aunt wears is made from the skins of great big cats like those he's seen at the circus. He loves Bambi and fears and hates the hunters who killed his mother, but soon he finds out that his favorite uncle is a deer hunter. The pet shop will have pretty bunnies hopping about. The butcher shop down the street will have them hanging on hooks.

Little by little a child will learn more and more about the more than 70 million animals killed in research each year, about cruel trapping techniques, about the killing of whales and porpoises and baby seals. He will discover that the oven cleaner his mother uses had to be sprayed in the eyes of unanesthetized rabbits before it could be sold to people; that the last few remaining great apes, our closest kin in the animal kingdom, are trapped and hunted to turn parts of their bodies into trinkets; and that researchers keep kittens awake for days until they die to study the effects of sleep deprivation.

He will also learn that some people care a great deal about animals and work hard—even risk their own lives—to prevent their suffering and slaughter. On the nightly news he will see protesters picketing a cosmetics company in an attempt to get it to stop testing its products on animals, and he will see programs about groups like Greenpeace whose members brave dangers to prevent the slaughter of whales and other animals.

If he is at all attentive to discussions about the plight of animals, he will become aware of the controversy over animal rights: Do we have a moral obligation to treat animals kindly? Or can we use them for any purpose we care to, regardless of the pain we inflict on them? Do animals have rights? Should we treat them as if they were *us?*

Your child may become distressed when he learns that the hamburger he eats is made from a cow or when he becomes aware of the various cruelties we inflict on animals for the sake of our amusement, vanity, and convenience. We recommend that you take his concerns about animal suffering seriously. If you tell him, "That's just the way things are" or "Nothing can be done," you will be teaching him that cruelty must be accepted passively. Obviously, there are people who don't accept it and who are trying to do something about it, either by doing their best not to contribute to the cruelty themselves (say, but not buying fur coats), or by actively working to change laws and practices. And they've had success. Cruel traps *have* been banned in many states; humane and endangered species laws *have* been passed; whaling *has* been reduced.

Keep in mind that your child may express the very same concerns when he becomes aware of examples of cruelty to human beings. Many people believed and told their children that "nothing could be done" about the cruel treatment of blacks in the south. Others refused to be cynical and went down south and marched alongside Dr. King and registered voters, and changed what many were certain couldn't ever be changed.

Similarly, if your child asks what can be done and you reply, "It's too much trouble to bother about," you will be communicating that while we *should* be opposed to cruelty, it's not worth inconveniencing ourselves for. (The very same issues will come up when your child asks you questions about cruelty to humans. He'll watch news reports about dictators and death squads—some installed and financed by our own government—and he'll wonder what he can do about it. Here, too, if you answer "Nothing," you are teaching him that serious cruelty must simply be accepted.)

When your youngster asks you questions about cruelty to animals (or to humans), do your best to discuss the issue as fully and frankly as possible, and review the options available to her. She can become a vegetarian, only use products that don't require testing on animals, contribute time or part of her allowance to a humane organization, or join a protest. Help her locate more information if she wishes. For example, if she is considering becoming a vegetarian, there are organizations that provide information on preparing healthful and tasty meatless meals.

If you are like most adults, you have mixed feelings about the treatment of animals. You don't want them to suffer, but you don't do much about it. A friend of ours loves animals, but she also loves her new beaver coat. She hates to think that beavers were killed for it, and she does her best not to think of it. If she had to personally drown a family of beavers in order to have the coat, she certainly would not do it. Yet, somehow, when the coat is already in the store and the animals are already dead, she finds it acceptable. Similarly, most consumers, we believe, would choose to have a smaller variety of household cleaning products available in their supermarkets if they themselves had to apply each new product to the corneas of dozens of rabbits and observe and record the degree of damage to their eyes (over 750,000 rabbits are used every year for these tests).

Whatever your own beliefs about the issue of animal rights and suffering, whatever your ambivalence and moral strengths and weaknesses, the best that you can do is help your children make up their own minds. We know families in which the parents eat meat and the children don't and other families in which the children eat meat and the parents don't. Cooking is a bit more time-consuming when everybody doesn't eat the same thing, but moral choices are not made for the sake of convenience.

## "BAD" LANGUAGE

Sometime during the middle childhood years you'll probably hear your child use language that is generally categorized as "dirty," "foul," or "obscene." Six-year-olds use such words to be grown-up (since they've probably heard adults or older children using them) or to be provocative (since parents often react with shock or amusement). The eleven-year-old uses "bad" language for the same reasons, but by that age it may have become part of his general expressive and social style—particularly if his friends reinforce tough talk.

Our society is far more accepting of strong language than it used to be, and there are probably a host of reasons for this. Men are no longer obsessed with protecting women from references to matters anatomical and sexual. "Polite society" no longer dominates cultural trends. Some anti-war activist groups in the sixties used "dirty" words to provoke society into recognizing that killing was the real obscenity to be confronted, not the words we use. Also, not many people believe in word magic anymore—that if you say "hell" and "damn," dire consequences will befall you.

The words a child uses become a moral issue only when they are used to hurt, and that's true whether she's using standard vocabulary or street language. If you teach your youngster not to intentionally hurt people, you will inevitably encounter the issue of hurting with words. Some parents tell their children, "You can call names or say whatever you want, but don't hit." Calling names may be less harmful than hitting, and it can certainly feel very satisfying to zap someone with the perfect cutting epithet, but it usually only escalates a conflict.

Our children will be better off if we teach them to handle their arguments with reason, by patiently explaining their side and genuinely trying to understand their opponent's side. When it's obvious that an opponent has no interest in being reasonable, it pays to just walk away rather than say anything to perpetuate the conflict. When reason fails, your youngster should call upon legitimate authorities to right any wrong he's suffered. With aggressive opponents who won't let him walk away, he may need an effective self-defense.

You may not want your child using curse words for reasons that have nothing to do with hurting anyone. You may have been brought up to find them offensive, and even though you know that there's nothing inherently bad about them, you still find yourself cringing whenever your child uses them. If this is the case, you have to decide whether you are going to adapt to your child or he's going to adapt to you. Either choice need not cause any serious problems.

If you decide to ask your child to refrain from using certain language in your presence, explain your reasons, even if they are only aesthetic ones. He's more than likely to try to accommodate you. If he doesn't, treat it as a sign that there's trouble in some other aspect of your relationship. Consider whether he is deliberately trying to provoke you or get some attention; or perhaps you have not yet taught him to be responsive to your feelings; or he might be feeling a need to assert his independence ("I have a right to say what I want").

You may not want your child to use curse words outside the home as well. You may feel it will reflect poorly on her and hurt her socially. "Bad" words, in this sense, are a form of bad manners. Most parents want their children to learn the various social conventions of their community: how to eat, dress, speak. These differ to varying degrees from community to community, group to group, and across generations. Some parents add that they also don't want their children to use curse words because they limit expression and reduce complex thoughts and feelings to the same few expletives.

If you explain your opposition to curse words in terms of social conventions—nothing more—with no moral overtones, your child is likely to go along with your request with little fuss. He'll learn to differentiate whom it's appropriate to use what language with, just as he learns when it's appropriate to wear dress clothes or play clothes. You'll probably get resistance, though, if you argue that speech manners (or any manners) are moral virtues. You're not likely to convince him that somehow he'll be a more righteous person if he keeps his language "clean."

## "I'M TELLING ON YOU": HOW TO HANDLE TATTLING

The good news is your child is learning right from wrong. The bad news is he is spotting everybody else's wrongs and telling on them. All children tattle to some degree and they start very young. The three-year-old delights in exposing the misdeeds of her older or younger siblings ("Tommy took a cookie"); the five-year-old eagerly broadcasts his playmates' transgressions on the playground ("She pushed in front"); and the seven-year-old takes pleasure in "snitching" to the teacher on a classmate ("He's passing notes").

Tattling is a natural byproduct of learning adult standards. The grown-ups set the standards of right and wrong and praise or scold according to whether their standards are met. But children don't merely want to be thought of as good; they want to be thought of as *best*. So tattling becomes a handy way to knock off any rivals for the "Best Kid" prize. It's also a useful tactic for recruiting the grown-ups to one's own side in a conflict ("Wait till I tell Mommy; she'll make you give it back to me").

An eight-year-old will ordinarily tattle only on children he doesn't like or with whom he is in direct competition, but preschoolers and young grade school children will even tattle on their closest friends or a beloved sibling. The younger children don't yet define friendship in terms of mutual obligations such as loyalty; nor do they recognize that a friend whom you tattle on isn't likely to remain your friend for long. Children of all ages are particularly prone to tattle when they themselves are in trouble. Every parent has heard something like, "Well, Melissa did it too" or "I know I cut a class, but Marty stole a kid's lunch."

Parents are often confused about how to handle tattling. They don't want to encourage their child's inclinations to get others in trouble, yet a blanket rule against tattling seems inappropriate since there *are* times when telling on others is legitimate (such as when a child sees another child about to harm someone or endanger himself). Parents also know that children can't always defend themselves from bossy or nasty peers and siblings, and need to be able to call for adult aid when necessary ("Mommy, he's hitting me"; "She took my ball"). Still, parents want their children to learn to handle the normal rough and tumble of childhood relationships without having to summon adult intervention for every quarrel or slight.

Tattling between siblings is usually the hardest type for parents to deal with. When they learn from one child of another's rule-breaking ("Mommy, Mommy, Brian didn't finish putting his toys away"), should they praise the tattler and scold the rule breaker—and thereby encourage tattling? Or should they regard any rule infractions learned through tattling as "inadmissible evidence"—which may lead the children to believe the rule wasn't very important.

All paths seem to have their pitfalls, yet the terrain is not as unmanageable as it first appears. When parents ask themselves, *"What do I want my child to learn from my response to her tattling?"* they quickly realize that children tattle for a number of different reasons and that each warrants a different response. The four main reasons why children tattle are:

1. to get another child in trouble ("You brought food into the living room and I'm telling"),
2. to obtain adult aid or protection for themselves ("It's my turn to pick the program and you're not letting me—and I'm telling"),
3. to prevent another child from doing harm, either to himself or someone else ("You're not supposed to cross the street alone and I'm telling"), and
4. to uphold the rules—more out of a need for orderliness than any commitment to the purpose behind the rules ("We're all supposed to walk in a line and you're not—and I'm telling").

Clearly, tattling for the first reason, to get another in trouble, is most disturbing to parents. They don't want their child to harm others intentionally or to seek to enhance his own status by lowering someone else's. So the first step for parents in responding to a tattle is to make a judgment about their child's intention. Why is he telling? Is it to help or harm?

If the tattling appears ill-intentioned (as in the case of the boy who announced that his brother didn't put his toys away), parents should make sure the child understands, not just their disapproval, but how they expect him to treat others. A parent could, for example, say, "You're not supposed to try to get Brian or anyone else in trouble. That's not being helpful. I'll find out soon enough if Brian did something he shouldn't have. Next time you see Brian doing something wrong, if you want to be a good brother, tell him the right thing to do and why he should do it, and if he needs help, help him. That's what brothers are supposed to do. And only tell me about it if he's doing something that could hurt someone or hurt himself."

The child who was tattled on, if he really broke a rule, should not be let off the hook either, but parents would do well to reprimand in a manner that affords the tattler as little satisfaction as possible. A direct and simple correction will usually suffice: "Brian, you know that you're supposed to put *all* your toys away when you clean up, so go to your room and finish." Avoid extra punishment for the rule breaker in these situations to keep from encouraging the tattler.

Parents should also help clear the air of bad feelings after a serious tattling incident between siblings (or friends), and use the incident for teaching important social and moral lessons, such as what it means to be a "brother" or "sister" or "friend" or "classmate." In other words, children need to understand why they shouldn't tattle —what's truly at stake that makes tattling wrong. For instance, a parent might say, "I expect my children to be on each other's side— not to try to get each other in trouble. We want to have a good, loving family, and that can only happen if everyone tries to help and take care of everyone else. In our family, we build each other up; we don't tear each other down. So now let's put this incident behind us and do something together that we can all enjoy." Children want to have a loving family and when they understand that that's what's at stake when they tattle, they become more receptive to parental prohibitions against tattling.

When parents aren't sure what a youngster's intentions are when he tattles, it is difficult to know how best to respond to him. For example, six-year-old Larry came running to his mother announcing that his older brother, Sam, had just taken a dollar from her purse. The mother had to decide whether Larry was tattling for a good reason (to protect her property) or for a bad one (to get Sam in trouble). Since Larry tattled on Sam with some frequency (lots of "Mommy, Sam didn't turn the water off," "Mommy, Sam didn't hang up his clothes"), she suspected that his primary interest was to get Sam in trouble.

Yet, in this instance she felt it was acceptable for Larry to tell on Sam since taking money without permission was a serious matter and broke a firm household rule for both children against taking anything from her purse (or anyone's belongings at all) without permission. She found herself unsure of whether to praise Larry for telling or reprimand him for tattling.

The best thing she could do was to be totally honest with Larry about her feelings, letting him know she was pleased that he told her about the money but that she was also concerned about his intentions. In this way she could explain that there are times when telling is the right thing to do, while still discouraging his ill-intentioned tattling in the future. She might say something like, "I'm pleased that you told me about Sam taking money from my purse because it's okay to tell on someone when they are doing harm— and taking somebody else's things without permission is doing harm. But I'm also concerned that since you tattle on Sam so often over every little thing, your reason for telling might not have been to be helpful but merely to get your brother in trouble. You have to think about which is the real reason you tattled. The only way I'll know is by what you do in the future. If you keep tattling over the things I've asked you not to, then it probably means that you were just trying to get him in trouble this time. And I hope that's not so."

She might then bring both children together to restate why taking things without permission is wrong, and why in particular she didn't want anything taken out of her purse. Then she could talk to Sam *privately* about why he took the money.

When a child tattles because her sense of order has been violated, parents need to let her know that correcting other children is not her job and is best left to the adults who are responsible for the rules. For instance, Monica frequently informed her first-grade teacher when her classmates didn't work on their journals as instructed. The teacher told her mother that she didn't believe Monica was out to harm the children but was simply upset that the teacher's rule wasn't being followed.

In this situation there was no reason to scold Monica as if she had done something bad. Monica believed in upholding rules if she thought they were good rules, so what she needed was a clearly stated and carefully explained rule about why children should leave the correcting of other children to the adults. So both teacher and mother explained that each child's work was his or her own responsibility, that the teacher would quickly learn who was and wasn't doing their journals, and that the class spirit would be ruined if children thought their classmates were trying to get them in trouble over things that weren't their business.

Obviously, when a classmate's irresponsibility does affect other children, as in a group project, then it would be appropriate for the children affected to inform the teacher. Here the motive for telling would be legitimate self-protection and not simply to do harm.

Children, even three-year-olds, are well aware of whether their actions are meant to harm or help. If parents make it clear that tattling to harm, like any harmful behavior, is not acceptable, if they explain why and promote their child's more good-natured inclinations, then it's unlikely that their child will have a long-lasting problem with tattling. The question of when it's appropriate to tell on others will remain an important topic for family discussions, without easy answers. Should your youngster report on a child who stole a library book? What if the thief is also the neighborhood bully who has warned him not to tell? These are serious issues that children and adults must sometimes face. We may honor the whistle blower but few are willing to take the same risks. Open family discussions can guide a child in these areas and help him define his own values.

## HELPING YOUR CHILD MEET RESPONSIBILITIES AT HOME, AT SCHOOL, AND IN THE COMMUNITY

### Home

Young children, starting at around two years of age, enjoy helping with chores, like clearing dishes from the table and making beds, as long as parents are patient and encouraging. If you blow up when your child drops a dish, he won't find clearing the table fun anymore. If helping your child develop confidence and competence is more important than a few pieces of china (even expensive ones), taking care of everyday chores will become part of his routine.

Expect a difference between getting your child to do chores with you and getting her to do them on her own. You are a big part of the fun and she wants to be with you and show off her growing skills. For example, she'll want to help you dust, but won't be as eager to put her blocks and toys away—unless you do it with her.

Some suggestions for chores:

**Start out doing chores with him.** "Let's put the toys away," will get a better response than "Go put your toys away." Then fade out your participation. "We'll do the ones in this corner together. Then I'll watch you do these on your own, and then we'll do the last corner together." A little later you can have him call you for an inspection (and a "Good job") when he's done. Ultimately, he'll do his chores all on his own. But remember, everyone likes some appreciation for a job well done.

**Break a chore down into small steps.** To make a bed well one has to go through a lot of steps and satisfy a number of criteria: corners neat, pillows stacked, cover smooth. Teach each step. And be patient and encouraging. Make learning a pleasure for your child. If *you* get frustrated and are about to scold, that's a signal for you to break that particular part of the task down into smaller steps for her. When a student isn't learning it's always easier to assume she is stupid or uncooperative than to look for ways to improve the lesson. If you need to, make a checklist describing each step in the task. Have her make sure that each item on the list is checked before your inspection. Then fade out your inspections so you only make them periodically and irregularly.

**Be flexible when possible.** As your child grows he will have more and more demands on his time. Some chores make sense only if they're done at certain times; it would be silly to make your bed right before going to sleep. Others need to be done sometime during the day, but it's less crucial when. Let your child choose his own time. He'll also develop his own way of doing things, sometimes not the most efficient way. If you know a better way, show him courteously, but if he wants to continue to do it his way, there is no reason not to let him if he gets the job done. Also, children may want to trade or rotate chores. Again, if they get the job done, why not?

**Present chores as one of the things one does to be a good family member.** Everyone pitches in so the burden is distributed fairly. Don't hesitate to say that it's unfair to you to have to clean up her toys after she finishes playing, that you have many other responsibilities, and that part of using something means putting it out of other people's way when you're done with it.

What about your child's room? Some children keep their rooms messy and dirty. Should they have a right to? Neatness and cleanliness are conventional issues, not moral ones. They are matters of aesthetics, without any objectively correct standard. If you are bothered by the way your child keeps his room, negotiate. If you or others have to enter his room or the mess or odor finds its way out, some change on his part would seem to be in order, as it would if he is so disorganized that he loses things or wastes so much time looking for things that he can't meet his responsibilities or is frequently late. When adults live together there is always some degree of adjusting to each person's sensibilities. We feel the same should hold between adults and children.

Sometimes children are uncooperative about chores because they feel used or not respected enough. Some friends of ours bought a country "dream" house and spent most weekends working on it with great joy. But they were hurt that their children, ages eleven, fourteen, and sixteen, had no interest in helping in the work and only pitched in after a lot of badgering. The children, we learned, were upset because they wanted to spend their weekends with their friends in the city and they felt they should have been consulted before the house was bought. What's more, the parents had very firm ideas about what their dream house should look like and the children were never even asked how they wanted their rooms decorated. Nor did their parents even take the time to try to explain what aesthetic vision lay behind their own decorating choices. Lack of cooperation seems quite inevitable under these circumstances.

## School

School problems rank high on the list of conflict areas between parents and children. These problems fall into two categories: disruptive behavior and poor achievement. If your youngster is disruptive or aggressive in school, it is obviously a moral problem since it means he is harming other students or teachers.

It's far less obvious, though, whether a child has a moral obligation to work to the best of his ability in school. Our society doesn't normally consider underachievement or truancy—behaviors that don't directly harm anyone except, perhaps, the student himself—to be moral infractions. But some cultures do, on the grounds that it is through school or other kinds of training programs that children acquire the skills and work habits to become self-sufficient adults who can contribute to their society. Without those skills and work habits a person has nothing useful to exchange with others and becomes a burden to everyone.

We believe that just as a child should be brought up to accept her share of family responsibilities, she should also be raised to become a contributing member of society—not just a taker. While school is not the only route toward solid citizenship (countless men and women who did poorly in school and who had no formal education at all have turned into responsible, productive, and creative adults), it's a safe bet that, as our economy becomes more dependent on complex technological skills, school achievement will become increasingly important for later success.

Without question education pays off for those who have it. The average college graduate earns a lot more than the average high school graduate. But it is also worth stressing to your youngster the moral (and not just the practical) side of preparing himself for his future as an adult—that he has an obligation to give something back for what he receives from others. Psychologists have found that when school children are told that their efforts will benefit others besides themselves, they work harder and show more self-control than children who only work for their own benefit.[18] It's also likely to be more inspiring for a child to think about preparing to partake in and contribute to one of the great civilizations of history than to think only about finding a job that pays well and provides long vacations.

Ours is an individualistic society; we ordinarily stress self-gain more than interdependence and mutual responsibility. Many parents might not feel comfortable teaching their children that they should work hard in school not just for their own good, but also for the good of the community. However, a sense of mutual obligation is not incompatible with basic American values—not when so many Americans, both young and old, were moved and inspired by John F. Kennedy's call to his countrymen to "Ask not what your country can do for you; ask what you can do for your country." The individualism we cherish is only in danger when the community gives itself the right to designate what form an individual's contribution must take and uses punishment to enforce its will.

***Motivating your child in school.*** School problems are far less likely to arise when a child's motivation to learn is strong. When children want to learn, they aren't going to be disruptive. This was demonstrated quite clearly by psychologists Teodoro Allyon and Michael Roberts. They set up a "token" system to motivate the five most disruptive boys in a fifth-grade reading class to improve their reading scores. The tokens could be traded in for various privileges including access to the game room, having a "good work" letter sent to parents, and becoming an "assistant" teacher. The boys' reading scores improved quickly and the amount of disruption fell almost to zero.[19]

As one would expect, though, as soon as the token system was withdrawn, reading scores went down and disruption increased markedly. These psychologists thus demonstrated that the motivation to learn can reduce problem behavior in school. But we also see that the effect will be short-lived if learning is merely a way to earn a material reward. For the effect to last, learning must become important to the child himself. Psychologists call this "intrinsic" motivation.

As we've pointed out, one way to increase a child's intrinsic motivation to learn is to stress his moral obligation to acquire skills that will enable him to contribute his fair share to the community. Another way is to nurture and channel his own natural curiosity. Young children want to know everything. They are relentless explorers, sometimes to their own jeopardy; and they ask a thousand questions, sometimes to their parents' annoyance.

If your fear for your child's safety or your own need for peace and quiet lead you to stifle his explorations and questions, then learning will not be the joy it should be. If he's afraid to ask you how an airplane flies or why a bird sings, then he may soon stop wondering about these things. He needs to sense that you want him to know everything. And don't feel embarrassed or defensive if you don't know the answers to his questions. You can set a good example by showing him that there's no shame in not knowing answers and that there is great joy to be found in searching for them. You'll find books in libraries and bookstores to help you answer questions that children commonly ask.

It's so easy to stimulate your child's curiosity and channel it into almost any area:

*Children naturally like to experience things they haven't encountered before.* Take your child to new places and also point out unnoticed aspects of familiar places. Even exploring the difference between the entranceway to your home or apartment building and the one next door is sufficient to spark a child's interest and open her eyes and mind to the relationship between the way things are built, the purpose they serve, and their attractiveness. Nothing is too trivial and nothing is intrinsically boring—not to a young and naturally curious mind.

*Children love to discover the ways that things are the same and the ways they are different.* A child starts categorizing and adjusting to sameness and difference right from birth,[20] and almost everything he learns will involve making these two kinds of comparisons. Any place you take him to and any object can provide a wealth of material for the exploration of sameness and difference.

*Children are natural scientists.* They want to know *why* about everything. Their earliest sentences show their interest in, and surprisingly good understanding of, causality.[21] If you show delight in your child's questions about why and how things happen, if you explain things to her patiently and help her explore how to find the answers you don't have, she will take pleasure in learning. School won't just be a place to endure for seven hours a day. It'll be a place you go to learn more about the world.

**Taking charge in the classroom: Setting learning goals.** In reality, not all schools are ideal places for learning. Some can be excessively regimented or too disorganized, or the atmosphere can be harsh and, nowadays, even dangerous. There are good and bad teachers and good and bad textbooks. Youngsters typically feel that they have no choice but to passively accept whatever their school sends their way. This is a self-defeating attitude. Children can set learning goals for themselves for every class, and those can be pursued even if the classroom environment is not what it should be. A child may, for instance, have a "boring" American History teacher who structures the course around memorizing names and dates. But there are so many fascinating things to learn about American History. If he sets his own learning goals, exploring questions like, What are the roots of today's political parties? and How have Central American governments reacted to the Monroe Doctrine?, he can structure a course that will hold some interest for him *and* make it easier to memorize the names and dates for the teacher.

It's worth the effort. A few interesting questions can mean the difference between your youngster wasting an entire semester grumbling impotently about her teacher or taking some control over her education to make every semester as worthwhile as possible. Working out the questions together and trying to figure out what she really wants to know can be an interesting educational time for both of you.

Industry has been using *goal setting* successfully for years to motivate employees. According to a recent review of findings in this area,

> Goals affect performance by directing attention, mobilizing effort, increasing persistence, and motivating strategy development. Goal setting is most likely to improve task performance when the goals are specific and sufficiently challenging, . . . [and] feedback is provided to show progress in relation to the goals.[22]

Similar procedures should help alter the role of the student from passive learner to active information seeker.

*Influencing teachers.* A student's behavior problems and his poor relationship with his teachers can also be improved if the student is not allowed to play the role of passive victim. Psychologists Thomas Sherman and William Cormier asked two highly disruptive fifth-graders what they could do to improve their relationship with their teacher. The students came up with an accurate list of "appropriate" behavior, including following instructions, paying attention to class discussions, having necessary materials on desk, raising hand, and not talking when the teacher is addressing the whole class.

They also came up with an accurate list of inappropriate behavior, the things that got them into trouble, including being out of one's seat, talking back, or talking out. These students obviously knew what their teacher liked and disliked, but taking responsibility to improve life in school was not part of their repertoire. The experimenters asked these students to try to get the teacher to treat them better. They agreed to try. The plan was to increase their "appropriate" behavior and decrease the "inappropriate."

The students didn't carry through immediately, but when the experimenters added a material incentive (a phonograph record or a toy car), they began to do more of what they expected their teacher would like and less of what she wouldn't like. The teacher, who had not been informed about the program, responded as the experimenters had hoped. She started to treat the students more positively within a short time and gave them a more favorable rating.[23] The lesson of the study: Students need to be taught that they can take action—legitimate action—to alter the way a teacher treats them.

Here are other practical steps you can take when your child starts school or when he or she is having problems there:

- *Make sure all assignments are completed.* If you take the time in the beginning to go over everything and insist that your child repeat inadequate work until she gets it right, she'll develop careful work habits.

- *Stress the joy of learning new information and skills* rather than simply fulfilling an unpleasant chore. Let your enthusiasm make learning a pleasure for her.

- *Keep in close contact with teachers.* If your child is having trouble, ask for a daily report from her teacher so that you know what areas to focus on at home. These reports will let you know if your efforts are succeeding. Most teachers will cooperate. A one- or two-sentence note or a simple checklist should be sufficient.

- *Make school a priority.* Don't take excuses. You want to convey to your youngster that school and learning are important—important enough for you to put a lot of your own time in with her. A number of studies show that you can improve a child's schoolwork by making her freedom to do some of the things that she wants to do, such as spending time with friends and watching television, dependent on getting better grades.[24] But be reasonable and realistic in your expectations. Don't require her to go from an F to an A in one leap in order to earn back a privilege.

- *If your child is having trouble understanding something, go over it with her step by step to find out where she goes astray.* It's hard to learn long division, but it's easy to learn any single step in the process. Go over each step as often as necessary. Drilling is part of learning, whether it's learning arithmetic or basketball.

- *Be encouraging.* You have to convince your child she can learn. She needs to understand that frustration and weariness are to be expected when learning new things. If she gets tired or confused it doesn't mean she's stupid or that she should give up.

- *Don't let her avoid meeting her responsibilities because she is in a "mood."* Everybody has his or her ups and downs. Part of becoming a responsible person is being able to meet obligations even when we're not in the mood to. It's easy to do well in short spurts when there aren't any difficult obstacles. The people who can be counted on hang in even when the going gets tough. On the other hand, there's no reason not to give some leeway to a youngster who has demonstrated her reliability. The goal isn't to turn her into a machine that never falters or needs a day off.

• *There are no boring subjects.* For every subject your child finds boring there are other children who are fascinated by it. If she's bored it means that she hasn't learned what questions to ask that will stimulate her curiosity. It is usually the child who is "boring" and not the subject. Boring people are the ones with no interests, enthusiasms or discoveries to share with us.

## Community Responsibilities

Your child will benefit greatly from putting some time in as a volunteer in a community organization. Hospitals, rescue squads, children's shelters, humane societies, and clean-up crews are a few possibilities. By participating in these kinds of organizations he will come face to face with real-world problems and learn the skills to handle them, including how to stay compassionate even when he's tired, frustrated, or repelled (this is a serious concern in some nursing colleges). Perhaps he'll also learn how political and bureaucratic disputes sometimes get in the way of good intentions—a worthwhile lesson. One hopes he will also find some compassionate adult role models, as well as meet other youngsters who are taking a constructive interest in community affairs and the needs of those around them.

There is another important benefit that comes from volunteering. Lizette Peterson of the University of Missouri has shown that children who have the skills required to help someone tend to offer help when it's needed. In her study she taught first- through sixth-graders how to work a safety release on a mechanical game and then left them alone to play. When these youngsters heard another child who was playing next door with the same game cry out that his finger was caught in the mechanism, most went to help. There were far fewer helpers among children who were shown how to play the game, but who were not taught about the safety release.[25]

In a helping organization your child will learn some specific helping skills, but of equal importance, she will get practice in helping. She will have the opportunity to develop a sense of herself as a competent helper, as someone who knows how to assess a situation and take effective action. Too many of our youngsters aren't given the opportunity to develop this sense of themselves.

By volunteering, your child will also have the opportunity to work side by side with adults. They will usually be her bosses, but she and they will be working together toward a common goal. This will be a very different role for her than that of student, son, or daughter. By working with adults she'll get a chance to see grown-ups working at jobs she otherwise would not have had the opportunity to encounter.

## GROUP IDENTITY

During the middle childhood years your child will learn who he is in the sense that he will begin to define himself in terms of his nationality, religion, race, sex, ethnic group, and community. He is also likely to join teams and clubs of various kinds. Little by little he will be exposed to the rituals and rites of these groups and what kinds of behavior and beliefs they find acceptable (*America stands for democracy. Boys don't play with dolls*). He will learn about the history and ideals of the groups he joins, their triumphs and heroes, and also whom they see as their enemies. Some of this information will come from you and other family members, some he will learn in school and religious instruction, and some he will get from the media and his friends.

As your youngster gets to know more about *his* group, he'll also learn about different groups. What he learns about them will have an enormous impact on how he feels they should be treated. As we discussed in the chapter on love, your child's ability to feel compassion and empathy for others ends at the boundary of "us." Those who are not *us* don't merit equal treatment; those labelled the enemy can be killed without any qualms.

Children naturally want to feel proud of their groups—proud to be an American or Italian or Bostonian. If their groups are worthwhile, *they* are worthwhile. Teach your child that an important reason for pride in his own group—his family, his country—is because of the moral standards that the group upholds, because it stands for things that are honorable. As a member of the group he is responsible for upholding those standards, too. Indeed, the ability of each member to feel that he or she belongs to a worthwhile group depends on everyone striving to live up to the group's ideals. When anyone acts otherwise, he or she lets the whole group down.

By the age of four, many children begin to evaluate themselves by comparing themselves to others.[26] When they become part of a group they start to compare it to others. Using other groups as a parameter and guide for achievement or status does not in itself cause any problems. After all, we can learn so much by observing other people's successes and failures. The trouble starts when, in order to elevate our own group, we look for ways to degrade others. Since your child will undoubtedly be exposed to chauvinist and anti-out-group propaganda from members of his own groups, you can help him rise above their propaganda by encouraging him to appreciate the differences between people, to be a good sport, and to develop bonds with people that extend beyond narrow group affiliations.

Among other specific lessons to teach your child are:

*Pride in your own group shouldn't prevent you from appreciating other groups.* This is true even if you are in competition with them. If a member of an opposing team in a game makes an extraordinary play, you should be able to appreciate and applaud him for it. Your desire to win should not destroy your love of the game and enjoyment of high quality play, regardless of which team it comes from.

*Your group deserves no special privileges.* Hitler's plan to enslave all humanity to serve the Aryan race is an example of the demand for special privileges carried to its most extreme. Two hundred years of black slavery and a hundred years of Jim Crow laws in America are another. One form the claim to special privileges takes is the belief that "God is on our side." This is something all sides claim. It's a handy device to induce young men to go to war because they needn't fear death or feel guilty for killing.

*Never assume members of other groups have less humanity than you.* In war the enemy is always characterized as having *no regard for human life* or believing that *life is cheap.* When a soldier on our side sacrifices his life for his comrades we honor him as a hero. When a soldier on their side does the same, he's called a fanatic or barbarian. People certainly differ in their views on life and death. Belief in an afterlife or reincarnation certainly affects people's conception of life and their attitude toward dying, and this can effect behavior in war.[27] But there is no reason to believe that any group of people value their own lives less or care less for their loved ones than we do.

*Never raise your group up by putting others down.* If you compete, do it fairly. If you lose, strive to improve. Be generous with other groups and they may reciprocate. Then everyone benefits. Because people are different doesn't mean they are inferior. This is a particularly important lesson for your child to learn when he begins to identify with his ethnic group. You can discourage negative ethnic stereotypes by teaching him positive things about the various groups he'll come across. Teach him to look for the good in "foreign" people, not the bad.

Today, on every populated continent of the globe, people are killing and torturing other people because they belong to a different nationality, religion, race, or ethnic group. During the 1980s there were over forty wars being fought simultaneously. Some of these conflicts go back hundreds of years. Generation after generation is brought up to right some ancient wrong or to guarantee that special privileges once gained are not lost. Yesterday, our daily newspaper had a front-page photo of a medic in one of these ever-warring lands carrying a six-month-old infant in his arms. The baby's legs had been blown off by a bomb. For what? What can be worth that?

We can put a halt to this legacy of hatred and slaughter if we teach our children that their first allegiance is to *mankind*. Place any other allegiance first—country, religion, you name it—and we always find a reason to hate and hurt each other. People protect their own. It is part of our nature. When members of our family or group are in trouble we come to their aid, even if it means risking our lives. But today, with thousands of weapons of mass destruction cocked and ready to be fired at a moment's notice, it is *mankind* that is in trouble. With nuclear weapons, in just a few agonizing minutes our species could disappear forever, and the only place in the vast universe that we are sure has life on it could become a charred, lifeless rock.

## EXPLAINING EVIL TO YOUR CHILD

When your child is nine or ten she might come home from school asking you about Hitler or some current demon or atrocity: "Why are people so cruel?" she'll ask.

One of the most painful responsibilities of parenting is teaching one's children about human cruelty—about genocide, slavery, warfare, torture, murder, rape, rapaciousness, and similar atrocities.

Children generally cannot fathom what motivates people to treat others so brutally. Even when children feel angry, envious, or covetous, it is not in their natures to plot or even fantasize such viciousness.

Most parents find they cannot protect their children from learning about human cruelty. It is featured on the nightly news, and in films and TV dramas and docudramas (as well as in the promotional ads for these shows, which are often aired during the early hours when many children are watching "children's" shows). They inevitably overhear adult conversations about heinous events, and by the third or fourth grade, they are reading about atrocities in assignments from school.

Parents are faced with the dilemma of how to prepare their children for these dreadful truths without terrifying or depressing them —without making them feel unprotected and helpless.

There are a number of ways parents can ease their children into this knowledge:

• By discussing the ways people have struggled successfully—and are still struggling—to prevent such atrocities.

• By specifically describing the institutions in our country that are designed to prevent individuals or groups of people from harming others (such as laws against slavery and the exploitation of children, and laws against discrimination and environmental pollution).

• By stressing that goodness eventually prevails over evil (that Hitler was defeated, communist totalitarianism was overthrown, democracy is on the rise, slavery was abolished, etc.).

• By taking actions together—and joining forces with others—in support of a human rights project or in protest against some atrocity.

• By stressing the predominance in everyday human interactions of kindness over unkindess (while pointing out that acts of kindness rarely make it into the news).

• By inspiring them with stories of courage even in the worst of times (such as stories of Christian rescuers of Jews during the Holocaust or the blacks who rescued whites during the Los Angeles riots).

• By teaching them "street-smart" safety strategies to make them feel less vulnerable in their communities.

• By helping them as well as you can to understand the motives behind such cruelties, and explaining that even adults often have trouble understanding how people can be so vicious.

It is unfortunate that one must teach one's children about the worst of humanity, but these are lessons they must learn so they will be better prepared to fight against the evils that they'll encounter during their own lives.

# 9

# Adolescence: The Difficult Transition to Adulthood

As everyone knows, adolescence can be a particularly stressful time for children and their parents. The influence of peers and hormones have begun to supplant the influence of parents. Competition is now intensified in many important arenas of the child's life, from school, to sports, to sex. The adolescent's inner conflicts, enthusiasms, and fears often seem excessive to parents. They commonly complain that their sweet child has turned into a self-centered and rude teenager who is overly dependent on friends and uncommunicative at home. For many parents the toughest hurdle of child-rearing is helping their surly and confused adolescent become a responsible and kind young adult.

From the adolescent's point of view the world is indeed a tough place. It is filled with rules not of his making. It presents him with moral conflicts that don't permit simple solutions. At times he finds himself virtually overwhelmed by sexual and romantic feelings. And he quickly discovers that he inhabits a society of peers in which drugs and alcohol are commonplace, yet illegal in the society at large.

In some settings he's encouraged to be kind and cooperative, yet the business of the world seems to be based on self-interest and competition. In addition, the religious beliefs and values that his parents try to hand down to him will often seem outdated or hypocritical. He's also likely to become aware of and concerned about the major moral issues of our civilization, including racial equality, poverty, peace, the preservation of the environment, and the exploitation of weak countries by the major powers. Informed and understanding parents can certainly make this time of passage easier for him. They can also try to make sure that his moral values don't get buried beneath the anxieties and harsh realities of daily life.

## SEX AND ROMANCE

Sex has traditionally been a major problem area for parents and their adolescents, especially their daughters. Teenagers have always spent a great deal of time thinking about sex. Their hormones have seen to that. But a substantial number of today's teenagers—both male and female—are actually having sex, many with regularity. In fact, the sexual revolution has now been around long enough for teenage sex to have become a pretty open matter, with a lot less strain between parents and adolescents over sexual matters than was the case a decade or two ago. Today, it's not uncommon for parents to take their teenage daughters for birth control counseling. This would have been unthinkable a generation ago.

Sexual conventions—society's rules about who should and shouldn't have sex with whom, under what circumstances, and in what form—vary from culture to culture and era to era. During the past few decades in the United States and most western countries, many former restrictions have been pretty much set aside. For example, during the late 1930s and 1940s Kinsey and his associates found that very few unmarried teenage girls were engaging in sexual intercourse. More recent surveys find things very changed: In the mid-1970s, 50 to 75 percent of female teenagers reported having had sexual intercourse.[1] Despite recent concerns about AIDS and other sexually transmitted diseases, the trend toward increased sexual activity at younger ages has continued.

Along with a change in sexual practices has come a change in the moral implications of sexual experience. Sex outside of marriage used to be considered immoral; and even within marriage, anything but the missionary position was looked upon as "unnatural." Church authorities taught that illicit sexual practices were a violation of God's law, a serious sin that deserved severe punishment. Sexual restrictions were even enacted into law. In many states in the country straightforward intercourse was the only legal form of sexual contact between adults. States felt an obligation to tell even married couples how they should and should not engage in sex in the privacy of their bedrooms and violations were punishable by long prison terms. Oral sex was punishable by fifteen years imprisonment in California.[2]

Morality is no longer tied to sex in quite the same way. For an increasingly sizable part of the population, sex outside of marriage and the exploration of sexuality are no longer in and of themselves looked upon as immoral. The burden of sexual morality always fell most heavily on women. But since the double standard is no longer standard, a young man can no longer "ruin" a young woman by having sex with her and then refusing to marry her. A woman's character is no longer judged primarily in terms of whether or not she has held out and remained a virgin. Previously, this one attribute overshadowed every other quality a young woman might possess.

The outcome of these changes is that men and women are far less able to use sex to exploit each other—a positive moral trend, in our estimation. These changes don't mean that morality has no relevance at all in sexual matters. It is still a significant and highly charged area for most adolescents and, therefore, concerns about kindness and justice are still highly relevant.

### The "New Morality" Versus the Old

Traditional western sexual morality was derived from religious doctrines, and questions about kindness and justice were not of prime concern. Rather, the central question was what kind of sexual relations God wanted men and women to have. Although interpretations of the Bible varied to some degree from era to era and sect to sect, by and large, sex didn't fare well. Saint Paul preached the virtues of celibacy and from then on western sexual morality tended to be defined in terms of the least sex possible, under the most restrictive conditions, solely for reproduction. All else was sin, particularly sex outside of marriage.

Changes in sexual mores during the past few decades—not just among teenagers, but in our population as a whole—can be attributed to a number of influences. Anthropologists made us aware of the diversity of sexual practices across cultures and taught us that there are no objective grounds for evaluating any culture's conventions, including our own, as better than any other. Kinsey and other researchers publicized that a large percentage of Americans weren't practicing what was being preached to them. There was a lot more sex around, including "illicit" sex, than had been suspected, without there being any obvious ill effects to the participants or to society. Psychoanalysts popularized the idea that too much sexual restraint was the cause of neurosis. It's a doubtful theory, but it opened the possibility that greater sexual freedom would lead to improved mental health. As women became more educated and assumed a more equal role in the economic life of the society, they began to demand more equality in the sexual area as well; they were no longer willing to accept the double standard or to deny their own sexual inclinations. New birth control devices made the avoidance of pregnancy easy and antibiotics made venereal diseases less frightening (before the AIDS epidemic). Obscenity laws were struck down in the courts as unconstitutional, making sexually stimulating material both legal and available. In the media sex was presented without the traditional moral overtones. The influence of religion declined, at least in certain practical areas of everyday life. When it comes to conventional rules, rules governing behavior that isn't intended to harm anyone—and religious-based sexual prohibitions fall into this category—fewer people are willing to accept their religion's directives as morally binding.

## Moral and Conventional Sexual Rules

There are two kinds of rules governing adult sexual behavior. Some are moral rules concerned with kindness and fairness—with respecting the other person's wishes and not exploiting him or her or breaking one's vows. Others are conventional rules based on custom, religious doctrine, and aesthetics; these define who one's partners can be and what kind of sex one can have with him or her. These two types of rules often get confused. A rule against rape is a moral rule since forcing sex on someone is unkind, to say the least. A rule against homosexual relations between consenting adults is a conventional rule, not intended to prevent people from treating each other unkindly. A rule against adults having sex with minors is a moral rule since its purpose is to prevent the exploitation of children. A rule against adultery is a moral rule since adultery breaks a vow to the spouse, while one against sex between unmarried consenting adults is a conventional rule since no one is hurt by the act.

What category do rules against sex between *unmarried consenting adolescents* fall into? There are two main arguments parents give children for postponing sexual relations. One is for religious reasons and is couched in moral language. But this argument isn't at all concerned with preventing teens from treating each other unkindly or unfairly. Rather it stresses that premarital sex is a sin, and against God's law. However, even in religious households these days the argument that God favors abstainers and punishes indulgers doesn't go over very big. We've educated our children to demand better explanations. They can accept that God is against killing since killing strikes them as intrinsically wrong, but before they'll accept that God is against premarital sex, they'll need some independent reason to convince them that it hurts people. Sex certainly has its complications for adolescents, but research shows that nowadays most don't think of it as morally wrong and few report any guilt feelings after having sex.[3]

The second kind of argument that parents give against sex before marriage is that it can be harmful socially, physically, and psychologically. In earlier generations one could make a good case for the position that having sex before marriage was socially harmful for teenagers—particularly teenage women. Virginity was an important criterion for marriageability, and the world of females was divided into "good" girls and "bad" girls, based on their sexual experience—although what made a young lady "bad" changed from time to time. In some eras a young woman who petted at all was a bad girl. In other eras, only if she petted "below the waist."

Daughters are not easily convinced these days that they'll ruin their chances for marriage if they lose their virginity. Although there has never been one sexual standard for all the diverse communities in America, it's safe to say that for large segments of our population today, a young woman does not automatically ruin her reputation or her marital prospects if she has had sex before marriage. A young woman who has sex indiscriminately because it seems the only way to get attention from young men may have a problem finding a long-term mate, but not because she is no longer a virgin.

With regard to physical harm from sex, most parents of adolescents are terrified about AIDS and other sexually transmitted diseases, as are many youngsters. Surveys report less promiscuity and more condom use, but most teenagers have not opted for abstinence.

Some parents argue that adolescents (again, primarily young women) may suffer psychological harm by having premarital sex. They believe that teenagers aren't ready to handle sex in a mature way. They worry that relationships involving sexual intercourse will become too deep, leaving their teenagers too vulnerable, or that sex will override all other aspects of a relationship and all other interests, or that sex might become trivial and separate from love. These arguments usually strike teens as unwarranted or hypocritical. Most say that their parents never tell them what they mean by handling sex in a "mature way" and that they don't try to teach them how to become more "mature." Teens usually take the "You're not ready to handle it" argument as an excuse adults use to impose outmoded standards on them.

Although parents' concerns may be legitimate, prohibiting sex is only one way to deal with them. Many teenagers who are having sexual relationships do learn to keep sex in perspective and maintain their ability to love. A recent study of college couples looked at the effects of sexual intimacy on their relationships. The researchers compared "traditional" couples that abstained from sex, "moderate" couples that delayed sex until strong bonds had developed, and "liberal" couples that started out having casual sex. They found "no evidence that early sex necessarily short-circuits the development of lasting commitments, nor that sexual abstinence or moderation consistently increases or decreases the development of a lasting relationship."[4] Whether your teenager can handle sex maturely will probably depend more on whether he or she has learned to handle social relationships, in general, maturely, than on anything special about sex itself.

In general, whatever you say to try to convince your teenager to refrain from sex, you'll probably encounter resistance and counterarguments. One mother who advised her teenage daughter to "save herself" for the right man received in reply that she didn't believe that there was one right man just made for her. She said she hoped one day to meet someone she loved enough to want to marry, but until that happens she wanted to learn as much as possible about handling relationships—and that included the sexual aspects.

One father told his teenage son that if he has different sexual partners or if he lives with a girl before marriage, he'll lose all interest in getting married and raising a family. In reply the son pointed out a number of examples of young men for whom that wasn't true. He felt it would be foolish and even immoral for him to marry someone and start a family with her without having lived with her first so he could learn what she was really like.

Most parents find that their teenagers aren't convinced by the reasons they give. Since their arguments aren't based on treating others kindly and justly, they don't carry the weight of moral imperatives. Many teens view parental injunctions against sex as simply an instance of one generation trying to impose its sexual conventions on another. It may feel like a moral issue to an adult who was brought up to believe that sex outside of marriage is sinful or dirty, but it's hard to convince today's teenagers of this.

Current sexual standards have changed certain aspects of male-female relationships while other aspects have remained the same. Since, on average, today's young men and women start having intercourse at an earlier age than that of earlier generations, many contemporary teens are not subject for quite as long as their predecessors to all the physical and emotional tensions that go along with restraint. There is obviously less of the constant pressuring by males on females to go "just a little further," and our impression is that fewer girls are agonizing over whether they'll lose their boyfriends if they don't give in—or if they do.

Things haven't changed quite as much for young teenagers. Before they have had their first sexual experiences, they go through many of the same phases of sexual exploration as teenagers of earlier generations, but now they pass through them more rapidly. Even for older adolescents who have already had sex, a lot has stayed the same. They still fall in and out of love with great intensity, still have good and bad relationships, still get hurt and jealous. They still date, feel lonely, and sometimes feel used, and at times become intimate with someone they aren't really interested in (in an earlier generation this kind of intimacy usually stayed precoital).

In sum, many of the most important aspects of adolescent relationships haven't changed at all. Teenagers of past generations had sex too, but then it was more likely to stop at some degree of petting. However, the moral questions—whether you treat your partner respectfully and honestly or deceive and exploit him or her—are just as pertinent whether you're petting or having intercourse.

As a parent, you may not be able to exert a lot of influence on your teenager's sexual activity. His or her sexual standards, like most other standards concerned with conventional behaviors, will evolve primarily out of peer interactions. But you can definitely have an influence on the moral aspects of your teenager's relationships— that is, on how sensitive he or she is to the feelings of girlfriends and boyfriends.

There are forms of sexual behavior that are definitely immoral and have always been so. Most of us would judge as immoral any behavior that takes advantage of people's weaknesses in order to have sex with them or that treats others as objects to be used for one's own pleasure. Lying and leading someone on or forcing or coercing them in order to get them to have sex with you are two examples of immoral practices. Another would be to knowingly pass on a sexually transmitted disease. A type of sexual abuse that has gotten a good deal of attention in the news lately is sexual exploitation on the job: demanding sex in return for employment, promotion, or salary increases.

Traditionally males have been looked on as the sexual exploiters, willing to use any tactic to seduce the resistant female. Certainly that still happens. But women can use sex in exploitative ways also. They can seduce a man for ulterior motives (for money, for power, to make a third party jealous), and both sexes are equally capable of deceiving and breaking vows.

There are lessons you can teach your children, whether they are at the kissing stage or are having intercourse, about treating boyfriends and girlfriends sensitively. Teach them not to think of sexual intimacy as *taking* but as *sharing*. Sharing means that you regard the other person as a whole person—not just as something for your enjoyment. When you treat someone as a whole person you must consider his or her feelings and goals and fears and what the consequences of your actions will be for him or her. Obviously, other people must decide for themselves about their own sexual behavior, but it's not fair to lead them to a decision through deception.

Try to be aware of how your teenagers are thinking about sex and relationships. Does your son talk about members of the opposite sex as if they were objects? Is your daughter manipulative and unkind once it's clear that a young man likes her? If she is "breaking up" with someone, is she sensitive to that person's feelings? Has your son started to annoy women on the street with catcalls and sexual invitations as a way to assert his masculinity?

If you observe your youngster engaging in these or any other insensitive and disrespectful behaviors, discuss their effects on the people to whom they are directed. Ask your child to put him- or herself in the other person's place. And don't be dissuaded by an "Oh, Mom (or Dad), you're square. It's no big deal. All the kids do it." It's important that you are firm about moral standards whenever you see your youngster treating others badly, *especially* when all the kids are doing it. When it comes to moral behavior, group norms or cultural standards are irrelevant. When we see bad intentions producing bad consequences, that's reason enough to define any action as immoral and to intervene. The anthropologist's notion of *cultural relativism*—which includes an injunction not to judge another culture or group according to one's own standards—doesn't apply to moral behavior. As any international human or animal rights organization will agree, cruelty is not justifiable simply because it's standard practice in a given culture.

Teaching your child to think of sex as sharing will also help protect him or her from being exploited. For example, young women often feel used if they find that a young man has lied about his feelings in order to have sex with them. They feel that they have been made a fool of. But no one can take from you that which you give willingly. If a young man is so desperate for sex and so insensitive that he doesn't consider the feelings of others, then he has degraded himself, not the young woman whose honest feelings led her to share an intimacy with him. (On the other hand, if the young woman was using sex to "catch" the man, then she is likely to wind up feeling cheated since she was bartering, not sharing.) You can help your children learn that the person who shares of him- or herself need never feel embarrassed because others are so selfish or desperate that they can only take.

It is particularly important for your children to learn how to say no when they don't want to have any, or a particular kind of, sexual contact with someone—and here we are talking about anything from a kiss to a touch to intercourse. Young women in particular need to understand that they have a right to say no. There are lots of reasons a woman will have sex when she doesn't really want it. She might be too embarrassed or afraid to refuse; she might feel sorry for the man or worry that he'll reject her; she might feel peer pressure or do it to spite someone else. If she has sex for any of these reasons, she's bound to feel bad about herself afterwards. None of these reasons has anything to do with sharing, with love, or with pleasure. A young woman will find it easier to say no if she understands that anyone who would put undue pressure on her, embarrass her, frighten her, or prey on her sympathies or affection to manipulate her into having sex deserves her scorn and not her body.

## Facing Rejection

Inevitably, when it comes to romance, all adolescents must learn how to face rejection. Losing someone you've cared for hurts. It's painful when someone who has brought joy and excitement into your life tells you he or she prefers spending time with someone else or just doesn't want to spend time with you anymore. Some teenagers have a hard time recovering from rejection. At those times they need parents to be understanding, even if it means leaving them alone for a few days should they request it. Finding words of comfort isn't easy at such a time. Anything that trivializes their suffering will certainly not be appreciated.

We all have to learn to accept the painful fact that every loving relationship ends. Someone leaves or dies, or feelings just fade as people change. Some youngsters have a hard time accepting this. They vow never to love again if the loss of love with its terrible pain is inevitable. Many an adolescent of an earlier era nodded in agreement while listening to Simon and Garfunkel express these feelings in song:

> Don't talk of love, well
> I've heard the word before,
> It's sleeping in my memory:
> I won't disturb the slumber
> Of feelings that have died.
> If I never loved, I never would have cried.
> I am a rock, I am an island.[5]

The only thing that makes the loss of love worth enduring is the joy of loving. The more your youngster understands that the great joy in love comes from feeling and giving love, the less he or she will focus on the fear of being rejected. And the more your youngster likes him- or herself, the less anxiety he or she will have over rejection, and the less devastating an actual rejection will be. It's when adolescents feel undeserving of someone's love that they fret endlessly over the possibility of losing it. In contrast, when they feel they are lovable and know that they have the resources to enjoy life and other interesting people, then they'll have confidence that their whole future does not depend entirely on any one person. Then when they love it won't be permeated with the kind of jealous fear and possessiveness that usually does wind up leading to rejection.

### Fidelity

What about fidelity in this era of sexual freedom? How does it fare among our youth? They still value it. Teenagers still go steady and make vows to be faithful. But sometimes, like adults, they find that other people are attractive also, and that they can even seriously love two people at once. Then the temptation to cheat becomes strong.

When your youngsters reach their "going steady" days, make sure they understand that breaking a vow betrays a trust and will hurt their friend a great deal if he or she finds out. If it's no longer the time for them to be going steady, then they should face that openly rather than try to get away with a double life that is bound to hurt those they care for and lower their own self-esteem. If they want to maintain their relationship, then the commitment to it needs to be reaffirmed regularly. Youngsters need to learn that being attracted to different people is nothing to feel guilty about and doesn't mean that they aren't really in love. The fact is that there are many people who have attractive qualities and one need not deny that in order to stay committed to one relationship.

### Teenage Pregnancy

If your daughter is having sexual intercourse, the possibility of pregnancy becomes an important concern for you and for her. For parents who are opposed to their daughter having intercourse but who suspect she is, this can become a very difficult issue. They worry about her becoming pregnant; yet if they suggest birth control, they fear it will seem as if they condone her sexual behavior. The best some parents do under these circumstances is to mutter a warning to the effect of "Make sure you don't get pregnant."

But many teenagers are getting pregnant these days. Both teenage pregnancy and abortion have increased substantially in recent decades. Some observers blame the welfare system for the rise in teenage pregnancy, particularly for the marked increase among young black women:

> . . . any girl is offered an irresistible solution (to being poor) by the U.S. Government. It presents her, at age sixteen, a chance for independence in an apartment of her own; free housing, medicine, legal assistance, and a combination of payments and food stamps with several

hundred dollars a month. There is only one crucial condition: She must bear an illegitimate child.

Other commentators dispute this explanation and blame the economy, racism, or the media. Still others have pointed to community and family influences.[6] Unfortunately, in the debate over which social institutions are to blame, the teenager's responsibility to her society gets lost. The obvious question, Why shouldn't unmarried teenagers have a child? doesn't get asked. And there are some very good reasons why they shouldn't. First, it places an unfair burden on other members of the community who must take care of both mother and child. Second, since the family is still the primary economic unit in our system, any goods and services received by "families" that make no economic contribution to the society are, from the standpoint of equitable distribution, undeserved. Finally, it brings a child into the world primarily to enhance one's own comfort, without sufficient regard for what one must do to prepare oneself to bring up a child who will be able to lead a happy and productive life. A recent *New York Times* editorial supplies some of the tragic statistics:

> More often than not, a pregnant teenager will drop out of high school. Because she has less education, she'll earn less than half the income of women who become mothers in their middle to late twenties. Their children will have an edge on hers. Her baby is more likely to have a low birth weight, have a lower I.Q., repeat at least one grade in school and not do as well on achievement test scores. The odds are two to one that she'll need welfare.[7]

In short, bringing a child into the world is an act with enormous moral implications because it has significant consequences for both current and future generations. And you can teach this to your teenagers—both daughters and sons—without waiting for the politicians and theorists to sort out which social institutions are at fault. As a society, we must be careful that in our zeal to correct economic and racial injustices we don't make the mistake of turning the moral obligations between the individual and his or her society into a one-way street with the community having obligations to the individual but the individual left free of any to the community (which, of course, is simply made up of other individuals).

Certainly any baby of an unmarried teenager must be taken care of, but just as certainly teenagers, male and female, should be encouraged to recognize their responsibility to their future children and community before they get pregnant (or make someone pregnant), and they should definitely not be rewarded for becoming pregnant. We will undermine all our attempts to make our social institutions more just and compassionate if we don't preserve, as an institution, a system of mutual obligations between the individual and his or her community. When individuals are not expected to meet community responsibilities, they are forced, in effect, to remain children, wards of the state, without dignity or respect. For adults there is no such thing as rights without responsibilities.

Our children are, of course, products of the environment we create for them. If we set up an environment in which they are not taught to recognize community obligations and are not held responsible for meeting those obligations then we will only have ourselves to blame for their self-indulgences.

Once a teenager becomes pregnant, she is faced with the decision of whether to have the child or have an abortion. There are many factors that she is likely to consider at that time, including religious standards, her relationship to the father and how he reacts to her pregnancy, her relationship to her parents, and how they react (if she tells them), economic concerns, career ambitions, peer advice and norms, her feelings about motherhood, and her thoughts about the morality of abortion. Science will be of no help to her on this last matter since it offers no criteria for defining when an embryo or fetus becomes "human."

If the baby is not wanted, then either alternative—to have the child or to abort it—is not a happy one. At that point the pregnant teenager will spend a lot of time wishing she had been more careful. There is evidence that the more openly parents discuss sex and contraception with their daughters, the more responsibly their daughters handle sexual matters. Psychologists Greer Litton-Fox and Judith Inazu, summarizing the research in this area, propose that

> . . . more frequent mother-daughter discussions about sex and birth control may allow the daughter to accept more easily her own sexuality, which appears to be a prelude for taking contraceptive responsibility. Further, it may be that frequent discussions of sex and birth control with the mother may desensitize the topics of sex and birth control sufficiently so that the daughter feels able to discuss them with her sexual partner also.[8]

Sex and birth control are difficult topics for many parents to bring up and discuss openly. One reason we've mentioned is parents' fear that they will appear to be condoning sex if they educate their children about it. But teenagers don't refrain from sex just because they are uninformed or unprepared. The consequences of their engaging in intercourse without adequate preparation are too costly—to themselves, their families, and their community—for parents to avoid the topic. If you want your children to refrain from having sexual intercourse, give them your reasons, but at the same time don't neglect to discuss contraception with them, as well as their responsibilities to sexual partners, their future children, and their community.

## ALCOHOL AND (OTHER) DRUGS

Regardless of whether your youngster has generally been a "good kid" or a "bad kid," there's a good chance that sometime during his adolescent years he's going to experiment with alcohol and drugs. Surveys show that 50 percent of high school students have smoked marijuana and drink occasionally. One out of five say they drink regularly. About the same amount have tried cocaine and other drugs.[9] Nowadays, drugs and alcohol are used commonly by adolescents from all social classes and from all regions of the country.

If immoral behavior is defined as behavior that intentionally harms others, then does putting substances of one kind or another into one's own body have any moral implications? It's not an easy question to answer. We've all known people who drink moderately without any harmful effects on their lives and without becoming abusive to others. And many of us have known people who use drugs periodically for relaxation, recreation, or "mind expansion," without any apparent problems arising from it. We may or may not respect their interest in or need for drugs, but it would be hard to fault them on moral grounds.

On the other hand, we've also known people whose lives have been shattered by alcohol and drugs and who, as a result, became a menace to everyone they came in contact with. According to a recent government report "alcohol abuse has been linked to half of all automobile accidents, half of all homicides, 25 percent of all suicides, and about 40 percent of all problems brought to family court." The report concludes that when you add the deleterious effects of alcohol on the job performance and physical health of the 10 to 15 million problem drinkers in this country, "the economic cost of alcohol abuse may be as high as $120 billion in the United States each year." The connection between addictive drugs like heroin and crime has always been strong, and recent surveys report that a substantial number of cocaine users are stealing to pay for their very expensive and very powerful habit.[10]

So with regard to adolescent alcohol and drug use, we have a situation in which the immediate consequences of any single episode of indulgence is usually not damaging to either the adolescent or anyone else. But a series of such episodes can lead to a tenacious physiological and/or psychological dependency that is unquestionably of great harm to the adolescent, and may turn him into a menace to those around him. Addicts and alcoholics characteristically become totally self-absorbed. Their friendships, family relations, savings, and careers all give way to the need to feed their habit. They use anyone and everyone they can. Fortunately, only a small proportion of teenagers who try drugs or alcohol become addicts or alcoholics. But because those who do become so miserable and mean, and because the "cure" rate is so low, parents have good reason to be alarmed when they discover their children using these substances.

### Preventing Addiction

Teenagers use and abuse alcohol and drugs for a variety of reasons—to gain acceptance from peers, to cope with rejection and loneliness, to reduce anxiety, to heighten experience, to overcome inhibitions, to feel adult, to ease frustrations, to escape responsibilities, to provoke parents, to emulate parents, to have "fun." But contrary to what many psychotherapists and social theorists would have us believe, the cure for an addiction doesn't usually lie in trying to undo these kinds of causes. People who use an addictive substance will always have more than one reason for using it. The cigarette "addict" will smoke when depressed, when celebrating, when doing hard work, when bored . . . you name the occasion or the psychological state and he or she will find it a good time to light up. The same goes for the food addict. And the same goes for the much more dangerous addictions to drugs and alcohol. There is no automatic connection between any emotional state or social condition and drug or alcohol abuse. Lots of people are depressed or anxious or poor, but most of them don't become alcoholics or drug addicts.

The best way to help your child handle alcohol and drugs responsibly is through helping him or her develop personal standards that are incompatible with abusing these substances. We can illustrate this process with some examples that David Premack compiled some years back of people who gave up cigarettes.[11] One man attributed his abstinence from smoking to the humiliation he experienced when he realized how readily he and the rest of the public let themselves be duped by greedy tobacco growers who sell a product they know causes cancer. He had an image of "those bastards down there sitting around a pool—Virginia, Kentucky—counting the loot, patting one another's back, laughing it up and not a one of them smoking. . . ." Another man said he quit after seeing an American Cancer Society film depicting a boy and his father on a stroll. In the film the boy imitates the father in various pleasant ways, and then the father takes out a cigarette to smoke as the boy watches. The ad had its intended impact on this man who had a son of his own and, as a physician, knew full well the harmful effects of smoking. Another man gave up smoking after he had kept his children waiting in the rain while he drove in another direction in order to get to the tobacco shop before it closed.

As Premack points out, each of these people had a standard of acceptable conduct (doing the best for one's children, not contributing to a company that knowingly markets a product that causes a deadly disease), and each came to realize that smoking made him behave in ways that were incompatible with that standard. As smokers they had become members of a class "repugnant" to them. The humiliation of that knowledge made them quit.

When it comes to addictions and habits, personal standards are far more likely to keep the person "straight" if they are established as part of a prevention program before any cravings have developed. Once habits and addictions are strong, people can usually manage to rationalize away any humiliation they might experience from violating a personal standard. For example, the physician might decide that it's all right to smoke as long as he doesn't do it in front of the children, or the man who didn't like tobacco growers could conclude that the profit their companies made from his two packs a day was miniscule.

Alcohol and drug dependencies are a lot stronger than a cigarette habit—so strong that successful treatment of any kind is highly uncertain. Prevention is therefore crucial. Once someone becomes addicted to drugs or alcohol and is bouncing back and forth between euphoric highs and despondent lows, she's not very responsive to outside influence; nor is she likely to be interested in or capable of taking constructive actions to overcome her problem. The adolescent who has begun to drink too much or take drugs regularly will usually feel that she can quit anytime she really wants to. But there is no warning signal when a dependency becomes too firmly entrenched to quit at will. The process is slow and insidious. Even after a full-fledged addiction is clearly established, the highs and lows associated with the cycles of craving and satisfaction make it difficult to recognize the reality of one's entrapment.

What kinds of personal standards are incompatible with addictions? The desire to be the kind of person who doesn't burden others; who doesn't look for excuses to do things he knows he shouldn't do ("I couldn't help it, I was drunk"); who tries to overcome weaknesses and faces obstacles directly rather than temporarily deluding himself into believing that they don't exist; who doesn't want to rely on crutches just to get through the day; who won't feel a sense of accomplishment from learning how to hold liquor or smoke a joint; who won't be content with gaining people's sympathy; who doesn't seek attention by playing "the bad boy"; who won't think of himself as daring and adventuresome because he gets drunk or stoned; who doesn't need to be in an altered state to feel attractive or sociable; who doesn't want his life controlled by the constant need for a substance or by the corrupt people who sell that substance; and whose curiosity about the world and ability to take pleasure in it are not so dulled or jaded that he can't find more interesting and pleasurable things to do with his time and mind than to get drunk or stoned.

As we've described in Chapter 4, you can foster the development of personal standards by helping your child develop ideals—images of the world as she would like it to be—and then by encouraging her to guide and evaluate her behavior in terms of those ideals. From a very young age—when she's six or seven—get her to think about the kind of person she has to be in order to help bring about the kind of world she'd like to live in. Also, point out people whose actions help bring this ideal closer and contrast them with those who make the world an unhappy and cruel place. Among the "repugnant" people (to borrow Premack's apt term) will be those who diminish their ability to lead constructive lives or to give of themselves by overindulging on drugs or alcohol.

Idealism comes very easily to most children. They want everyone to be good and kind, they always want the good guy to win, and they want to be on the side of right. They don't always act according to these ideals, but reminding them of their ideals will usually bring their behavior back into line. This early idealism is part of what we commonly call the "innocence" of children. Children need never lose that innocence. Of course, they'll have to learn that bad guys win a lot of the time, and that sometimes it's not even easy to know what the most kind or just action in a situation is. But they need never lose their faith that the world can be better, nor their desire to help make it better. Learning about the harsh realities of life need not make a youngster cynical, mean, or self-indulgent.

**What is overindulgence?** You'll have to give serious thought to how you want to define overindulgence. Is it anything but total abstinence? Or is occasional and moderate alcohol and drug use acceptable? What about getting drunk or stoned once in a while? Every parent will have to come to his or her own conclusion. But remember, whatever definition of overindulgence you decide on, you'll have to convince your youngster that your position is reasonable. At a minimum, overindulgence should mean drinking or taking drugs to the point that one becomes a burden or danger to others (passing out, throwing up, getting into fights, drunken driving, stealing), or fails to fulfill responsibilities to oneself or others (poor school grades, falling asleep at work, forgetting promises), or is in danger of developing a physiological dependency.

Your arguments will be more convincing if you stay realistic. Not all substances are equally harmful. One drink doesn't make an alcoholic. Nor do most adolescents today think of taking a drink or a drug as immoral in and of itself.[12] On the other hand, teenagers tend to underestimate the harmful effects of alcohol and drugs. The typical teenager feels she knows "the score," and that she can keep her interest in drugs under control. Unfortunately, the more she indulges the more in control she feels. Cocaine, for example, was one substance that most adolescents underestimated. Even many drug experts thought of it as a mild, nonaddicting "recreational" drug. Recent reports show this to be wrong. The development of an addiction to cocaine may be slow and imperceptible or (with "crack" cocaine) rapid and overwhelming. In either case, as thousands of broken lives attest, the craving for cocaine soon becomes virtually one's only goal in life.

If your child overindulges, *your* life will be greatly and adversely affected. Therefore it's important to communicate your limits clearly and forcefully. Let him know that you're not going to clean up after him, or make excuses for him to other people, or excuse him from meeting his obligations at home. Also let him know that you don't intend to live with someone who can't interact normally with you because he's usually stoned or has a hangover. Your youngster should understand that if he loses control over his life, you will take whatever steps are necessary to help him regain it and to prevent him from hurting others—including committing him to an institution.

While you are trying to discourage your teenagers' interest in drugs and alcohol, there will be other influences working against you. Peers will offer them alcohol and drugs and may ridicule them for refusing. Beer commercials will try to make them believe that no joyful occasion is complete without a six-pack. They'll read about their favorite rock stars and athletes taking drugs. Perhaps some diehard from the 1960s drug culture will try to convince them that drugs are "mind-expanding." And keep in mind that aside from what you say to your youngsters about drugs and alcohol, they will also be strongly influenced by their observation of the role these substances play in your life.[13] The more important drugs and alcohol are to you, the more acceptable they are likely to be to them.

We've already discussed that children need to learn how to say no. When you can't say no, you wind up doing things you feel are wrong just because an authority tells you to; you spend time and even have sex with people you don't want to be with; you buy things from salesmen that you don't want and can't afford; you drink or take drugs when you'd really rather not.

Talk to your child about situations in which she's likely to be encouraged to take a substance she'd rather not take: at a party, after a game, before school. Help her put into words the pressure she'll feel when someone offers her a drink or when a marijuana cigarette is passed her way. Will her friends think she's square, not cool, frightened, prudish, a baby? Then remind her to remind herself of what her ideals are, of the kind of person she wants to be, of what she stands for. The purpose of these reminders is to replace her imagery of the snickers and sarcasm she anticipates from her friends if she declines their offers, with good thoughts about staying "straight."

Also make sure your youngster understands that if her friends are *really* her friends, they won't make her feel bad for refusing their offers. A peer who makes fun of her if she chooses not to indulge is showing that she isn't much of a friend. Review how your youngster might refuse an offer. Even practicing a simple, direct "No thanks, I'd rather not" may be enough to give her the confidence to refuse. She might also poke fun at the offerer: "I'll just watch you get stoned. It's fun to see you sink into a stupor." You should also discuss how she might respond to further pressure. A straightforward statement of her position, such as "You've made your choice, I expect you to respect mine," should be sufficient. She'll find that most people do respect a firmly stated choice. If a stronger assertion is needed, she might say, "I'm doing fine without it and I intend to stay that way," or simply, "I want you to stop bothering me."

When it comes to beer commercials and other media messages that link alcohol and fun, make sure your youngster understands that most people do not consider drinking beer the high point of their day. A lot of people do enjoy a beer now and then and others drink it regularly. But those who drink a great deal of it regularly don't look like the virile, lively, fun-loving folks in the ads. The big drinkers are usually the ones with the paunches who tend to be either ornery or lethargic and can most often be seen heading for the bathroom.

Now that so many popular athletes and entertainers take drugs, there's a danger that our children will think that drug use will help them become more like these role models. Adolescents tend to idolize their favorite athletes and entertainers. The term *halo effect* applies well to this kind of idolization: if someone excels in one area, we assume he or she has good attributes in others. Because someone sings a song well or can sink a jump shot from twenty feet, we assume he or she is unquestionably worth emulating. In truth, there's no reason to believe that talented people are any wiser or kinder than anyone else, and our children need to learn this.

## Drugs and the Law

One of the facts of life in our society is the possibility of arrest for using illicit drugs. Your youngster will know, though, that most people don't get arrested. The illegal drug industry is one of the largest in the world, and could not have gotten that way if users were getting thrown in jail. A recent report reveals that:

> In the United States, Exxon is the sole corporation with annual revenues in excess of the $79 billion that, according to the Drug Enforcement Administration's last estimate, is generated every year by the sale of illicit drugs. And the National Organization to Reform Marijuana Laws reports, marijuana is currently our second largest cash crop nationally, after corn and just ahead of soybeans.

Another report estimates that "cocaine traffic in the State of New York exceeded $7 billion a year."

The drug trade is like any other retail business. Its product has to be available to the public or it can't survive. And illicit drugs are available everywhere. You can go into virtually any city or college campus in the nation and with a few inquiries you can find dealers to sell you practically any drug you want. "The National Institute of Drug Abuse estimates that 56 million Americans have smoked marijuana and 22 million have ingested cocaine."[14] The only people who don't seem to know where to find the drug dealers are the drug enforcement authorities. Keeping drugs both illegal and easily available is as disastrous an arrangement as our society could come up with. The price of drugs is kept exorbitantly high, forcing people with dependencies to take extreme measures to support their habits; few are deterred from taking drugs since few get arrested, and huge sums of money are diverted into an underworld economy.

Government officials are also accused of being lax when it comes to legislating and enforcing drunk driving laws—some feel because of pressure from the liquor lobby. Over twenty-five thousand people are killed and maimed by drunk drivers every year, and a substantial number of these accidents are caused by teenagers. One group (Mothers Against Drunk Drivers), reacting to the unconscionably light penalties for drunk driving, has called drunk driving "the only socially acceptable form of homicide in our society."

You can be sure that if your youngster comes to handle drugs and alcohol responsibly it's not likely to be because of laws or government policy. It'll primarily be because of the values he or she learned at home.

## RELIGION AND MORAL TRAINING

We know parents who are upset because their children don't believe in God. And we know parents who are upset because their children do. Some of those how want their children to believe in God feel it is a prerequisite for leading a moral life, that a person can't be considered moral unless he or she believes. To them it's an essential part of the definition of morality. This requirement obviously has nothing to do with the definition of morality we are using in this book—treating others kindly and fairly.

Another reason some parents give for linking belief in God with morality is that without this belief there would be no reason to be moral. Without the fear of God, they say, we would have no reason to suppress our basic selfish impulses. But treating others well out of fear of punishment is just the opposite of what we ordinarily think of as morally motivated behavior. It doesn't take a moral sense to behave honestly when a gun is put to your head. That's just self-preservation. We call someone moral when he can be trusted to do the right thing even when he can get away with doing otherwise. Those who believe in a punitive God are convinced they can never ultimately get away with doing the wrong thing. In a sense, the gun is always pointed at them. One can't sneak past God, they believe, and He has all eternity to make you pay for your sins. Since He can read minds, even bad thoughts are dangerous. The belief in a punishing God can have a powerful controlling effect on behavior, but it has nothing to do with encouraging good intentions toward others.

There is another side to religious training, though—one that teaches love for one's fellow human beings, although indirectly, through the love of God. Most children are not just brought up to fear God; they are also taught to love Him, and many go through phases when they do with great intensity. God becomes very personal to them. They want desperately to please Him by following His commandments, doing good deeds, and thinking good thoughts. They believe that God has feelings and they empathize with the pain He feels when He witnesses how cruel humans can be toward each other. God says they should love their fellow man, so they do. Through their love of God, they *internalize* His code of right and wrong.

As we have described in Chapter 2, a child's love for her parents leads her to internalize their standards of good conduct. In precisely the same way, a child's love of God will lead her to internalize her religion's code of right and wrong. This is the primary way religion teaches morality. But as we have seen, internalization is only one of the ways to develop moral standards and come to care about others. It is an important part of early moral training, but as a child develops, one hopes that her moral motivation will be based increasingly on empathy and personal standards rather than on living up to parental rules and directives. Similarly, a child doesn't need to want to please God, or even believe in God, in order to develop moral standards, good intentions, or empathic feelings toward others.

Parents who don't want their children to believe in God mention a number of reasons for their position. They want their children to care about others directly, without any intermediary. They don't want them to have to rely on any authority to tell them what is morally right and wrong. They cite the atrocities committed in the name of religion, including "holy" wars (both ancient and current), the burning of heretics, and the suppressing of man's greatest ideas and thinkers, from Galileo's trial by the Inquisition to recent "creationist" attacks on Darwin and evolutionary theory. And many parents would feel like hypocrites asking their child to believe in something that they don't believe in themselves.

Our position is that there is no inevitable connection between religious belief and morality. While one can cite ignoble acts derived from religious beliefs, one must also remember that some of man's most noble humanitarian achievements have been inspired by religion. Gandhi was inspired by his religious beliefs, but so was the man who assassinated him.

A child need not be taught to believe in God in order to develop into a moral person. Just as there are men and women of high moral character who believe in God, so there are others who don't. For instance, American children are often surprised to learn that many of the men we honor as the "founding fathers" of our country—including Washington, Franklin, Jefferson, Madison, and Adams—did not believe in conventional religion. They were deists espousing a philosophy that maintained that there is an order to nature, but which rejected the ideas of a supernatural God who interacts with man and rewards and punishes him. They also rejected traditional notions of heaven, hell, and Christ as the son of God, as well as the divine inspiration of the Bible. Their idealism and commitment to establishing a just society was based on their feeling for man and not on religious belief. Indeed, because they had witnessed so much religious intolerance in the various colonies, most of which had official state religions, they wrote a clause into the First Amendment of the Constitution to prevent religious groups from having any secular power in the new union.

The moral lessons that religions teach can be undermined by other aspects of religious belief, and it's important to make your children aware of these. One obvious way is when believers are taught to hate nonbelievers—when they learn to regard members of a different religion as sinful and deserving of punishment not because they treat people badly, but because they view God in a different way.

Religious practice can also become harmful when it seeks to benefit the "soul" at the expense of the body. Under ordinary circumstances when we want to treat someone well, it is taken for granted that he or she is the ultimate judge of what *well* means. To use a mundane illustration, a person is not likely to perceive it as an act of kindness toward him if you try to force him to eat something he dislikes because *you* like the taste of it. We only give ourselves the right to force on people what we believe to be in their interest when our intervention is necessary—when, for instance, they are minors or ill. Even then, we can evaluate the correctness of our judgment sometime in the future (we can observe whether the child we forced to take medicine gets well).

When it comes to benefiting souls, though, no evaluations are possible. Whether a soul is improved in this life or not, or the "next one," is not open to inspection. That an action is good for the soul —ours or someone else's—must simply be *accepted* on faith, because a religious authority (a priest or the Bible) tells us so. This can cause problems. The days of torturing bodies to save souls are gone in our part of the world. But other practices based on the same principle persist. For example, the birth control policy of the Catholic Church is not based on the visible well-being of human populations. The Bible is interpreted as being against birth control; therefore, for the benefit of the souls of the faithful, birth control is defined as immoral while the miseries of overpopulation are deemed less important. For similar reasons, the Church labels masturbation "a grave moral disorder." Masturbation is an act that cannot possibly be considered immoral in terms of doing intentional harm to others. But because it violates the Church's interpretation of "the design of God," it is therefore condemned.[15] The Church committee that issued the decree is interested in saving souls. Whether people who masturbate (almost everyone) are harmed by being stigmatized as suffering from "a grave moral disorder" is not its concern.

Since people are generally uncertain about what is good and bad for their souls, opportunities for charlatans abound. Someone who manages to get himself officially designated as the interpreter of God's word or who simply succeeds in convincing believers that he has special spiritual insights or powers, becomes, in essence, the gatekeeper to heaven. He knows things they can't know and "sees" and "hears" things they can't see or hear. He then is in a very powerful position which he can use for humanitarian purposes or for self-aggrandizement, wealth, and political manipulation.

While some religious groups work untiringly for the benefit of mankind—promoting peace, aiding the ill and the poor, and offering kindness and comfort to anyone in need—others preach only about personal salvation. They warn that the nuclear Armageddon is imminent (which was, of course, prophesied in such and such chapter and verse) and insist that only by believing in the one true religion—their's, obviously—can anyone be saved. While true-believers enter the kingdom of heaven, the unbelieving rest of mankind deservingly gets wiped out. Morality, in these groups, thus gets twisted into a philosophy of "every man for himself."

We suggest that you teach your children to distinguish the *moral* aspects of their religion, those that set forth high standards for how people should treat each other and that focus on easing human suffering, from the doctrinal aspects, those that stress unquestioning obedience to church doctrine, building the church as an institution, and personal salvation. These two aspects are not necessarily incompatible, but if you are bringing your children up within a religious framework, it's worth checking to make sure that the moral side is not neglected. Indeed, there is evidence that how churchgoers treat their fellow man is related to which of these aspects they emphasize. For instance, some early psychological studies found that churchgoers were on the average more prejudiced than non-churchgoers. But upon closer examination, it turned out that prejudice was only high in those whose religious motivation stressed the doctrinal aspects, those for whom personal salvation and the church as a social institution were of primary importance. Churchgoers who looked to religion for moral guidance in their daily lives were not high in prejudice.[16]

***Moral instruction and religion.*** Moral instruction has traditionally been taught within a religious framework, but if you aren't bringing up your child within such a framework, moral instruction will be your responsibility alone. There are no other institutions in our society today that provide moral training, except, of course, the family. Schools used to, but as our society began to define moral infractions as either psychological or social deviancy, they became uncomfortable with that role. The solutions to deviant behavior were to be found in psychotherapy and social reform, not in moral training with its emphasis on individual responsibility. With the growing crime rate among our youth, schools have recently reintroduced some formal moral instruction. A number of school systems have even gone back to using the old McGuffey readers (first used in 1836) with their traditional moral lessons.

If you are basing moral training on religion, there are two possible predicaments worth anticipating. If your adolescent has learned to value reason, don't be surprised if he comes home one day armed with persuasive antireligious arguments—perhaps culled from Thomas Paine's *The Age of Reason,* or some similar treatise—and wants to debate with you about the Bible. Many adolescents go through periods when faith is sufficient to sustain their religious beliefs, and other periods when they need to anchor their beliefs in reason. You may or may not be inclined to enter a debate with your child, but you won't be doing him justice or be supporting your religious goals for him if you belittle or condemn him for his doubts. Don't assume he is turning away from religion irrevocably. Many people with strong religious beliefs have gone through periods of doubt and questioning in search of their own paths to faith. You may want to advise him to talk to a clergyman, but don't just pass him on to others. Use his questions as an opportunity to share your experience of religion with him. That way even if he does reject religion for himself, he will have an understanding of the value it has in other people's lives.

Also, don't be too surprised if one day your child tells you she's joining a religious cult. This is something thousands of parents have faced and it's usually alarming news for them. They fear their child has been duped or even brainwashed, that her religious beliefs have been distorted, that her psychological weaknesses have been exploited, and that she will be used for sinister ends. Although we suspect most parents won't be comforted by this information, it's worth remembering that today's major religious institutions once started out as "cults," and that the fervor and tight discipline of these groups is characteristic of ultra-orthodox believers of any faith.

Young men and women have many different motives for joining cults. One that often goes unmentioned is that they are looking for a place to practice goodness. For many of our youth, the competitive worlds of college, business, and dating appear to offer little prospect for leading a virtuous life. To some these new religious groups seem to provide a community of people actively doing God's work on earth. Traditional religious establishments often appear too comfortable for them, too involved with internal politics, too tame to have an impact on the problems of the world. You may have good reason to doubt the sincerity of the various cult leaders, and may even be shocked by your own child's sudden strong religious and humanitarian interests. Whatever your reaction, a respectful dialogue will do more good than hysterical condemnations.

If the cult leaders' claims are to be countered, you'll need to consider what to teach your child about spotting "false prophets." If you've taught him and he's accepted that God interacts with people, and that in the past prophets have been charged with revealing His word, then it may not seem farfetched to him to have another prophet among us today.

Your child's ultimate religious beliefs will depend on a number of influences, including what you've taught her, what she's learned in formal religious instruction, what she's learned about religion in school, what her friends believe, and various cultural trends. During recent decades we've seen increased interest in mysticism, Eastern religion, cults, religious communes, and fundamentalism. Overall, though, surveys report a decline in religious belief among our youth during these decades, and few now feel it is morally "wrong" not to believe in God.[17] If this decline is the trend of the future, parents will obviously not be able to rely as heavily on religion for moral training.

**Morality and Meaning.** One of the things religion provides is *meaning* to life. One feels sponsored, with a significant place in a grand and rational scheme. Belief in an afterlife and a God who rewards and punishes means that the sum of one's acts adds up to something, that one's life has an ultimate consequence. We have evolved to be exquisitely responsive to the consequences of our actions. We experience life as meaningful when the positive and negative outcomes that follow our actions make a difference to us. Then we strive to increase the positive and decrease the negative. When the outcomes are *of no consequence* to us or positive outcomes appear impossible, we experience life as meaningless, we feel hopeless, depressed, even suicidal.

One of the characteristics that sets we humans apart from other animals is that we respond to extremely distant consequences (a thirty-year-old saves for his retirement thirty-five years hence). Religion builds on this ability to project our fates into the future, and extends the time-line for rewards and punishments not merely to the end of our lives, but into the "next life"—into eternity. At the threshold of the next life, the sum of our acts in this life—the good and bad we've done—is tabulated to determine how we'll spend eternity. Preparing for eternity can provide a great sense of purpose.

For the nonreligious, purpose must be found elsewhere. It can be found by experiencing one's life as a part of history and the great human struggle to create a more humane, just, and beautiful world. You can help your children experience their lives as meaningful by giving them a sense of obligation to those in the past who forged and fought for the "good" that they now enjoy—the artists and artisans, the philosophers and farmers, the physicists and physicians, all who left the world a better place than they found it. And include ordinary people, those who never achieved fame, but who fulfilled their responsibilities to others and made the world a better place for those around them.

Talk about the good you received from your parents and what they received from theirs. In other words, you want to give your children a sense of their place in history, teaching them that their life continues a magnificent story that started long before they were born and will go on long after they are gone—and that their chapter in this grand saga will certainly make a difference in how the story turns out, that how they conduct their lives will have an impact on many people now and in the future, including, someday, their own children.

If you can give your children a sense that the torch of civilization is being passed into their hands, and that they have an obligation to keep it bright and pass it on, they will experience their lives as meaningful, whether or not they believe in a literal afterlife.

## RULES, RULES, RULES

Mrs. Sanchez learned that Robert, her teenage son, was borrowing his friend Louis' membership card to a health club in order to use the facilities on days that Louis couldn't go. She asked Robert if the club had a rule against members loaning their cards. He replied that they did. "Then you shouldn't borrow the card," his mother said. "But I'm not hurting anyone," the boy answered. "Louis can't go some nights, so I'm just taking his place. What's wrong with that? It's not as if I were keeping anyone else out."

Mrs. Sanchez explained her reasons: "First, the people who run the club established the rule that cards shouldn't be loaned, and they have a right to make the rules. That's their job, not yours. Second, they might have taken in more members than their facilities can accommodate at one time on the assumption that everyone wouldn't show up at the same time. So when you show up in Louis' place, you might very well be taking time away from other paying members." Robert cut in with, "But it's never very crowded. There's more than enough equipment for everyone."

Mrs. Sanchez had other objections. "I assume that if you get caught, Louis would lose his membership." Again, Robert defended himself: "They never look at anyone. All you do is hold your card up so they can see the expiration date." Mrs. Sanchez had one last point to make: "We do only what we can afford to do, and we don't try to sneak our way into places we can't afford to pay for. That's on principle, so we can respect ourselves."

Robert agreed that his mother's arguments were reasonable, yet he still felt he wasn't doing anything wrong by borrowing the card. He didn't think that breaking the club's rule was bad because he wasn't hurting anyone by doing so.

Virtually all aspects of our children's lives—indeed all of our lives—are governed by a plethora of rules. There are family rules, school rules, playground rules, work rules, church rules, community rules (otherwise known as laws). It's important to think about what kind of attitude you want your child to have toward the rules she'll encounter. Should all rules be inviolable? And if not, when is it okay to break one?

When we look at community rules, we find that they fall into three categories: rules of proper treatment, rules of order, and rules of access. What you teach your child about rules is likely to depend on the kind of rule you are referring to.

## Proper Treatment Rules

These are society's basic moral rules on how to treat others. They typically take the form of prohibitions against harming others intentionally ("Thou shalt not . . ."), although some are stated as prescriptions or obligations to do good. Among the common prohibitions are rules against killing, stealing, and libeling. An example of a prescriptive moral rule would be a "good samaritan" law requiring individuals to come to each other's aid in certain emergencies.

Parents in our society generally accept these proper treatment rules and want their children to adhere to them. It's the rare parent who actually encourages his or her child to harm others. Thus, parents and society at large present a united front when it comes to teaching children proper treatment rules. In addition, it's fairly easy for parents to be sure when this type of rule has been violated.

Sometimes, though, parents will find that the proper treatment rules of their society don't coincide with their personal moral standards. For example, if you lived in Hitler's Germany you may not have agreed with your society's rules for the proper treatment of non-Aryans. Similarly, there are South Africans today who are against apartheid; and there are Iranians who disagree with what the Ayatollahs maintain are the proper treatment rules for women. When parents disagree with their society's proper treatment rules they are faced with the dilemma of having to teach their children either to uphold rules that they themselves despise, or to oppose those rules—with all the risks that that entails.

## Rules of Order

These are conventional rules instituted to make life safer and more efficient. "Drive on the right," "Cross at the green," "When the whistle blows, line up for a head count" are examples of a few such rules. Breaking a rule of order doesn't generally constitute a moral violation except when, as in driving rules, there is implicit in the rule the responsibility to consider the safety of others.

Rules of order don't usually cause confusion for parents or children. They generally apply to everyone equally and the reasons for them are obvious. For instance, when your teenager starts to drive he's not likely to question the rule to drive on the right.

For the most part, rules of order only lead to problems when they become ends unto themselves. For instance, your child might encounter an overzealous school principal or camp director who likes the "look" of disciplined children, and for no useful reason insists that his charges march from place to place in neat lines and stand at attention for long periods of time. Your youngster may complain to you, but this need not cause any conflict between you—unless you too like the look of disciplined children marching in neat lines or you believe that children should simply do whatever adults tell them.

If your youngster complains to you about, say, her school principal's rules, the best thing to do is discuss them. They may be more reasonable than she thinks. If not, then work through together what options for change are available to her. These might include sending a committee of students to present their grievances to the principal or lodging a complaint against him with the school board. If the board isn't sympathetic, she can work to elect different members of the board, or organize a public act of civil disobedience or switch schools, or decide simply to bear it. The point here is that when it comes to rules of order there's no reason for you and your child to be on opposing sides. They are simply conventional rules. Presumably, the principal's intention is not to harm the students. Your youngster needs to learn that she doesn't have to accept the rules passively, but that she won't always be able to change them to her liking.

### Rules of Access

Here's where the problems come in. Rules of access define the requirements we must meet to gain access to the things we want. Recall the story of Mrs. Sanchez and her son, Robert. He wanted to use the health club facilities but wasn't a member, so he borrowed his friend's card. Robert didn't see the issue as a moral one since he wasn't hurting anyone. He wasn't arguing that it was right to borrow the card, only that it was not morally wrong to do so. To his mother, it was a moral issue since he was, in essence, denying the club managers their right to run their club as they wanted. He was trespassing on private property, and that was wrong "on principle."

Problems arise with rules of access because it's not always clear whether violating them constitutes a moral infraction. Here's another example to illustrate this dilemma.

Mr. Simmons told us that his son, Carl, managed to get his driver's license a year early by altering the date on his birth certificate. The boy did this in order to get a job delivering newspapers by truck on weekends—a job that paid much more than he could have earned elsewhere. His father was pleased. He said, "The boy is ambitious and he's smart, and he's already a safer driver than most adults on the road."

Carl's mother wasn't so pleased. She worried that her son was setting a bad precedent for himself. She didn't want him to think that he could disobey society's rules whenever it suited him.

As we talked to the parents we learned that Mr. Simmons wasn't advocating indiscriminate rule breaking; nor was Mrs. Simmons in favor of following any and all rules regardless of circumstances. In this particular instance the father felt that the age requirement for a driver's license was arbitrary and unreasonable, based on a meaningless criterion (chronological age), and not on how well and responsibly a person handles a car. He believed that when a rule is unreasonable and when violating it doesn't hurt anyone, it's okay to try to get around it. You may get in trouble if you get caught, but it's not a moral issue.

Mrs. Simmons disagreed. She wasn't so sure that there wasn't some sense in setting an age requirement for drivers, since younger drivers have the most accidents and she knew of no way for driving examiners to judge whether a particular young man will turn into an irresponsible driver once he's passed his exam. More importantly, she felt that Carl didn't have the right to decide which laws he would follow and which he would not—not in a democracy in which the people participate in making the law by electing representatives. "What if everybody did it?" she asked.

Her husband laughed and replied, "Good, then maybe they'd change the law." She replied, "But we have procedures for changing laws, and if our society is going to work, we have a moral obligation to obey the law while we use legitimate means to change the ones we don't like." Her husband told her that she wasn't being practical. "By the time you get the law changed, he'll be too old to benefit from it," he said. She knew that, she replied, but it didn't change her mind about what was right. "Perhaps," she added, "if he needed money for an emergency, then breaking this kind of law in which no one gets hurt in any immediate way would be more excusable, but it's still wrong in principle."

We believe that under most conditions rules of access should be obeyed—but there are exceptions. The following are some guidelines we suggest you teach your children and why they make sense to us:

*When you think a rule is reasonable and fair, follow it even if you can get away with breaking it.* We assume that Robert didn't believe that the health club managers were unreasonable in setting up a rule against members loaning their cards. Presumably if he ran a health club he would set up similar rules for a variety of practical reasons, from insurance considerations to the depreciation of equipment.

It's tempting to want to violate rules of access when we know we can get away with it, even when we believe the rules are perfectly reasonable. But when we break such rules, we trespass on other people's rights—we use their property and services without their permission and without giving anything back in return. When people learn that they are being cheated, they usually take self-protective measures (for example, by tightening security at the entrance to the health club). When a lot of people in a community feel that they must protect themselves from other members of the community, the quality of everyone's life is ultimately diminished.

*When you think that a rule is unreasonable but applied fairly, follow it if it was enacted legitimately.* Mr. Simmons (and presumably Carl) felt the driving age rule was unreasonable. Yet we're sure they would agree that the government does have the right to establish such rules. If they accept the legitimacy of the government, then they have an obligation to uphold its laws. If they don't accept the legitimacy of the government—say a military junta has overthrown their elected leaders—then we don't believe they have any obligation to uphold its laws or rules, regardless of whether they are applied fairly.

In establishing a minimum legal driving age and any other laws that affect adolescents, the question of legitimacy has obvious relevance since adolescents before the age of eighteen don't have any say in enacting the laws that they are supposed to obey. They are too young to vote or hold public office. Like any disenfranchised group, they may feel they have no obligation to obey laws that are imposed on them without their representation. To date, adolescents in our society have generally accepted their status as minors in the legal sense (meaning they have no right to participate in government). But when and if they cease to, the minimum age for driving is only one of a number of laws that are likely to be re-evaluated.

Mrs. Simmons raised an interesting issue when she said that if her son had needed money for an emergency there might be some excuse for his behavior. In essence, she was recognizing that there are times when *extenuating circumstances* can affect our judgment of an act's morality. Imagine, for example, that your teenager tells you that his math teacher's lectures are so unfathomable, his exams so unreasonable, and his manner so authoritarian that the only way to get a decent grade is to cheat. Let's assume also that math is an important course for your youngster because she is applying to engineering college, and that you have good reason to trust her interpretation of the situation. Technically, the teacher is the legitimate authority and cheating is the wrong way to pass an exam. Yet if an otherwise responsible young woman cheated under these circumstances, a parent might not view it as harshly as the more typical case of cheating to compensate for not keeping up with schoolwork.

***When you think a rule is both unreasonable and unfair, do your best to oppose it.*** Not very many years ago, in many states in this country, black Americans on a bus could only sit in the seats at the back. They couldn't drink from the same water fountain as whites or sit at the same lunch counters. Opposing these rules was risky business for blacks and whites; nevertheless, such rules were certainly worth opposing. When a law is harmful or oppressive, the only moral thing to do is oppose it. In the past it has been legal to throw Christians to the lions and Jews into ovens, and the moral action was to oppose these laws.

We would like to believe that it is obvious to everyone that *moral* obligations are not the same as *legal* obligations and that when the two are in conflict the moral obligation should prevail. But not everyone agrees. The following quote expresses an opposing point of view:

> To despise legitimate authority, no matter in whom it is invested, is unlawful; it is rebellion against God's will.

This was said by Pope Leo XIII about one hundred years ago.[18] Unfortunately, similar sentiments are still expressed today: God supports the president, so it's against God's will to oppose the president. Therefore, the morality of the president's policies are to be taken for granted. (Whatever happened to the unknowability of God's will?) One also hears more sophisticated versions that attempt to justify cruelty in the name of order.

One can oppose an immoral law in various ways, including legal redress (trying to have the law declared unconstitutional), rousing public support for its repeal (rallies and marches), civil disobedience (such as sit-ins), and armed revolution (as in 1776). If you want your child to oppose unjust laws, which form should his opposition take? When a legal system has mechanisms for changing laws and redressing grievances as ours does, litigation, we hope, would be the first choice, reserving more disruptive tactics for times when the harmful effects of a law are severe and imminent or when the government is unapproachable.

There are usually many steps that can be taken before resorting to violence. For instance, the civil rights and peace movements of recent decades were effective, though largely nonviolent, using legal channels, public protests, and civil disobedience—though activists were often the recipients of violence. There's no way to know whether your children will come of age during an era of movements and social unrest. But if they do, how they react will be greatly affected by what you've taught them about their responsibility to the suffering of others and what one should do when one's conscience and the law are in conflict.

A dramatic and ironic example of how parents influence their children was reported in a *New York Times* story about the Morales family in 1981.[19] The father was a member of the ruling junta in El Salvador and part of that country's wealthy elite. Two of his sons had joined the revolutionaries and were dedicated to overthrowing the government. The irony comes from the fact that the sons, one of whom was in jail, claimed that they were only living up to the ideals they had learned from their father. One son wrote to his father and accused him of betraying those principles: "The least you could do at this point is to act in a way that is faithful to the principles you taught me."

A number of studies have found that young men and women who were active in the peace and civil rights movements, fighting to change laws they considered unjust, had been strongly influenced by the values of their parents. Early attempts to characterize these social activists as rebellious were mistaken. On the contrary, they were actually putting their time, energy, and often their lives on the line in order to uphold what they had been taught were the most fundamental of American values: equality and freedom. They felt it was the government, not them, that was rebelling against America. Some of their parents had already become cynical about the possibility of change, and feared that their children would be harmed while accomplishing nothing. But the moral lessons these parents had taught—often through their own earlier participation in humanitarian causes—had already gotten through.[20]

Like the parents in these studies, you too—whether you intend to or not—are sending your children messages about what ideals are worth fighting for, what tyrannies are worth opposing, and what risks are worth taking for the sake of others. It's a good idea to clarify these beliefs for yourself to make sure that you are communicating what you truly believe.

# 10

# When Morals and Other Values Collide: Helping Your Child Maintain Morals in the "Real" World

Although parents today are concerned about the moral training of their children, it has been our experience that few are interested in encouraging their children to devote themselves totally to helping others. They may admire the extraordinary devotion to others of Mahatma Gandhi, Albert Schweitzer, or Mother Theresa, but leading a moral life is not only defined in those exceptional terms. Caring about people and taking pleasure in their pleasure does not mean we can't have other concerns and joys as well. All of us have to make decisions about how much time and effort we want to devote to others, and we have to judge at what point doing for them means we are no longer being fair to ourselves.

Children go through many kinds of moral dilemmas, such as whether to report a friend who has done something wrong or whether to risk being a good samaritan in a dangerous situation. There are no universally right answers to these kinds of moral dilemmas. Each individual must find his or her own path. But parents can prepare their children for these decisions by helping them clarify their goals and appreciate the consequences of the different choices they may make.

## MORAL CONFLICTS

Your daughter's friend, who is on the verge of flunking out of school, asks to be tutored for a surprise exam announced for the next day. But your daughter has a front-row seat, purchased with her own savings, to see her favorite group in concert tonight. What should she do?

Your son sees an older youth break into a school locker. The older boy threatens him with, "If you tell anyone, I'll get you." What should he do?

Your teenage daughter gets a Christmas job in a department store and discovers that the manager of her section, who hired her and treats her well, is defrauding the company of money. What should she do?

Your daughter is walking with a friend, and a derelict asks them for a quarter. She reaches in her purse, but her friend says, "If people give him money for begging, he'll never have a reason to find a job." What should your daughter do?

Your son's friend asks him to place his exam paper near the edge of the desk so he can copy the answers. What should your son do?

Your son is on the school football team in a championship game. The coach calls for a maneuver which could seriously injure a player on the opposing team. What should your son do?

Your daughter's sorority sisters take a secret vote to keep minority groups out. She is opposed to the policy, but her friends will get in trouble if she reports them. What should she do?

Your teenager passes an alley and hears a call for help. He sees a man beating someone on the ground. What should he do?

Your son is offered a good job with the government, but he must first sign a loyalty oath and take a lie-detector test. He believes that loyalty oaths insult loyal citizens for no purpose since the disloyal would not hesitate to lie. He also feels that lie-detectors contradict our justice system by forcing people to prove their innocence even though they haven't been accused of any crime and by taking away their constitutional right not to incriminate themselves. But he wants the job. What should he do?

Your children are bound to encounter many of these kinds of moral conflicts throughout their lives. They'll face situations in which they'll have to choose between:

- doing for oneself (going to a concert) or doing for others.
- meeting one's obligations to society (reporting a thief) or protecting oneself.
- loyalty to friends (giving exam answers) or violating one's own standards of honesty.

- obeying authority (following the coach's orders) or adhering to personal standards against doing harm.
- allegiance to a group (sorority sisters) or allegiance to personal standards of fairness.
- coming to someone's aid (in an alley) or one's own safety.
- giving someone immediate help that may do harm in the long run (a quarter to a derelict) or letting the person suffer now because it will have a long-term benefit.
- exposing wrongdoing (the section manager's embezzling) or minding one's own business.
- advancing one's own interests (taking the lie-detector test) or upholding one's personal standards of justice.

Deciding what to do in any of these situations isn't easy. In all of them it is assumed that the child has no ill intentions toward anyone and that he or she wants to do "the right thing." Still, there are no formulas or equations you can give your youngster for balancing his obligations to himself against his obligations to others, nor for any of the other kinds of conflicts described. How should your daughter decide if she should give up her concert ticket to tutor a friend? Certainly seeing a concert is not a life-and-death issue, and the consequences of missing it will not be as serious as the consequences to the friend of flunking out of school. Yet other considerations might also pass through your daughter's mind: was an earlier offer to tutor her friend refused? Is her friend habitually self-indulgent and always burdening others with last-minute emergencies? Has her friend been there for her when she has been in need? Is it even realistic for the friend to believe she can learn enough in one night to pass the exam? Would it be good for her friend to face the consequences of her irresponsibility?

A particularly difficult decision for parents to make is how brave and self-sacrificing they want to encourage their children to be. Many parents teach brothers and sisters to stick up for each other and come to each other's aid if harmed, but they are less likely to want their children to put themselves in danger for a stranger. What about for a friend or neighbor? It's hard to draw a clear line. Parents generally wish to raise children who will fight for what they believe in, yet who aren't foolhardy; who are cooperative, yet able to say *no* when necessary; who are good team members, yet unafraid to stand on their own, even against the crowd; who have concern for others, yet not an easy mark. That is, they want to help their youngsters find a position somewhere between selfishness and selflessness.

Again, there is no formula for finding the "right" decision in moral conflict situations (notwithstanding the attempt by the philosopher Immanuel Kant to devise such a formula. The philosophically minded might try applying his *categorical imperative* to the question of whether or not to expose a person who has confided to you his intention to commit a crime. You'll get two different answers depending on whether you use his "inflexible" or his "meritorious" test of duty). A classic example of a moral conflict in which both alternatives seem equally right (or wrong) is the triage dilemma faced by overworked medical staff during war and disasters: Should they help those who are the most seriously hurt but who have the least chance of surviving even with medical care, or those who are far less hurt and have a good chance of surviving if they get medical attention?

By exposing your child to other people's attempts to find satisfactory solutions to real-life moral conflicts, you'll help prepare her for similar conflicts that will inevitably arise in her own life. Too often children enter adolescence expecting only obvious, black-and-white alternatives. Disillusionment quickly sets in, often followed by inclinations to "turn off," "drop out," or simply "look out for number one."

Newspapers and newsmagazines will provide many examples of real-life moral conflicts that you can discuss with your child. In one recent example, hundreds of American churches of various denominations disobeyed a U.S. government ruling and gave sanctuary to thousands of illegal aliens who had fled the dictatorships in Guatemala and El Salvador. Some church leaders saw this as the U.S. Immigration Service versus the Gospel; they chose the Gospel.[1]

In teaching your child to consider the moral implications of alternatives in conflict situations, suggest that he start by asking himself about his own motivation, whether he harbors any ill intentions toward any of the parties concerned that might influence his decision one way or the other. For instance, if the young woman who is asked to tutor her friend envies the friend's looks or popularity, she might take some satisfaction in seeing her fail the exam.

Assuming there are no such ill intentions, here are some guidelines you can teach your child to use when faced with moral conflicts:

**1. How would she want to be treated if she were in the other person's place?** Here we have the "Do unto others . . ." dictum turned into the question, How would I want to be treated?

It's easy for a child to let her own immediate desires color her view of a moral conflict. For instance, a youngster's desire to go to a concert she has saved for is likely to be a lot stronger and more immediate than her desire to help her friend. Therefore it's important that she take time to put herself in her friend's place before deciding on the "right," as opposed to the most immediately satisfying, action. Putting oneself in the other person's place has two components: First you try to experience the other person's situation as he or she feels it. Then you ask yourself what *you* would expect of others if you were in their shoes. This might clarify for you what you think is fair.

For instance, if your daughter experiences her friend's situation from her friend's perspective, she may appreciate the degree of the friend's need or fear. This might make her more inclined to give aid or it might make her realize that the friend is overreacting, failing to consider all the possibilities (for example, that the teacher allows students to offset a failed exam by handing in a term paper). Then, to get an idea of what she thinks is fair, she should imagine herself in the same predicament as her friend and ask herself how she would expect a good friend to treat her. She might realize that she would never ask someone to do what her friend is asking her to do —that when she gets herself into trouble, she accepts the consequences without burdening others. She could see this as the "right" way to behave, and thus conclude that her friend is being unfair to her. Or she might decide that her personal choice to "take the consequences" has nothing to do with fairness, but is based on her preference for an independent and self-reliant lifestyle, with no moral implications at all.

**2. How severe are the consequences to each party?** Few of our children, we hope, would equate missing a concert with flunking out of school. Yet, as we pointed out, other circumstances may make a teenager decide that her friend's request for tutoring is unfair—for instance, if her earlier offer of help had been refused. Still a young woman in this situation might conclude that the damage to her friend if she flunks out will be so severe that the question of what's fair is no longer important—that the friend needs to be rescued, even from her own irresponsibility, and that the concert must be foregone.

*3. What are the implications for the community at large?* What if nobody came to anyone's aid? What if all witnesses to crimes refused to testify in court because it was inconvenient or because they feared they would be putting themselves in danger? What if no one stood up for his or her rights or for the rights of others?

Our acts (as well as our failures to act) have immediate consequences for ourselves and for the individuals with whom we are in direct contact; they also set off reverberations in the entire community. All our deeds and misdeeds add up to what is sometimes called community morale or spirit. If we don't help a friend, it will have an impact on our group of friends. If we don't report a thief, our community will become a more suspicious, self-protective, and dangerous place.

When morale is high we feel we live in a place where people are well-intentioned, can be trusted, and will come to each other's aid. A young woman named Kitty Genovese didn't live in such a place. In 1964 she was repeatedly assaulted and eventually murdered by a man on a street in New York City. At least thirty-eight people heard or saw the attack from their apartment windows. No one went to her aid. No one even called the police for over half an hour. The entire nation was shocked by this incident. How could it have happened? What kind of people had we become? Had we lost all sense of obligation to each other?

In many moral conflict situations it's easy to feel *Why me?* Why should I be the one to take a stand? Why should I be the one to take a risk and put my job or life in jeopardy? If that's the way the system works or if others don't feel obliged to act, why should I—and what good can I do on my own, anyway? Thus one way out of taking a moral stand is to pass the responsibility off onto others, to assume they are in a better position to do something, and if they don't, then there must be good reason not to. The Kitty Genovese incident provoked a series of social psychology studies on people who don't help others, on those whom researchers call "unresponsive bystanders." This research has demonstrated how pervasive the "Let someone else do it" attitude is.[2] Yet other people do help, and our children can be taught to see their acts as contributing to the morale and morals of the community at large. We can teach them that every act counts and that one person *can* make a difference.

Check your daily newspaper with your child for confirmation of the fact that caring individuals can indeed have a significant impact on their society. For example, news stories recently covered the one-man crusade of Ernest Fitzgerald, "a stubborn enemy of Pentagon waste," as the *New York Times* called him. The government fired him after he exposed billions of dollars in cost overruns. He sued to get his job back, was reinstated after years of litigation, and is back on the job fighting now to make the entire military procurement system accountable. If he succeeds, the government will no longer be able to spend up to $10,000 for an item that anyone can buy in a hardware store for a few dollars.

Another article described the efforts of the Reverend Leon H. Sullivan to change the economic conditions of blacks in South Africa. His strategy? Get American corporations that do business there to pay and treat blacks and whites equally. In only seven years, 120 of America's largest companies, including General Motors, IBM, Mobil, DuPont, and ITT, had become signatories to the "Sullivan principles."[3]

One may agree or disagree with what Fitzgerald and Sullivan are doing, but they are standing up for their convictions and their individual lives are making a difference in the community at large, affecting the well-being of people they'll never know and who won't ever have heard of them. In both cases, how easy it would have been for them to turn their backs on their ideals and shrug cynically, "Change South Africa? Never." "Change the Pentagon? Never."

Our children need these kinds of humanitarian models. A young black college student who participated in the first student sit-in of an "all white" lunch counter in the South—an act that set off a chain reaction of civil rights protests that altered the very social structure of the nation—said he was first inspired by reading about Gandhi at the age of fifteen. "What makes a guy like this tick?" he wondered. "He goes to prison and then gets out and then he does the same thing again immediately. . . . He was a pretty amazing guy to me, so faithful to his people. . . . I began to wonder sometimes why couldn't I be a Gandhi myself, doing something for the race."[4]

The news media tend to report only the big stories of general interest. We suggest you teach your children that the morale and spirit of our society is just as dependent on the efforts of ordinary people in everyday situations—on whether we each uphold our ideals in our daily interactions.

## MONEY AND MORALS IN A COMPETITIVE SOCIETY

At some point during her adolescence or early adulthood, your youngster will begin to take her place in the economic life of our society. She will find employment, start to build a career, and may someday even employ others. Half of her waking life will be spent exchanging her skills or the product of her skills for money. If you've brought her up to care about being kind, she'll have to face the question of whether it is possible to be kind and still profit in a competitive economic system.

Whatever career your child enters, it won't take her long to discover that although there are business ethics and rules on how one may and may not compete, the code contains no requirement for kindness. When she's competing with someone for the same dollar, she's not expected to be concerned about that person's needs. In a competitive system like ours one is rarely faulted for pursuing too much wealth.

Businesses create ethical codes (for example, delivering goods when promised, paying bills within thirty days) and governments create business laws (paying employees at least the minimum wage, requiring that products meet safety standards) in recognition of the obvious fact that the way in which individuals conduct their business affects the well-being of others. But beyond those codes and laws, it's no holds barred. If one businessman drives his competitors out of business, their loss is his gain. Their financial setback is *their* problem, not his. In essence, competition prevents the bonds between people that promote kindness.

Our businessman might argue that he prevailed over his competitors because he was, in fact, being kinder to his customers by giving them a better product or price. Sometimes that will be the case, and it is one of the major virtues of a competitive system—you must always please the customer. Often this leads to better products, but sometimes one can hook customers through better packaging and marketing while actually offering an inferior product. If this turns out to be the case, one would still not be violating any business ethics. Kindness, unfortunately, is not factored into the "bottom line."

Think about whether or not what you teach your child about morality is compatible with how he'll have to behave in order to have a successful career. If he's concerned about behaving morally, without question he'll face many moral conflicts in the business world. For instance, a young woman we know took a summer job doing piecework in a factory—so much pay for so many pieces completed—and found herself embroiled in a common labor-management dispute over pay rates. After a few days on the job a regular employee asked her to slow down, explaining that the workers had an understanding among themselves not to finish more than a certain number of pieces per hour. "Otherwise the company lowers the pay scale, forcing us all to work at breakneck speed all day for the same pay," her co-worker explained. The young woman needed as much money as possible for her college tuition, and she also felt obliged to do her best for the company. However, she didn't want to make life difficult for her fellow employees whose working conditions year-in and year-out depended on the piece rate. She had entered a setting in which there was no clear moral position. When labor and management are adversaries, as they usually are, all one can do is take a side. One can't be kind to both parties.

Business is rife with difficult moral dilemmas. If you're hired away from one firm to work for a competitor, are you obliged to keep the secrets of your former employer or to divulge them to your new employer?

Even when behavior is clearly illegal, the moral implications are not always black and white. A building contractor described how he could not do business in his city if he didn't pay off the various building code inspectors. Did he feel it was wrong? "Yes," he said. "I hate being part of a corrupt system, but I can't see risking my whole business on this issue. I never give an inspector money in order to get away with using inferior materials or to do anything that would endanger anyone. It's just that they expect to be paid, and there is so much red tape that if they want to, they can stall a project for years. It's easy for an outsider who hasn't spent twenty years of hard labor working his way up in this business to say that I should fight them and refuse to pay. It just isn't worth it."

Another moral dilemma in the business community recently set off considerable public debate because it emerged out of an international scandal. The basic issue was whether or not it should be illegal for American businessmen to bribe foreign officials and purchasing agents in order to make sales in countries where bribery, although ostensibly illegal, is standard business practice. Some businessmen claimed that if the same laws that govern the way Americans do business with each other were applied to overseas operations in countries with different standards, American companies would be at a disadvantage. How would you want your child to handle this situation if he or she were selling products overseas?

Like many young men and women, your child may someday find him- or herself working for a company that is engaged in questionable moral and legal practices, and he or she may get a clear message that employees are expected to participate in, or at least shut their eyes to, the practice or lose their jobs. It's not an uncommon occurrence; nor are the violations likely to be trivial. In a recent analysis of corporate ethics and crime, sociologist Marshall Clinard reports that:

> Nearly two-thirds of the Fortune 500 corporations were charged with violations of corporate law over a two-year period (1975–1976); one-half of these were charged with a serious or a moderately serious violation. . . . A . . . recent study found that 115 corporations of the Fortune 500 had been convicted between 1970 and 1979 of at least one major crime or had paid civil penalties for serious illegal behavior. Allowing for size, the larger of the Fortune 500 corporations have been found to be the chief violators.
>
> The corporate violations have resulted in enormous economic losses to consumers and the government. . . . Such illegal practices include price-fixing, false advertised claims, the marketing of unsafe products, environmental pollution, political bribery, foreign payoffs, disregard of safety regulations in manufacturing cars and other products, the evasion of taxes, and the falsification of corporate records to hide illicit practices. There have also been injuries (and even deaths) among citizens and employees because of unsafe drugs and other products, pollution, and unprotected work conditions. Such serious illegal acts, knowingly committed against consumers, their own workers, their competitors and even against foreign nations, have often involved tremendous sums of money.[5]

Clinard interviewed a considerable number of retired middle management executives who had worked for major companies. The majority said that the pressure to engage in unethical behavior comes down from the top. As one respondent put it, "Top management is responsible for whether a corporation is unethical or ethical. Top management wants to be surrounded by persons who follow their ideas and patterns of behavior. . . ." Another said, "Some middle management were forced, for example, to deal unethically with labor problems that interfered with production."

The former executives cited "competition and greed" as the primary motives for engaging in unethical behavior and most (71.5 percent) said that government regulation is necessary to protect the public. One man summed up his experience this way: "You start out of college with high ideals and due to pressures these ideals deteriorate during one's corporate experience."

How can your child keep his ideals and still succeed in the hard-edged, competitive world of business? The Clinard study confirms that some businessmen do. One manager, for example, referred to his company as "a good, honest corporation. The founder was a very ethical man, and later top management followed his views." Another said, "It largely depends upon the ethics of the person; some middle management can resist pressures and others cannot."

Obviously, one factor that will determine how your child handles his business dealings will be how important money is to him compared to other values. This will depend to a good degree on what he's learned at home. We recently heard a mother encourage her son, who was becoming a physician, to volunteer time to work in a clinic in a poor neighborhood. We also remember another mother of a medical student discouraging her child from the same with the quip, "Don't rich people need good doctors just as much as poor people?"

As in any moral conflict situation, you are not likely to have absolute answers to give your child about just how much personal wealth to pursue and at what cost to herself and others. It's not easy to sort out one's obligations to employers, employees, fellow workers, customers, the general public, and oneself. But these are important areas to discuss together. Since similar issues are likely to have arisen in your own life, you might want to discuss how you handled them.

Although your child may never be asked or tempted to violate any laws and may consistently meet the ethical standards of her occupation, she will still have to deal with the question of whether *morality* is possible in a competitive economic system. Not long ago, a lot of our young men and women decided that it wasn't and they "dropped out," hoping to find an alternative lifestyle (usually in a communal setting) that would not pit them against their fellow man. One hears less these days about formal dropping out, but many young men and women—particularly those brought up to behave morally—are still wondering whether morality and career success are compatible.

Don't be surprised if your young man or woman raises this question with you. A more concrete way of asking about morality in business is, *Can the business of society be conducted in such a way that people can pursue profits without profiting at each other's expense?* Devout capitalists and communists both claimed that this is exactly what their respective systems strive toward. The capitalist explained that in a "free market" economy you only profit by giving people value for their money, never at their expense. If you give them less, they won't buy from you. Similarly, you pay people exactly what their labor is worth. If you pay them less, they won't work for you.

One reason that things aren't quite so rosy in practice—why people certainly seem to be profiting at each other's expense—is because to the capitalist the value of a person's product or labor is by definition exactly the price someone pays for it. If you paid $400 per month for your apartment last year, $400 was its exact value. If your landlord raised the rent to $800 this year, and you (or someone else) paid it, then $800 is its exact value this year. You may have kept the apartment because all the landlords were raising rents and you couldn't find a cheaper one. It doesn't matter why. From the capitalist, free market perspective, you are getting exact value for your dollar and the landlord has not profited *at your expense.*

From your perspective, though, if you find you can no longer afford to get your shoes repaired and are eating only canned soup for dinner every night, while your landlord has traded in his Ford for a Mercedes, it will certainly seem to you that he has profited at your expense. And it's not probable that your landlord will lower his rent to accommodate your plight, not if he can get his full price from someone else if you move out. A competitive system doesn't foster the kinds of bonds between people that would make that likely. As we've mentioned, capitalism has difficulty accommodating kindness. When you are competing with someone, you are not inclined to be concerned with his or her happiness.

In a competitive system the notion of fairness gets reduced to the market principle: the fair price is whatever price the market will bear. Or else fairness gets tied to arbitrary criteria, such as whom you compare yourself to. For instance, firemen maintain that it's only fair that they get paid the same as policemen, but policemen claim they deserve more since their job is more demanding and their contribution to the community greater. Firemen disagree. Imagine the chaos in municipal budgets if both groups decided that their contributions to the community were on a par with, and there-

fore deserved the same pay as, the politicians, bureaucrats, and at-
torneys sitting in judgment on their salaries.

The capitalist might reply to these criticisms by asserting that the
moral lapses of capitalism are trivial compared to the moral virtues
of a system that provides so amply for the needs of so many people,
reminding us that even with the great disparity of incomes that capitalism produces, most people—even the poor—live in relative comfort compared to the way people live under other systems. Thus,
looking out for number one becomes a moral position because self-
interest, through the "invisible hand" of market forces, promotes
the general welfare. Yet there may be a way of providing for people's
material needs without undermining their bonds to their fellow citizens.

Communism made a strong claim that its citizens could not possibly profit at each other's expense. Marx believed that a society based
on the principle "From each according to his ability, to each according to his need" would curb the heartlessness of capitalism, do
away with the great discrepancy between rich and poor, and foster
bonds between members of the community. He argued that only
when the workers become owners will they reap the full profits of
their own labor, and then the class structure that divides society will
disappear. In the Communist ideal each person's labor contributes
to the shared wealth of the community, so an individual's economic
condition improves only as everybody else's condition improves.
Thus no one is in competition.

In practice, though, this gave the community great power over the
individuals in it. When you work for the community you do what *it*
tells you (that is, what the central committee tells you). You as an
individual are only important through what you contribute to the
group. So the individual freedoms that we cherish so much and that
are quite compatible with capitalism got sacrificed in Communist
countries "for the good of the State."

Communist states claimed that their citizens couldn't profit at
each other's expense, but many of their citizens felt they weren't
profiting at all in the sense of being able to run their own lives and
pursue their own interests without coercion from the state. So large
numbers of citizens tried to defect and the state erected walls along
heavily guarded borders to keep them from fleeing. Eventually, almost all Communist governments were overthrown by their citizens.

An economic system that simultaneously promotes productivity,
individual freedoms, and moral interactions between people is still a

thing of the future. One development we see as a positive trend is the growing number of corporations in which workers own a significant part of the company, participate in its management, and share directly in the profits earned. The traditional antagonism between owners and workers appears to be diminished through these practices. A news article on one such company illustrates our point:

> Two years ago, when the Lincoln Electric Company's sales were sagging because of the recession, fifty factory workers volunteered to help out.
>
> After a quick sales training course, they took to the road, their only compensation $18^1/2$ cents a mile for expenses, with no money for lodging or meals. Their objective: to help sell the company's Model SP200, a small welder. . . .
>
> The tactic worked. People who had been plant workers all their lives walked into body shops all over the country and said, "Hi. I'm a factory worker from Lincoln Electric. I've got a welder I'd like to sell you." The pitch brought in $10 million in new sales and the small arc welder is now one of Lincoln's best-selling items.
>
> An unusual scenario, perhaps, in American industry where, often as not, a company and its workers are at odds.[6]

One of the reasons the article cites for this unusual and highly successful relationship is that "workers have shared in the company's fortunes. Under an employee stock purchase plan, about 75 percent of the workers own about 40 percent of the stock." They also earn high wages "which include a substantial annual bonus based on the company's profits. While the average Lincoln worker earned about $44,000 in . . . 1981, half of that was in bonus."

Another reason cited for the company's success is employee participation in decision-making. Since 1914 an advisory board of employees' representatives has met twice a month with top officers. Other important reasons include guaranteed employment (no worker has been laid off in forty years), and promotion almost exclusively from within based on merit (the company's seventy-five-year-old chairman and chief executive started as a production worker in 1929 and "eats with the rest of the workforce in the company cafeteria").

Some labor leaders who see the relationship between employers and workers as inherently antagonistic worry that these "reform" management schemes are just new ways to exploit workers. There are also industrialists who believe that workers are basically lazy and irresponsible, and that giving them any power will work against company interests. But over fifty years of research in industrial psychology indicates that worker participation systems can be devised that benefit both the company and the workers simultaneously. In one pioneering study done back in the 1940s, Lester Coch and John French demonstrated that when workers and management cooperate to meet each other's goals, both productivity and worker satisfaction increase. These findings have been confirmed many times.[7]

Our children will one day be conducting the business of our society. If we bring them up to recognize the benefits of cooperation rather than competition and to consider the impact of their business activities on others, then perhaps a new economic system in which morality has a larger place will evolve.

## CITIZENSHIP AND IDEOLOGY

As your youngsters move into adulthood they will begin to take part in the political life of our society and encounter moral issues on every front. Some will be local (Should the community assume any responsibility for its indigent members, for example, by building a shelter for the homeless?); some will be national (What should our government do, if anything, about the 35 million Americans who live below the poverty level?); some will be global (Should it be our policy to overthrow governments we don't like—even democratically elected ones—and replace them with friendly military dictatorships?); some will concern our basic identity as a nation (If our government conducts secret wars—secret from our people, certainly not secret from the people we are fighting against—can we still claim to have government *by the people*?).

Your children's stands on these kinds of issues will depend to a large degree on their understanding of the forces that determine people's behavior and the social conditions they live under—that is, on their answers to the questions, What makes people rich or poor, and what makes them violent or peaceful? For instance, are people poor because of their own inadequacies, because of an inadequate upbringing, or because of unfair economic conditions? Is a revolution in Central America a just reaction to an oppressive political and economic system, or a product of left-wing ideologies such as socialism or liberation theology?

If your child blames the poor for their poverty (they are lazy, unthrifty, or lack ability), he'll be less likely to support antipoverty programs than if he blames society.[8] Similarly, when he reads about a ghetto teenager robbing and killing a storekeeper, he will be in favor of a stiff jail sentence and perhaps capital punishment if he blames the teenager himself for being heartless and cruel. If, instead, he blames the teenager's social circumstances—such as a childhood spent in poverty with abusive parents and inadequate schools—he will be in favor of rehabilitation programs and expanded social services in the ghetto. Likewise, if he reads about a wealthy Central American landowner hiring gunmen to kill off union organizers, he'll want the man brought to trial if he places the blame on that particular landowner. If he blames the country's feudal economic and social system for the landowner's action, he'll support revolution there.

This question of *blame* has always been central to our moral, as well as our legal, system. If we can't blame a man for his destructive actions (because he has a brain tumor, or he was forced into the action, or we consider him mentally incompetent), we don't feel moral outrage over what he did and don't want to see him punished.

Can the social sciences (psychology, sociology, anthropology) be of any help in determining where the blame for a given action lies? For the most part, their influence has been to remove blame from the individual. To sociologists and social psychologists individual action is generally looked on as a product of social factors like poverty, family structure, and racial prejudice. Even psychotherapists and personality psychologists, whose area of study is the individual, don't blame people for their behavior. If a person is extremely aggressive, for instance, they see it as a symptom of disturbances *within* the person—simply the natural outcome of his psychological condition, which is presumed to be beyond his control and, therefore, not something to blame him for.

We have a problem here: How do we maintain a moral (or legal) system if individuals are held blameless—if we attribute their acts to forces, both within and without, that are beyond their control? It's an important question because psychologists and sociologists often have an influence in designing and implementing social and economic programs, and their focus on forces beyond the individual's control may inadvertently lead them to neglect one of the most important influences on an individual's actions: holding him or her *personally responsible* for what he or she does.

There is a way, though, to bring personal responsibility back into our theory and practices while still taking account of social forces. We must get rid of the idea of blame. In traditional moral and legal systems, when a person acted badly he was blamed. But blame implies that we believe that the person could have done otherwise, yet chose to do what he did anyway. However, from a scientific point of view, it makes no sense to say that a person could have acted otherwise or done anything other than exactly what he did. Physicists and botanists would obviously never say that an apple that fell from a tree could have done otherwise. All they can do is try to account for the forces that led to the apple falling.

The same is true for social scientists studying human behavior. It's not a matter of whether or not scientists believe in free will. Science (and any other method of inquiry) has no way to determine whether a person could have acted differently from the way he acted. All science, including human science, starts with the assumption that an event occurs because of the particular conditions that existed just prior to it. The more closely you duplicate those conditions, the more likely the same event (or, in modern physics, probability distribution of events) will occur. If you want something else to happen, you have to change the prior conditions. Someone might argue that a person acts a particular way because he chose to, that his choice was the prior event. But to scientists, *choice* is not a final cause; they will still want to know what conditions led up to that particular choice.

Are we saying, then, that social conditions *are* to blame for what we do? From a scientific point of view it makes as little sense to blame society as it does to blame an individual. The behavior of parents, public officials, teachers, and businessmen, is as much a product of prior conditions as the behavior of, for instance, a delinquent teenager. True, we can change the teenager's behavior by changing the social conditions he lives under, perhaps by convincing his parents to apply firmer discipline and treat him more affectionately. But that doesn't mean we blame his parents. Nor does it mean—and this is of great importance—that we shouldn't hold him responsible for his actions.

Of all the social conditions affecting anyone's behavior, including poverty and parental neglect or abuse, none is more important than being held responsible for the impact of one's actions on others. We've all read about young criminals who commit crime after crime as they pass in and out of the courts, family service organizations, and rehabilitation centers. When other youths see these youngsters roaming free in the neighborhood, they too learn that our society is timid about holding even serious offenders responsible for their actions. Psychologists may try to "cure" them and social workers may try to get them job training and reconcile them with their families. Both will generally treat them "professionally," which means nonjudgmentally. No one will try to make them feel that they are bad people because they try to hurt others; no one will give them moral training to help them develop empathy and moral standards.

In order to judge a delinquent teenager's behavior as immoral and hold him responsible for his acts, we don't need to "blame" him or assume that he could have done otherwise. We just need to believe two things: 1) that he intended to do harm (or in the psychologist's more objective terminology, that doing harm was the reinforcer for his act); and 2) that holding him responsible by making sure he suffers negative consequences for doing harm, will improve his behavior in the future, or at least prevent the misbehavior of others like him who will see that they too will be held responsible. Our moral outrage at his acts and the consequences we set up to induce him to act otherwise in the future must always be tempered by legal and just procedures. But moral outrage has a value. It communicates to those who would harm us that we will not allow ourselves to be victimized. Only if someone's behavior can't be changed by consequences (for example, his acts derive from a brain tumor) will holding him responsible be inappropriate.

Well, what about social conditions like poverty, political oppression, and racial prejudice? Don't these affect behavior? Most certainly they do. Holding individuals responsible generally means only punishing them for their misdeeds. It has nothing to do with setting up fair incentives and rewards so that people want to behave responsibly and amiably. When people are impoverished, oppressed, and discriminated against, they will inevitably engage in behavior that threatens and offends the dominant segment of society. If an individual can't get ahead using legitimate means, no one should be surprised when that person resorts to illegitimate means.

An instructive example of the importance of incentive conditions was reported by sociologist Allan Holmberg (as described in an article by John Kunkel).[9] Holmberg worked with an impoverished community of Peruvian Indians. When he arrived he found little in the way of "positions of responsibility in public affairs [or] . . . adequate leadership . . . and almost no public services were maintained." In addition, "cooperation within the community was the exception rather than the rule, and resistance to the outside world was high. Attitudes toward life were static and pessimistic." Most Indian peasants worked slowly, producing barely enough to meet the minimum necessities. To some observers, they were simply lazy and ignorant. Holmberg's assessment was different.

Until 1952 the fate of the Indians depended largely on the whims of the "patron" of the hacienda, who made all major decisions for them and for whom they had to work without pay. Holmberg concluded that the Indian "is not willing to labor long and well under all conditions. In most instances, he will do so only when he is working for himself or within his own culture. When working outside this framework, under conditions in which he is held in disrespect and generally receives little in the way of reward, he usually tries to get by with as little effort as he can."

When the social conditions were changed, the Indians changed. When they got paid for their labor, were allowed to keep what they produced, and were given responsibility for making their own decisions, they became more industrious, seeking out training to increase the productivity of their farms, and began to develop effective community structures. The rapid change was attributed, in part, to the fact that the villagers participated in determining how all new programs would be carried out. A paternalistic "welfare approach" was rejected on the grounds that it would not root the program "in the desires and responsibilities of the community itself." Thus, the Indians were given responsibility for both the successes and failures of their actions. By 1957, the community gained complete self-control and ran the hacienda on its own.

To prepare your youngsters for their adult responsibilities as citizens who will be making decisions on political officials and social and economic programs, we suggest you teach them that any program that fails either to provide people with adequate and fair incentives or to hold them responsible for their actions has little chance of succeeding.

We suggest that you also try to make your children aware of the major political issues of the day. A *New York Times*-CBS Poll in July 1983 found that only 8 percent of Americans knew that the Reagan administration supported the government in El Salvador and opposed the government in Nicaragua. Given the fact that our government's actions were life-and-death issues for the people of those countries and involved us in wars that were costing us hundreds of millions of dollars, one would hope for more interest on the part of our citizenry. It's hard to have government by the people when the people remain willfully uninformed (it goes without saying that one can't have government by the people when the government deceives the people or keeps fundamental policies secret). Our children need to appreciate that because we are a global power the actions of our leaders affect the quality of people's lives all over the world. Sometimes our leaders have pursued "our interests" in ways that have had devastating consequences for others. And sometimes we have done great humanitarian service.

By discussing important political issues with your child and exploring their moral implications, you will not only be preparing him to take his place as a responsible citizen. You will also be opening up a dialogue that, if handled with mutual respect, will bring the two of you closer together. In general, by bringing moral training into the home in a thoughtful and systematic way, parents will enrich both their children's and their own lives, and will open up wonderful, often joyful avenues of interaction for all family members. They will also be taking a significant step toward promoting the kind of society they want their children to inherit.

# NOTES

## NOTES TO CHAPTER 1

1. Weiss, R.F., Buchanan, W., Alstatt, L., and Lombardo, J.P. Altruism is rewarding. *Science*, 1971, 171, 1262–1263.
2. Strayer, F.F., Wareing, S., and Rushton, J.P. Social constraints on naturally occurring preschool altruism. *Ethology and Sociobiology*, 1979, 1, 3–11.
3. MacDonald, K. Warmth as a developmental construct: An evolutionary analysis. *Child Development*, 1992, 63, 753–773.
   Weiss, B., Dodge, K., Bates, J.E., and Pettit, G.S. Some consequences of early harsh discipline: Child aggression and a maladaptive social information processing style. *Child Development*, 1992, 63, 1321–1335.
4. Masters, J.C., and Furman, W. Popularity, individual friendship selection and specific peer interaction among children. *Developmental Psychology*, 17, 344–350.
   Hartup, W.W., Glazer, J.A., and Charlesworth, R. Peer reinforcement and sociometric status. *Child Development*. 1967, 38, 1017–1024.
   Kurdek, L.A. and Krile, D. A developmental analysis of the relation between peer acceptance and both interpersonal understanding and perceived social self-competence. *Child Development*, 1982, 53, 1485–1491.
5. Freud, S. *Group psychology and the analysis of the ego.* New York: Bantam Books, 1960. (Original German edition, 1921)
6. Walters, J., Pearce, D., and Dahms, L. Affectional and aggressive behavior of preschool children. *Child Development*, 1957, 28, 15–26.
   Hay, D.F. and Rheingold, H.L. The early appearance of some valued social behaviors. In D.L. Bridgeman (ed.), *The nature of prosocial development: Interdisciplinary theories and strategies.* New York: Academic Press, 1984, Chapter 3.
7. Piaget, J. *The moral judgment of the child.* New York: Free Press, 1965.

8. Karniol, R. Children's use of intentional cues in evaluating behavior. *Psychological Bulletin,* 1978, 85, 76–81.

   Armsby, R.E. A re-examination of the development of moral judgments in children. *Child Development,* 1971, 42, 1241–1248.

9. Durkin, D. The specificity of children's moral judgments. *Journal of Genetic Psychology,* 1961, 98, 3–13.

   Grinder, R. Relations between behavioral and cognitive dimensions of conscience in middle childhood. *Child Development,* 1964, 35, 881–892.

   Ford, M.E. The construct validity of egocentrism. *Psychological Bulletin,* 1979, 86, 1169–1188.

   Borke, H. Interpersonal perception of young children: Egocentrism or empathy. *Developmental Psychology,* 1971, 5, 263–269.

   Likona, T. Research on Piaget's theory of moral development. In T. Likona (ed.), *Moral development and behavior: Theory, research, and social issues.* New York: Holt, Rinehart and Winston, 1976, Chapter 12.

10. Kohlberg, L. Stage and sequence: The cognitive developmental approach to socialization. In D.A. Goslin (ed.), *Handbook of socialization theory and research.* Chicago: Rand McNally, 1969, Chapter 6.

11. Severy, L.J. and Davis, K.E. Helping behavior among normal and retarded children. *Child Development,* 1971, 42, 1017–1031.

    Strayer, F.F., et al, *op cit.*

    Eisenberg-Berg, N. and Neal, C. Children's moral reasoning about their own spontaneous prosocial behavior. *Developmental Psychology,* 1979, 15, 228–229.

12. Campagna, A.F. and Harter, S. Moral judgment in sociopathic and normal children. *Journal of Personality and Social Psychology,* 1975, 31, 199–205.

13. Likona, T. *Raising good children.* New York: Bantam Books, 1983.

    Kohlberg, L. Moral stages and moralization: The cognitive developmental approach. In T. Likona (ed.), *Moral behavior and development: Theory, research, and social issues.* New York: Holt, Rinehart and Winston, 1975, Chapter 2.

14. Kohlberg, L. Stages of moral development as a basis for moral education. In C.M. Beck, B.S. Crittenden, and E.V. Sullivan (eds.), *Moral education: Interdisciplinary approaches.* Toronto: University of Toronto Press, 1971, pp. 23–92.

    Selman, R.L. Social-cognitive understanding: A guide to educational and clinical practice. In T. Likona (ed.), *Moral development and behavior.* New York: Holt, Rinehart, and Winston, Chapter 17.

    Radke-Yarrow, M. and Zahn-Waxler, C. Dimensions and correlates of prosocial behavior in young children. *Child Development,* 1976, 47, 118–125.

    Bar-Tal, D., Raviv, A., and Goldberg, M. Helping behavior among preschool children: An observational study. *Child Development,* 1982, 53, 396–402.

    Staub, E. A child in distress: The influence of age and number of witnesses on children's attempts to help. *Journal of Personality and Social Psychology,* 1970, 14, 130–140.

15. Skinner, B.F. *Beyond freedom and dignity.* New York: Knopf, 1971.

**16.** Kirigan, K.A., Braukmann, C.J., Atwater, J.D., and Wolf, M.M. An evaluation of teaching-family (Achievement place) group homes for juvenile offenders. *Journal of Applied Behavior Analysis,* 1982, 15, 1–16.

## Notes to Chapter 2

**1.** Meichenbaum, D. *Cognitive-behavior modification: An integrative approach.* New York: Plenum Press, 1977.

Luria, A.R. *The role of speech in the regulation of normal and abnormal behavior.* New York: Liveright, 1961.

Skinner, B.F. *Verbal behavior.* New York: Appleton-Century-Crofts, 1957, Chapter 19.

O'Leary, S.G. and Dubey, D.R. Applications of self-control procedures by children: A review. *Journal of Applied Behavior Analysis,* 1979, 12, 449–465.

Furrow, D. Social and private speech at two years. *Child Development,* 1984, 55, 355–362.

**2.** Aronfreed, J. *Conduct and conscience.* New York: Academic Press, 1968.

**3.** Hart, C.H., DeWolf, D.M., Wozniak, P., and Burts, D.C. Maternal and paternal disciplinary styles: Relations with preschoolers' playground behavioral orientations and peer status. *Child Development,* 1992, 63, 879–892.

Stayton, D., Hogan, R., and Salter-Ainsworth, M. Infant obedience and maternal behavior: The origins of socialization reconsidered. *Child Development,* 1971, 42, 1057–1069.

Londerville, S. and Main, M. Security of attachment, compliance, and maternal training methods in the second year of life. *Developmental Psychology,* 1981, 17, 289–299.

Minton, C., Kagan, J., and Levine, J.A. Maternal control and obedience in the two-year-old. *Child Development,* 1971, 42, 1873–1894.

Sears, R.R., Maccoby, E.E., and Levin, H. *Patterns of child rearing.* New York: Row, Peterson, 1957, Chapter 10.

McCord, W., McCord, J., and Howard, A. Familial correlates of aggression in nondelinquent male children. *Journal of Abnormal and Social Psychology,* 1961, 62, 79–93.

**4.** Wolfe, D.A., Katell, A., and Drabman, R.S. Parents and preschool children's choices of disciplinary child rearing methods. *Journal of Applied Developmental Psychology,* 1982, 3, 167–176.

**5.** Zahn-Waxler, C., Radke-Yarrow, M., and King, R. Child-rearing and children's prosocial initations toward victims in distress. *Child Development,* 1979, 50, 319–330.

Sears, R.R., et al, *op cit.*

Grusec, J. The antecedents of self-criticism. *Journal of Personality and Social Psychology,* 1966, 4, 244–252.

**6.** Bretherton, I. and Beeghly, M. Talking about internal states: The acquisition of an explicit theory of mind. *Developmental Psychology,* 1982, 18, 906–921.

Hood, L. and Bloom, L. What, when, and how about why: A longitudinal study of early expressions of causality. *Monographs of the Society for Research in Child Development,* 1979, 44 (6, Serial No. 181).

Crockenberg, S. and Litman, C. Autonomy as competence in 2-year-olds: Maternal correlates of child defiance, compliance, and self-assertion. *Developmental Psychology,* 1990, 26, 961–971.

Dunn, J. and Munn, P. Development of justification in disputes with mother and sibling. *Developmental Psychology,* 1987, 23, 791–798.

7. Pikas, A. Children's attitudes toward rational versus inhibiting parental authority. *Journal of Abnormal and Social Psychology,* 1961, 62, 315–321.

Anderson, W.H., Jr. and Moreland, K.L. Instrumental versus moralistic self-verbalizations in delay of gratification. *Merrill-Palmer Quarterly,* 1982, 28, 291–296.

8. Krebs, D.L. Empathy and altruism. *Journal of Personality and Social Psychology,* 1975, 32, 1134–1146.

Houston, D.A. Empathy and the self: cognitive and emotional influences on the evaluation of negative effects in others. *Journal of Personality and Social Psychology* 1990, 59, 859–868.

9. Bretherton, I. and Beeghly, M., *op cit.*

Borke, H. Interpersonal perception of young children: Egocentrism or empathy? *Developmental Psychology,* 1971, 5, 263–269.

Dunn, J., Brown, J., Slomkowski, C., Tesla, C., and Youngblade, L. Young children's understanding of other people's feelings and beliefs: Individual differences and their antecedents. *Child Development,* 1991, 62, 1352–1366.

Barnett, K., Darcie, G., Holland, C.J., and Kobasigawa, A. Children's cognitions about effective helping. *Developmental Psychology,* 1982, 18, 267–277.

Toi, M. and Batson, C.D. More evidence that empathy is a source of altruistic motivation. *Journal of Personality and Social Psychology,* 1982, 43, 281–292.

10. McCord, W., McCord, J., and Howard, A., *op cit.*

11. Baumrind, D. Current patterns of parental authority. *Developmental Psychology Monographs,* 1971, 4 (1, Whole Pt. 2).

McCord, W., McCord, J., and Howard, A., *op cit.*

12. Sears, R.R., et al., *op cit.*

13. Radke-Yarrow, M. and Zahn-Waxler, C. Roots, motives, and patterns in children's prosocial behavior. In J. Reykowski, J. Karylowski, D. Bar-Tal, and E. Staub (eds.). *The development and maintainance of prosocial behaviors: International perspectives.* New York: Plenum Press, 1984.

14. Siegel, A.E. and Siegel, S. Reference groups, membership groups, and attitude change. *Journal of Abnormal and Social Psychology,* 1957, 55, 360–364.

Newcomb, T.M. Attitude development as a function of reference groups: The Bennington study. In G.E. Swanson, T.M. Newcomb, and E.L. Hartley (eds.), *Readings in social psychology,* rev. ed., New York: Holt, Rinehart & Winston, 1952.

15. Harris, M.B. Reciprocity and generosity: Some determinants of sharing in children. *Child Development,* 1970, 41, 313–328.

Rosenhan, D. and White, G.M. Observation and rehearsal as determinants of prosocial behavior. *Journal of Personality and Social Psychology*, 1967, 5, 424–431.

Staub, E. A child in distress: The influence of nurturance and modeling on children's attempts to help. *Developmental Psychology*, 1971, 5, 124–132.

Grusec, J.E., Kuczynski, L., Rushton, J.P., and Sumutis, Z.M. Learning resistance to temptation through observation. *Developmental Psychology*, 1979, 15, 233–240.

Allen, M.K. and Liebert, R.M. Effect of live and symbolic deviant modeling cues on adoption of a previously learned standard. *Journal of Personality and Social Psychology*, 1969, 11, 253–260.

Bryan, J.H. and Walbek, N.H. The impact of words and deeds concerning altruism on children. *Child Development*, 1970, 41, 747–757.

Bryan, J.H. and Walbek, N.H. Preaching and practicing generosity: Children's actions and reactions. *Child Development*, 1970, 41, 329–353.

Midlarsky, E., Bryan, J.H., and Brickman, P. Aversive approval: Interactive effects of modeling and reinforcement on altruistic behavior. *Child Development*, 1973, 44, 321–328.

16. Midlarsky, E. and Bryan, J.H. Affect expressions and children's imitative altruism. *Journal of Experimental Research in Personality*, 1972, 6, 195–203.

17. Porterfield, J.K., Herbert-Jackson, E., and Risley, T.R. Contingent observation: An effective and acceptable procedure for reducing disruptive behavior of young children in a group setting. *Journal of Applied Behavior Analysis*, 1976, 9, 55–64.

## NOTES TO CHAPTER 3

1. Stotland, E., Mathews, Jr., E.E., Sherman, S.E., Hansson, R.O., and Richardson, B.Z. *Empathy, fantasy and helping*. Beverly Hills, CA: Sage, 1978.

2. Cole, D.L. Perceptions of war and participants in warfare: A ten year replication. *International Journal of Peace Research*, 1973, 10, 115–118.

3. Toi, M. and Batson, C.D. More evidence that empathy is a source of altruistic motivation. *Journal of Personality and Social Psychology*, 1982, 43, 281–292.
Batson, C.D. How social an animal? The human capacity for caring. *American Psychologist*, 1990, 45, 336–346.

4. Leiman, B. Affective empathy and subsequent altruism in kindergartners and first graders. Paper presented at the meeting of the American Psychological Association, Toronto, Canada, August 1978. Cited in M. Hoffman, Is altruism part of human nature? *Journal of Personality and Social Psychology*, 1981, 40, 121–137.

5. Peterson, L. Role of donor competence, donor age, and peer presence on helping in an emergency. *Developmental Psychology*, 1983, 19, 873–880.
Staub, E. Helping a person in distress: The influence of implicit and explicit "rules" of conduct on children and adults. *Journal of Personality and Social Psychology*, 1971, 17, 137–144.

6. Hoffman, M.L. Empathy, its development and prosocial implications. In

C.B. Keasey (ed.), *Nebraska symposium on motivation, vol. 25.* Lincoln: University of Nebraska Press, 1977, pp. 169–218.

7. Simner, M.L. Newborn's response to the cry of another infant. *Developmental Psychology,* 1971, 5, 136–150.

   Martin, G.B. and Clark, III, R.D. Distress crying in neonates: Species and peer specificity. *Developmental Psychology,* 1982, 18, 3–9.

   Sagi, A. and Hoffman, M.L. Empathic distress in newborns. *Developmental Psychology,* 1976, 12, 175–176.

   Field, T.M., Woodson, R., Greenberg, R., and Cohen, D. Discrimination and imitation of facial expressions by neonates. *Science,* 1982, 218, 179–181.

   Cohn, J.F. and Tronick, E.Z. Three-month-old infants' reaction to simulated maternal depression. *Child Development,* 1983, 54, 185–193.

   Young-Browne, G., Rosenfeld, H.M., and Horowitz, F.D. Infant discrimination of facial expressions. *Child Development,* 1977, 48, 555–562.

   Barrera, M.E. and Maurer, D. The perception of facial expressions by the three-month-old. *Child Development,* 1981, 52, 203–206.

   Bretherton, I. and Beeghly, M. Talking about internal states: The acquisition of an explicit theory of mind. *Developmental Psychology,* 1982, 18, 906–921.

8. Hoffman, M.L. Empathy, role-taking, guilt and development of altruistic motives. In T. Likona (ed.), *Moral development and behavior: Theory, research and social issues.* New York: Holt, Rinehart & Winston, 1976, Chapter 7.

9. Zahn-Waxler, C., Radke-Yarrow, M., Wagner, E., and Chapman, M. Development of concern for others. *Developmental Psychology,* 1992, 28, 126–136.

10. Johnson, D.B. Altruistic behavior and the development of the self in infants. *Merrill-Palmer Quarterly,* 1982, 28, 379–388.

    Borke, H. Interpersonal perception of young children: Egocentrism or empathy? *Developmental Psychology,* 1971, 5, 263–269.

    Stewart, R.B. and Marvin, R.S. Sibling relations: The role of conceptual perspective-taking in the ontogeny of sibling caregiving. *Child Development,* 1984, 55, 1322–1332.

11. Zahn-Waxler, C., Friedman, S.L., and Cummings, E.M. Children's emotions and behaviors in response to infant's cries. *Child Development,* 1983, 54, 1522–1528.

    Johnson, D.B., *op cit.*

    Eisenberg-Berg, N. Development of children's prosocial moral judgment. *Developmental Psychology,* 1979, 15, 128–137.

    Eisenberg-Berg, N. and Geisheker, E. Content of preachings and power of the model/preacher: The effect on children's generosity. *Developmental Psychology,* 1979, 15, 168–175.

    Rosenhan, D.L. Some origins of concern for others. In P. Mussen, J. Langer, and M. Covington (eds.), *Trends and issues in developmental psychology.* New York: Holt, Rinehart, & Winston, 1969.

    Sims, S.A. Induction, self-induction and children's donation behavior. Paper presented at the 49th Annual Meeting of the Eastern Psychological Association, Washington, D.C., March 1978. Cited in E. Staub, *Positive social behavior and morality, Volume 2: Socialization and development.* New York: Academic Press, 1979.

12. Hoffman, M.L. Parent discipline and the child's consideration for others. *Child Development,* 1963, 34, 573–588.

    Hart, C.H., DeWolf, D.M., Wozniak, P., and Burts, D.C. Maternal and paternal disciplinary styles: Relations with preschoolers' playground behavioral orientations and peer status. *Child Development,* 1992, 63, 879–892.

    Hoffman, M.L. Moral internalization, parental power, and the nature of parent-child interaction. *Developmental Psychology,* 1975, 11, 228–239.

    Bearison, D.J. and Cassel, T.Z. Cognitive decentration and social codes: Communicative effectiveness in young children from differing family contexts. *Developmental Psychology,* 1975, 11, 29–36.

13. Zahn-Waxler, C., Radke-Yarrow, M., and King, R.A. Child rearing and children's prosocial initiations toward victims in distress. *Child Development,* 1979, 50, 319–330.

14. Mallick, S.K. and McCandless, B.R. A study of catharsis of aggression. *Journal of Personality and Social Psychology,* 1966, 4, 591–596.

    Frodi, A. Effects of varying explanations given for a provocation on subsequent hostility. *Psychological Reports,* 1976, 38, 659–669.

15. Chandler, M. Egocentrism and antisocial behavior: The assessment and training of social perspective-taking skills. *Developmental Psychology,* 1973, 9, 326–332.

16. Iannotti, R.J. Effect of role-taking experiences on role-taking, empathy, altruism, and aggression. *Developmental Psychology,* 1978, 14, 119–124.

    Chalmers, J.B., and Townsend, M.A.R. The effects of training in social perspective taking on socially maladjusted girls. *Child Development,* 1990, 61, 178–190.

17. Johnson, D.W. Cooperativeness and social perspective taking. *Journal of Personality and Social Psychology,* 1975, 31, 241–244.

    Buckley, N., Siegel, L.S., and Ness, S. Egocentrism, empathy, and altruistic behavior in young children. *Developmental Psychology,* 1979, 15, 329–330.

    Feshbach, N.D. Learning to care: A positive approach to child training. *Journal of Clinical Child Psychology,* 1983, 12, 266–271.

    Klemchuk, H.P., Band, L.A., and Howell, D.C. Coherence and correlates of Level 1 perspective taking in young children. *Merrill-Palmer Quarterly,* 1990, 36, 369–387.

18. Barnett, M.A., Howard, J.A., King, L.M., and Dino, G.A. Antecedents of empathy: Retrospective accounts of early socialization. *Personality and Social Psychology Bulletin,* 1980, 6, 361–365.

    Fabes, R.A., Eisenberg, N., and Miller, P.A. Maternal correlates of children's vicarious emotional responsiveness. *Developmental Psychology,* 1990, 26, 639–648.

    Aronfreed, J. and Paskal, V. The development of sympathetic behavior in children: An experimental test of a two-phase hypothesis. Unpublished manuscript, University of Pennsylvania, 1966. Described in J. Aronfreed, *Conduct and Conscience.* New York: Academic Press, 1968, Chapter 6.

Hoffman, M.L. Altruistic behavior and the parent-child relationship. *Journal of Personality and Social Psychology,* 1975, 31, 937–943.

19. Barnett, K., Darcie, G., Holland, C., and Kobasigawa, A. Children's cognitions about effective helping. *Developmental Psychology,* 1982, 18, 267–277.

20. Polirstok, S.R. and Greer, R.D. Remediation of mutually aversive interactions between a problem student and four teachers by training the student in reinforcement techniques. *Journal of Applied Behavior Analysis,* 1977, 10, 707–716.

21. Lochman, J.E., Burch, P.R., Curry, J.F., and Lampron, L.B. Treatment and generalization effects of cognitive-behavioral and goal-setting interventions with aggressive boys. *Journal of Consulting and Clinical Psychology,* 1984, 52, 915–916.

Forman, S.G. A comparison of cognitive training and response cost procedures in modifying aggressive behavior of elementary school children. *Behavior Therapy,* 1980, 11, 594–600.

22. Shirer, W. *The rise and fall of the third reich.* New York: Fawcett-Crest, 1959, p. 1463.

## NOTES TO CHAPTER 4

1. Weston, D. and Turiel, E. Act-rule relations: Children's concepts of social rules. *Developmental Psychology,* 1980, 16, 417–424.

Tisak, M.S., and Turiel, E. Variations in seriousness of transgressions and children's moral and conventional concepts. *Developmental Psychology,* 1988, 24, 352–357.

Tisak, M.S. Children's conceptions of parental authority. *Child Development,* 1986, 57, 166–176.

2. White, R.W. Motivation reconsidered: The concept of competence. *Psychological Review,* 1959, 66, 297–333.

3. DiVesta, F.J. and Stauber, K.A. Identification of verbal concepts by preschool children. *Developmental Psychology,* 1971, 5, 81–85.

Masters, J.C., Furman, W., and Barden, R.C. Effects of achievement standards, tangible rewards, and self-dispensed achievement evaluations on children's task mastery. *Child Development,* 1977, 48, 217–224.

Mischel, W. and Liebert, R.M. Effects of discrepancies between observed and imposed reward criteria on their acquisition and transmission. *Journal of Personality and Social Psychology,* 1966, 3, 45–53.

Locke, E.A., Shaw, K.N., Saari, L.M., and Latham, G.P. Goal setting and task performance: 1969–1980. *Psychological Bulletin,* 1981, 90, 125–152.

Eisenberger, R. and Masterson, F.A. Required high effort increases subsequent persistance and reduces cheating. *Journal of Personality and Social Psychology,* 1983, 44, 593–599.

4. Gouldner, A.W. Norm of reciprocity: A preliminary statement. *American Sociological Review,* 1960, 25, 161–178.

Greenglass, E.R. Effects of prior help and hindrance on willingness to help another: Reciprocity or social responsibility. *Journal of Personality and Social Psychology,* 1969, 11, 224–231.

DePaulo, B.M., Brittingham, G.L., and Kaiser, M.K. Receiving competence-relevant help: Effects on reciprocity, affect, and sensitivity to the helper's nonverbally expressed needs. *Journal of Personality and Social Psychology,* 1983, 45, 1045–1060.

Levitt, M.J., Weber, R.A., Clark, M.C., and McDonnell, P. Reciprocity of exchange in toddler sharing behavior. *Developmental Psychology,* 1985, 21, 122–123.

5. Blackwood, R. The operant conditioning of verbally mediated self-control in the classroom. *Journal of School Psychology,* 1970, 8, 251–258.

MacPherson, E.M., Candee, B.L., and Hohman, R.J. Comparison of three methods for eliminating disruptive lunchroom behavior. *Journal of Applied Behavior Analysis,* 1974, 7, 287–297.

6. Williamson, G.M., and Clark, M.S. Providing help and desired relationship type as determinants of changes in moods and self-evaluations. *Journal of Personality and Social Psychology,* 1989, 56, 722–734.

Bridges, K.B. Emotional development in early infancy. *Child Development,* 1932, 3, 324–341.

7. Makarenko, A. *The road to life* (trans. Ivy and Tatiania Litvino). Moscow: Foreign Language Publishing House, 1951.

Bronfenbrenner, U. Soviet methods of character education: Some implications for research. *American Psychologist,* 1962, 17, 550–564.

Bowen, J. *Soviet education: Anton Makarenko and the years of experiment.* Madison, Wisconsin: Univ. of Wisconsin Press, 1962.

8. Hood, L. and Bloom, L. What, when and how about why: A longitudinal study of early expressions of causality. *Monographs of the Society for Research in Child Development,* 1979, 44 (6, Serial No. 181).

9. Eisenberg-Berg, N. and Neal, C. Children's moral reasoning about their own spontaneous prosocial behavior. *Developmental Psychology,* 1979, 15, 228–229.

Dreman, S.B. and Greenbaum, C.W. Altruism or reciprocity: Sharing behavior in Israeli kindergarten children. *Child Development,* 1973, 44, 61–68.

10. Tapp, J.L. and Kohlberg, L. Developing senses of law and legal justice. *Journal of Social Issues,* 1971, 27(2), 65–91.

Tapp, J.L. A child's garden of law and order. *Psychology Today,* 1970, 4(7), 29–31, 62–64.

11. Elder, G. Parental power legitimation and the effect on the adolescent. *Sociometry,* 1963, 26, 50–65.

Dekovic, M., and Janssens, J.M. Parent child-rearing style and child's sociometric status. *Developmental Psychology,* 1992, 28, 925–932.

Coch, L. and French, J.R.P. Overcoming resistance to change. *Human Relations,* 1948, 1, 512–532.

White, R. and Lippitt, R. *Autocracy and democracy: An experimental inquiry.* New York: Harper, 1960.

Lind, E.A., Kanfer, R., and Early, P.C. Voice, control, and procedural justice: Instrumental and noninstrumental concerns in fairness judgments. *Journal of Personality and Social Psychology,* 1990, 59, 952–959.

12. Olijnik, A.B. and McKinney, J.P. Parental value orientation and generosity in children. *Developmental Psychology,* 1973, 8, 311.

 Casey, W.M. and Burton, R.V. Training children to be consistently honest through verbal self-instruction. *Child Development,* 1982, 53, 911–919.

13. McGuire, W.J. Inducing resistance to persuasion: Some contemporary approaches. In L. Berkowitz (ed.), *Advances in experimental social psychology, Vol. 1.* New York: Academic Press, 1964.

14. Pikas, A. Children's attitudes toward rational versus inhibiting parental authority. *Journal of Abnormal and Social Psychology,* 1961, 62, 315–321.

15. Rokeach, M. *The nature of human values.* New York: Free Press, 1973.

 Greenstein, T. Behavior change through value self-confrontation: A field experiment. *Journal of Personality and Social Psychology,* 1976, 34, 254–262.

 Tetlock, P.E. A value pluralism model of ideological reasoning. *Journal of Personality and Social Psychology,* 1986, 50, 819–827.

16. Neimark, E.D. and Slotnick, N.S. Development of the understanding of logical connections. *Journal of Educational Psychology,* 1970, 61, 451–460.

17. Grusec, J.E., Kuczynski, L., Rushton, J.P., and Simutis, Z.M. Modeling, direct instruction, and attributions: Effects on altruism. *Developmental Psychology,* 1978, 14, 51–57.

 Miller, R.L., Brickman, P., and Bolen, D. Attribution versus persuasion as a means for modifying behavior. *Journal of Personality and Social Psychology,* 1975, 31, 430–441.

 Jensen, A.M. and Moore, S.G. The effect of attribute statements on cooperativeness and competitiveness in school-age boys. *Child Development,* 1977, 48, 305–307.

 Toner, I.J., Moore, L.P., and Emmons, B.A. The effect of being labeled on subsequent self-control in children. *Child Development,* 1980, 51, 618–621.

 Perry, D.G., Perry, L.C., Bussey, K., English, D., and Arnold, G. Processes of attribution and children's self-punishment following misbehavior. *Child Development,* 1980, 51, 545–551.

18. Grusec, J.E. and Redler, E. Attribution, reinforcement, and altruism: A developmental analysis. *Developmental Psychology,* 1980, 16, 525–534.

19. Bryan, J.H. and Walbek, N.H. Preaching and practicing generosity: Children's actions and reactions. *Child Development,* 1970, 41, 329–353.

20. Marcus Tullius Cicero, *De republica,* 1. New York: Liberal Arts Press, 1960. (Original: C. 50 B.C.)

 Locke, J. *Two treatises on government.* Cambridge: Cambridge University Press, 1962, Chapter 2. (Original: 1690)

21. Zellman, G. and Sears, D. Childhood origins of tolerance for dissent. *Journal of Social Issues,* 1971, 27 (2), 109–136.

 Sullivan, J.L., Pierson, J.E., and Marcus, G.E. Political tolerance: The illusion of progress. *Psychology Today,* 1979, 12(3), 86–91.

 Wilson, W.C. Belief in freedom of speech and press. *Journal of Social Issues,* 1975, 31(2), 69–76.

22. Freud, S. *New introductory lectures on psychoanalysis.* New York: W.W. Norton, 1933. (Original German edition, 1933)

23. Wilhelm II. Speech, 1891. In G. Seldes (ed.), *The great quotations.* New York: Pocket Books, 1967, p. 46.

24. *New York Times,* Nov. 25, 1969, p. 16.

25. Milgram, S. *Obedience to authority.* New York: Harper & Row, 1974.

26. London, P. The rescuers: Motivational hypothesis about Christians who saved Jews from the Nazis. In J. Macauley and L. Berkowitz (eds.), *Altruism and helping behavior.* New York: Academic Press, 1970, pp. 241–250.
    Oliner, S.P., and Oliner, P.M. *The altruistic personality: Rescuers of Jews in Nazi Europe.* New York: The Free Press, 1988.

27. Schwartz, S.H. Words, deeds and the perception of consequences and responsibility in action situations. *Journal of Personality and Social Psychology,* 1968, 10, 232–242.

28. Brehm, J.W. *A theory of psychological reactance.* New York: Academic Press, 1966.

29. Staub, E. A child in distress: The influence of nurturance and modeling on children's attempts to help. *Developmental Psychology,* 1971, 5, 124–132.

30. Laupa, M. Children's reasoning about three authority attributes: Adult status, knowledge, and social position. *Developmental Psychology,* 1991, 27, 321–329.

31. Baumrind, D. Current patterns of parental authority. *Developmental Psychology Monographs,* 1971, 4 (1, Whole Pt. 2).
    Peck, R.F. and Havighurst, R.J. *The psychology of character development.* New York: Wiley, 1960.
    Baumrind, D. Some thoughts about childrearing. In U. Bronfenbrenner (ed.), *Influences on human behavior.* Hinsdale, Ill.: Dryden Press, 1972, pp. 396–409.

32. Zellman, G. and Sears, D., *op cit.*

33. Hess, R.D. and Torney, J.V. *The development of political attitudes in children.* Garden City N.Y.: Anchor-Doubleday, 1968.

34. Hoffman, M. Altruistic behavior and the parent-child relationship. *Journal of Personality and Social Psychology,* 1975, 31, 937–943.

35. Calhoun, J.C. Speech to Senate. In G. Seldes (ed.), *The great quotations, op cit.,* p. 865.

36. Vishinsky, A. The law of the Soviet state, 1938. In G. Seldes (ed.), *The great quotations, op cit.* p. 395.

37. Kodroff, J.K. and Roberge, J.J. Developmental analysis of conditional reasoning abilities of primary-grade children. *Developmental Psychology,* 1975, 11, 21–28.
    Schulman, M. *The passionate mind: Bringing up an intelligent and creative child.* N.Y.: The Free Press, 1991.

## NOTES TO CHAPTER 5

1. Schulman, M.S. Love training: Behavior therapy with an aggressive child. *The Behavior Therapist,* 1978, 1, 16–17.
2. Brown, P. and Elliott, R. Control of aggression in a nursery school class. *Journal of Experimental Child Psychology,* 1965, 2, 103–107.
3. Alley, T.R. Head shape and the perception of cuteness. *Developmental Psychology,* 1981, 17, 650–654.
4. Anisfeld, E. The onset of social smiling in preterm and full-term infants from two ethnic backgrounds. *Infant Behavior and Development,* 1982, 5, 387–395.
   Wolff, P.H. Observations on the early development of smiling. In B.M. Foss (ed.), *Determinants of infant behavior, Vol. 2.* New York: Wiley, 1963, pp. 113–134.
5. Rheingold, H.L., Hay, D.F., and West, M.J. Sharing in the second year of life. *Child Development,* 1976, 47, 1148–1158.
   Rheingold, H.L. Little children's participation in the work of adults, a nascent prosocial behavior. *Child Development,* 1982, 53, 114–125.
   Lennon, R., and Eisenberg, N. Emotional displays associated with preschoolers' prosocial behavior. *Child Development,* 1987, 58, 992–1000.
6. Bridges, K.M.B. Emotional development in early infancy. *Child Development,* 1932, 3, 324–341.
   Zahn-Waxler, C. and Robinson, J. The development of empathy in twins. *Developmental Psychology,* 1992, 28, 1038–1047.
   Eckerman, C.O., Whatley, J.L., and Kutz, S.L.K. Growth of social play with peers during the second year of life. *Developmental Psychology,* 1975, 11, 42–49.
   Walters, J., Pearce, D., and Dahms, L. Affectional and aggressive behavior in preschool children. *Child Development,* 1957, 28, 15–26.
7. Hoffman, L. The father's role in the family and the child's peer group adjustment. *Merrill-Palmer Quarterly,* 1961, 7, 97–105.
   Hoffman, M.L. Parent discipline and the child's consideration for others. *Child Development,* 1963, 34, 573–588.
   Brown, A.W., Morrison, J., and Couch, G.B. Influence of affectional family relationships on character development. *Journal of Abnormal and Social Psychology,* 1947, 42, 422–428.
   McCord, W., McCord, J., and Howard, A. Familial correlates of aggression in nondelinquent male children. *Journal of Abnormal and Social Psychology,* 1961, 62, 79–93.
8. Hess, R.D. and Camara, K.A. Post-divorce family relationships as mediating factors in the consequences of divorce for children. *Journal of Social Issues,* 1979, 33(4), 79–96.
9. Thomas, A. and Chess, S. *Temperament and development.* New York: Brunner/Mazel, 1977.

10. Hay, D.F. Cooperative interaction and sharing between very young children and their parents. *Developmental Psychology*, 1979, 15, 647–653.

    Piaget, J. *The moral judgment of the child.* New York: Free Press, 1965.

    McClintock, C.G. and Moskowitz, J.M. Children's preferences for individualistic, cooperative, and competitive outcomes. *Journal of Personality and Social Psychology*, 1976, 34, 543–555.

11. Thomas, A. and Chess, S., *op cit.*

12. LaGreca, A.M. and Santogrossi, D. Social skills training with elementary school students: A behavioral group approach. *Journal of Consulting and Clinical Psychology*, 1980, 48, 220–227.

    Ross, D.M., Ross, S.A., and Evans, T.A. The modification of extreme social withdrawal by modeling with guided participation. *Journal of Behavior Therapy and Experimental Psychiatry*, 1971, 2, 273–279.

13. Hartup, W.W. Peer interaction and social organization. In P.A. Mussen (ed.), *Carmichael's manual of child psychology, Vol. 2.* New York: John Wiley, Chapter 24.

    Ladd, G.W. and Oden, S. The relationship between peer acceptance and children's ideas about helpfulness. *Child Development*, 1979, 50, 402–408.

    Dodge, K.A. Behavioral antecedents of peer social status. *Child Development*, 1983, 54, 1386–1399.

14. Feinman, S. Social referencing in infancy. *Merrill-Palmer Quarterly*, 1982, 28, 445–470.

15. Hartup, W.W. Aggression in childhood: Developmental perspectives. *American Psychologist*, 1974, 5, 336–341.

16. Lerner, M. The justice motive: Equality and parity among children. *Journal of Personality and Social Psychology*, 1974, 29, 539–550.

    Nelson, S. and Dweck, C. Motivation and competence as determinants of young children's reward allocations. *Developmental Psychology*, 1977, 13, 192–197.

    Thorkildsen, T.A. Pluralism in children's reasoning about social justice. *Child Development*, 1989, 60, 965–972.

17. Stewart, R.B. Sibling attachment relationships: Child-infant interactions in the strange situation. *Developmental Psychology*, 1983, 19, 192–199.

18. Hovland, C.I. and Sears, R.R. Minor studies of aggression: Correlation of lynching with economic indices. *Journal of Psychology*, 1940, 9, 301–310.

    Bettelheim, B. and Horowitz, M. Ethnic tolerance: A function of social and personal control. *American Journal of Sociology*, 1949, 55, 137–145.

    Tenenbaum, S. *Why men hate.* New York: Beechurst Press, 1947.

19. Staats, A.W. and Staats, C.K. Attitudes established by classical conditioning. *Journal of Abnormal and Social Psychology*, 1958, 57, 37–40.

    Razran, G.H.S. Conditional response changes in rating and appraising sociopolitical slogans. *Psychological Bulletin*, 1940, 37, 481.

20. *New York Times*, April 3, 1984, p. A17.

21. Harkness, S., Edwards, C.P., and Super, C. Social roles and moral reasoning: A case study in a rural African community. *Developmental Psychology*, 1981, 17, 595–603.

22. Merton, R. *Social theory and social structure*, rev. ed. New York: Free Press, 1957.

Kramer, R.M. and Brewer, M.B. Effects of group identity on resource use in a simulated commons dilemma. *Journal of Personality and Social Psychology*, 1984, 46, 1044–1057.

23. Byrne, D. *The attraction paradigm*. New York: Academic Press, 1971.

Karylowski, J. Self-esteem, similarity, liking, and helping. *Personality and Social Psychology Bulletin*, 1976, 2, 71–74.

Kaufmann, H. and Marcus, A. Aggression as a function of similarity between aggressor and victim. *Perceptual and Motor Skills*. 1965, 20, 1013–1021.

Krebs, D.L. Empathy and altruism. *Journal of Personality and Social Psychology*, 1975, 32, 1134–1146.

24. Rokeach, M. *Beliefs, attitudes and values*. San Francisco: Jossey-Bass, 1968.

Silverman, B. Consequences, racial discrimination and the principle of belief congruence. *Journal of Personality and Social Psychology*, 1974, 29, 497–508.

25. Allport, G. *The nature of prejudice*. Reading, Mass.: Addison-Wesley, 1954, Chapter 16.

Dubois, R. *Neighbors in action*. New York: Harper, 1950.

26. Katsh, A.I. A survey of racial prejudice. *Educational Forum*, 1941 (March).

Williams, E. Facts and democratic values reduce racial prejudice. *Social Education*, 1946 (April).

27. Attributed to Pastor Martin Neimoeller. In E. Morison Beck (ed.), *John Bartlett's familiar quotations*. Boston: Little, Brown & Co., 1980, p. 824.

28. Katz, P.A. and Zalk, S.R. Modification of children's racial attitudes. *Developmental Psychology*, 1978, 14, 447–461.

29. Cullen, C. "Incident." *On these I stand: Selected poems*. New York: Harper, 1947.

30. Sherif, M. and Sherif, C.W. *Groups in harmony and tension*. New York: Harper, 1953.

31. Snyder, M. Self-fulfilling stereotypes. *Psychology Today*, 1982, 16(7), 60–68.

## Notes to Chapter 6

1. Underwood, B. and Moore, B.S. The generality of altruism in children. In N. Eisenberg (ed.), *The development of prosocial behavior*. New York: Academic Press, 1982, Chapter 2.

Hartshorne, H. and May, M.A. *Studies in the nature of character. Vol. 1: Studies in deceit*. New York: Macmillan, 1928.

Yarrow, M.R. and Waxler, C.Z. Dimensions and correlates of prosocial behavior in young children. *Child Development*, 1976, 47, 118–125.

2. Freud, S. *The ego and the id*. London: The Hogarth Press, 1927. (Original German edition, 1923)

Lorenz, K. *On aggression*. New York: Harcourt, Brace & World, 1963.

3. McCord, J. Some child-rearing antecedents of criminal behavior in adult men. *Journal of Personality and Social Psychology*, 1979, 37, 1477–1486.

Patterson, G.R. and Stouthamer-Loeber, M. The correlation of family management practices and delinquency. *Child Development*, 1984, 55, 1299–1307.

Loeber, R. and Dishion, T. Boys who fight at home and school: Family conditions influencing cross-setting consistency. *Journal of Consulting and Clinical Psychology*, 1984, 52, 759–768.

Borduin, C., Pruitt, J., and Henggeler, S.W. Family interaction in Black, lower-class families with delinquent and nondelinquent adolescent boys. *Journal of Genetic Psychology*, 1986, 147, 333–342.

4. Ferster, C.B. A functional analysis of depression. *American Psychologist*, 1973, 28, 857–870.

Tavris, C. *Anger: The misunderstood emotion.* New York: Simon and Schuster, 1982.

5. Schulman, M. Expectancies as cues for predicting the reaction to failure. *The Psychological Record*, 1972, 22, 267–276.

6. Homans, G.C. *Social behavior: Its elementary forms.* New York: Harcourt Brace Jovanovich, 1974.

Azrin, N.H., Hutchinson, R.R., and Hake, D.F. Extinction-induced aggression. *Journal of Experimental Analysis of Behavior*, 9, 191–204.

Davies, J.C. Toward a theory of revolution. *American Sociological Review*, 1962, 27, 5–18.

Feierabend, I.K. and Feierabend, R. Aggressive behaviors within polities, 1948–1962: A cross-national study. *Journal of Conflict Resolution*, 1966, 10, 249–272.

7. Adams, J.S. Inequity in social exchange. In L. Berkowitz (ed.), *Advances in experimental social psychology, Vol. 2.* New York: Academic Press, 1965.

8. Pastore, N. The role of arbitrariness in the frustration-aggression hypothesis. *Journal of Abnormal and Social Psychology*, 1952, 47, 728–731.

9. Karniol, R. Children's use of intention cues in evaluating behavior. *Psychological Bulletin*, 1978, 85, 76–85.

Piaget, J. *The moral judgment of the child.* New York: The Free Press, 1965. (Original edition, 1932)

Jensen, L.C. and Hughston, K. The effect of training children to make moral judgments which are independent of sanctions. *Developmental Psychology*, 1971, 5, 367–368.

Olthof, T., Ferguson, T.J., and Luiten, A. Personal responsibility antecedents of anger and blame reactions in children. *Child Development*, 1989, 60, 1328–1336.

10. Shure, M.B. and Spivack, G. *Problem-solving techniques in childrearing.* San Francisco: Jossey-Bass, 1978.

Novaco, R.W. Stress inoculation: A cognitive therapy for anger and its application to a case of depression. *Journal of Counseling and Clinical Psychology*, 1977, 45, 600–608.

Rahaim, S., Lefebvre, C., and Jenkins, J.O. The effects of social skills training on behavioral and cognitive components of anger management. *Journal of Behavior Therapy and Experimental Psychiatry*, 1980, 11, 3–8.

Kaufman, L.M. and Wagner, B.R. Barb: A systematic treatment technology for temper control disorders. *Behavior Therapy,* 1972, 3, 84–89.

11. Strober, M. and Bellack, A.S. Multiple component behavior treatment for a child with behavior problems. *Journal of Behavior Therapy and Experimental Psychiatry,* 1975, 6, 250–252.

    McCullough, J.P., Huntsinger, G.M., and Nay, W.R. Self-control treatment of aggression in a sixteen-year-old male. *Journal of Counseling and Clinical Psychology,* 1977, 45, 322–331.

12. Goodwin, S.E. and Mahoney, M.J. Modification of aggression through modeling: An experimental probe. *Journal of Behavior Therapy and Experimental Psychiatry,* 1975, 6, 200–202.

    Forman, S.G. A comparison of cognitive training and response cost procedures in modifying aggressive behavior of elementary school children. *Behavior Therapy,* 1980, 11, 594–600.

    Lochman, J.E., Nelson III, W.M., and Sims, J.P. A cognitive behavioral program for use with aggressive children. *Journal of Clinical Child Psychology,* 1981, 10, 146–148.

13. Tanner, U.L. and Holliman, W.B. Effectiveness of assertiveness training in modifying aggressive behaviors of young children. *Psychological Reports,* 1988, 62, 39–46.

    Foy, D.W., Eisler, R.M., and Pinston, S. Modeled assertion in a case of explosive rages. *Journal of Behavior Therapy and Experimental Psychiatry,* 1975, 6, 135–137.

14. Dawe, H.C. An analysis of two hundred quarrels of preschool children. *Child Development,* 1934, 5, 139–157.

15. Chittenden, G. An experimental study of measuring and modifying assertive behavior in young children. *Monographs of the Society for Research in Child Development,* 1942, 7(1, Serial No. 31).

16. Kuo, Z.Y. Studies on the basic factors in animal fighting: (VII) Interspecies coexistence in mammals. *Journal of Genetic Psychology,* 1960, 97, 211–225.

17. Azrin, N.H. and Lindsley, O. The reinforcement of cooperation between children. *Journal of Abnormal and Social Psychology,* 1956, 2, 100–102.

18. Mischel, W. and Ebbesen, E. Attention in delay of gratification. *Journal of Personality and Social Psychology,* 1970, 16, 329–337.

19. Chittenden, *op cit.*

20. Henderson, J.Q. A behavioral approach to stealing: A proposal for treatment based on ten cases. *Journal of Behavior Therapy and Experimental Psychiatry,* 1981, 12, 231–236.

    Henderson, J.Q. Follow-up of stealing behavior in 27 youths after a variety of treatment programs. *Journal of Behavior Therapy and Experimental Psychiatry,* 1983, 14, 331–337.

    Nietzel, M.T. Social learning applications for the criminal justice system. Address to the Second Congress for Clinical Psychology and Psychotherapy, German Association for Behavior Therapy, 1982.

21. Olejnik, A.B. and McKinney, J.P. Parental value orientation and generosity in children. *Developmental Psychology,* 1973, 8, 311.

22. Whiting, J.W.M. and Whiting, B. *Children of six cultures.* Cambridge, Mass: Harvard University Press, 1975.

Staub, E. A child in distress: The effects of focusing responsibility on children on their attempts to help. *Developmental Psychology,* 1970, 2, 152–153.

Bathurst, J.E. A study of sympathy and resistance (negativism) among children. *Psychological Bulletin,* 1933, 30, 625–626.

Geer, J.H. and Jarmecky, L. The effect of being responsible for reducing another's pain on subject's response and arousal. *Journal of Personality and Social Psychology,* 1973, 26, 232–237.

Tilker, H. Socially responsive behavior as a function of observer responsibility and victim feedback. *Journal of Personality and Social Psychology,* 1970, 14, 95–100.

Berkowitz, L. and Connor, W.H. Success, failure, and social responsibility. *Journal of Personality and Social Psychology,* 1966, 4, 664–669.

Peterson, L. Influence of age, task competence, and responsibility focus on children's altruism. *Developmental Psychology,* 1983, 19, 141–148.

Moriarty, T. Crime, commitment, and the responsive bystander: Two field experiments. *Journal of Personality and Social Psychology,* 1975, 31, 370–376.

23. Kinnard, E.M. The psychological consequences of abuse for the child. *Journal of Social Issues,* 1979, 35(2), 82–100.

Hollin, C.R. and Wheeler, H.M. The violent young offender: A small group study of a Borstal population. *Journal of Adolescence,* 1982, 5, 247–257.

Hoffman-Plotkin, D. and Twentyman, C.T. A multimodal assessment of behavioral and cognitive deficits in abused and neglected preschoolers. *Child Development,* 1984, 55, 794–802.

24. Parke, R.D. Some effects of punishment on children's behavior. *The young child: Reviews of research, Vol. 2.* Washington, D.C.: The National Association for the Education of Young Children, 1972, pp. 264–283.

Hart, R.J. Crime and punishment in the army. *Journal of Personality and Social Psychology,* 1978, 36, 1456–1471.

Aronfreed, A. *Conduct and conscience.* New York: Academic Press, 1968.

25. Goranson, R.E. and Berkowitz, L. Reciprocity and responsibility reactions to prior help. *Journal of Personality and Social Psychology,* 1966, 3, 227–232.

Eisenberg, N., Cameron, E., Tryon, K., and Dodez, R. Socialization of prosocial behavior in the preschool classroom. *Developmental Psychology,* 1981, 17, 773–782.

Charlesworth, R. and Hartup, W.W. Positive social reinforcement in the nursery school peer group. *Child Development,* 1967, 38, 993–1002.

26. Rushton, J.P. and Teachman, G. The effects of positive reinforcement, attribution, and punishment on model induced altruism in children, *Personality and Social Psychology Bulletin,* 1978, 4, 322–325.

Bryan, J.H. and Walbek, N.H. Preaching and practicing generosity: Children's actions and reactions. *Child Development,* 1970, 41, 329–353.

27. Hay, J. A study of principled moral reasoning within a sample of conscientious objectors. *Moral Education Forum,* 1982, 7(3), 1–8.

28. Eisenberg-Berg, N., Haake, R.J., and Bartlett, K. The effects of possession

and ownership on the sharing and proprietary behaviors of preschool children. *Merrill-Palmer Quarterly*, 1981, 27(2), 61–68.

29. Heisler, G. Ways to deter law violators: Effects of levels of threat and vicarious punishment on cheating. *Journal of Clinical and Consulting Psychology*, 1974, 42, 577–582.

30. Reisman, J.M. and Schorr, S.I. Friendship claims and expectations among children and adults. *Child Development*, 1978, 49, 913–916.

31. Hunter, F.T. and Youniss, J. Changes in functions of three relations during adolescence. *Developmental Psychology*, 1982, 18, 806–811.

    Henggler, S.W., Rodnick, J.D., Borduin, C.M., Hanson, C.L., Watson, S.M., and Urey, J.R. Multisystemic treatment of juvenile offenders: Effects on adolescent behavior and family interaction. *Developmental Psychology*, 1986, 22, 132–141.

    Berndt, T.J. Developmental changes in conformity to peers and parents. *Developmental Psychology*, 1977, 15, 608–616.

    Alexander, J.F. and Parsons, B.B. Short-term behavioral interactions with delinquent families: Impact of family process and recidivism. *Journal of Abnormal Psychology*, 1973, 81, 219–226.

    Patterson, G.R. Interventions for boys with conduct problems: Multiple settings, treatments, and criteria. *Journal of Consulting and Clinical Psychology*, 1974, 42, 471–481.

32. Deluty, R.H. Children's evaluations of aggressive, assertive, and submissive responses. *Journal of Clinical Child Psychology*, 1983, 12, 124–129.

33. Milgram, S. *Obedience to authority*. New York: Harper & Row, 1974.

34. Alexander, R., Corbett, T.F., and Smigel, J. The effects of individual and group consequences on school attendance and curfew violations with predelinquent adolescents. *Journal of Applied Behavior Analysis*, 1976, 9, 221–226.

    Speltz, M.L., Wenters-Shimamura, J., and McReynolds, W.T. Procedural variations in group contingencies: Effects on children's academic and social behaviors. *Journal of Applied Behavior Analysis*, 15, 533–544.

    Switzer, E.B., Deal, T.E. and Bailey, J.S. The reduction of stealing in second graders using a group contingency. *Journal of Applied Behavior Analysis*, 1977, 10, 267–272.

35. Cheyne, J.A. and Walters, R.H. Intensity of punishment, timing of punishment, and cognitive structure as determinants of response inhibition. *Journal of Experimental Child Psychology*, 1969, 7, 231–244.

    Verna, G.B. The effects of four-hour delay of punishment under two conditions of verbal instructions. *Child Development*, 1977, 48, 621–624.

36. Mayer, G.R., Butterworth, T., Nafpaktitis, M., and Sulzer-Azaroff, B. Preventing school vandalism and improving discipline: A three-year study. *Journal of Applied Behavior Analysis*, 1983, 16, 355–369.

37. Stark, R. and McEvoy III, J.M. Middle class violence. *Psychology Today*, 1970, 4(Nov.), 52–54, 110–112.

    Bandura, A. and Walters, R.H. *Adolescent aggression*. New York: Ronald Press, 1959.

Bandura, A. *Aggression*. Englewood Cliffs, N.J.: Prentice-Hall, 1973.

38. Borden, R.J. Witnessed aggression: Influence of an observer's sex and values on aggressive responding. *Journal of Personality and Social Psychology*, 1975, 31, 567–573.

Short, Jr., J.F. Collective behavior, crime, and delinquency. In D. Glaser (ed.), *Handbook of criminology*. Chicago: Rand McNally, 1974, pp. 413–454.

Deluty, R.H. Cognitive mediation of aggressive, assertive, and submissive behavior in children. *International Journal of Behavioral Development*, 1985, 8, 355–369.

39. Bandura, A., Ross, D., and Ross, S.A. A comparative test of the status envy, social power, and secondary reinforcement theories of identificatory learning. *Journal of Abnormal and Social Psychology*, 1963, 67, 527–534.

Eisenberg-Berg, N. and Geisheker, E. Content of preachings and power of the model/preacher: The effect on children's generosity. *Developmental Psychology*, 1979, 15, 168–175.

40. Cummings, E.M., Iannotti, R.J., and Zahn-Waxler, C. Aggression between peers in early childhood: Individual continuity and developmental change. *Child Development*, 1989, 60, 887–895.

Heusmann, L.R., Eron, L.D., Lefkowitz, M.M., and Walder, L.O. Stability of aggression over time and generations. *Developmental Psychology*, 1984, 20, 1120–1134.

Robins, L.N. *Deviant children grown up*. Baltimore: Williams & Wilkins Co., 1966.

41. Azrin, N.H. Pain and aggression. *Psychology Today*, 1967, 1(May), 26–33.

Thompson, W.C., Cowan, C.L., and Rosenhan, D.L. Focus of attention mediates the impact of negative affect on altruism. *Journal of Personality and Social Psychology*, 1980, 38, 291–300.

42. Eliot, T.S., "East Coker." *The complete poems and plays*. New York: Harcourt, Brace and World, 1952.

43. Ferster, C.B. and Skinner, B.F. *Schedules of reinforcement*. New York: Appleton-Century-Crofts, 1957.

44. Meichenbaum, D.H. and Goodman, J. Training impulsive children to talk to themselves: A means of developing self-control. *Journal of Abnormal Psychology*, 1971, 77, 115–126.

45. Eisenberger, R. and Masterson, F.A. Required high effort increases subsequent persistence and reduces cheating. *Journal of Personality and Social Psychology*, 1983, 44, 593–599.

46. Hartup, W.W., Glazer, J.A., and Charlesworth, R. Peer reinforcement and sociometric status. *Child Development*, 1967, 38, 1017–1024.

Coie, J.D. and Dodge, K.A. Multiple sources of data on social behavior and social status in the school: A cross-age comparison. *Child Development*, 1988, 59, 815–829.

Hayes, D.S. Cognitive basis for liking and disliking among preschool children. *Child Development*, 1978, 49, 906–909.

47. *Time*, Aug. 15, 1983, p. 15.

48. Patterson, G.R., Littman, R.A., and Bricker, W. Assertive behavior in chil-

dren. *Monographs of the Society for Research in Child Development,* 1967, 32, (4, Whole No. 113).

49. Miller, W.B., Geertz, H., and Cutter, H.S.G. Aggression in boys' street corner groups. *Psychiatry,* 1961, 24, 283–298.

50. *New York Times,* Aug. 3, 1983, p. B4.

## NOTES TO CHAPTER 7

1. Mehler, J. and Bever, T.G. Cognitive capacity of very young children. *Science,* 1967, 158, 141–142.

   Piaget, J. and Inhelder, B. *The psychology of the child.* New York: Basic Books, 1969.

   Piaget, J. *The construction of reality in the child.* New York: Basic Books, 1954.

2. Staats, A.W. *Child learning, intelligence and personality: Principles of a behavioral interaction approach.* New York: Harper & Row, 1971, Chapter 14.

3. Ford, M.E. The construct validity of egocentrism. *Psychological Bulletin,* 1979, 86, 1169–1188.

   Borke, H. Interpersonal perception of young children: Egocentrism or empathy? *Developmental Psychology,* 1971, 5, 263–269.

   Bretherton, I. and Beeghly, M. Talking about internal states: The acquisition of an explicit theory of mind. *Developmental Psychology,* 1982, 18, 906–921.

   Hood, L. and Bloom, L. What, when, and how about why: A longitudinal study of early expressions of causality. *Monographs of the Society for Research in Child Development,* 1979, 44(6, Serial No. 181).

   Berzonsky, M.D. The role of familiarity in children's explanations of physical causality. *Child Development,* 1971, 42, 705–715.

   Karniol, R. Children's use of intentional cues in evaluating behavior. *Psychological Bulletin,* 1978, 85, 76–85.

   Tapp, J.L. and Kohlberg, L. Developing senses of law and justice. *Journal of Social Issues,* 1971, 27(2), 65–91.

4. Waters, E., Wippman, J., and Sroufe, L.A. Attachment, positive affect, and competence in the peer group: Two studies in construct validation. *Child Development,* 1979, 50, 821–829.

   Lieberman, A.F. Preschoolers' competence with a peer: Relations with attachment and peer experience. *Child Development,* 1977, 48, 1277–1287.

   Paster, D.L. The quality of mother-infant attachment and its relationship to toddler's initial sociability with peers. *Developmental Psychology,* 1981, 17, 326–335.

5. Stayton, D., Hogan, R., and Salter-Ainsworth, M. Infant obedience and maternal behavior: The origins of socialization reconsidered. *Child Development,* 1971, 42, 1057–1069.

   Londerville, S. and Main, M. Security of attachment, compliance, and maternal training methods in the second year of life. *Developmental Psychology,* 1981, 17, 289–301.

6. Etzel, B.C. and Gewirtz, J.L. Experimental modification of caretaker-maintained high-rate operant crying in a 6- and a 20-week-old infant (Infans tyrannotearus): Extinction of crying with reinforcement of eye contact and smiling. *Journal of Experimental Child Psychology*, 1967, 5, 303–317.

   Bell, S.M. and Salter-Ainsworth, M.D. Infant crying and natural responsiveness. *Child Development*, 1972, 43, 1171–1190.

7. Klein, R.P. and Yarrow, L.J. Maternal behavior and sharing by toddlers. *Psychological Reports*, 1980, 46, 1057–1058.

8. Williams, C.D. The elimination of tantrum behavior by extinction procedures. *Journal of Abnormal and Social Psychology*, 1959, 59, 269.

9. Gesell, A. The ontogenesis of infant behavior. In L. Carmichael (ed.), *Manual of child psychology*, second edition. New York: Wiley, 1954, Chapter 6.

10. Holden, G.W. Avoiding conflicts: Mothers as tacticians in the supermarket. *Child Development*, 1983, 54, 233–240.

    Clark, H.B., Greene, B.F., MacRae, J.W., McNees, M.P., Davis, J.L., and Risely, T.R. A parent advice package for family shopping trips: Development and evaluation. *Journal of Applied Behavior Analysis*, 1977, 10, 605–624.

    Sanders, M.R. and Dadds, M.R. The effects of planned activities and child management procedures in parent training: An analysis of setting generality. *Behavior Therapy*, 1982, 13, 452–461.

11. Zeece, P.D. and Crase, S.J. Effects of verbal warning on compliant and transition behavior of preschool children. *Journal of Psychology*, 1982, 112, 269–274.

12. Nucci, L.P. and Turiel, E. Social interactions and the development of social concepts in preschool children. *Child Development*, 1978, 49, 400–407.

    Nucci, L.P. and Nucci, M.S. Children's social interactions in the context of moral and conventional transgressions. *Child Development*, 1982, 53, 403–412.

    Smetana, J.G., Kelly, M., and Twentyman, C.T. Abused, neglected, and nonmaltreated children's conceptions of moral and social-conventional transgressions. *Child Development*, 1984, 55, 277–287.

13. Siegal, M. and Rablin, J. Moral development as reflected by young children's evaluation of maternal discipline. *Merrill-Palmer Quarterly*, 1982, 28, 499–509.

14. Sidel, R. *Women and childcare in China: A first hand report.* New York: Penguin Books, 1982 (revised edition).

15. Midlarsky, E. and Bryan, J.H. Affect expressions and children's imitative altruism. *Journal of Experimental Research in Personality*, 1972, 6, 195–203.

16. Lytton, H. Disciplinary encounters between young boys and their mothers and fathers: Is there a contingency system? *Developmental Psychology*, 1979, 15, 256–268.

    Russo, D.C., Cataldo, M.F., and Cushing, P.J. Compliance training and behavioral covariation in the treatment of multiple behavioral problems. *Journal of Applied Behavior Analysis*, 1981, 14, 209–222.

17. Timberlake, W. and Allison, J. Response deprivation: An empirical ap-

proach to instrumental performance. *Psychological Review,* 1974, 81, 146–164.

18. Van Houten, R., Nau, P.A., MacKensie-Keating, S.E., Sameoto, D., and Colavecchia, B. An analysis of some variables influencing the effectiveness of reprimands. *Journal of Applied Behavior Analysis,* 1982, 15, 65–83.

   Forehand, R., Roberts, M.W., Doleys, D.M., Hobbs, S.A., and Resnick, P.A. An examination of disciplinary procedures with children. *Journal of Experimental Child Psychology,* 1976, 21, 109–120.

   Jones, F.H. and Miller, W.H. The effective use of negative attention for reducing group disruption in special elementary school classrooms. *The Psychological Record,* 1974, 24, 435–448.

   Wahler, R.G. Oppositional children: A quest for parental reinforcement control. *Journal of Applied Behavior Analysis,* 1969, 2, 159–170.

   Gardner, H., Forehand, R., and Roberts, M. Time-out with children: Effects of an explanation and brief parent training on child and parent behavior. *Journal of Abnormal Child Psychology,* 1976, 4, 277–288.

   Olson, R.L. and Roberts, M.W. Alternative treatments for sibling aggression. *Behavior Therapy,* 1987, 18, 243–250.

19. Bretherton, I. and Beeghly, M. Talking about internal states: The acquisition of an explicit theory of mind. *Developmental Psychology,* 1982, 18, 906–921.

   Weiner, B., Graham, S., Stern, P., and Lawson, M.E. Using affective cues to infer causal thoughts. *Developmental Psychology,* 1982, 18, 278–286.

   Masters, J.C. and Carlson, C.R. Children's and adults' understanding of the causes and consequences of emotional states. In C.E. Izard, J. Kagan, and R.B. Zajonc (eds.), *Emotions, cognitions, and behavior.* New York: Cambridge University Press, 1984, Chapter 14.

   Barnett, K., Darcie, G., Holland, C.J., and Kobasigawa, A. Children's cognitions about effective helping. *Developmental Psychology,* 1982, 18, 267–277.

20. Burleson, B.R. The development of comforting communication skills in childhood and adolescence. *Child Development,* 1982, 53, 1578–1588.

   Johnson, D.B. Altruistic behavior and the development of the self in infants. *Merrill-Palmer Quarterly,* 1982, 28, 379–388.

21. Fellner, C.H. and Marshall, J.R. Kidney donors revisited. In J.P. Rushton and R.M. Sorrentino (eds.), *Altruism and helping behavior: Social, personality, and developmental perspectives.* Hillsdale, N.J.: Lawrence Erlbaum Associates, 1981, Chapter 17.

   Fox, R.C. A sociological perspective on organ transplantation and hemodialysis. *Annals of the New York Academy of Science,* 1970, 169, 406–428.

22. Eisenberg, N. Children's differentiations among potential recipients of aid. *Child Development,* 1983, 54, 594–602.

23. Wilson, E. The genetic evolution of altruism. In L. Wispe (ed.), *Altruism, sympathy and helping: Psychological and sociological principles.* New York: Academic Press, 1978, Chapter 1.

24. Nelson, S.A. and Dweck, C.S. Motivation and competence as determinants

of young children's reward allocation. *Developmental Psychology*, 1977, 13, 192–197.

Eckerman, C.O., Whatley, J.L., and McGehee, L.J. Approaching and contacting the object another manipulates: A social skill of the one-year-old. *Developmental Psychology*, 1979, 15, 585–593.

Eckerman, C.O. and Whatley, J.L. Toys and social interaction between infant peers. *Child Development*, 1977, 48, 1645–1656.

Grusec, J.E. and Abramovitch, R. Imitation of peers and adults in a natural setting: A functional analysis. *Child Development*, 1982, 53, 636–642.

Rhine, R.J., Hill, S.J., and Wandruff, S.E. Evaluative responses of preschool children. *Child Development*, 1967, 38, 1035–1042.

25. Irwin, D.M. and Moore, S.G. The young child's understanding of social justice. *Developmental Psychology*, 1971, 5, 406–410.

## NOTES TO CHAPTER 8

1. Selman, R.L. and Selman, A.P. Children's ideas about friendship: A new theory. *Psychology Today*, 1979, 13(4), 70–80, 114.

   McGuire, K.D. and Weisz, J.R. Social cognition and behavior correlates of preadolescent chumship. *Child Development*, 1982, 53, 1478–1484.

   Reaves, J.Y. and Roberts, A. The effect of type of information on children's attraction to peers. *Child Development*, 1983, 54, 1024–1031.

   Bigelow, B. and LaGaipa, J.J. Children's written descriptions of friendship. *Developmental Psychology*, 1975, 11, 857–858.

   Gottman, J., Gonso, J., and Rasmussen, B. Social interaction, social competence, and friendship in children. *Child Development*, 1975, 46, 709–718.

   Masters, J.C. and Furman, W. Popularity, individual friendship selection and specific peer interaction among children. *Developmental Psychology*, 1981, 17, 344–350.

   Ladd, G.W., Price, J.M., and Hart, C.H. Predicting preschoolers' peer status from their playground behavior. *Child Development*, 1988, 59, 986–992.

2. Hay, D.F. Cooperative interaction and sharing behavior between very young children and their parents. *Developmental Psychology*, 1979, 15, 647–653.

   Howes, C. and Rubenstein, J.L. Toddler peer behavior in two types of day care. *Infant Behavior and Development*, 1981, 4, 387–393.

   Sackin, S. and Thelen, E. An ethological study of peaceful associative outcomes to conflict in preschool children. *Child Development*, 1984, 55, 1098–1102.

3. Nelson, L. and Madsen, M.C. Cooperation and competition in four-year-olds as a function of reward contingency and subculture. *Developmental Psychology*, 1969, 1, 340–344.

4. Martin, R.A. and Lefcourt, H.M. Sense of humor as a moderator of the relation between stressors and mood. *Journal of Personality and Social Psychology*, 1983, 45, 1313–1324.

5. Lorenz, K. *On aggression.* New York: Harcourt, Brace & World, 1966.

6. Andreas, C. War toys and the peace movement. *Journal of Social Issues,* 1969, 25(1), 83–99.

   Editorial, *Toys and Novelties,* April, 1966. Cited in C. Andreas, ibid.

7. Reilly, T.P., Hasazi, J.E., and Bond, L.A. Children's conceptions of death and personal mortality. *Journal of Pediatric Psychology,* 1983, 8, 21–31.

8. Eron, L.D., Huesmann, L.R., Brice, P., Fischer, P., and Mermelstein, R. Age trends in the development of aggression, sex typing, and related television habits. *Developmental Psychology,* 1983, 19, 71–77.

   Rubinstein, E.A. Television and behavior: Research conclusions of the 1982 NIMH report and their policy implications. *American Psychologist,* 1983, 38, 820–825.

   Feshbach, S. and Singer, R.D. *Television aggression: An experimental field study.* San Francisco: Jossey-Bass, 1971.

   Sebold, H. *Adolescence: A social psychological analysis.* Englewood Cliffs, N.J.: Prentice-Hall, 1977.

9. Bryan, J.H. and Schwartz, T.H. The effects of film material upon children's behavior. *Psychological Bulletin,* 1971, 75, 50–59.

   Forge, K.L. and Phemister, S. The effect of prosocial cartoons on preschool children. *Child Study Journal,* 1987, 17, 83–88.

   Ahammer, I.M. and Murray, J.P. Kindness in the kindergarten: The relative influence of role playing and prosocial television in facilitating altruism. *International Journal of Behavioral Development,* 1979, 2, 133–157.

   Gorn, G.J., Goldberg, M.E., and Kanungo, R.N. The role of educational television in changing the intergroup attitudes of children. *Child Development,* 1976, 47, 277–280.

10. Surgeon general's scientific advisory committee on TV and social behavior, TV and adolescent aggressiveness, vol. 3, Washington, D.C.: Government Printing Office, 1972.

   Eron, L.D. Parent-child interaction, television violence, and aggression of children. *American Psychologist,* 1982, 37, 197–211.

   Huesmann, L.R., Eron, L.D., Klein, R., Brice, P., and Fischer, P.F. Mitigating the imitation of aggressive behavior by changing children's attitudes about media violence. *Journal of Personality and Social Psychology,* 1983, 44, 899–910.

   Diener, E. and DeFour, D. Does television violence enhance program popularity? *Journal of Personality and Social Psychology,* 1978, 36, 333–341.

11. Weiner, B., Graham, S., Stern, P., and Lawson, M.E. Using affective cues to infer causal thoughts. *Developmental Psychology,* 1982, 18, 278–286.

   Rothenberg, B.B. Children's social sensitivity and the relationship to interpersonal competence, interpersonal comfort, and intellectual level. *Developmental Psychology,* 1970, 2, 335–350.

12. Kifer, R.E., Lewis, M.A., Green, D.R., and Phillips, E.L. Training delinquent youths and their parents to negotiate conflict situations. *Journal of Applied Behavior Analysis,* 1974, 7, 357–364.

   Bright, P.D. and Robin, A.L. Ameliorating parent-adolescent conflict with problem-solving communication training. *Journal of Behavior Therapy and Experimental Psychiatry*, 1981, 12, 275–280.

Alexander, J.F. and Parsons, B.B. Short-term behavioral interventions with delinquent families: Impact of family process and recidivism. *Journal of Abnormal Psychology*, 1973, 81, 219–226.

13. Peterson, C.C., Peterson, J.L., and Seeto, D. Developmental changes in ideas about lying. *Child Development,* 1983, 54, 1529–1535.

14. Kunda, Z. and Schwartz, S.H. Undermining intrinsic moral motivation: External reward and self-presentation. *Journal of Personality and Social Psychology*, 1983, 45, 763–771.

15. Sachs, D.A. The efficacy of time-out procedures in a variety of behavior problems. *Journal of Behavior Therapy and Experimental Psychiatry*, 1973, 4, 237–242.

16. O'Brien, T.P., Riner, L.S., and Budd, K.S. The effects of a child's self-evaluation program on compliance with parental instructions in the home. *Journal of Applied Behavior Analysis*, 1983, 16, 69–79.

Wood, R. and Flynn, J.M. A self-evaluation token system *versus* an external evaluation token system alone in a residential setting with predelinquent youths. *Journal of Applied Behavior Analysis*, 1978, 11, 503–512.

Seymour, F.W. and Stokes, T.F. Self-recording in training girls to increase work and evoke staff praise in an institution for offenders. *Journal of Applied Behavior Analysis*, 1976, 9, 41–54.

Bonjean, C.M. and McGee, R. Scholastic honesty among undergraduates in differing systems of social control. *Sociology of Education*, 1965, 38, 127–137.

17. Lerner, M.J. *The belief in a just world.* New York: Plenum, 1980.

18. Kazdin, A.E. and Geesey, S. Simultaneous-treatment design comparisons of the effects of earning reinforcers for one's peers versus oneself. *Behavior Therapy*, 1977, 8, 682–693.

Wolf, M.M., Hanley, E.L., King, L.A., Lachowicz, J., and Giles, D.K. The timer-game: A variable interval contingency for the management of out-of-seat behavior. *Exceptional Children*, 1970, 37, 113–117.

19. Allyon, T. and Roberts, M.D. Eliminating discipline problems by strengthening academic performance. *Journal of Applied Behavior Analysis*, 1974, 7, 71–76.

20. Gross, G.S. Categorization in one- and two-year-olds. *Developmental Psychology*, 1980, 16, 391–396.

21. Hood, L. and Bloom, L. What, when, and how about why: A longitudinal study of early expressions of causality. *Monographs of the Society for Research in Child Development*, 1979, 44(6, Serial No. 181).

22. Locke, E.A., Shaw, K.N., Saari, L.M., and Latham, G.P. Goal setting and task performance: 1969–1980. *Psychological Bulletin*, 1981, 90, 125–152.

23. Sherman, T.M. and Cormier, W.H. An investigation of the influence of student behavior on teachers. *Journal of Applied Behavior Analysis*, 1974, 7, 11–21.

24. Atkeson, B.M. and Forehand, R. Home-based reinforcement programs de-

signed to modify classroom behavior: A review and methodological evaluation. *Psychological Bulletin,* 1979, 86, 1298–1308.

25. Peterson, L. Role of donor competence, donor age, and peer presence on helping in an emergency. *Developmental Psychology,* 1983, 19, 873–880.

26. Ruble, D.N., Feldman, N.S., and Boggiano, A.K. Social comparison between young children in achievement situations. *Developmental Psychology,* 1976, 12, 192–197.

   Morris, W.N. and Nemcek, Jr., D. The development of social comparison motivation among preschoolers: Evidence of a stepwise progression. *Merrill-Palmer Quarterly,* 1982, 28, 413–425.

27. Henderson, W.D. The Vietnamese army. In M. Janowitz and S.D. Wesbrook (eds.), *The political education of soldiers.* Beverly Hills, CA: Sage, 1983, Chapter 5.


NOTES TO CHAPTER 9

1. Kinsey, A.C., Pomeroy, W.B., Martin, C.E., and Gebhard, P.H. *Sexual behavior in the human female.* Philadelphia, PA: W.B. Saunders, 1953.

   Hopkins, J.R. Sexual behavior in adolescence. *Journal of Social Issues,* 1977, 33(2), 67–85.

   *New York Times,* November 20, 1983, p. A1.

2. Katchadourian, H.A. and Lunde, D.T. *Fundamentals of human sexuality.* New York: Holt, Rinehart & Winston, 1972.

3. Peplau, L.A., Rubin, Z., and Hill, C.T. Sexual intimacy in dating relationships. *Journal of Social Issues,* 1977, 33(2), 86–109.

   Goertzel, T. Changes in the values of college students, 1958 to 1970/71. *Pacific Sociological Review,* 1972, 15, 235–244.

4. Peplau, *op cit.*

5. Simon, P. *I am a rock.* Eclectic Music Co., 1965.

6. Gilder, G., quoted in *New York Times,* Breakup of Black Family Imperils Gains of Decades. November 20, 1983, pp. 1, 56.

   Russell, C.S. Unscheduled parenthood: Transition to "parent" for the teenager. *Journal of Social Issues,* 1980, 36(1), 45–63.

7. *New York Times,* December 13, 1983, p. A30.

8. Litton-Fox, G. and Inazu, J.K. Patterns and outcomes of mother-daughter communication about sexuality. *Journal of Social Issues,* 1980, 36(1), 7–29.

9. New York Times Metropolitan Area High School Survey, *New York Times,* July 19, 1981, pp. 1, 38.

10. *New York Times,* October 30, 1983, p. 17.

    Cocaine Survey Points to Widespread Anguish, *New York Times,* January 3, 1984, p. C1.

11. Premack, D. Mechanisms of self-control. In J.M. Foley, R.A. Lockhart, and D.M. Messick (eds.), *Contemporary readings in psychology.* New York: Harper & Row, 1970, pp. 451–463.

12. Nucci, L., Guerra, N., and Lee, J. Adolescent judgments of the personal,

prudential, and normative aspects of drug usage. *Developmental Psychology*, 1991, 27, 841–848.

13. Newcomb, M.D., Huba, G.J., and Bentler, P.M. Mothers' influence on the drug use of their children: Confirmatory tests of direct modeling and mediational theories. *Developmental Psychology*, 1983, 19, 714–726.

14. Falco, M. The big business of illicit drugs. *New York Times Magazine*, December 11, 1983, pp. 108–112.
*New York Times*, December 11, 1983.

15. Educational Guidance in Human Love. Issued by the Sacred Congregation for Catholic Education, excerpted in *New York Times*, December 2, 1983.

16. Allport, G.W. and Ross, J.M. Personal religious orientation and prejudice. *Journal of Personality and Social Psychology*, 1967, 5, 432–443.
Brannon, R.C.L. Gimme that old-time racism. *Psychology Today*, 1970, 3(11), 42–44.

17. Goertzel, *op cit.*
Yankelovitch, D. *The new morality: A profile of American youth in the 1970s.* New York: McGraw-Hill, 1974.
Nucci, L. Children's conceptions of morality, societal convention, and religious prescription. In C. Harding (ed.), *Moral dilemmas.* Chicago: Precedent Press, 1985.

18. Leo XIII. Immortale Dei, On the Christian Constitution of States, Nov. 1, 1885. In A. Seldes (ed.), *The great quotations.* New York: Pocket Books, 1972, p. 66.

19. *New York Times*, June 4, 1981.

20. Keniston, K. The sources of student dissent. *Journal of Social Issues*, 1967, 23(3), 108–137.
Rosenhan, D.L. The natural socialization of altruistic autonomy. In J. Macauley and L. Berkowitz (eds.), *Altruism and helping behavior.* New York: Academic Press, 1970, 251–268.
Flacks, R. The liberated generation: An exploration of the roots of student protest. *Journal of Social Issues*, 1967, 23(3), 52–75.

## NOTES TO CHAPTER 10

1. *New York Times*, April 10, 1983, p. E4.

2. Latane, B. and Darley, J.M. *The unresponsive bystander: Why doesn't he help?* New York: Appleton-Century-Crofts, 1970.

3. *New York Times*, November 13, 1983, p. A1.
*New York Times*, November 6, 1983, Section 3, p. 1.

4. Solomon, F. and Fishman, J.R. Youth and social action: II. Action and identity-formation in the first student sit-in demonstration. *Journal of Social Issues*, 1964, 20(2), 36–45.

5. Clinard, M.B. *Corporate ethics and crime: The role of middle management.* Beverly Hills, CA: Sage, 1983.

6. *New York Times*, January 15, 1984, p. F4.

7. Coch, L. and French, Jr., J.R.P. Overcoming resistance to change. *Human Relations,* 1948, 4, 512–533.
Tannenbaum, A.S. *Social psychology of the work organization.* Belmont, CA: Wadsworth, 1966.

8. Feagin, J.R. Poverty: We still believe that God helps those who help themselves. *Psychology Today,* 1972, 6 (Nov.), 101–110, 129.

9. Holmberg, A.B. Changing community attitudes and values in Peru. In R.N. Adams (ed.), *Social change in Latin America today.* New York: Harper, 1960.
Kunkel, J.H. Some behavioral aspects of social change and economic development. In R.L. Burgess and D. Bushell, Jr. (eds.), *Behavioral sociology: The experimental analysis of social process.* New York: Columbia University Press, 1969, Chapter 15.

# INDEX